A Sociology of International Investment Law

THE HISTORY AND THEORY OF INTERNATIONAL LAW

In the past few decades, the understanding of the relationship between nations has undergone a radical transformation. The role of the traditional nation state is diminishing, along with many of the traditional vocabularies which were once used to describe what has been called, ever since Jeremy Bentham coined the phrase in 1780, 'international law.' The older boundaries between states are growing ever more fluid, and new conceptions and new languages have emerged which are slowly coming to replace the image of a world of sovereign independent nation states which has dominated the study of international relations since the early nineteenth century. This redefinition of the international arena demands a new understanding of classical and contemporary questions in international and legal theory. It is the editors' conviction that the best way to achieve this is by bridging the traditional divide between international legal theory, intellectual history, and legal and political history. The aim of the series, therefore, is to provide a forum for historical studies, from classical antiquity to the twenty-first century, that are theoretically informed and for philosophical work that is historically conscious, in the hope that a new vision of the rapidly evolving international world, its past and its possible future, may emerge.

PREVIOUSLY PUBLISHED IN THIS SERIES

The Unseen History of International Law
Mark Somos, Matthew Cleary, Pablo Dufour, Edward Jones Corredera, and Emanuele Salerno

The New Haven School
American International Law
Rián Derrig

Socialism and International Law
The Cold War and Its Legacies
Raluca Grosescu and Ned Richardson-Little

Odious Debt
Bankruptcy, International Law, and the Making of Latin America
Edward Jones Corredera

A Century of Anarchy?
War, Normativity, and the Birth of Modern International Order
Hendrik Simon

The Individual in International Law
Anne Peters, Tom Sparks

A Sociology of International Investment Law

Themes from Max Weber

David Schneiderman

OXFORD
UNIVERSITY PRESS

OXFORD
UNIVERSITY PRESS

Great Clarendon Street, Oxford, OX2 6DP,
United Kingdom

Oxford University Press is a department of the University of Oxford.
It furthers the University's objective of excellence in research, scholarship,
and education by publishing worldwide. Oxford is a registered trade mark of
Oxford University Press in the UK and in certain other countries.

Published in the United States of America by Oxford University Press
198 Madison Avenue, New York, NY 10016, United States of America.

British Library Cataloguing in Publication Data
Data available

Library of Congress Control Number: 2026933549

ISBN 9780198982708

DOI: 10.1093/9780198982739.001.0001

Printed and bound by
CPI Group (UK) Ltd., Croydon, CR0 4YY

MIX
Paper | Supporting
responsible forestry
FSC® C013604

The manufacturer's authorized representative in the EU for product safety is
Oxford University Press España S.A. of Parque Empresarial San Fernando de Henares,
Avenida de Castilla, 2 – 28830 Madrid (www.oup.es/en or product.safety@oup.com).
OUP España S.A. also acts as importer into Spain of products made by the manufacturer.

To my family

Acknowledgments

I was prompted to think with Max Weber only because I happened to be browsing through a second-hand copy of the English-language translation of his essays in *From Max Weber* (to which the sub-title of this book pays tribute).[1] I initially undertook no systematic reading of Weber but, browsing through this tattered copy, I happened to stumble upon an excerpt addressing means-ends rationalizing. I discovered that there were affinities between his account of bureaucratic rationality and the modern way of resolving constitutional disputes by way of proportionality analysis. Over the course of years, as I dived further into Weber's *ouevre*, it became clear to me that Weber was a legal thinker—that much of his social theorizing was grounded in his legal training.[2] It was easy to then connect the dots between Weber's innovative and provocative methods to many of the controversies arising out of the sub-field of international law with which I have been preoccupied over many years. This book is the final product of that first coincidence.

I am grateful to the numerous colleagues who read or commented upon parts of this encounter between Max Weber and international investment law. Among them are Olabisi Akinkugbe, Julian Arato, Nehal Bhuta, Phillipp Dann, Laura Ford, Ben Heath, Moshe Hirsch, Dimitris Kontogiannis, Jedediah Kronke, Michael Rask Madsen, Federico Ortino, Nicolás Perrone, Lauge Poulsen, Sonia Rolland, Mavluda Sattorova, Thomas Schultz, Greg Shaffer, Celine Tan, Dave Trubek, Paolo Vargiu, Sam Whimster, Jason Yackee, Fuad Zarbiyev, and Velimir Živković.

I was fortunate to be able to present chapters to various audiences including those at the Academic Forum Conference, University of Michigan Law School; IEL Collective at Warwick University; iCourts, University of Copenhagen; Faculty of Law, Humboldt University Berlin; Faculty of Law, University of Geneva; Dickson Poon School of Law, King's College London; International Law and Society Conference in Lisbon, Portugal; International Law and Sociology Conference at the University of Toronto; the Purdy Crawford Workshop on International Business Law at Schulich School of Law, Dalhousie University; and the Centre for European Law and Internationalisation, University of Leicester.

I also had the benefit of student research assistance from Emily Rand, Jacob Lokash, and Bjorn Wagenpfeil. At Oxford University Press, I had the privilege of working again with Fay Gibbons. The general editors of the History and Theory of International Law deserve special thanks for accepting this book

[1] Gerth and Mills (1946).
[2] Turner and Factor (1994).

into their series. An earlier version of Chapter 1 appeared in Moshe Hirsch and Andrew Lang (eds) *Research Handbook on the Sociology of International Law* (Edward Elgar 2018) 232–51. A longer version of the argument in the first part of Chapter 2 appeared in *Max Weber Studies* (2024) 24: 183–216. A few passages in Chapter 3 are drawn from my contribution to Supreme Court Law Review (2d) (2013) 63: 557–77.

Finally, I am pleased to acknowledge funding in support of this project from the Social Sciences and Humanities Research Council of Canada. This book is dedicated to my family, both past and present. I treasure all of them dearly. Special thanks to Thelonious Monk for providing the soundtrack.

Contents

Introduction

I. Prologue

The Gods remain at war.[1] Citizens pray at the altar of competing ideological deities.[2] Their governments, too, remain at odds over trajectories for social and economic betterment. Though there is the appearance of coalescence around the fundamentals by which to alleviate economic disparities—those proffered, for instance, by the prophets of austerity[3]—paths forward remain contentious. For Max Weber, it is a stubborn fact of modern life that conflict is endemic. The best we can do, Weber claims, is to scrutinize the means that we choose in light of our inevitably conflicting ends.

International investment law aims to settle many of the contentious questions that have preoccupied international political economy throughout much of the twentieth century. 'Third world' states sought, for instance, to elevate to international law the standard of 'appropriate compensation' in the case of nationalization and expropriation, taking into account 'all circumstances that the State considers pertinent.'[4] This formulation was fiercely resisted by powerful first-world states, the United States among them, for seemingly rejecting stricter rules of international law.[5] The rule of international law, as defined by these states, required nothing less than full (or 'just') compensation at fair market value.[6] That debate, it is said, has now been settled. The compensation rule, as laid down in some 3,000 bilateral investment treaties and regional trade and investment agreements,

[1] Weber (1919b) at 348 (the 'gods are in conflict—unceasing conflict—with each other') and (1916) at 79 (one must 'choose which of these gods he will serve ... [but] at all times he will find himself engaged in a fight against one or other of the gods of this world, and above all he will always find that he is far from the God of Christianity'). See Jameson (1973) at 61–62.

[2] Ideology is understood here to be capacious, as in Shklar (1964) at 4 (referring to 'political preferences') and Kennedy (1997) at 41–42 (ideology as 'project'). Larrain (1979) at 76–77 attributes to Lenin the movement away from ideology as the 'distortion' of knowledge to a 'concept which covers a whole range of social and political thought.'

[3] For critiques, see Dardot and Laval (2019) and Streeck (2014).

[4] As stated in the 1974 Charter of Economic Rights and Duties of States, UN Doc A/RES/3281(XXIX), GAOR 29th Session Supp 31 vol 1, 50.

[5] For discussion, see Perrone and Schneiderman (n.d.).

[6] This is the standard associated with US Secretary of State Cordell Hull when seeking compensation for Mexican oil nationalizations. See Hull (1938).

A Sociology of International Investment Law. David Schneiderman, Oxford University Press.
 DOI: 10.1093/9780198982739.003.0001

reflects how the high standard, alleged to represent international law, espoused by capital-exporting states emerged victorious.

The legal order to protect foreign investors abroad now has a global reach. Constructed principally in the period after the fall of the Soviet Union, it is one of the most legally muscular forms of international law in the world. It has also given rise to considerable controversy by reason of the breadth of investor protections, as interpreted by investment arbitration tribunals, and the resulting contraction of policy space in countries both in the Global North and Global South.[7] The United Nations Conference on Trade and Development has gone so far as to describe the regime as at a crossroads. The question is not whether to reform or not, but what direction reform will take.[8]

The investment law regime entitles foreign investors to launch disputes for compensation should states run afoul of laconic standards of treatment. Such treaty standards are intended to shield investors from legal and policy change—what is labeled 'political risk.' Once established within a host state, investments are considered immobile and vulnerable to that sort of risk. Investment treaties commit host states mostly to freeze regulatory environments and, if not, to compensate investors for the diminution in the value of an investment. Investment tribunals are authorized under treaty to award compensation to investors because, among other things, investors' legitimate expectations have been upset.[9] The 'theoretical basis' for this approach, the tribunal in Suez v. Argentina declared:[10]

> no doubt is found in the work of the eminent scholar Max Weber who advanced the idea that one of the main contributions of law to any social system is to make economic life more calculable and [who] also argued that capitalism arose in Europe because European law demonstrated a high degree of "calculability." An investor's expectations, created by law of a host country, are in effect calculations about the future.

The tribunal's invocation of Weber's sociological approach to legal norms and forms, even if uncommon, should not be all that surprising. What Weber characterized as 'formally rational law' facilitated the rise of modern markets because it respected property and contracts. A staple in the law and development

[7] Though perhaps too crude a distinction, I consider this binary synonymous with those of rich and poor and developed and underdeveloped states. It cannot be controversial to claim that investment disciplines result in the contraction of policy space—that is their intended consequence.

[8] UNCTAD (2015) 213 ('a shared view is emerging that reform is needed').

[9] Under the standards of protection concerning expropriation, minimum standard under international law and fair and equitable treatment. See discussion in Schneiderman and Van Harten (2024).

[10] Suez v. Argentina, Decision on Liability, ICSID Case No. ARB/03/19 (July 30, 2010) at para. 222. The passage was cited with approval in 'Dissenting Opinion of Mr. Gary Born' at para. 32, fn. 46, p. 12 in Antaris GmbH and Göde v Czech Republic, Award, PCA Case No 2014-01, IIC 1413 (May 2, 2018).

literature,[11] Weber's analysis of the conditions giving rise to capitalism in the 'West' often is conscripted to advance arguments that less developed and developing states need only mimic those same paths to economic success. But things are not that simple. Weber's contributions to a variety of fields of knowledge (law, economics, sociology, methodology) equip us with tools of analysis that are largely overlooked in the field of investment law.

This book aims to scrutinize the field of investment law in a sociological light, informed by the social theory of Max Weber. Methodologically, Weber purported to be doing 'value-free' social science, untainted by political or economic ideology. Weber's sociology describes forms of legal rule that reach their apogee in developed capitalist economies. Formal legal rationality, encompassing private law rules that generate calculability and predictability for economic actors was, for Weber, the most precise form of legal rule known to the occidental world.[12] Weber was preoccupied with understanding the rise of this particular phenomenon in the West.[13] Claims that these same rules will promote free markets are made today. Moreover, there is an insistence that there should be no debate about the merits of spreading a capitalist spirit globally. All that needs discussing today are the procedural means for facilitating the movement of capital across borders and the legal resolution of disputes should they arise. The book offers an exploration of the commonalities, differences, and blind spots shared by this relatively new international legal field with one of the most influential theorists of modernity.

II. Weber's Methods

Weber's training in law and legal history left its 'mark on all his future work.'[14] It helps to explain why Weber was deeply interested in legal thought and legal education, even as he remained frustrated by doctrinaire (what he labeled 'dogmatic' and 'intrajuristic') thinking that was predominant in legal thought. Writing in tumultuous times, both before and after the First World War, this 'gloomy nineteenth-century man' was preoccupied with modern threats to formal law.[15] The pursuit of substantive ends through law, Weber believed, concerned matters of social policy that 'cannot be settled on the basis of purely technical considerations.' Rather, questions concerning the proper ends of legal rules (which he associated with 'values') inevitably will 'be the subject of *dispute*.'[16] Scrutinizing the relationship between ends

[11] Trubek (2006) at 74 (Weber 'has continued to fascinate scholars' of law and development) and Trubek (1972b) at 15. D'Aspremont (2020) at 332 writes that Weber's work even 'has enjoyed dramatic popularity among international lawyers.'

[12] *Präziseste* has been translated as 'precise.' See, for example, Weber (1956) at 469.

[13] Jaspers (1989) at 81.

[14] Rheinstein (1954) at xxv and Ford (2020).

[15] Hennis (1986) at 175.

[16] Weber (1904) at 104 (emphasis in original).

and means is all that could be expected of social scientific inquiry. Interpretation of this sort could not answer contentious questions about preferred ends that ought to be pursued.[17] Instead, all that social scientists, legal scholars included, could do was evaluate the means adopted to pursue those a priori chosen ends.

Weber's sociology is replete with this distinction between ends and means. Meaning can be given to social action by evaluating the mechanisms chosen to achieve certain ends. Interpretation of 'such rationally purposeful action possesses, for the understanding of the choice of means, the highest degree of verifiable certainty.' Conversely, he adds, 'ultimate ends ... often cannot be understood completely,' though we may be able to intuit those objectives intellectually.[18] Means and ends can have a relationship that is familiar 'on grounds of experience,' as when the choice of means is almost 'inevitable.'[19] Human action, in this way, is better understood if the preferred end sought is known (though this may be obscure to observers and, sometimes, even to actors). No certainty can be attached to the interpretation of human action. Rather than causal certainty, all an observer can claim is a 'peculiarly plausible hypothesis' about sought-for ends.[20]

In Weber's sociological terminology, 'instrumentally rational action' reveals the means chosen to pursue 'calculated ends.' 'Value-rational' action, by contrast, reflects the conscious choice of ends, typically having to do with some ethical, aesthetic, religious, or other value postulates.[21] Instrumentally rational action is where individuals, acting within particular social contexts, account for the ends, means, and side effects of their behavior. Value rationality, by contrast, is almost always 'irrational,' from an instrumentally rational point of view.[22]

The dyads rational/irrational, means/ends, in addition to substantive/formal, serve as heuristic aids to Weber's sociology of law.[23] This is a chapter included among texts collected by Marianne Weber in *Economy and Society* (*Wirtschaft und Gesellschaft*) that he completed and made ready for publication prior to his death in 1920.[24] Law can be either irrational or rational in substantively and formally different ways.[25] I elaborate on the formulations in the course of this book's argument. All that needs to be said, in the meantime, is that characteristics associated with

[17] Weber (1910a).
[18] Weber (1978) at 5.
[19] Weber (1978) at 18.
[20] Weber (1978) at 9.
[21] Weber (1978) at 24–26. I draw here upon Kalberg (1980). See also Swedberg and Agevall (2016) at 173.
[22] Weber (1978) at 26. See Swedberg and Agevall (2016) at 165–67.
[23] Treiber (2020) at 25 (describing his 'contrastive pairs').
[24] Mommsen (2005) at 89 writes that the only chapter among Weber's older texts 'that he appears to have considered ready for publication was "Economy and Law" (*Wirtschaft und Recht*), the so-called "Sociology of Law" (*Rechtssoziologie*).' Kronman (1983) at 2 describes it as one of his 'least finished works.' On Marianne Weber's role in facilitating its publication, see Hanke (2009). Treiber (2020) at 8 estimates its having been completed by early- to mid-1913.
[25] See Weber (1978) at 656–57 and discussion in Kalberg (1980) and Kronman (1983).

the spread of formally rational law, interpreted and enforced by bureaucratic machinery, were, for Weber, irreversible.[26]

This reading of investment law, through a Weberian lens, can be understood as being both *for* and *against* investment law.[27] Weber can be read as *for* investment law in so far as his tools of analysis can be characterized as offering scaffolding that supports the spread of the regime's legal constraints. As mentioned, Weber's thought has been viewed as so supportive that it has been conscripted, even if rarely, by investment arbitrators as offering rationales for their findings that favor investors.[28] Scholars, too, have been quick to absorb readings of Weber that buoy their accounts of investment law.[29] He can be read *against* investment law in so far as, both methodologically and prescriptively, Weber offers tools of analysis that generate powerful critiques of the field's presuppositions. These are appraisals that the carriers of investment law—the field's scholars, lawyers, and arbitrators—have hardly grappled with.

It might be thought that a German sociologist writing at the turn of the century—associated with the 'protestant ethic,' 'ideal types,' and 'disenchantment'—will have little to contribute to contemporary debates about investment law. This book is premised on the belief that theory informs practice and that conscripting aspects of Weber's work illuminates the contemporary practice of, and debates over, international investment law. It means to demonstrate that Weber's scholarship generates insights into some of international investment law's blind spots while at the same time laying the groundwork for a better understanding of the regime's contemporary defenders.

Briefly consider, by way of illustration, the 'decades' old view that there is an 'interrelation' between signing investment treaties and promotion of the rule of law.[30] This is the claim that investment law 'furthers' procedural aspects of the rule of law *external* to states, at international levels,[31] and enhances respect for the rule of

[26] Weber (1918a) at 279 and Weiss (1987) at 160 (irreversible in the sense that thinking actors would not choose to reverse course).

[27] Though not perfectly analogous, Beetham (1989) describes Weber as being a problem *for* liberalism (in his preference for strong leadership) and problem *of* liberalism (by diagnosing the erosion of the social basis for liberal rule). If signaling ambivalence, this two-sidedness can also be understood as evidence of Weber's unrelenting insistence on being open to myriad explanations for any particular social phenomena. Jaspers (1989) at 131 explains this as Weber's 'floundering ... at the boundaries in order to set free the expanse for deeper truth in action and existence.'

[28] As in the Suez v. Argentina award and in the dissent in Antaris GmbH v. Czech Republic, in text associated with fn. 5, supra.

[29] See, for instance, Potestà (2013) at 94 and fn. 30, Salacuse (2000) at 399, and Wälde (2006) at 455. These authors are discussed further in the opening paragraph of Chapter 6.

[30] Calamita and Berman (2022) at 299 and Reinisch and Schill (2023) at 3. Authors typically distinguish between a 'procedural conception' of the rule of law, associated with 'independent, impartial, neutral, predictable, and overall fair justice,' and 'substantive' or 'material conceptions' that concern compliance with human rights such as the right to property (see Reinisch and Schill [2023] at 4).

[31] According to recitals to an International Law Association resolution of 2024: '8. CONVINCED that certain substantive standards of treatment in international investment law can be seen as expressions of the rule of law,' reproduced in Reinisch (2024) at 477.

law *internal* to states host to foreign investment.[32] The procedural features associated with the rule of law idea—take predictability and consistency, for example—are hardly values dominant in investment arbitration (discussed in Chapter 6).[33] Given the decentralized, revolving, and ad hoc nature of investment treaty arbitration, consistency and predictability have proven to be so problematic as to be identified as priority agenda items at the UN Working Group tasked with considering its reform.[34] Also weak, and largely unsubstantiated, is the alleged correlation between participating in the regime for investment protection and enhancing the procedural side of the rule of law within states. Calamita and Berman conclude their study of eight Asian states as producing 'no evidence to support the systemic claims of the rule of law theory.'[35] As Sattorova maintains, 'investment treaties and arbitration have traditionally been concerned with providing redress to disaffected investors, not with incentivizing host States to respect the rule of law.'[36] Or consider the associated claim that investment treaties enhance 'good governance.' Capital-importing states are likely to internalize legal rules and adjust their behavior to avoid investment claims, it is said.[37] One practicing lawyer alleges that signing investment treaties can alter behavior and 'sometimes have significant effects on governance.'[38] Yet this claim, too, is revealed to be weakly supported by the evidence and largely dependent on bureaucratic capacity, more robust in rich Northern states.[39] It is apparent that, for many capital-importing states, investment claims have not resulted in adjustments to internal policy deliberation.[40] Despite this empirical reality, international investment lawyers and scholars continue to promote legal protections for investors as a means of enhancing the rule of law and, thereby, improving the conditions to attract new foreign investment.[41] Even if this were substantiated by the evidence—and, to repeat, it is not—it turns out to be law reform for the privileged few.[42]

[32] Schill (2010) at 180–81.

[33] Or consider the absence of procedural safeguards for judicial independence in investment arbitration, in Van Harten (2010). Brekoulakis and Howard (2024) at 398 treat separation of powers doctrine as unsuitable for arbitration as that authority rests upon an agency or fiduciary relationship. I address the weakness of the principal-agent analogy in Chapter 5.

[34] The UN working group has been tasked with prioritizing 'consistency, coherence, [and] predictability' in its deliberations. See UNCITRAL Working Group III (Investor–State Dispute Settlement Reform) Thirty-sixth session, Vienna, October 29—November 2, 2018, 'Possible reform of investor-State dispute settlement (ISDS): Consistency and related matters. Note by the Secretariat,' August 28, 2018, A/CN.9/WG.III/WP.150. For an opposing view, see Reinisch (2023) at 234, who maintains that 'arbitral outcomes have been fairly consistent.'

[35] Calamita and Berman (2022) at 303.

[36] Sattorova (2023) at 367.

[37] Schill (2010).

[38] Krishan (2011) at 130.

[39] See, for example, Van Harten and Scott (2016) and discussion in Berge and Berger (2021).

[40] Sattorova (2018) and Calamita and Berman (2022).

[41] Bjorklund (2023) at 466 (on the external rule of law); Reinisch and Schill (2023) and Echandi (2011) at 15 (on the internal rule of law).

[42] Rodríguez (2001) at 39. This argument is developed further in Chapter 2.

Weber's probabilistic approach to legal rules better accounts for the variable outcomes within states. He insists that the causal effects of legal rules cannot be identified simply by taking notice of their content. We cannot identify empirical reality merely with reference to existing laws.[43] Nor does legal or economic development proceed along some 'biological scheme of development' that follows a path of 'law-like necessity.'[44] In other words, just because a law is enacted does not mean that individual behavior will adapt—there is only an 'objective probability' that individuals will behave as imagined.[45] There exists an 'empirically valid chance,' Weber maintains, of seeing expected conduct realized in practice.[46] Weber, therefore, envisages the likelihood of 'disharmonious development' as between law and economy.[47] In other words, Weber insists that correlations between law and conduct are not exact—the 'empirical legal order' is 'but one of the determinants of the behaviour of the acting human being.'[48] Weber's caution suggests that claims made by international investment law scholars and lawyers are causally inadequate.[49] What is proffered by them is a form of substantive reasoning, driven by an ethic of conviction, rather than one produced by knowledge of empirical realities.[50]

III. The Book's Methods

This relationship between Weberian sociology of law and investment law will not be as apparent to many as it has been to me. The burden of this book is to convince readers that such an inquiry proves fruitful. To be sure, there are weaker and stronger linkages but, in each such instance, Weber provokes deeper thinking about a number of the presuppositions at work in this regime.[51] What is assumed here is that there are 'elective affinities' between Weberian sociology and the operative assumptions of international investment law.[52] Having its source in chemistry

[43] Weber (1907) at 218 and Gephart (2015) at 51.
[44] Weber (1904c) at 19.
[45] Weber (1913b) at 291 and Weber (1906). On Weber's probabilistic approach, see Freund (1968) at 75.
[46] Weber (1913b) at 291.
[47] Käsler (1988) at 27.
[48] Weber (1907) at 220. Weber's response was to offer up ideal types with which to test historical developments. See Scaff (1989) at 39.
[49] Weber (1904) at 118 speaks of causally adequate connections. Generally, see Turner (2019).
[50] This argument is taken up further in Chapter 3.
[51] Weber (1919b) at 351 ('No science is completely without presuppositions'). These often are the product of value choices that are not entirely proved in Weber (1904a) at 116 and (1919b) at 345–46. According to Malczewski (2019) at 365, by 'presupposition' Weber refers to 'a set of organizing principles partaking of the nature of an axiom or constituting a postulate (whether empirically or logical in nature) posited to condition an entity or event of interest.' Weber expects science to be without presuppositions, the 'ethical correlate' of which was 'to think lucidly and to be intellectually honest' in Treiber (1985) at 831. Alexander (1983) devotes a volume to excavating Weber's presuppositions—his 'multidimensional understanding'—of 'action and order' (at 56).
[52] Some investment law scholars have taken note of these affinities, for example, Potestà (2013) at 94 and fn. 30, Salacuse (2000) at 399, and Wälde (2006) at 455 (discussed further in Chapter 6).

in the eighteenth century (and then given literary form in Goethe),[53] Weber invoked 'affinities' but in a vague and undisciplined manner. In its simplest formulation, affinity underscores a 'relationship,' 'correspondence,' or 'intersection' of ideas. Though the attraction between ideas and interests can produce something new,[54] Weber's usage stops short of identifying a 'necessary link' or 'direct causality' between the two.[55] Rather than reciprocal influence, the term implies a 'prior distance' or 'spiritual gap' that is conceptually filled by this research method.[56]

A particular challenge is the lack of familiarity legal scholars working in the English language have with Weber's sociology. His work is not typically taught in Anglo-American law schools, and scholarly work that discusses his legal sociology in depth are few in number.[57] Trubek's early contributions more closely line up with this book in so far as he applies Weber's legal sociology to the question of law and the quest for economic improvement.[58] Others have made important contributions to understanding Weber's sociology of law, though few have deployed his methods and arguments in order to grasp recent developments in international law.[59]

Moreover, Weber is considered a notoriously difficult writer, and his unfinished work, *Economy and Society*, is challenging and hard to navigate. There is, however, a vast secondary literature that has proven not only to be helpful but also sharpens thinking about investment law. Though I take issue with some of these interpretations, my intention is not to contribute to that body of work. Nor am I preoccupied with periodizing Weber's works or tracing the course of their development. Rather, the ambition is to provide an innovative avenue—'a valuable vantage point'[60]—for thinking about this sub-field of international law. Though there remains some controversy over what Weber meant on some questions, my

[53] Howe (1978) and Goethe (1960) at 38 ('where four substances, up to now linked together in two pairs, are brought in contact with each other, abandon their previous union and bind themselves together afresh ... the invented words "kinship by choice" [are] wholly justified'). Treiber (1985) at 811 complains that it is 'misleading to make use of Goethe's meaning of the term ... to interpret the term as used by Weber.'

[54] McKinnon (2010) at 122, 124.

[55] Weber (1910b) at 284 and Löwy (1992) at 12. See also Löwy (2004) at 102 ('de processus d'interaction qui ne relèvent ni de la causalité direct, ni du rapport "expressif" entre forme et contenu'). Weber (1910b) goes so far, however, as to claim that he had identified, in the 'ethic of calling,' a 'constituent component' in the rise of 'capitalist spirit.'

[56] Löwy (1992) at 12 and Treiber (1985) at 810 ('a train of thought with a large number of gaps'). For example, there is a large gap, though an 'elective affinity,' between religious sects that prefer 'direct democratic administration' while rejecting the charisma of office (such as the Puritans) and 'political democracy,' in Weber (1978) at 1208.

[57] Most helpful have been Rheinstein (1954), Trubek (1972a), Kronman (1983), Kennedy (2004), Sahni (2006, 2009), and Coutu (2018). Translated into English are Treiber (2020) and Gephart (2015).

[58] Trubek (1972a) and Trubek (1972b).

[59] See authors in fn. 57, *supra*. Hirsch (2015) devotes a chapter to international investment law and its connection to human rights law in his book on the sociology of international law. He does not focus particularly on Weber's sociology of law.

[60] 'Almost all of the sciences are indebted to dilettantes for achievements of some sort, and often for the contribution of quite valuable vantage points' in Weber (1920a) at 218.

object is not to conclusively resolve ongoing debates over his meaning but to explore their implications for thinking about international investment law. To this end, the book positions Weber as generating resources for thinking about modern law and, thereby, renders Weber relevant for our times.[61]

The object, however, is not merely a descriptive one. Evaluating investment law presuppositions in the light of socio-legal methods has the benefit of revealing numerous weak links in the chains of legitimation claimed by investment law professionals.[62] I have adopted these means with this particular end in mind. It is a value choice made by all researchers: by serving the god of critique, I necessarily will offend other gods.[63] I do not purport to be undertaking value-free determinations but, instead, am driven by concerns that have preoccupied me as a researcher.[64] I even hope to chase after something original by 'relating *known* facts to *known* viewpoints but nevertheless creating something new.'[65]

Such knowledge, Weber warns, becomes obsolete 'in ten, twenty or fifty years,' giving rise to new 'questions' which demand that its results 'be surpassed and rendered obsolete.'[66] The thirst for knowledge articulates well the aspiration I have for this book. 'To be surpassed in the field of science is not only the fate that we all share,' he writes, 'it is the goal that we all work towards.'[67]

IV. The Book's Outline

The first chapter explores suppositions at work in Weber's description of formally rational law that are also at play in investment law. Weber famously described formally rational law as the most exacting form of law, where 'definitely fixed legal concepts in the form of highly abstract rules are formulated and applied.' Formally rational law facilitates economic development by providing continuous, predictable, and efficient administration of justice. Formally rational law can only thrive if substantive elements exogenous to the legal system, such as those advanced

[61] Others note that 'many significant problems of Weber's era have begun to re-emerge and dominate public discussion,' including 'questioning of capitalism in its current globalized incarnation' in Hanke, Scaff, and Whimster (2019) at 6 or that Weber's preoccupations 'anticipate our own' so that scholars of today will utilize 'Weberian ideas from the past to illuminate a present problem' in Chalcraft (2008) at 1, 2.

[62] Those who 'challenge the dominant presuppositions' are labeled 'political' or 'ideological,' per Wolin (1991) at 197, as they do not assume the 'legitimation struggle is over.'

[63] Paraphrasing Weber (1919b) at 350. On the choices available to scholarly inquiry that lie within the realm of 'value ideas,' see Weber (1904) at 121.

[64] Weber (1910) at 365. See Kronman (1983) at 33–34. If asked to blurb previous work, I would describe it as preoccupied with 'others' who typically don't count within, and are provided with little solicitude by, the investment law system. See, for instance, the last section of Chapter 2 ('Unprivileged Others').

[65] Weber (1904) at 138.

[66] Weber (1919b) at 341.

[67] Weber (1919b). For an elaboration, see Oakes (1977) at 12.

by certain class interests or ideological movements, are kept at a safe distance. I trace how investment lawyers, scholars, and arbitrators conceive of this regime as exhibiting features of formally rational law. They also resist the substantively irrational—pejoratively labeled 'politics'—from entering investment law's domains. I argue that keeping substantive values at bay is impossible, not only because of pressures generated by states and citizens alike, but because the system itself is saturated with substance, in much the same way as Weber's higher form of law.

By what means are legitimate legal orders maintained? Weber described legitimacy as resting, in part, upon a 'belief' in legal authority. Two principal ways of understanding Weber's description of legitimate law have been offered to date. The first ascribes to Weber an empty formality that is satisfied merely by the fact that law is duly enacted in accordance with rules previously laid down. The second reads Weber's legitimate law as founded upon a normativity that is appealing to law's subjects. There are, according to this second reading, *reasons* that sustain the legitimacy of legality rather than merely the fact of procedural correctness. In Chapter 2, I offer up a reading of Weber that leans in the direction of a modestly normative account, one that navigates between the two poles, and which emphasizes both process and form. In order to elucidate this aspect of Weber's legal sociology, I contrast Weberian legitimacy with Lon L. Fuller's criteria of legality. In so far as it can be said that Fuller infused law with an internal morality, and should Weber's and Fuller's portrayals of law overlap, then Weber, too, can be treated as having adopted a moral view of law. This discussion sets the stage for the second half of the chapter, which examines the role that the requirement of generality plays in investment law's universalizing ambition. Though purporting to serve the 'rule of law,' the generality of investment law conceals the politics underlying investment law, projects a false universality, and promotes freedom for only a privileged few, disguising the regime's principal concern of protecting foreign investors.

At the urging of a number of academic commentators, and in some instances directed to do so by treaty text, arbitration tribunals have had recourse to a ubiquitous methodology for resolving contentious constitutional questions, namely, proportionality analysis. A focus on means-ends scrutiny is described as a 'tailor-made solution' for investment arbitration that will enhance the reputation of ISDS. Chapter 3 evaluates the success of proportionality in light of the imperatives that drive investment arbitration. These are imperatives that I associate with, in Weber's terms, an 'ethic of conviction.' This is an ethical ambition that prefers to secure the attainment of chosen ideal ends—namely, the protection of foreign investors—irrespective of the means chosen. Proportionality is less likely to succeed, I argue, when arbitrators strive to secure the regime's ambitious ends despite its consequences for diminishing state policy capacity in the pursuit of the public interest. This is contrasted with Weber's 'ethic of responsibility,' which considers the consequences of decision making, particularly having regard to the interests of all those affected by ISDS. Arbitrators, I argue, apply proportionality analysis without attention to consequences because their goal-oriented ethic of conviction overwhelms their analysis of chosen means.

Weber placed universities and legal training as central to his account of the growth of formally rational law. Legal educators were critical 'social carriers' for the spread and success of Western legal institutions and norms. Chapter 4 therefore asks: are legal educators complicit in securing the spread and arguable success of international investment law? In order to better understand the value orientation of these teachers, three overlapping, ideal types are selected as representative of thinking in this field. First are the 'cold warriors'—those who conceive of the field as an obstacle to the rise of socialism or communism within states that threaten the future of global capitalism. Investment law, in this sense, serves as a bulwark against the rise of conflict associated with the Cold War between Russia and the West. Second are those who move between the academy and arbitral practice. They will be called 'charismatics' as they offer justifications for the regime by having recourse to their own authority and expertise—like the charismatic authority of a judge. Charisma gets routinized, even bureaucratized, over time, resulting in seemingly legitimate authority that is productive of a belief necessary to sustain legitimacy over time. Last to be considered are the 'moralists,' who conceive of investment law as a means of ensuring a just world order. They issue moral verdicts founded upon ex cathedra pronouncements, concluding that extant legal rules achieve justice in the contemporary world. No independent fact-based empirical inquiry is undertaken; instead, the system is appraised in universalizable and self-evident terms. Regrettably, their versions of international legal morality leave things pretty much intact, serving as an excuse for the field's morally deficient status quo.

Weber characterizes bureaucratic power as one of the most 'fateful' forces in modern life. Accompanying the rise of formally rational law was a staff of well-trained and independent bureaucrats who administer and enforce it. Weber does not distinguish sharply between the figures who enforced the administration of justice. He subsumes judicial machinery under the larger body of officials that administer justice, among other things. In Chapter 5, I consider whether investment arbitration is a form of bureaucratic justice understood in Weberian terms. In this chapter, I take up this question, first, by summarizing Weber's worry about bureaucracy and, second, by examining scholarship that considers ways in which the authority of international adjudicators, operating in a wide variety of settings, can be reined in. Finally, in the third part, I consider ways in which investment arbitration fits into the machinery for international justice for foreign investors, serving at the apex of investment law's bureaucracy. The aim is to portray investment arbitration as not just bureaucratic in style but political in substance.

Chapter 6 turns to a question that Weber did not precisely ask: can ideal typical formally rational law alone produce economic development? Even if there is much in Weber's account that lends support to investment law's presuppositions, it is mistaken, I argue, to expect legal reforms to trigger investment for economic development. Even if it is tempting to read Weber as mapping a pathway for development that others simply can mimic, I argue that this constitutes an unfortunate misreading. Weber's conclusions are more cautious and tentative. Only detailed historical studies could explain patterns of development arising out of unique locales. There were no universal pathways to development that could be prescribed. Indeed, it would be irresponsible for social scientists to do so. Investment law professionals, for this reason, are too quick to inflate their ideal—promoting the rule of law by signing investment treaties—with the real. They should instead be more tentative and careful about the expected benefits arising out of investment treaty commitments. In short, they must be more forthright about the ethical stance that determines the object and purpose of the investment treaty disciplines: to vindicate the interests of foreign investors.

Weber famously describes the contemporary world as 'disenchanted.' By this, he meant to say that, rather than being ruled by magic and spirits, we are now governed by 'technology and calculation.' No longer can we rely upon prophets to direct the conduct of our everyday lives. Instead, individuals are forced to choose those gods—those 'ultimate standpoints'—they wish to follow. In addition to summing up the book's main arguments, the Conclusion argues that lawyers, state officials, and even citizens continue to be enchanted by international investment law. This is achieved by eliding many of the difficulties that a Weberian frame illuminates, including the role of charisma in legal rule, the assumed correlation between legal rules and economic development, and governance by investment law professionals. In other words, the Conclusion argues that the modern world is not so much disenchanted as enchanted by a legal technology that exhibits features associated with Weber's formally rational law. It is by carefully interrogating the regime's presuppositions, I contend, that one can come to a better understanding of investment law's flaws.

1
At the Barricades of Formal Law*

The community of scholars, lawyers, and arbitrators promoting the distinct system for resolving disputes between foreign investors and states—investor–state dispute settlement (ISDS)—characterizes investment law as a form of higher law. Rejected is the lowest common denominator of protections for foreign investors. Investors are granted, instead, property, contract, and due process rights akin to standards available to citizens within influential capital-exporting states.[1] ISDS offers, they say, a mode of depoliticized dispute resolution in which objective criteria are applied to resolve disputes in much the same way as judges perform lawfinding functions within the courts of investor home states. Arbitrators describe investment tribunals as offering 'independence and detachment from domestic pressures.'[2] This has distinct advantages over what they view as compromised dispute resolution processes available within states.

This self-description has an affinity with the higher form of law described by Max Weber in his chapter on the sociology of law, posthumously published in *Economy and Society*.[3] Weber famously characterizes formally rational law as the highest form of law, facilitating capitalist relations of production by providing unambiguous, continuous, and efficient administration of justice.[4] It is advantageous in modern capitalist societies, he maintains, to have legal orders promoting a regime of 'dispassionate legality'[5] that enforces 'calculable' legal rules.[6] It is a continual challenge, however, to keep at bay what Weber characterizes as 'substantive' values—things he claims that are external to law, such as ethical imperatives, utilitarian motives, or material justice—from creeping into its domains.[7]

* Adapted from David Schneiderman, 'International Investment Law as Formally Rational Law: A Weberian Analysis' in Moshe Hirsch and Anthony Lang (eds), *Research Handbook on the Sociology of International Law*. © The Editors and Contributing Authors Severally 2018. All rights reserved. Reproduced with permission of the Licensor through PLSclear.

1 Vandevelde (2017) at 20–27.

2 Clayton v. Canada (2015) Award on Jurisdiction and Liability, Permanent Court of Arbitration (PCA) Case No. 2009-04 (17 March) at para. 439.

3 Weber (1978), chap. 8.

4 Weber (1978) at 800 describes Roman forms of action as having achieved the 'highest level' of legal thinking, 'within the range of the purely analytical method' and, at 810, contrasts ecclesiastical and patrimonial hierarchies with 'achieving the highest degree of formal juridical precision which would maximize the chances for correct prediction of legal consequences and for the rational systemization of law and procedure.' On the rational administration of justice, see Weber (1978) at 974.

5 Weber (2009) at 147.

6 Weber (1920a) at 215.

7 Weber (1978) at 657.

A Sociology of International Investment Law. David Schneiderman, Oxford University Press.
© Oxford University Press 2026. DOI: 10.1093/9780198982739.003.0002

Weber accepted as representative of modern law features associated with the nineteenth-century rule of law state (*Rechtsstaat*).[8] The fear was that calculable law was being compromised by norms intended to address power imbalances endemic to modern capitalism, via the social state (*Sozialstaat*).[9] Yet Weber offers few means in his legal sociology by which the law can fend off new demands being made upon it other than by simply barricading established legal forms from competing values. In this chapter, I attribute a similar failure to international investment law. The regime purports to offer up an objectively neutral means of resolving disputes between investors and host states, yet does not do so well in mediating disputes with logics not associated with mere business morality.

One needs, of course, to approach cautiously Weber's analysis, given the difficulties of translation, much of the work's unfinished state, the immense amount of detail, and subtle shifts in argumentation.[10] Investment arbitration also serves as an imperfect model for Weber's rationally formal law, given its informal tendencies, such as unpredictable and contradictory outcomes.[11] Despite these impediments, there are features of Weber's analysis that map on well to justifications that are offered in support of investment law's system of dispute resolution. This is a legal mechanism that applies abstract norms, typically found in more 'advanced' legal systems, enforced by impartial administrators who resist the encroachment of substantive (viz. political) values that will undermine, if not destroy, the regime.[12] These are constituent elements of what Trubek calls the 'core conception of modern law,' deviations from which are intolerable, and that correspond to Weber's system of rational law.[13]

This chapter proceeds in four parts. I outline, first, Weber's argument about the rise of formal law and then turn to descriptions of international investment law that have been offered up by some of its leading advocates that appear to mirror Weber's own. In the penultimate part, I consider the limits to Weberian methods by identifying the values, associated with modern capitalism, Weber advances via formally rational law despite an insistence that his method is value free. These prescriptive defects appear to be reproduced by investment law's partisans, a discussion to which I turn in the last part.

[8] Though he 'hardly' invokes the term, per Eliaeson (2000) at 137. Weber also lacked the 'euphoria of liberal apologists' for the 'state based upon the rule of law,' argues Anter (2014) at 178. Nevertheless, Anter (2014) at 61 claims, the 'principles of legal rule Weber put forward are at root also those based upon the rule of law.' Weber had 'implicit faith in legality' and the rule of law, adds Whimster (2025) at 236.

[9] McCormick (2007) at 78.

[10] Baier, Lepsius, Mommsen, and Schluchter (2000). See Mommsen (2005) at 89 on its relatively finished state, though the chapter on sociology of law was one of the most complete.

[11] Schneiderman (2010). Compare Schultz (2014a). This is discussed further in Chapter 5.

[12] Weber (1978) at 647.

[13] Trubek (1972b) at 4, 13.

I. Modern Law as Formal Law

As mentioned in the Introduction, one of the keys to Weber's analyses in a variety of fields (social action, economics, and law) is the distinction between two ideal types of rationality, the first formal and, the second, substantive. The former is associated with the pursuit of impersonal and logically verifiable action; the latter is associated with the pursuit of some ultimate value against which results are measured.[14] In the legal field, degrees of formality are determined by whether outcomes are guided by an identifiable system of rules laid down in advance and generalizable.[15] In his sociology of law, Weber distinguishes between two types of formalism: (i) empirical formalism, where the utterance of words or attachment of a signature gives rise to legal consequences (the most 'rigorous form' perceptible as 'sense-data,' such as a signature on a document) and (ii) logical formalism where 'definitely fixed legal concepts in the form of highly abstract rules are formulated and applied' to 'legally relevant' facts (achieving 'the highest measure of methodological and logical rationality').[16] Because of its reliance on judgment rather than 'extrinsic elements,' the latter 'softens the rigidity of concrete formalism.'[17] Substantively rational law, by contrast, is concerned with values that are exogenous to a formal system of legal ordering. It is influenced 'by norms different from those obtained through logical generalization of abstract interpretations of meaning.'[18] These extra-legal considerations have to do with things such as ethics, utilitarianism, or 'political maxims' that are divorced from the 'peculiarly professional, legalistic, and abstract approach to law in the modern sense.'[19]

It is the ideal type of formal law that facilitates modern capitalism by ensuring that state law takes shape in calculable and predictable rules. '"Equality before the law" and the demand for legal guarantees against arbitrariness demand formal and objective and rational "objectivity" of administration,' Weber maintains.[20] It is this form of legality—general rules made pursuant to constitutionally sanctioned processes—that characterizes legal systems in the modern era.[21] It is not only law in this abstract and general sense that Weber admires, however. He also appreciates highly rationalized forms of justice developed by specialized courts serving specifically commercial needs.[22] These are specialized fields attending to

[14] Weber (1978) at 85.

[15] Weber (1978) at 657.

[16] Weber (1978) at 657, associated with Pandect's civil law. See discussion in Weiacker (1995) chap. 23.

[17] Weber (1978) at 657.

[18] Weber (1978) at 657. See also Kronman (1983) and Trubek (1972a).

[19] Weber (1978) at 657.

[20] Weber (1978) at 979. Arbitrariness is described as a 'total disregard' for rules in Weber (1978) at 645.

[21] Weber (1978) at 644 and Anter (2014) at 61.

[22] Weber (1978) at 858 and Treiber (2011) at 35 (e.g., 'commercial law and the law of negotiable instruments').

the 'economic needs' of 'bourgeois interests,' a form of 'modern particularism.'[23] Though departing from the requirement of generality, they produce a semblance of certainty in market relations.

Particular features associated with Weberian formally rational law deserve emphasis in light of the discussion that follows. Three features are highlighted: (i) professionalization, (ii) irreversibility, and (iii) the challenge to formal law by anti-formalist tendencies. First, the development of formally rational law requires the agency—the 'decisive cooperation'—of legally trained specialists.[24] Accompanying the increasing rationalization of law, Weber observes, is an increasing professionalization for which 'specialized, i.e. rational, training is an ineluctable requirement.'[25] Weber, in contrast to Marx, insists that such developments cannot be reduced to merely the product of economic and social conditions. Economic interests only indirectly influence the direction law takes—'they were not the exclusive, or even the primary causal forces' of the rise of a powerful stratum of jurists.[26] Instead, Weber insists that rationalization develops 'intrajuristically,' and so places emphasis on the then 'prevailing' type of legal education and professional training.[27] The growing demand for specialized knowledge was a response to 'the significance of commerce and those participating in it.'[28] While the daily needs of legal practitioners and their clients contributed to legal developments, it was not solely their needs that influenced the content of formally rational law.[29] Weber identifies the legal profession as the principal agents ('social carriers')[30] in the proliferation of rational law in the West.[31] They were 'more important than any other factor.'[32]

The rise in specialization of legal professionals is for Weber a process parallel to the increasing professionalization of the administrative state. Indeed, Weber assimilates legal professionals, in both their 'law making' (legislative) and 'law finding' (judicial) functions, to the rise of a 'specialized officials' we associate with bureaucracy—the 'modern "servant of the state".'[33] Weber goes so far as to liken the judge to a 'kind of legal paragraph machine into which one throws the documents on a case together with costs and fees so that it will then spit out a judgment along with some more or less valid reasons for it.'[34] Tendencies toward

[23] Weber (1978) at 880. 'Systematization and codification without loss of practical adaptability' was achieved 'because compelling and clearly defined economic needs were operative' in Weber (1978) at 858.

[24] Weber (1978) at 775.

[25] Weber (1978) at 775, discussed in more detail in Chapter 3.

[26] Weber (1920a) at 215.

[27] Weber (1978) at 776.

[28] Weber (1978) at 775.

[29] Gephart (2015) at 99. It was the confluence of states adopting Roman law's formal jurisprudence that indirectly precipitated the rise of capitalism, in Weber (1920b) at 343.

[30] Weber (2009) at 152 and Bendix (1962) at 85–87.

[31] Weber (1920a) at 215.

[32] Weber (1978) at 776.

[33] Weber (1919) at 322; Weber (1978) at 35; Weber (1919) at 312.

[34] Weber (1918b) at 148–49. Elsewhere, Weber analogizes the modern lawyer to a 'slot machine' in which one deposits a fee in order to 'have it spew out' a decision in Weber (1978) at 886. References to

the bureaucratization of power via this 'living machine' are 'inescapable,' its rule 'absolutely unbreakable' and 'hardest to destroy.'[35] 'The future belongs to bureaucratization,' Weber declares.[36] This was the 'steel-hard casing' (translated by Parsons as 'iron cage') that Weber both documented and problematized.[37] Constitutional reforms proposed by Russian liberals that would preserve the Tsar's authority meant 'irrevocably' joining European processes.[38] Even socialism could not escape this inevitable increase in officialdom.[39] Though expressing a great deal of ambivalence about such developments—chafing against Weber's insistence on careful historical study—the trajectory appeared to be irreversible.[40]

Finally, the principal challenge to formally rational law is the encroachment of substantive elements, exogenous to the legal system, addressing such matters as ethics, emotions, or politics.[41] These tendencies, concerning themes 'directed against the dominance of a mere business morality,' had to be kept at a safe distance.[42] Just as 'modern-rational industrial capitalism ... requires calculable technical means in order to organize work, [it] also needs a calculable law and administration that function according to formal rules.'[43] Formal law is the law of the balance sheet.[44] In his 1920 lectures on general economic history, Weber maintains that markets 'must be able to depend on calculable adjudication and administration.'[45] What capitalism requires, he declares, is 'law that can be counted upon, like a machine; ritualistic and magical considerations must be excluded.'[46] Anti-formalist tendencies—the pursuit of material or class justice—were a threat to the supremacy of a system of formally rational law. What was required were laws devoid of all 'sacredness of content.'[47] Emotions could not overtake reason.[48] The depoliticization of law was critical to this endeavor.

the machine-like qualities of law as modern bureaucratic apparatus appear in myriad places in Weber's writings. See Weber (1920a) at 207; Weber (1978) at 893, 895, 979, 1394; Weber (1895b) at 244; and Weber (2009) at 417.

35 Weber (1918a) at 156, 157; Weber (1978) at 987.
36 Weber (1918a) at 156.
37 Weber (2009) at 158. A more literal translation is offered by Sayer (1991) at 144 ('the shell [also *Gehäuse*] on a snail's back').
38 Weber (1906b) at 73. Weber predicted liberal constitutional reforms were doomed to fail because of both fiscal incapacity and the diminished political capacity of liberal reformers.
39 Weber (1918a).
40 Not entirely, however, if thinking individuals decided otherwise. See discussion in Weiss (1987).
41 Weber (1978) at 656.
42 Weber (1978) at 886.
43 Weber (1920a) at 215.
44 Weber lectured that 'a rational capitalistic establishment is one with capital accounting, that is, an establishment which determines its income yielding power by calculation according to the methods of modern bookkeeping and the striking of a balance' in Weber (1920b) at 275. On Weber's emphasis on the calculable needs of economic actors, see Kronman (1983) at 132–37.
45 Weber (1920b) at 277.
46 Weber (1920b) at 342–43.
47 Weber (1978) at 895.
48 Weber (1978) at 980.

II. Investment Law as Formal Law

It is no mere coincidence that the claimed benefits of investment law in the late twentieth century parallel many of those identified by Weber in the early twentieth century. For one thing, Weber's narrative about the legal structures accompanying the rise of modern capitalism helped to frame the first law and development movement and continues to influence its discourse, now emphasizing the 'rule of law' and principles of 'good governance.'[49] His account provides, according to Trubek, 'the most convincing and coherent analysis of the causal relationship between law and development in the West.'[50] As discussed later in this book, the faulty casual assumption that the adoption of investment treaty commitments facilitates economic development and promotes the rule of law continues to dominate the field. These claims will often be made without any empirical evidence offered in support. It is simply assumed that the 'protection offered by investment treaties is tangible enough to feature in the investor's calculus of investment risks.'[51] This assumption is not only empirically flawed but also contradicts Weber's own methods, which resist any assumed correlation between law and economic outcomes.[52]

Turning to the three features of professionalization, irreversibility, and social questions, much of the literature on international investment law is of a technical nature and generated for professional insiders. It resembles what Weber derisively labels 'legal dogmatics'[53]—what falls within the definition of investment, the application of most favored-nation clauses, or the scope of umbrella clauses are some examples of the field's main preoccupations. These are important matters, to be sure, and reveal something of the field's operating presuppositions. Recent initiatives responding to, what the United Nations Conference on Trade and Development describes as, the regime's 'legitimacy crisis'[54] reveal other trend lines. The record of proceedings at the United Nations Commission on International Trade Law (UNCITRAL) Working Group III signals some desire, confined to modest procedural reforms, to revive the regime's credibility.[55] The resulting 'disenchantment' has given rise to new treaty texts intended to better balance foreign

[49] Davis and Trebilcock (2008) at 901 describe an instrumentalist account in modernization theory that is influenced by Weber. They are rightly skeptical about these claims, just as Weber, who resisted causal chains between law and behavior, would have been.

[50] Trubek (1972b) at 15. On the influence of Parsons' interpretation of Weber in development discourse, see Thomas (2006).

[51] Douglas (2009) at 1–2. Given the 'highly competitive market' for foreign direct investment, 'stability and predictability' of the domestic legal environment are 'always important and often decisive,' Douglas writes, echoing Weber's claims about capitalism's need for calculability.

[52] On the unreliability of this assumption, see Yackee (2011) and compare with Lajour and Salfi (2015). This is further discussed in Chapter 6.

[53] Weber (1910a) at 365–66, associated with 'pure' questions of law.

[54] UNCTAD (2015a) at 128.

[55] For example, an arbitrator code of conduct, alternative dispute resolution mechanisms, and a multilateral investment court. See discussion of this proceduralist mandate in Polonskaya (2020).

investor rights against the state 'right to regulate.'[56] Such strategies are meant to serve as a way of reasserting state control over treaty outcomes.[57] Others, however, deny that there is any legitimacy problem that needs addressing. Crisis tendencies have prompted something of a rearguard action by the status group of investment lawyers and arbitrators who seek to preserve their power over the law that they administer. This posturing is instructive in so far as it yields evidence of how these legally trained professionals sustain the regime, insist on the regime's irreversibility, and resist anti-formalist pressures.

This is a group that self-identifies as a professional class with the requisite training and exclusive ability to administer a complex set of legal rules. Its method of dispute resolution promotes a model of private law in which actors are free to arrange their 'affairs as they see fit.'[58] Arbitrators supervise enforcement of these arrangements. They are described as 'professional cosmopolitans.'[59] They liken themselves to judges in national state contexts[60] but, unlike local judges, uncorruptable.[61] Not only do they perform their adjudicative functions efficiently, but they also provide a 'competent, neutral, and independent' method of international adjudication.[62] They are also specialists. There is no room for 'amateurs,' they say.[63] Arbitrators will look to like-minded scholars to assist in their interpretive tasks. Scholars 'may be key to the development of essential common principles,' declares Paulsson.[64] Douglas' *The International Law of Investment Claims* provides one such attempt at 'codifying a specialist domain of international law'[65] and to which Paulsson, as an arbitrator, will have recourse.[66] As if to prove the point being made here, Paulsson describes arbitral institutions as 'organs of justice' exhibiting 'the invaluable qualities that Max Weber ascribed to sound bureaucracies, essential to successful modern societies.'[67]

Investment lawyers, scholars, and arbitrators are those best positioned, in short, to interpret and render coherent the 'codification of customary international law'—'proto-constitutional rules for the global economy'—intended to protect and promote foreign investment.[68] This is an ensemble of impersonal rules that need to be administered impartially. Even if some of these rules had no prior cognizable

[56] Sornarajah (2015) at 5, 9.
[57] Langford, Behn, and Fauchauld (2018).
[58] Paulsson (2013) at 2.
[59] Paulsson (2013) at 274.
[60] Paulsson (2013) at 9.
[61] Paulsson (2013) at 259 and Schwebel (2015) at 10.
[62] Paulsson (2013) at 258.
[63] Weber (1918b) at 277.
[64] Paulsson (2013) at 298.
[65] Douglas (2009) at xxiv.
[66] For example, Pantechniki SA Contractors and Engineers v Albania (2009) Award, ICSID Case No ARB/07/21 (30 July) at para. 36.
[67] Paulsson (2013) at 286.
[68] Wälde and Kolo (2001) at 846, 822.

content (e.g., fair and equitable treatment[69]), they have the virtue of being directed at guaranteeing contractual expectations and non-arbitrariness. They enable states to make 'reliable promises,'[70] ensuring 'stability and predictability of the existing regulatory regime.'[71] Investment treaties have the principal function of serving to 'stabilize the favorable investment climate that exists as a matter of policy in the host state at the time the host state enters into the BIT.'[72] It is a matter of the 'governed' holding the 'state accountable in law.'[73] Wälde and Kolo liken the regime to a 'prosperity- and civilization-creating machine.'[74] So common sense is the set of legal obligations promoted by investment law professionals, governments that resist them should be treated akin to '"minors" without full legal capacity'—as 'juveniles' in the international arena.[75]

Arbitrators are not biased nor do they direct state policy. All they do is enforce binding international commitments.[76] The prospects of having states control treaty principles by drawing up new text or issuing interpretive directives—a proposal issuing out of many quarters[77]—is anathema. This would 'dispense of the rule-based system of independent and impartial, hence, apolitical, investment dispute resolution.'[78] The European Federation for Investment Law and Arbitration (EFILA) argues that 'arbitral tribunals' freedom of interpretation of the treaties should be safeguarded' rather than constrained.[79] For this reason, the European Commission proposal for a so-called investment court, a version of which has been incorporated into the Canada-EU Comprehensive Economic Trade Agreement (CETA)[80] and other European treaties, remains a threat. Even though the adjudicative mechanism leaves interpretive control to a sub-set of the investment arbitration bar, on permanent retainer, it is considered to be a 'radical departure' in the direction of greater state control over arbitral appointments.[81] In the bellicose style preferred by some investment law professionals, arbitrator Brower describes the investment court as an 'invasive species ... endeavoring by constriction to kill its prey, namely the existing investor/State arbitration system, and then go on, like a classical Colonizing Great Power, to press the vast non-EU majority of the world to accept its suzerainty.'[82]

69 Mann (1981) at 243.
70 Paulsson (2005) at 265.
71 Douglas (2009) at 1.
72 Vandevelde (1998a) at 523.
73 Hart and Dymond (2002) at 150, 170.
74 Wälde and Kolo (2001) at 814.
75 Wälde and Weiler (2002) at 163.
76 Paulsson (2005) at 263.
77 Ortino (2013); Roberts (2010); UNCTAD (2015a) at 132–35; Yackee (2012).
78 Brower and Blanchard (2014) at 696.
79 See EFILA (2014) at 4 ('The process of appointment ensures selection of independent and impartial arbitrators and there is no need to limit their freedom of interpretation').
80 In treaties with Canada, Mexico, Singapore, and Vietnam but not in the EU's treaty with Japan. See Bungenberg and Reinisch (2020) at 2287, 2304 fn. 17.
81 For example, Lalonde (2016) and American Bar Association (2016).
82 Brower (2024) at xxiv.

Repoliticization, in other words, is to be avoided at all costs. Describing as 'ideologically-driven polemics' arguments that are giving rise to ongoing legitimacy problems in the field, Brower and Blanchard purport to provide a value-free evaluation that moves from the unfounded fears of critics to 'observed experience with the existing system.'[83] Though acknowledging that the system is not perfect, the authors proclaim (without empirical evidence in support) that the system of investment arbitration 'improve[s] domestic governance' and 'strengthens the rule of law domestically and internationally.'[84] No other knowledge, other than that which promotes business morality, is admissible. Other professional logics, such as human or social rights, must be kept at a safe distance.[85]

The regime of investment law, together with its system of ISDS, it is claimed, is largely irreversible. Investment law entrepreneurs have good reason to feel confident about their future. It is, after all, an impressive victory by a group of lawyers to have convinced states to precommit to enforceable investment treaty norms on a worldwide scale. Though its origins lie in international law for the diplomatic protection of aliens, the doctrinal ambit of modern international investment law is far more expansive and its protections more powerful than any previously observed regime. By most measures, it is a truly remarkable achievement secured by this status group. Though standards of protection might change, admits Lauterpacht, 'it seems much less likely that the procedural advances will be reversed.' 'It is an old maxim that freedom once conferred cannot be withdrawn,' he observes.[86] Even if treaties can be rescinded on relatively short notice, established investments continue to take advantage of treaty protections for ten to fifteen years, on average, into the future. Even denunciations of, amounting to withdrawal from, the International Convention for the Settlement of Investment Disputes will not have quite the desired effect for established investments. Such methods, Schreuer writes, are not likely to give rise to 'quick and decisive results.'[87] Sornarajah acknowledges that the investment law project will continue to mutate, making reversal more difficult. He argues that the system, nevertheless, is now in crisis, particularly as not only developing, but also developed, states are expressing doubts about the regime's utility. 'Now that the boot is on the other foot,' Sornarajah cautions, 'it is beginning to feel the pinch quite a bit.'[88] Regime 'collapse' is 'imminent.'[89] This may only be wishful thinking. Despite the array of countries having second thoughts, including the countries of the European Union by withdrawing from the Union's Energy Charter Treaty,[90] there are powerful forces

[83] Brower and Blanchard (2014) at 700.
[84] Brower and Blanchard (2014) at 755, 760. I provide a preliminary response to this claim in the Introduction and, more fully, in Chapter 6.
[85] Hirsch (2015) chap. 5.
[86] Lauterpacht (1997) at 276.
[87] Schreuer (2011) at 794.
[88] Sornarajah (2013) at 476.
[89] Sornarajah (2015) at 47.
[90] Schneiderman (2024a) at 51, protecting European investors in the energy sector.

at work, including investment law professionals themselves, working to preserve the 'gains' made after the fall of the Berlin Wall. They will have 'valid intellectual and mercenary reasons,' Sornarajah proclaims, to continue to prop up the regime.[91] It seems premature to write off the impact such forces will have on the struggle over determining the future of international investment law.

If this discussion is not meant to be exhaustive of those features of investment law that have an affinity with Weber's ideal of rationally formal law, we should also not overstate the degree of resemblance. In many respects, investment law doctrine does not live up to Weber's ideal typical formulation. Too much discretion is granted to arbitrators to interpret laconic investor treaty protections. Investment tribunals have displayed resistance to adapting to new textual directives, despite efforts to rebalance treaty obligations so that they grant states regulatory room to maneuver.[92] The Eco Oro award is exemplary in this regard.

Despite the expressed wish of the parties to exempt measures necessary to protect the environment in treaty text, the Eco Oro tribunal insisted that compensation still be paid to the foreign investor, regardless. This was due to the cancellation of licences, granted by Colombian authorities, to exploit an ecologically sensitive alpine watershed system (the páramo) that serves as a primary source of fresh drinking water for 70 percent of the country. The text of the treaty's exceptions clause seems expressly intended to preclude the payment of compensation to an investor whenever the state takes bona fide measures to protect the environment.[93] The tribunal's interpretation of the clause declares otherwise—Colombia was required to show that the measure was not only necessary to protect the environment but also that it was necessary to pay for it. To not have provided compensation amounted to violation of the state's obligation of fair and equitable treatment.[94] This interpretation directly contradicts the treaty's message. The Eco Oro award indicates that there are few escape routes from the heightened liability rules investment tribunals seek to impose on states. The award renders less predictable the negotiated treaties that are meant to settle state expectations.

The Eco Oro award is better interpreted as ensuring the consistent enforcement of obligations owed to investors. The empirical data reinforce this impression. That

[91] Sornarajah (2015) at 54. On lawyers as playing a dominant role as professional politician, see Weber (1918b) at 217 and Weber (1919a) at 319. For analogizing professional politicians to entrepreneurs, see Weber (1919a) at 320, 338.

[92] Alschner (2022a).

[93] Article 2201(3) of the Free Trade Agreement Between Canada and Colombia (signed November 21, 2008, and in force August 15, 2011) provides that 'nothing in this Agreement shall be construed to prevent a Party from adopting or enforcing measures necessary' to protect the environment. See Garden (2023) on the state party submissions which, applying the clause, would erase state liability under the FTA.

[94] Eco Oro (2021) at para. 832. See discussion in Schneiderman (2024a) at 113–14. The tribunal in Montauk Metals (2024) at paras. 982–83 agreed with this interpretation but concluded that there was no breach, in this instance, of the Canada-Colombia FTA that would give rise to the obligation to provide compensation.

record reveals that investment tribunals behave reflexively, attentive to their institutional environment, responding to concerns expressed by influential states.[95] It also turns out that investment tribunals are more interested in securing consistency of interpretation—a hallmark of rationally formal law—than correctness, even in disputes that concern dissimilar treaties.[96] Not only are powerful capital-exporting states more advantaged by holding the pen in the course of treaty negotiations,[97] but tribunal outcomes are more likely to favor investors from capital-exporting states.[98] In addition, tribunals are more likely to prefer wealthy individual investors and large companies over less wealthy and less large investors.[99] In other words, the regime to protect foreign investment is not entirely bereft of calculability and predictability. It, instead, exhibits features that both adhere to and abjure Weber's ideal type. The regime imperfectly reflects Weber's 'utopian' view of law. Indeed, as Freund admits, any purely formal law that 'dispenses with any concern extraneous to law, has never existed and doubtless never will.'[100]

III. Managing Change Through Legal Forms?

Though the preeminent chronicler of the rise of modern law and its associated bureaucratic apparatus, Weber exhibits a great deal of ambivalence about it. If an admirer of routinized rationality, he also displays 'strong note[s] of ambiguity and soft whispers of pathos.'[101] In his writings on politics, Weber insists that political leadership, exhibiting an 'ethic of responsibility' that can hold officialdom to account, is appropriate to the task of checking the steel-hard casing of modernity.[102] The problem is that Reichstag parliamentarians were, at the time, constitutionally incapable of performing this function and so failed to attract responsible leadership. Weber, for this reason, condemned the German political branches for their 'ignorance' and 'amateurish stupidity.'[103] What he sought to adapt to German circumstances were functions already performed by the English Parliament—ones that provided the 'counterbalance of publicity' to rule by officials.[104]

Indeed, Weber admired more than English forms of parliamentary rule. Weber also admired English judges.[105] Because of the disdainful way in which Weber describes English judging in his sociology of law, Trubek understands Weber as

[95] Langford and Behn (2018) at 579.
[96] Alschner (2020).
[97] Sattorova (2022).
[98] Van Harten (2012).
[99] Van Harten and Maylsheuski (2022).
[100] Freund (1968) at 254.
[101] Wolin (2004) at 379.
[102] Weber (1919) at 352.
[103] Weber (1918a) at 178–79.
[104] Weber (1918a) at 185.
[105] Sahni (2006) at 188.

having an 'England problem.' This is because the English system of justice in the early twentieth century looked less like a rule-bound, abstract, and codified system (as on the Continent) and more like a precedent-based and discretionary system of situational justice.[106] Weber derisively labels this 'Kadi justice'—rule by 'informal judgments rendered in terms of concrete ethical or other practical valuations.'[107] The 'problem' was that England had a highly developed system of law that facilitated the rise of modern capitalism,[108] in which case, market relations did not require logically formal or codified law, only calculable law.[109] That is, given the English bar's intimate connection to business, it could reliably articulate a predictable set of norms to complement the extra-legal norms that promoted economic success. So long as the legal order reduced business risk by being 'as free as possible of surprises,' economic activity could confidently advance.[110]

England turned out to be much less of a problem for Weber. In his 1895 essay on '"Roman" and "Germanic" Law,' Weber even expresses admiration for English judges, who were no mere 'paragraph and precedent machine' crying out for 'formal characteristics,' as they were on the Continent.[111] Instead, English judges were prepared to take on a 'larger and more honourable role' which rendered them superior to their 'relatively modest' Continental counterparts.[112] 'According to a great tradition,' Weber writes, 'the English administration of justice does not avoid (in certain cases) the ethical consideration of economic events.'[113] English judges were not merely 'badly-paid civil servants' as they were on the Continent.[114] Not only did English justice promote modern capitalism, it was also in a position to thwart the bureaucratization of justice.[115] It was unlikely, however, that English judges would be able to continue along this path for much longer: 'As the bureaucratization of formal legislation progresses, the traditional position of the English judge is also likely to be transformed permanently and profoundly.'[116]

[106] Trubek (1972a) at 746–48. Neumann (1936) at 246 argues otherwise, maintaining that English law resembles Weberian continental law. The common law, he writes, 'is a closed system, a final body of rules, without gaps, so that any decision must be reached—in so far as statute law does not apply—on the basis of previously made decisions.' He concludes that, from 'this sociological view-point ... there exists neither a structural difference nor a sociologically relevant distinction between English and Continental law; or if they do exist, then only in the sense that the German, for instance, is far less rigid than the English law.'

[107] Weber (1978) at 976.

[108] Weber (1978) at 890.

[109] Treiber (2011) at 50.

[110] Kronman (1983) at 122.

[111] Weber (1895b) at 244. I am indebted here to the analysis in Sahni (2009).

[112] Weber (1895b) at 245.

[113] Weber (1895b) at 244.

[114] Neumann (1986) at 262.

[115] Stinchcombe (2001) at 79 reads Llewellyn (1960) as having replied to Weber's 'England problem.' For Llewellyn, appellate courts fill in gaps and respond to new situations by generating new formal categories ('all formal abstraction comes from informal details' at 183). The system thereby is rendered 'gapless.' Stinchcombe does not seem to have been aware of Weber's 1895 essay (1895b), which devises a response not unlike what he reads into Llewellyn.

[116] Weber (1978) at 894. If for Weber, modern law is 'in a particularly high degree jurists' law,' he also views the enactment of law (as revealed in the above quote) as becoming 'increasingly bound' to the

The real 'problem' is that Weber had no other prescription for resisting the encroachment of values alien to business morality—no way of channeling, within legal forms, claims to 'substantive justice by certain social class interests and ideologies.'[117] In other words, Weber did not manage the challenges of change very well. His ultimate message was one of 'resignation.'[118] McCormick's reading of Weber aids in thinking through this impasse. Weber, he argues, took as representative of modern law those features associated with the nineteenth-century rule of law state (*Rechtsstaat*) which, by this time, was being overtaken by the law of the social state (*Sozialstaat*) intended to partly address the power imbalances endemic to modern capitalism.[119] Like other good nineteenth-century liberals, Weber was determined to preserve 'status quo neutrality'—shielding existing baselines for the distribution of property, legal entitlements, and so on, from social pressures[120]—in his legal sociology. This is a mistake, observed Hale, in so far as it disregards the fact that law is not 'natural' but performs distributive functions dependent upon the 'relative power of coercion which the different members of the community can exert against one another.'[121]

Can we fairly accuse Weber of naturalizing the law associated with the rise of modern markets?[122] Weber adopts an anthropological approach to the rise of modern capitalism, favoring influences other than purely economic ones, in deliberate opposition to Marx. In which case, he could claim that the rise of formally rational law was not determined by economic and social circumstances; rather, there were other more important factors giving rise to its spread, including the 'intrajuristic' ones mentioned above (namely, the legal profession and legal education).[123] Extra-juristic influences (political and social conditions) were only indirect, contributing to the 'systematization' of law and 'intensifying' its 'institutionalization.'[124] Economic factors did not 'create' legal techniques, they

specialized minds of jurists, per Habermas (1984) at 256. Kennedy (2004) at 1064 argues otherwise, that Weber was already 'disenchanted' with lawmaking but held out hope for logical formal rationality reigning in interpretation (or lawfinding).

[117] Weber (1978) at 894.
[118] Mommsen (1984) at 62.
[119] McCormick (2007) at 78. But note, again, that Weber steers clear of these terms, per Eliaeson (2000) at 137.
[120] A stance associated, in the English-speaking world, with classical legal thought. See Kennedy (2004) at 1035 and Sunstein (1993) at 3. On the difficulty of preserving laws' autonomy from social forces, see Unger (1976) at 200 (it is no more than an ideal 'which the liberal form of social life makes necessary to entertain but impossible to achieve').
[121] Hale (1923) at 478.
[122] A proposition that would be vehemently resisted by Weber (1978) at 874, as the 'axioms of natural law have lost all capacity to provide the fundamental basis of a legal system.' Weber characterizes natural law as 'the sum total of all those norms which are valid independently of, and superior to, any positive law and which owe their dignity not to arbitrary enactment but, on the contrary, provide the very legitimation for the binding force of positive law' (Weber 1978 at 867).
[123] Weber (1978) at 776.
[124] Weber (1978) at 655.

only contributed to their 'dissemination,' Weber maintains.[125] Law adapted to its circumstances, developing a 'technical means' of finding a 'compromise between conflicting interests' and thereby influencing the development of modern capitalism.[126]

On the other hand, Weber appreciated the commonplace realist insight that law 'influences' the distribution of power.[127] By placing legal practitioners among society's 'conservative forces,' Weber more than hints at formal law having a structural tilt.[128] The 'propertyless masses' are not well served by 'equality before the law' and 'the "calculable" adjudication and administration demanded by bourgeois interests,' Weber admits.[129] While formally rational law ostensibly serves the interests of all, it is 'accessible only to the owners of property and thus in effect support their very autonomy and power positions.'[130] Similarly, the right of association offers, for workers, 'only formal legality' which, apart from a few cases, cannot 'serve as a means of struggle because their dispersion permanently obstructs constructive use of such a right.'[131] The 'large and unpropertied masses of the nation,' Weber acknowledges, 'can only to a limited extent experience civil law in its immediate and imperceptible importance.'[132] Underprivileged classes could not safely assume, in other words, that they would benefit from the application of formally rational law.[133] Weber, in this way, accepted a number of the social critiques of classical legal thought that were already in circulation.[134]

If Weber acknowledges the class bias of modern law, he chooses not to place too much emphasis on it.[135] Löwith's verdict, that Weber 'misunderstands himself as a specialised scientist' by denying the 'substantive character' and 'value-relatedness' of his approach to rationality, appears too harsh.[136] So too is Marcuse's pointed criticism of Weber in the 1964 conference celebrating the centenary of his birth: 'Weber's analysis was not value-free enough, in that it imported values and norms specific to capitalism into the "pure" definitions of formal rationality.'[137] In

[125] Treiber (2011) at 39 and Weber (1920a) at 215.

[126] Weber (1978) at 875 and Trubek (1972b) at 15. Lechner (2023) at 331 nevertheless observes that the links Weber draws out between law and economy appear 'strangely indefinite.'

[127] Weber (1978) at 924.

[128] Weber (1978) at 875.

[129] Weber (1978) at 980.

[130] Weber (1978) at 730.

[131] Weber (1894) at 182.

[132] Weber (1895b) at 244.

[133] In such passages, McCormick (2007) at 103 observes, Weber 'suddenly goes "red," or at least a dark shade of pink.' Sayer (1991) at 143, more to the point, describes Weber as being 'eminently consistent with Marx's view.'

[134] Kennedy (2004). See Ehrlich (1936) at 430.

[135] Colliot-Thélène (1992) at 222 comes to a similar verdict (it 'does not belong to the heart of Weber's theory of legitimacy').

[136] Löwith (1982) at 39. What Weber accuses others of 'holds equally true for himself: ultimate presuppositions and *Weltanschauungen* extend right into the "logical" structure' of his work (Löwith 1982 at 39).

[137] Marcuse (1971) at 149 and, slightly modified, Marcuse (1968) at 223. Marcuse had earlier credited Weber for having alerted readers to the connection between 'mass democracy and bureaucracy'

so far as Weber admits that formal law grants advantages to powerful economic interests—that it transmits values preferring market morality—then these charges miss their mark.[138] On the other hand, as Treiber warns, Weber continually 'takes sides.'[139] In the last part of his sociology of law, Weber valiantly aims to fend off further encroachment upon formal law by interests opposed to the logic of markets. He is 'prone,' Treiber writes, 'to the same "mixture" of ideal-typical conceptualization and evaluative judgement against which he himself warned so emphatically.'[140] His 'ambiguous position'—one could even say hostility—'toward recent trends' in law and legal theory 'are at odds with the empirical character he claims for the sociology of law,' contends Colliot-Thélène.[141]

The idealized version of the conceptual jurisprudence in which Weber was schooled[142] was 'consistently and deliberately elevated' as representing values 'worthy of being defended.'[143] As legal positivists of the nineteenth century insisted, the legal system is a 'closed' one, 'independent' of social relations, and impervious to being perturbed by extra-legal values.[144] There could be no hint of raw political power displayed in legal forms.[145] The emphasis was on preserving 'ideological neutrality' by 'locking in a set of assumptions and values and locking out all others.'[146] Though modern law is capable of transmitting a range of values,

and for having been alive to the 'material fate of the masses' being 'increasingly dependent upon the continuous and correct functioning of the increasingly bureaucratic order of private capitalistic organizations' in Marcuse (1941) at 57, quoting Weber's *Wirtschaft und Gesellschaft* (1922) at 669. For Marcuse's critique at the Heidelberg conference, see Kellner (1985) at 104–5 and Zimmerman (2006) at 74. Nelson's (1971) at 171 hostile response to Marcuse, describing the latter's intervention as a 'polemic' which has 'no place' in Weber's 'scientific method or scientific reality,' does not respond directly to Marcuse's charge. There is only this: 'The mis-steps he [Weber] made in all good faith in responding to the awesome challenges of his day do not weigh heavily in the balance against the immense services he rendered to mankind.' As for Marcuse's relationship to Weber, Bottomore (1984) at 36–38 identifies affinities between Weber and Frankfurt School theorists while Villa (2018) at 268 attributes to Weber 'the foundation and basic conceptual structure of much, if not all, of their work.' One can surmise that Weber would have treated with disdain many of the conclusions offered by this first generation of critical theorists in the absence of adequate empirical support.

138 Alexander (1983) at 117 accuses these authors of reading Weber with 'polemical intent.'

139 Treiber (2011) at 238 and Treiber (2011) at 64.

140 Treiber (2020) at 163. See also Treiber (2008) at 240, Treiber (2023) at 361, and Lechner (2023) at 330. Mommsen (2021) at 24 similarly describes the 'fairly intimate connexion between Weber's scholarly work and his political creed,' the former 'substantially stimulated by political considerations of a very fundamental nature.' It is 'doubtful,' Aron (1970) at 303 adds, that 'Max Weber refrained from all value judgment.'

141 Colliot-Thélène (2008) at 85.

142 Ghosh (2014) at 111 and Treiber (2008) at 237.

143 Treiber (2008) at 237 and Treiber (2011) at 64.

144 Weiacker (1995) at 343.

145 Weiacker (1995) at 347.

146 Merryman (1985) at 65. Working folks were particularly not well served by the judicial branches, explains Wehler (1985) at 128. They were so 'influenced by the partisan interests and ideologies of the ruling class ... that, despite the formal application of the law, the oppressed classes were adversely affected by the manipulation of justice' (quoting Fraenkel on 'class justice'). On Fraenkel's ambivalence toward formally rational law, see Scheuerman (2000) at 79–81.

including those associated with social protection, it inevitably gets processed through forms rendering them compatible with the system as a whole.[147]

An insistence on dampening legal aspirations comes through clearly in Weber's favorable review of Lotmar's book, *The Labour Contract*.[148] Weber admitted that, as 'appealing as Lotmar's social and political ethos appears,' transposing his 'concepts into the area of judicial practice *today* would necessitate radical changes to the entire character of our judicature, namely, the *abolition of its formalist basis*, in other words, a transition to "Kadi justice".'[149] The personnel staffing the judicial branch seem 'poorly qualified' to undertake this task, he writes, and, if they were to do so, would 'immediately find themselves torn apart in the whirlwind of class struggle.'[150] The only means by which working-class interests could be inserted into the extant legal frame would be 'in an impartial manner .... avoiding hasty value judgments,' working logically with 'existing legal norms according to its formal method and thereby distancing ... this method from arbitrariness, including that form of arbitrariness which disguises itself as social and ethical considerations.'[151]

Technical rationality associated with the modern pursuit of profit 'becomes the definitive standpoint from which everything is assessed'[152]—it embodies 'a commitment to ... the ideal of individual freedom,' and thus rests upon a 'substantive postulate,' writes Kronman.[153] If formally rational law can only be defended as the product of valid legal processes, rather than the product of scientific thought, dissensus provides the backdrop against which formal law is the product. It is inevitable, then, that substantive presuppositions (*weltanschauungen*) extend into the 'logical structure' of his sociology of law. It is plain from Weber's own thinking that formal law's suppositions are derived independently of rule positivism—that the ends we pursue are the product of values adopted before commencing social scientific inquiry. For this reason, it can be said that law is inevitably partial simply due to the fact that legal forms promote 'political preferences.'[154] We should not expect

[147] This was due to the influence and 'relative autonomy of jurisprudence.' Legal scholars served as the originators, arbitrators, and interpreters of the law, especially the civil law' in Kelly (1979) at 58.

[148] Weber (1902).

[149] Coutu (2009) at 577, translating Weber (1902) at 152 (emphasis added). Treiber (2008) at 239, fn. 35, describes Weber's attitude to Lotmar as 'ambivalent' whose proposal, if introduced into legal practice, would be 'foundation shaking.'

[150] Weber (1902) at 152–53 (translation by Google Translate).

[151] Weber (1902) at 149–50 (translation by Google Translate). Similarly, Hayek (1982) at 28 insists that the test of the appropriateness of a rule is the extent to which it is compatible 'with the rest of the accepted system of rules or values.' Beirne (1979) at 121 maintains that Weber did not oppose incorporation of substantive values due to his own 'political preferences' but due to an 'independent' construction of a rational legal order. This comports with Weber's skepticism of Lotmar's proposed labor law reforms, but it is hard to square with Weber's acknowledgment of rational law's class bias.

[152] Beetham (1985) at 275.

[153] Kronman (1983) at 95.

[154] Shklar (1964) at 4 who suggests that such partiality is inevitable in so far as values give 'any thinking person a sense of direction.' Similarly, see Kennedy (1997) at 41–42 (ideology as 'project'). Cotterrell (1983) at 80 claims that natural law was the 'only form of "legal ideology"' that Weber recognized. As natural law's influence dissipated, losing 'all capacity' to ground the modern legal system (Weber [1978] at 874), so did the 'ideological functions of law.'

legal formalism to 'yield,' as a consequence, 'socially neutral results.'[155] It seems inescapable to conclude that Weber's rational law, in both its procedural and substantive dimensions, 'cannot be,' as Schluchter maintains, 'without some elements of substantive rationality.'[156]

Weber vigorously defended the legal ramparts of modern capitalism against values considered extraneous to the autonomous development of the law. For this reason, his acknowledgments about class bias seem secondary to the heightened importance placed on preserving the characteristics he associated with formally rational law.[157] Weber can, therefore, fairly be accused of coming 'perilously close' to endorsing a definition of law that 'can never redistribute wealth or regulate prices.'[158]

By resisting the forces agitating for deformalized law, Weber could not—at the time he completed the chapter on the sociology of law in 1913[159]—envisage law adapting to new political and social contexts. While acknowledging formal law's limitations, he did not 'make a serious effort to come to grips' with its failings.[160] Weber, instead, hoped that political leadership could manage those forces pushing for change.[161] It was, ultimately, the heroic and charismatic individual who would be expected to take responsibility for the fate of the nation.[162] Yet Weber recognized elsewhere in his legal sociology the virtues of managing social change through law. He looked again to the English system for precedent. There were '[s]afety valves' against the effects of legal formalism, such as the use of civil juries, that represented a 'softening of rationality in the administration of justice.'[163] Elsewhere in *Economy and Society* (in the chapter on 'legitimate domination'), Weber acknowledges that there exists a 'considerable arbitrary element in the decisions of [English] justices of the peace, but only insofar as they concerned pure "police cases" *not* involving interests of the propertied.'[164] The English managed demands for substantive justice by instituting a form of 'dualism' in the administration of justice—formal law

[155] Shklar (1964) at 107. It is merely 'one morality among others,' she writes (Shklar 1964 at 109). Legal theory, 'openly or not, is conditioned at every point by ideological commitments' (Shklar 1964 at 223).

[156] Schluchter (1981) at 117. Habermas (1984) at 309, by contrast, describes modern law as 'uncoupled from ethical motives.' Weber conceives of 'modern law and legal domination ... so narrowly that the need for a principled mode of justification is shaded out in favor of sheer positivism,' reducing 'it to a rationalization of means-ends relations' in Habermas (1984) at 262.

[157] The case is further made in Chapter 2, where Weber's formally rational law is shown to resemble Fuller's inner morality of law. This reading continues to be resisted, however. See, for instance, d'avray (2023) at 66 who claims that *Wirtschaft und Gesellschaft* 'is astonishingly free from value judgements or even clues as to Weber's personal convictions.'

[158] McCormick (2007) at 84, fn. 20.

[159] Treiber (2020) at 8.

[160] Kennedy (2004) at 1055. Weber 'presents few means by which workers can forestall the authoritarian powers of command imposed upon them' in Cohen (1985) at 290.

[161] Müller (2011) at 42.

[162] Löwith (1982) at 57.

[163] Weber (1978) at 891.

[164] Weber (1978) at 271 (emphasis in original).

for the economically powerful and another ('Kadi' justice) for the weaker strata.[165] This helped to ensure the maintenance of 'juristic precision' in the fields that counted most, namely, commercial ones.[166]

In journalism published immediately after the war, Weber even included himself among those striving for 'very radical social democratization,'[167] expressing concern that popular referenda could 'obstruct socialization,'[168] and that profits not be allowed to 'get out of hand.'[169] Germany's future economy would be 'determined by both the *previous* financial burdens [namely, paying down war debt] and the *intended* socialization.'[170] 'Property was no longer sacrosanct,' observes Whimster.[171] Weber may have been strategic in his concessions to socialism, however.[172] Concerned about attracting foreign investment to rebuild Germany's economy after the war, he warns that 'a purely *proletarian* government, even the best, is *not credit worthy to foreigners*.' 'Only a bourgeois government,' Weber advises his readers, 'obtains reconstruction credit, as we need it.'[173] He remained, declares Roth, 'a liberal critic of the emerging welfare state and its pendant, the militarized state economy,' a view Roth characterizes as 'anti-anti-capitalist.'[174]

IV. Investment Law as Formal Law's Last Gasp?

In this last part, I undertake a parallel inquiry into how well investment lawyers and arbitrators are managing the pressures being brought to bear by forces wishing to alter the regime in the pursuit of logics different from the ones underlying investment law.[175] Without going into great detail about the abundant fissures that continually erupt, it should suffice to say that the regime has continually been under this sort of pressure—to accommodate interests beyond those that typically count within the investment treaty system—and that the response of the regime's actors has been varied and, arguably, ineffectual. I focus on a few of those responses here.

165 Treiber (2011) at 53.
166 Weber (1978) at 894.
167 Weber (1918c) at 25.
168 Weber (1918c) at 52.
169 Weber (1918c) at 36. See also references to Weber's support for workers and unionism in Smith (2023) at 204.
170 Weber (1918c) at 53 (emphasis in original).
171 Whimster (2021) at 12 (Weber 'steels his readers for swingeing wealth taxes and redistribution for returning troops as well as reparations').
172 Weber's appeals to social democracy are described by his translator, Sam Whimster, as being, 'in part, tactical' and partly due to the 'exigency of having to rebuild the Germany economy' in (1918c) at 25, fn. 7.
173 Weber (1918c) at 34, 35. Weber worried about proposed 'confiscations' that would arouse suspicions about Germany's credit worthiness (Weber 1918c at 34).
174 Roth (2002) at 517.
175 I have documented these sorts of pressures elsewhere. See, for example, Schneiderman (2016). Also see Hirsch (2015: chap. 5).

There is no question that, for most of the relevant actors operating within the system, the disintegration of international investment law would be intolerable. Investment lawyers are partisans of the system and, in so acting, partisans for their own cause. This helps to explain the enthusiasm with which empirical studies revealing the absence of northern 'bias' in investment treaty interpretation are embraced[176] and, conversely, the indifference with which empirical studies revealing that investment tribunals, to a statistically significant degree, prefer the interests of capital-exporting states over capital-importing ones are greeted.[177] Arbitrators are not biased and do not direct state policy, they insist. All that they do is give effect to voluntarily entered into international agreements.[178] Investment law's promoters maintain that the system is 'becoming more "democratic" than it once was and that investor-state arbitrations are not likely to be one-sided courts for capital.'[179]

For many lawyers and arbitrators, it is anathema to do anything more than to tweak some of the system's deficiencies by offering up procedural modifications—for instance, an end to unilateral appointments,[180] allowing the imposition of security for costs,[181] or preventing overcompensation in damages awards.[182] What is not permitted, for many, is to have states interfere in such ways as to disturb the preserve of arbitrators and lawyers.[183] The hyperbolic nature of resistance to change reached its apogee when Gary Born likened the establishment of an investment court, along the lines proposed by the European Commission and incorporated into some European trade and investment agreements, as resurrecting Nazi-era prohibitions on party-appointed arbitration.[184] For others, it is permissible for states to 'recalibrate' investment treaty obligations by offering up new treaty text or permitting the system to 'evolve' and, thereby, improve.[185] Alvarez goes so far as to liken these developments to a 'double movement,' analogous to the rise of the social welfare state that represented the second wave of Polanyi's countermovement.[186]

For many of them, the social critique of investment arbitration is nothing but a bundle of mistruths. Critics are described as 'shrill' and 'misguided'

[176] For example, Franck (2009).
[177] Van Harten (2012) at 233–34.
[178] Paulsson (2005) at 263.
[179] Alvarez (2010b) at 636.
[180] Paulsson (2013) at 278.
[181] Schwebel (2015) at 10.
[182] Ballantyne (2023).
[183] Brower and Blanchard (2014).
[184] Born (2021) at 418. For National Socialists, '[c]ontrolling the administration of justice and adjudication of disputes was central to those totalitarian efforts' in Born (2021) at 420. But see Živković (2022).
[185] Alvarez (2010a).
[186] Alvarez (2010b) 640; Polanyi (2001) at 138–39; Dale (2010) at 205. It can be said that, for Polanyi, 'recalibration' of a system that separate markets out from politics does not represent well the organizing principle he associated with the second of his 'double movements' in Polanyi (2001) at 234. See discussion in Schneiderman (2013a) at 7–9.

'propagandists'[187] who engage in 'ideologically driven polemics,' having 'no discernable basis in reality,' based on 'nothing more than empty rhetoric'—at bottom they are 'ignorant,' charge Brower and Blanchard.[188] Investment lawyers and arbitrators, by contrast, are virtuous and impartial, promoting a version of civilized justice that banishes politics from investment disputes. In light of these flights of rhetorical fury, one could say that they do not manage the challenge of change very well.[189]

They man the barricades of change by, in part, relying on formalistic conceptions of legitimacy that are familiar to Weberian legal thought. Procedurally correct legal forms, enacted by states, have secured the international regime for the protection of foreign investment. In this way, they remain faithful to the Weberian narrative about states having a monopoly on the legitimate use of force.[190] This is an argument that has seduced even sophisticated minds, like Habermas who, while worrying about democratic deficits at the European level, insists that international regimes are not wholly without legitimacy but are the 'fruits of political voluntarism.'[191] They were not imposed unilaterally by the United States, Habermas maintains, but were the consequence of 'cumulative negotiated agreements ... coordinated in concessive negotiations between a large number of individual governments.' Rolling back this kind of negative integration stands 'no chance of success,' he concludes.[192]

Legitimacy, for this reason, should not be a problem. Yet legitimacy problems continue to dog the regime (as argued in Chapter 4, below). This helps to explain why, for some of the 'propagating strata,' it is important to emphasize that investment law goes no further than standards of protection available to citizens within national constitutional systems.[193] This has featured prominently in U.S. debates around granting fast-track authority to the executive branch, as when President Barack Obama sought authorization to complete negotiations leading toward a Trans Pacific Partnership Agreement (TPP).[194] A group of some fifty law professors, in an open letter on ISDS directed at Congressional leadership, made this claim precisely as a way of pacifying concerns about investment law's breadth.[195]

It also helps to explain the importance of having states internalize practices of 'good governance' associated with investment treaty norms. Rather than having special rules available only to foreign investors, it would be preferred if this law

[187] Paulsson (2005) at 233.
[188] Brower and Blanchard (2014) at 699, 711, 717, 720.
[189] I have documented this 'paranoid style' elsewhere. See Schneiderman (2016).
[190] Weber (1978) at 54.
[191] Habermas (2002) at 224.
[192] Habermas (2004) at 224.
[193] Parvanov and Kantor (2012). Compare Johnson and Volkov (2013).
[194] USTR (2014).
[195] Akhavam et al. (2015) ('Many of these rights are similar to those guaranteed by the U.S. Constitution, but they might not be guaranteed in foreign countries').

were available equally to all. Some will even admit that this precisely is investment law's end game: to have investment disciplines apply to all economic regulation within the host state, irrespective of whether economic actors are foreign or domestic.[196] We can surmise that Weber would not have found this development unwelcome. If he expressed admiration of specialized courts serving specifically commercial needs, 'i.e. commercial law and the law of negotiable instruments,'[197] Weber preferred conformity with characteristics of the ideal type—that formal law be expressed in general terms and applied to all, even if all do not enjoy the fruit of its benefits.

V. Conclusion

Though they might be unaware of it, international investment lawyers, arbitrators, and scholars are partly carrying out the project that Weber envisaged one hundred years ago. Though not a perfect transcription—there is perhaps much room for discretion in the interpretation of investment treaty norms—their project approximates well Weber's own of spreading rationally formal law as a corollary to the promotion of economic security for the already powerful.

The *Sozialstaat* ultimately prevailed over Weber's formally rational law. Might history repeat? There is good reason to believe that it will not be easy to roll back investment law's strictures. The determined resistance of investment law's social carriers (scholars, lawyers, and arbitrators) to such an outcome ensures that such a struggle will be long and exhausting. Weber, for example, pointed (with some disdain) to the English bar's success in repelling departures from traditional forms of procedure or to the institution of a land registration system as examples of resistance whenever 'lawyer's material interests are threatened.'[198] This is a profession, after all, that he admired for its 'training in *fighting*'[199]—one well equipped to engage in the rearguard politics of self-defense. Moreover, even in cases where treaties are denounced, they will continue to protect investments well into the future. With a world wide web of thousands of bilateral and regional investment treaties currently in force, it seems less likely that the system will collapse in on itself.[200] Indeed, despite efforts by some political leadership, it will take a Herculean effort to dispose of it.

196 Hart and Dymond (2002) at 168 and Vandevelde (1998b) at 639.

197 Weber (1978) at 858 and Treiber (2011) at 35.

198 Weber (1978) at 788.

199 Weber (1918a) at 217 (emphasis in original).

200 It would be a mistake to read denunciations of the European Energy Charter Treaty as evidence of imminent collapse. The withdrawal of European states from investor protection for Europeans in the energy sector is meant to preserve freedom to maneuver for European states, not for those poorer states that are receptive to capital from European investors. See the discussion in Schneiderman (2024a) at 50–51.

2

Initiating and Maintaining Legitimacy

Investment law professionals have been guarding the regime's barricades for several decades. It was only after the passage of some twenty years, from the regime's take-off in the mid-1990s to its 2015 *World Investment Report*[1] that the United Nations Conference on Trade and Development (UNCTAD)[2] announced that the regime suffered from a 'legitimacy crisis.'[3] Among the shortcomings enumerated in UNCTAD's annual report were 'unforeseen' legal and financial risks without accompanying additional foreign direct investment (FDI) flows, conferring greater rights on foreign than domestic investors, creating the risk of 'regulatory chill' on 'legitimate government policymaking,' and generating procedural deficiencies such as inconsistent awards and 'due process' failures.[4] There was now an emerging 'shared view ... on the need for reform.'[5] How could this new international legal order have so quickly lost its legitimacy? Did the regime ever have it?

Whenever scholars begin to contemplate grounds for legitimacy, they are obliged to move into Max Weber's 'sphere of influence.'[6] This is because Weber addresses, however imprecisely, the means by which legitimate legal orders are maintained. Weber described legitimacy as resting, in part, upon a 'belief' (*glauben*) in legal authority.[7] Two principal ways of understanding Weber's account have been offered to date that elucidate what it means to believe in legitimate law. The first ascribes to Weber's treatment a formalism that is satisfied merely by the fact that law is enacted in accordance with rules previously laid down. The second reads Weber's legitimate law as founded upon a normativity that is appealing to law's subjects. There are, according to this second reading, reasons that sustain the legitimacy of legality rather than merely the fact of procedural correctness.[8]

1 UNCTAD (1915a) at 123 reports that the regime 'substantially gained momentum in the 1990s,' after the fall of the Berlin Wall and collapse of the Soviet Union.

2 Reports which encouraged entering into investment treaty commitments. See Perrone (2018).

3 UNCTAD (2015a) at 128.

4 UNCTAD (2015a) at 128 and UNCTAD (2015b) at 85.

5 UNCTAD (2015a) at 120. UNCTAD (2020) at 2 called for states to 'accelerate reform of old- generation treaties and thereby reduce the risk of ISDS cases against State measures in pursuit of legitimate public policy objectives.'

6 Habermas (1974) at 199.

7 Weber (1978) at 215.

8 For the first reading, see Habermas (1984) and, for the second, Schluchter (1981). Representative scholarship is discussed further in Section I.

A Sociology of International Investment Law. David Schneiderman, Oxford University Press.
 DOI: 10.1093/9780198982739.003.0003

The first reading is the commonly accepted view of Weber's condensed discussion of legitimacy. The weight of authority urges us to adopt this reading as Weber eschewed normative evaluations of legitimate law. According to this value-free formulation,[9] so long as law is enacted in accordance with formally valid criteria then it qualifies as legitimate. Obedience is then owed to legal authority because it establishes an 'impersonal order' which extends to officials authorized to issue commands.[10] There is an additional ingredient to Weber's formulation, however, often glanced over. To qualify as legitimate, there must be a 'belief in the legality of enacted rules.'[11] Might belief require something more than compliance with 'formally correct procedures'?[12]

There is good reason to think that Weber's approach to legitimacy requires something more than simply conforming to established legal processes. Consider how new international economic legal orders, such as the regime to protect foreign investors, suffer from ongoing legitimacy problems. It is not enough that rules to promote international economic cooperation are authorized by valid legal processes available in national and international fora. The response of publics in the United Kingdom (Brexit), the United States (Trump), and the rise of populism, generally, reveal significant skepticism about deferring to international regimes simply because they adhere to legally correct processes. This 'transfer of authority,' a group of American conservatives complain, 'pretends to high moral legitimacy even as it weakens representative government.'[13] Formal legality seems incapable of attracting, at least to date, an allegiance that otherwise sustains this kind of legal-rational rule over time.[14]

In this chapter, I offer up a reading of Weber that leans in the direction of a modestly normative account, one that navigates between the two dominant poles, emphasizing process and form. To elucidate this aspect of Weber's legal sociology, I contrast Weberian legitimacy with legal philosopher Lon L. Fuller's criteria of legality. Fuller is credited with having defended, in a famous debate with H. L. A. Hart, the 'values' that inhere in law.[15] In order to be regarded a system of law, rules must satisfy a number of formal characteristics specified by Fuller, among them generality and predictability. Without satisfying such criteria of 'excellence,' no

[9] Weber (1978) at 311–12.
[10] Weber (1978) at 215–16.
[11] Weber (1978) at 215.
[12] Weber (1922b) at 132 and Weber (1978) at 37.
[13] See National Conservatism (2022) ('we oppose transferring the authority of elected governments to transnational or supranational bodies—a trend that pretends to high moral legitimacy even as it weakens representative government, sows public alienation and distrust, and strengthens the influence of autocratic regimes').
[14] The regime does seem capable of continuing to enchant. See discussion in Conclusion.
[15] See Hart (1965) and Fuller (1969a) chap. 5.

'properly called' legal system could be said to exist.[16] It is upon these procedural grounds that Fuller claims to have infused law with an internal morality. If Weber's and Fuller's ideal characteristics of law overlap,[17] then Weber, too, can be treated as having subscribed to a distinctive moral view of law.[18] That is, in order to reveal the values that lie at the core of Weber's legitimate law, I piggyback on Fuller's view of legal legitimacy.[19] Even if Weber's ideal-typical features of legitimate law do not map perfectly on to Fuller's criteria of legality, there is sufficient overlap to suggest that one can claim that there is a modest normative core to Weber's account. Having identified the presence of this normative nucleus, the discussion turns to a principal virtue that is relied upon to help sustain investment law's legitimacy, namely, its generality. I argue that an emphasis on generality elides the politics underlying investment law, projects a false universality, and promotes freedom for only a privileged few, disguising the regime's principal concern of protecting foreign investors. Legitimation problems will endure so long as public—all those others who are affected by rule under investment law—are absent from the discussion.[20]

The chapter proceeds as follows: After outlining the debate over values within Weber's discussion of legitimacy, the next part turns to some of the 'easily comprehensible connections' between Weber and Fuller.[21] This is a discussion that sets

[16] Fuller (1969a) at 39 (it cannot 'properly be called a legal system at all'). In addition to generality, laws must be public, non-retroactive, clear, non-contradictory, capable of compliance, stable, and congruity between law and official action (which I associate with reciprocity). See Sciulli (1992) at 112–13. Note that Hart agrees that rules 'must satisfy certain conditions: they must be intelligible and within the capacity of most to obey, and in general they must not be retrospective, though exceptionally they may be' in Hart (1961) at 202. If this is the content of the inner morality of law, Hart says, then 'we may accept it,' also at Hart (1958) at 59 and Hart (1965) at 347, 350. On the commonalities between Hart and Fuller, see Postema (2010).

[17] Fuller's use of ideal types, if 'popularized' by Weber, is attributed to Hegel's influence on Fuller in Summers (1983) at 12. Yet his characterization of these ideals, which are 'never attained perfectly,' is redolent of Weber in Fuller (1958b) at 91. Fuller also maintained, as did Weber, that 'thought constructs' only emphasize 'a single aspect of reality and concentrates attention on it to the neglect of other aspects' in a letter to Joseph C. Hutchinson (July 5, 1932) quoted in Winston (1988) at 332, fn. 9. For a discussion of ideal types as a 'one-side accentuation,' see Weber (1904) at 125.

[18] Fuller devoted little attention to Weber even though he was familiar with continental legal theory. For passing references to Weber, see, for example, Fuller (1968) at 89 and Fuller (1969) at 143, 148–49, n. 58.

[19] It is regrettable that affinities between Weber and Fuller have not previously been the subject of much scholarly inquiry. See their consideration in Ketchen (2003) at 19 and Dyzenhaus (1997) at 148–49, who both conclude that Weberian legitimacy concerns only compliance with formally correct procedures. See also Sciulli (1992) chap. 6, who does not attend to any of the points on which they might intersect.

[20] The public interest is an elusive and contested concept, to be sure. See, for example, the essays collected in Friederich (1967), some of which rely upon formal legality as the sole criterion. Here, I follow Dewey (1927) at 15–16 ('the public consists of all those who are affected by the indirect consequences of transactions to such an extent that it is deemed necessary to have those consequences systematically cared for'). An 'all-affected principle' is elaborated upon in Habermas (2001) at 70 and in Fraser (2007) at 21. That principle helped give shape to the proposal developed in Schneiderman (2017b) and to the analysis in the second part of this chapter. Being attentive to the consequences of political action is precisely what Weber calls for in his vocation of politics lecture in Weber (1919a).

[21] Treiber (1985) at 811 describes 'elective affinities,' in part, as 'an intellectual construct for producing easily comprehensible connections.'

the stage for the second half of this chapter which interrogates one of the principal features of international investment law, namely, its ostensible 'generality.'[22] If Weber's legitimate law has a modest normative core, then investment law's legitimacy cannot rest simply upon the fact of its legality. It must also cultivate belief in its legitimacy. By shedding a spotlight on one of its purported virtues—an impartiality generated by abstract and general rules—one learns how well the regime creates and sustains legitimacy. The regime's problem is that its benefits cannot be felt outside of a narrow and privileged class of economic actors. The chapter offers a reminder that legitimate law requires something more than legally binding rules to endure.

I. Values

Theorizing of legitimacy almost always begins with Weber's ideal (or 'pure') types.[23] They serve, however, as less than adequate instruments for evaluating what is 'legitimate' and what is not.[24] His account of legitimacy, observe Turner and Factor, leaves a great deal to be desired.[25] Weber did not define or elucidate what he meant by legitimacy.[26] Nor are criteria provided with which to evaluate legitimate as opposed to illegitimate rule.[27] Though he is a stickler for defining concepts, legitimacy remains 'unclear.'[28] The absence of a 'fuller discussion' in his sociology of law is 'perplexing.'[29]

Weber insists that rule (*Herrschaft*) is not sustainable without legitimacy.[30] Every system of rule—whether old or new, public or private—aims to 'cultivate

[22] Readers less interested in Weberian normativity, internal to debates within the scholarship, should move on to the second half of the chapter where features of investment law's normativity are placed under the microscope.

[23] Loewenstein (1966) at 88 ascribes to Weber's three ideal types of legitimate rule 'his greatest achievement in political sociology.' Hennis (1976) at 89 declares that '[w]herever the category of legitimacy turns up in modern social science it is at root Weber's concept.' Indeed, it can also serve as a 'conceptual focus for the whole' of *Economy and Society*, claims Beetham (1985) at 257.

[24] Hyde (1983) at 426 goes so far as to accuse Weber's legitimacy frame as insufficient to explain compliance (it 'exhibits a sterile functionalism and blinds researchers to the possibility that law merely is a terrain of combat').

[25] Turner and Factor (1984) at 73. Contrast with Rheinstein (1954) at xxxi who describes these passages as offering great 'precision.'

[26] Friedrich (1963) at 201. It is a concept that is 'defined is nowhere in his writings,' observes Anter (2014) at 54.

[27] Anter (2014) at 61.

[28] Anter (2014) at 58. Hanke (2001) at 31 explains that Weber's typology of legitimacy was not a primary concern in his early writings on domination. This deficiency may be due to the fact that it is only after the First World War that dynastic forms of rule became 'widely discredited.' It is the case, after all, that democracy was not widespread even in early twentieth-century Europe and so did not call for 'justifications for political rule' that are now commonplace. See also Müller (2011) at 3 and Hennis (1976) at 88, 102 (an 'absolutist mode of rule remains the foil for the concept up to the present day').

[29] Adair-Toteff (2017) at 83.

[30] Weber (1978) at 213.

belief in its legitimacy.'[31] Legitimacy gives rise to the 'probability' that the 'governed' will follow the rules laid down.[32] In contrast to traditional and charismatic authority,[33] rational legal rule, the most 'modern form of administration,' is associated with a 'belief in the legality of enacted rules and the right' of those authorized to rule to 'issue commands.'[34]

By operating at such high levels of abstraction, readers are left with the impression that Weber intends his discussion of legitimate rule to be 'value-free.'[35] This is with good reason, as Weber insists that he undertakes no normative evaluation.[36] So long as the legal order enjoys the requisite 'prestige of being considered binding,' then it will enjoy legitimacy.[37] In the case of legal authority, 'obedience is owed to the legally established impersonal order.' It is 'by virtue of the formal legality of their commands' that obedience will be expected.[38] Attempts at reading in any sort of normative element into Weber's schema is described as 'an ill-fated enterprise.'[39] Weber leaves us with the impression that whatever may be law's normative appeal, it plays no role in his discussion of ideal types of rule.[40] In Weber's formulation, nothing more seems to be required other than that law has been enacted following correct legal processes.[41] No reasons or justifications for rule contribute to the system of belief.

This has prompted complaints about the thinness of Weber's account of legitimate legal rule.[42] Accusing Weber of characterizing formal law as normless, Habermas chides him for 'shading' out principled modes of justification in 'favour

[31] Weber (1978) at 213. *Glauben* is here translated into 'belief.'

[32] Weber (1978) at 31. Weber (1907) at 218–19, 225 observes the distinction between logical validity (associated with legal dogmatics) and empirical acceptance (causally influencing conduct). See also Bruun (2007) at 198–99 and Schluchter (2002) at 270–72. Radbruch (1932) at 114 similarly distinguishes between factual validity and normative validity.

[33] Swedborg and Agevall (2016) at 189–91. These categories are described in Weber (1978) at 215 and Weber (1919a) at 311–12.

[34] Weber (1978) at 217, 215.

[35] For example, Mommsen (1984) at 403–4 and his 'digression' on Winckelmann's attempt at reading Weber's legitimacy as tied to value-rational beliefs (at 448–53). Reading substantive values into Weber's discussion of legitimate law 'has been rejected by the majority of scholars,' admits Beetham (1985) at 265.

[36] Weber (1978) at 311–12. His approach takes the world as it actually is—the world of 'is' rather than one of 'ought.' The intrajuristic view of law is concerned, by contrast, with 'what normative meaning ought to be attributed' to legal propositions (at 311). See also Weber's last critique of Stammler in Weber (1978) at 325–27.

[37] Weber (1978) at 31.

[38] Weber (1978) at 215–16. Note that Weber (1919a) at 311–12 outlines three types of legitimate rule but without mentioning the need to cultivate belief.

[39] Anter (2014) at 61. Rasmussen (2023) at 98 emphasizes the structures of authority that legitimize belief rather than 'good arguments.' He refers to Hennis (1976) at 108, who takes up Smend's formulation of 'legitimation by structure' (at 104). There is some ambivalence here, as Rasmussen maintains that legitimate orders will have 'normative authority' ([2023] at 99).

[40] According to Taylor (1985) at 65, Weberian legitimacy addresses not people's attitudes but concerns an 'objective evaluation of regimes.' Taylor associates Weber's view with seventeenth-century uses of the term legitimacy.

[41] Legal validity, per Gardner (2012) at 21, 'depends on its sources, not its merits.'

[42] Kumm (2004) at 920.

of sheer positivism'—he 'neglects the moment of a need for rational justification.'[43] For Habermas, this constitutes an embarrassing omission. Criticism of Weber's normless legality is 'almost unanimous,' observes Anter.[44] In a pointed critique, Beetham argues that Weber obscures the distinction between belief and justification. The governed do not view exercises of authority over them as legitimate just because they believe it to be so, rather, it is because 'it *can* be *justified in terms of their* beliefs.'[45] What needs determining is the degree to which power conforms to the 'the normative expectations' of those subject to authority, he maintains. This calls for an evaluation of the degree of 'congruence' (or its lack) between power and the 'belief, values and expectations' of law's addressees.[46] Beetham therefore proposes filling out criteria by which belief in legitimate rule can be justified.[47]

Others seek to read values into Weber's account of legitimacy. Schluchter claims that what is sought by Weber is a 'principle of justification that permits a normative orientation and a corresponding motivation on the part of the ruled.'[48] This is a reading of Weber conducted through the lens of the Weimar-era legal theorist Hermann Heller.[49] Schluchter insists that in order to be 'believable,' law 'must give expression to basic rules.' There must be substantive, in addition to formal, elements in order for those authorized by law to rule, among them the separation of powers, self-determination, and respect for equality.[50] This is the only basis for creating a belief in legality that creates 'durable' legitimacy.[51] Other commentators agree. Some mode of justification is expected for legitimate rule under law, Kronman insists, some 'reason' to explain the plight, for instance, of materially subordinate classes.[52] Coutu adds that formal legality for Weber 'cannot be the definitive, let alone the sole criterion of legitimacy' but 'must be supplemented by substantively rational elements.'[53] Even Weber's sympathetic translator, Rheinstein, would not concede that a 'purely formal' systemized law could exist without consideration of 'some social policy, that is, of substantive rationality.'[54] It

[43] Habermas (1984) at 262. Ford (2025) at 112ff explains why Weber is not quite a legal positivist.
[44] Anter (2014) at 60.
[45] Beetham (1991) at 11 (emphasis in original). Simmons (1999) at 132–33 characterizes this as an attitudinal approach to legitimacy, which he associates with Taylor (1985) at 65–66 (legitimacy is defined with reference to 'attitudes and beliefs which dispose them to assume or refuse to assume the disciplines and burdens of membership in a given society').
[46] Beetham (1991) at 11.
[47] Beetham (1991) at 16 (that it conforms to 'established rules,' 'justified by reference' to widely shared beliefs, and there is evidence of 'consent' by subordinates to the 'particular power relation').
[48] Schluchter (1981) at 85.
[49] See Heller (1996) and Schluchter (1981) at 109.
[50] Schluchter (1981) at 109. Dyzenhaus (1997) at 213–15 reads Heller similarly and in ways that are compatible with Fuller's inner morality of law.
[51] Schluchter (1981) at 109. Heller, in his Weimar-era writing, declares that state power can only enjoy legitimacy to the degree it is able to secure 'recognition' by the law's addressees. Greater degrees of 'voluntary recognition' will be displayed when the state, 'for the sake of its self-preservation,' aims for an 'ethical justification' for the exercise of power, in Heller (1996) at 1187, 1179–80.
[52] Kronman (1983) at 41.
[53] Coutu (2018) at 83–84.
[54] Rheinstein (1954) at xlix.

is inevitable, in other words, that substantive values lie at the foundation of law's formal rationality.[55]

The presence of these opposing readings reveals the inadequacy—the 'chronic elusiveness'—of Weber's account of legitimacy.[56] This lack is underscored by the severed connection to religious belief.[57] Breuer maintains, for instance, that legal legitimacy is defined 'by its diametrical opposition to sacredness or charisma.'[58] It is this connection to Weber's sociology of religion that largely escapes discussions of legally legitimate rule. Hanke suggestively credits Weber's typology of legitimate rule to his thinking about charismatic rule. 'Max Weber's preoccupation with Sohm's "charismatic organization" of the early Christian church could have led to the idea of linking ideas of legitimacy and forms of domination,' she surmises.[59] In this way, his studies on sociology of religion and domination can be 'traced back to a common core.'[60] Ford similarly points to religious rule as the exemplar for Weber's formulation of legitimacy.[61] Could it be that traditional and charismatic forms of rule have not been overcome entirely by the ascendance of rationally formal law?[62] As Breiner suggests, might traditional rule, in particular, 'fill a legitimacy deficit' that operates in the 'interstices' of modern law?[63]

Little's study of religion and law in pre-revolutionary England is suggestive of this connection between belief and something more than normatively hollow legitimacy. Invoking Weber as his source, Little maintains that any authority—'whether it be a king, religious leader, or a parliament—will inevitably seek to validate its right to command by reference to some higher set of loyalties.' Weber, he writes, expects every society to face the task of 'arranging itself' so that 'its patterns of authority fit into an ultimate frame of meaning that commands the loyalty of

[55] Cotterrell (1983) at 83 insists that both '[f]ormal rationality and substantive rationality … are necessarily present in any legal system made up of rules aimed at the regulation of social life.' Atiyah and Summers (1987) at 2, describe law as 'an admixture of certain formal attributes on the one hand, and substantive reasoning on the other.' D'Avray (2010) at 151–52 calls attention to the role that formal law plays in 'furthering … certain explicit or unspoken values and convictions.' He also points out that Atiyah and Summers are 'unaware' of their affinities to the Weberian tradition ([2010] at 146, fn. 3).

[56] Geertz (1983) at 121 (referring to charisma but also mentioning legitimacy).

[57] According to Ghosh (2014) at 219, 'religion was the true centre of all Weberian thought.' Belief, of course, is a keyword in religious studies. It has become 'something of a habit,' writes Bell (2014) at 88, to refer to it as 'the problem of belief.'

[58] Breuer (2019) at 240.

[59] Hanke (2001) at 32 (translation by Bjorn Wagenpfeil).

[60] Hanke (2001) at 32 and Treiber (2005) at 142. Parsons (1968) at 665 emphasizes the connection between charisma and legitimate rule ('the quest of the source of legality always leads back to a charismatic element') but overstates that element in modern legal rule (the source of legality under rational bureaucratic rule is, 'in the last analysis, charismatic').

[61] Ford (2020) at 102.

[62] Parsons (1968) at 660, 665 insists that Weber envisages traditional and charismatic rule encompassing what is 'generally called religion' by linking, in Weber (1978) at 215, 'sanctity' to tradition and charisma.

[63] Breiner (2023) at 382–83, 389 (speaking of the tension between rational formal state rule and popular sovereignty).

its members.'[64] Appealing to this 'higher' frame, by which powers successfully can rule, makes some sense when speaking of religious values. Faith conditions the frame of meaning, generating the 'ultimate values' by which legitimacy is gained. Little, similarly, connects Weber's three forms of legitimate rule to religious belief—they 'were invariably treated in connection with an analysis of religion,' he declares.[65]

Does Weber, then, lean in the direction of something more than legal formalism? Legal legitimacy, complains Poggi, remains only a 'weak, legitimizing force.'[66] What then explains the resilience of legal rule. Can normatively empty legality, alone, succeed in cultivating legitimacy? Does it produce 'articles of belief' in modern societies?[67] Weber acknowledges that it is a condition of any durable rule, 'even the best organised, that it should enjoy a certain measure of inner assent from at least those sections of the ruled who carry weight in society.'[68] The problem for Little, as for many other readers, is that Weber pays little attention to the content that drives that consent. In so far as theological motivations were in play, Weber preferred to leave that to others, like his friend Ernst Troeltsch, to elucidate.[69]

Weber does not directly address the question of whether the law can generate an allegiance similar to compliance that is 'religiously conditioned.'[70] Instead, he resorts to an appeal to mere legal formality. Modern law offered logical and calculable ways of organizing social life,[71] in the same way as protestant ascetism offered believers a 'methodical' and systematized way of pursuing a spirit of 'dispassionate legality.'[72] Protestants testified 'through action' to their 'belief.'[73] Do modern subjects testify to their belief in legality by virtue of compliance? As Weber would be quick to remind us, the analysis cannot be a 'one-sided' one.[74] There may be any number of 'equally possible' factors that contribute to modern legal legitimacy.[75] However, by forsaking religion or alternative sources of value as a basis for Weber's legitimate legal rule, might we be missing a piece of the puzzle?

64 Little (1969) at 7.
65 Little (1969) at 9.
66 Poggi (1978) at 107.
67 Little (1969) at 8.
68 Weber (1918b) at 165.
69 As in Troeltsch (1931).
70 Weber understood, in an 1884 letter to his brother Alfred, that the source for modern rational rule could be found in Christianity, quoted in Ghosh (2014) at 92.
71 Legal formalism has the benefit of 'controlling the anarchy presented by plural and competing value systems' in Ghosh (2014) at 118.
72 Weber (1920) at 120, 145, 147 and Ghosh (2014) at 120.
73 Weber (1920) at 121. Kalberg (1990) at 58 suggests that salvation religions 'may endow action with continuity and even rationalize action.'
74 See Weber (1907) at 187–88 on Stammler's materialist conception of history (it is 'hopeless' to 'present historical formations as being solely determined and qualified by one single component').
75 Weber (1920) at 159 (emphasis in original removed). The subjective motivations for rule following can range widely, from 'pure expediency' to custom or habit.

Turning to Fuller's internal morality of law reveals some of the normativity that may be lingering under the surface of Weber's account. Consider, first, some selected affinities between Weber's and Fuller's legal thought.[76] On a close reading, it turns out that Weber and Fuller were not that far apart on some academic controversies they each encountered. It might be thought 'untenable' to claim that there are affinities in their legal thought.[77] Weber appears to represent a type of legal formalism that Fuller decried as impossible in legal orders that are attuned to the lives of its subjects. Despite this perceived discord, consider, first, how their views on natural law overlap. Though Weber insists that the influence of natural law had 'disintegrated,'[78] he does not deny that its content was assimilated into formally rational law. Weber acknowledges natural law as having a decisive influence on contemporary legal production and interpretation.[79] He associated the rise, in the seventeenth and eighteenth centuries, of freedom of contract with a 'universal formal principle of natural law construction.'[80] It is this species of natural law that was adopted by the US Supreme Court in the late nineteenth century, Weber notes, that gets relaxed only after 1937.[81]

Fuller, for his part, describes his project as reviving a version of natural law that denies a 'rigid separation' between the law as it is and the law as it ought to be.[82] Natural law thinking, for Fuller, represents a freer and more open style of thinking, less inhibited by disciplinary boundaries and 'unhampered by positivistic restraints.'[83] His version of natural law, however, is not that typically associated

[76] These are discussed more fully in Schneiderman (2024c).

[77] Sciulli (1992) at 88 describes it as 'untenable' to cite Fuller while retaining Weber's 'basic concepts' of his sociology of law. But see Schauer (2024) at 119, who suggests that Fuller, in describing a system without rules as no legal system at all, was 'implicitly following' what Weber described as Kadi justice.

[78] Weber (1978) at 873. Troeltsch (1922) at 212 similarly describes the 'total and fundamental dissolution of the idea of a universal Natural Law.' He distinguishes between the 'natural rights of man' tradition in Europe and its disappearance 'almost completely in Germany' by the Romantics and, ultimately, displaced by 'de-moralised law' represented by a 'stern realism' ([1922] at 207–14). Unlike Weber, Adair-Toteff (2017) at 82 notes, Troeltsch held 'natural law in high esteem.'

[79] Weber (1978) at 873. Weber describes a 'shift' from the 'ethical and juristically formal to the utilitarian and technically substantive.' See also Weber (1918a) at 329 (discussing jurists responsible for secularizing 'theories of natural law born from legal and Christian thinking').

[80] Weber (1978) at 869. These are norms, Weber quotes anonymously, which not 'even God himself could change' (at 896). The 'quasi-religious' element of modern commercial law is emphasized in Ford (2019) at 101–2.

[81] Weber appears to be speaking of the Lochner era, named after the infamous ruling in *Lochner* v. *New York*, 198 US 45 (1904) which constitutionally invalidated a New York labor law legislating maximum hours of work. The Lochner era gave expression to a 'kind of quasi-religious support for "free competition",' in Ford (2019) at 102. Weber describes judicial interpretation as being premised on a natural law reading of 'preambles to the constitutions' ([1978] at 869). This is inaccurate. The period was defined by interpretations of the US Constitution's fifth and fourteenth amendments.

[82] Fuller (1940) at 5–6. Even H. L. A. Hart acknowledged a 'core of good sense' in natural law and whose 'minimum content' informs modern law in Hart (1961) at 188–95 (as regard rules 'respecting persons, property and promises,' at 193).

[83] Fuller (1940) at 104 and Fuller (1968) at 181 (describing his version of natural law as a more 'modest form,' rejecting the 'dogmatisms' associated with an eternal and unchanging natural law).

with its dominant 'higher law' variants.[84] Fuller calls out those, working within the natural tradition, who rely on 'firm, incorrigible rules' that abstracted means from ends.[85] Natural law writers are content simply to 'lay down rules about what is right' without explaining the mechanics of 'how you get there,' a complaint that would have been welcome to legal positivists.[86] Fuller's aim is to bring to the surface hidden, substantive elements in systems of law, but it was a 'procedural or institutional kind of natural law.'[87] As Selznick describes it, Fuller's is a 'morality of good practice, of means rather than ends.'[88]

If Weber denies being committed to values in his legal sociology,[89] Fuller similarly denies advancing substantive ends, bracketing features of valid law from moral considerations.[90] Issues such as 'polygamy, the study of Marx,' or 'the worship of God' are resolved with reference to a morality that is 'external' to law, he says.[91] Nevertheless, Fuller was entangled in debates over collapsing the 'chasm' between 'is' and 'ought,'[92] a divide that Weber sought vigorously to defend.[93] Fuller, however, did not want to be understood as claiming that 'what ought to be can be deduced from what is.'[94] Rather, he sought to emphasize the 'goal-directed' nature of human conduct and that goals, or purposes, assist interpreters in vicariously understanding the meaning of human action.[95] In this way, Fuller's purposive approach to action is congenial to Weber's method of interpretive understanding (*verstehen*), where regularities in human conduct make it meaningfully possible to discern the values that motivate behavior.[96]

[84] As Shklar (1986) at 68 emphasizes, there is a great degree of 'diversity and incompatibility among the various schools of natural law.'

[85] Winston (2021) at 670.

[86] Letter from Fuller to B. R. Inagaki (April 6, 1969) quoted in Rundle (2017) at 430 and in Winston (2021) at 671.

[87] Fuller (1969a) at 184. For this reason, Fuller's approach would not have appeased Strauss (1950) at 42, who accused Weber's 'thesis [of] necessarily lead[ing] to nihilism.' For a more sympathetic natural law reading of Fuller, see Finnis (1980) at 274.

[88] Selznick (1965) at 948. Raz (1979) at 224 claims that Fuller's argument, that law is necessarily moral, 'fails.' At most, Fuller's instrumental account reveals the 'value' or 'virtue' of the rule of law but not its moral virtue.

[89] But see Cohen (1972) at 85 ('certainly his categories are not value free').

[90] Fuller (1954a) at 480 (his studies implied 'no commitment to "ultimate ends"').

[91] Fuller (1969a) at 96 (including 'progressive income tax, or the subjugation of women'). Reminiscent of Weber, Fuller (1956) at 702 writes that the 'validity of human ends and "values" is not a matter of reasoned demonstration' but decided by 'some fiat of the will.'

[92] See the debate between Nagel (1958) and Fuller (1958b). Chasm is from D'Entrèves (1970) at 151.

[93] For Weber (1913a) at 310, the scholarly mixing up of facts and values 'constitute the most reprehensible of all [possible] abuses.' See also Weber's criticism of Stammler in Weber (1978) at 326 and discussion in Coutu (2013). Weber (1910a) at 365, in reply to Kantorowitz, declares that whether the value of a legal norm is 'desirable ... cannot be resolved by the kind of work that we want to pursue.' According to Kronman (1983) at 86, for Weber, 'values do not inhere in facts.'

[94] Winston (1988) at 332.

[95] Fuller (1956) at 697, 699.

[96] Weber (1978) at 18, Ghosh (2014) at 130–31 ('that is, [conduct] measured according to the degree of its rationality'), and Oakes (1975) at 33–37.

If moral concerns are walled off, Fuller nevertheless problematizes the distinction between ends and means. That ends can be pursued regardless of the choice of means retains a 'curious vitality,' observes Fuller. The separation of 'ends-setters' from 'means-specialists' assumes that social institutions are 'infinitely pliable' and so can be 'shaped to any desired end.'[97] Complaints about the separation of ends and means is, of course, prominent in Weber's methodological writings. He provides no warrant to those who use any means in the pursuit of chosen ends. If violence is the specific means available to politics, then political leadership having an ethic of responsibility will attend to the foreseeable consequences of ends that are being pursued. A shared cautious liberalism that breaks down the distinction between values and processes animates both Fuller and Weber.[98] This is made most evident in their shared interest in the features associated with properly enacted law.

Fuller firmly believed that something more than mere formal correctness was required for law to be considered legitimate. What is called for were benchmarks that regulate lawmaking activities.[99] Fuller offers up a number of criteria more likely to produce 'good' law.[100] As mentioned, he does not embrace a version of natural law guided by some external or transcendent authority.[101] His, instead, is a version insistent upon the capacity of men to 'reason,' to be 'responsible' agents,[102] and committed to keeping open the 'channels of communication' by which we convey to others what we 'perceive, feel and desire.'[103]

To the extent that Weber's rationally formal law exhibits characteristics that resemble some of Fuller's 'utopia' of eight principles of legality, there are grounds to think that we can ascribe to Weber the promotion of certain values associated with validly enacted law.[104] Among them, and repeatedly emphasized by Weber,

[97] Fuller (1956–57) at 63, 56. For discussion, see Westerman (1999). Any disagreement with H. L. A. Hart melted in this respect as well. Hart (1958) at 86 pleads for a corrective to the view that there is a sharp separation between ends and means and that 'rational argument is reserved for discussion [only] of "means".'

[98] According to Nagel (1958) at 81, Fuller (1956) at 702 exhibited a naivete that value conflicts, in course of collaborative processes, could be overcome.

[99] Fuller (1958a) at 641.

[100] Fuller (1958a) at 636. On 'fidelity' to law producing good effects, see Fuller (1958a) and Fuller (1954a) at 468. Though 'bad' law, it is not necessarily legally invalid in Fuller (1969) at 123. It must amount to a 'sufficiently gross departure from the principles of legality' to amount to 'not law at all,' in Fuller (1969) at 170. For discussion, see Summers (1984) at 71.

[101] Fuller's understanding of natural law rejected guidance from an 'authoritative' source, denied any resemblance to a 'written code,' and spurned anything like a transcendent 'higher law' in Fuller (1958b) at 84. Instead, Fuller contemplated 'natural laws associated with a particular kind of human undertaking,' namely, subjecting human conduct to legal rules, what he would come to call 'eunomics.' See Fuller (1969) at 96 and Mootz III at 428. West (2011) at 45 maintains that the divide between Fuller and Catholic natural law scholars was greater than that between Fuller and Hart. The worry, for Catholic legal thinkers like Finnis (1980) at 274, is that although there is value to Fuller's 'desiderata,' they do 'not guarantee every aspect of the common good, and sometimes it does not secure even the substance of the common good.'

[102] Fuller (1969) at 162.

[103] Fuller (1969) at 186.

[104] Fuller (1969a) at 42.

are generally enacted rules that are more likely to bring about the impartial administration of justice.

Generality

For Weber, the outstanding feature of modern legal rule is that it operates without regard to 'personal considerations' or to 'personalistic status order.'[105] Legitimate law establishes an 'impersonal order' of abstract rules.[106] These typically will be 'legal precepts' following principles which are 'capable of generalized formulation . . . . approved' by the 'governing' group.'[107] Law 'creation' exhibits the characteristics of legitimate law when 'general rules' are promulgated, addressing 'typical situations rather, than merely intervening in specific cases.'[108] Obedience is not owed to those with authority to enforce or administer law, however, but to that 'impersonal order' itself.[109] There will also be an expected congruence between lawmaking and lawfinding (interpretation and enforcement).[110] '[O]bservance by the government of the rules is regarded as the ordinary thing,' Weber maintains, and 'disregard' of the rules 'would ordinarily' be characterized as '"arbitrary" conduct.'[111]

This approach mirrors at least one of the eight principles—seemingly one of the central features—associated with the rule of law enumerated by Fuller.[112] This is the 'requirement of generality,' which demands the faithful application of rules 'previously declared as those to be followed.'[113] This feature of traditional liberal legal thought is envisaged as a guide for human affairs.[114] The law, Fuller writes, 'does not tell a man what he should do to accomplish specific ends set by the lawgiver,' rather, 'it furnishes him with baselines against which to organize his life with his fellows.'[115] This requirement does not deprive legal authorities, whether they be courts or tax adjudicators, from issuing commands directed against specific persons. Rather, an insistence on generality serves as a precondition for individuals

[105] Weber (1978) at 225, 600.
[106] Weber (1978) at 215, 217.
[107] Weber (1978) at 217.
[108] Weber (1978) at 645.
[109] Weber (1978) at 218. This is presented as 'the modern form of reason—as objective scientific rationality' in Cohen (1972) at 86.
[110] On 'lawmaking' (creation) vs. 'lawfinding' (application), see Weber (1978) at 653–54 and, relatedly, on legislation vs. adjudication, see Weber (1978) at 644–45.
[111] Weber (1978) at 645, discussed further below under 'Reciprocity.'
[112] On the role of generality, see Rundle (2012) at 9 ('the other seven principles . . . follow naturally, because, together, it is observance of these requirements that makes governance through general rules not just effective, but possible').
[113] Fuller (1969a) at 46. Fuller emphasizes that there 'must be rules of some kind' ([1969a] at 46).
[114] Winston (1981) at 38.
[115] Fuller (1969b) at 234. Fuller (1936) at 195–96 associates 'congruence between legal rules and ways of life' with Llewellyn's version of legal realism. See Llewellyn (1989) at 82.

who desire to be free to steer the lives in whichever direction they wish. One is thereby not 'told at each turn what to do' but furnished only with a 'baseline for self-directed action.'[116] So long as formally rational law exhibits a semblance of generality, then a wider ambit of freedom of choice is left to the individual, even if, as Weber admits, it is the propertied classes who are more likely to benefit from this sort of freedom.[117]

There will be an opportunity to elaborate upon this later in the chapter but, to sum up this point, among the formal prerequisites for the exercise of legislative power, for Fuller, is that it be exercised 'impersonally.'[118] The requirement of generality, which is a central feature of Fuller's internal morality of law, is also vital to Weber's description of formally rational law that has the most probability of achieving legitimacy and, therefore, compliance. Consequently, to claim that there is no normative content to Weber's idea of legal legitimacy belies, one could say, belief.

Predictability

That law be predictable is another feature of rationally formal law that helps to sustain belief in its legitimacy. In contrast to the capricious and arbitrary features of law associated with, what Weber derisively labels, Kadi justice, the consistency with which bureaucratic staff applies law to particular cases is a feature of secularized legal administration.[119] This is allied to the needs of modern business which insists on a prompt and 'predictably functioning legal system.'[120] Business firms cannot prosper under capricious justice, Weber insists. Instead, the 'modern capitalist enterprise rests primarily on calculation and presupposes a legal and administrative system, whose functioning can be rationally predicted, at least in principle, by virtue of its fixed general norms, just like the expected performance of a machine.'[121]

A number of Fuller's criteria of legality correspond to Weber's emphasis on predictability. Among them, the need for constancy and coherence, and the expectation that no one is above the law.[122] Associated with predictability is an insistence on stability. No properly called legal system can withstand a 'daily stream

[116] Fuller (1969a) at 210.
[117] Kronman (1983) at 95 and Trubek (1985) at 931. Individual freedom modeled upon market transactions is mostly available to the propertied classes who can take advantage of these lawmaking powers in Weber (1978) at 699.
[118] Winston (1981) at 38.
[119] Weber (1978) at 217.
[120] Weber (1978) at 337.
[121] Weber (1978) at 1394.
[122] These are associated with the criteria of clarity, stability, and congruence between law and official action. See the criteria mentioned in *supra*, fn. 9.

of amendments,' Fuller declares.[123] Nor can a system properly be called law if it were to apply rules differentially or inconsistently.[124] Any functioning legal system requires a 'sound and stable framework' for interactions between citizens and government.[125] A preference for stability is connected to the systemic bias against retrospective laws, another of Fuller's criteria of legality. This 'reliance' factor does not render the legal status quo immutable. Instead, what is required is that 'some warning is given of the impending change and the change itself does not become effective so swiftly that an insufficient time is left for adjustment to the new state of the law.'[126] Weber, too, cannot conceive of a fully rationalized system of law that does not meet these formal requirements.[127] It would be hard to sustain belief in a system so bereft of predictability.

Reciprocity

One particular feature of Fuller's account, not expressly accounted for in his criteria of legality but presupposed by many of them, concerns the principle of reciprocity.[128] This principle, Fuller declares, lies at the intersection between 'the morality of duty and the economics of exchange.' It is represented by Jesus's teachings in the Sermon on the Mount: do unto others as they do unto you.[129] This 'bond of reciprocity' unites us, Fuller says, in 'anonymous collaboration' not only in the pursuit of market exchanges but in rule following.[130] Too often, law creation is viewed as simply the 'exercise of authority' exhibiting none of the 'interplay' of reciprocity between enacted law and citizen. Typically, the 'law does not invite the citizen to interact with it; it acts upon him.'[131] These interactions, 'once central,' have been 'pushed to the periphery,' Fuller complains.[132]

This amounts to a bargain of a sort: a 'relatively stable reciprocity of expectations' which underlies relations between 'lawgiver and subject.' It is 'part of the

[123] Fuller (1969a) at 37 (describing a regime led by a mythical King Rex that could not properly be called law).
[124] As in King Rex's exercise in codification, which did not correspond to Rex's own rulings, in Fuller (1969a) at 38.
[125] Fuller (1969a) at 210.
[126] Fuller (1969a) at 80.
[127] Weber (1978) at 886 worried, however, that anti-formal pressures upon rationally formal law could not be resisted.
[128] Fuller (1969a) at 61 (once made explicit, [reciprocity] can be extended to all eight principles of legality"). Waldron (2010) at 153 writes that the requirements of consistency and congruence make sense when 'we begin to understand law as a more-or-less horizontal enterprise of reciprocity between law-maker and law-subject.'
[129] Matthew 7:12. Fuller's is a much less demanding version than Weber's, who maintains that Jesus's sermon makes 'unworldly demands' on us in Weber (1919) at 364.
[130] Fuller (1969a) at 22–23, 40.
[131] Fuller (1969b) at 231.
[132] Fuller (1969b) at 232.

very idea of a functioning legal order.'[133] In the usual case, legal subjects 'must of necessity accept *on* faith that his government is playing the game of law fairly.'[134] A 'functioning legal system,' Fuller concludes, 'depends upon a cooperative effort—an effective and responsible interaction—between' ruler and subject.[135] Failure to follow the dual obligations of generality and not abiding by the system's 'own declared rules' amounts to no system of law at all.[136] It is with this interactional view of law in mind, Fuller insists, that 'many things' become clear that are 'now obscured by the prevailing conception of law as a one-way projection of authority.'[137]

Is there an element of reciprocity in Weber's account of legitimate law? Weber's sociology of law accentuates some of these same features by indicating that government be bound by its own legal norms and 'limited by vested rights.' These are 'restraints' upon government's own freedom of action 'to which it must adjust itself.'[138] But his emphasis upon the ruler and not upon the ruled accentuates the unidirectional authority of law that Fuller laments. 'To the government,' Weber writes, 'the individual and his interests are in the sense legal objects rather than the bearer of rights.'[139] Rulers act upon subjects of law rather than the ruled acting as subjects participating in law creation and law application. For Weber, reciprocal relations are confined to the private sphere, 'for instance, in the agreement of two business partners concerning the division of work and profits between them and their legal position within and outside the firm.'[140] There are, nevertheless, intimations of reciprocity in Weber's account of legitimate law that can be drawn out.

The Subjects of Law

We are left with the impression that when Weber addresses 'belief' in legitimate rule, he is preoccupied with the belief of ruling authorities rather than the belief of the subjects of rule.[141] For instance, Weber prefers to emphasize the role of charismatic leadership or of bureaucratic *fonctionnaires*. Yet even charismatic authority, Weber admits, 'rests entirely on recognition by the ruled.'[142] It is this other side to

[133] Fuller (1969a) at 209.
[134] Fuller (1969b) at 235.
[135] Fuller (1969a) at 219. Fuller (1969a) at 39, fn. 1 and at 61, fn. 19 acknowledges the influence of Simmel (1950) at 186.
[136] Fuller (1969b) at 235.
[137] Fuller (1969a) at 221. Governance can never be a 'top-down project' writes Rundle (2021) at 191 of Fuller.
[138] Weber (1978) at 644.
[139] Weber (1978) at 645.
[140] Weber (1978) at 699.
[141] For example, Kalberg (2017) at 53–54, who names bureaucratic organization as the most 'widely discussed type of rulership.'
[142] Weber (1978) at 266.

Weber's account of legitimacy that a comparison with Fuller draws out, namely, the role played by the subjects of rule. Weber's reference to 'belief' as 'the basis of every authority and, correspondingly, every kind of willingness to obey' calls attention to this perspective.[143] Belief may be 'guaranteed' by either 'purely subjective' internal effects or the 'expectation of specific external effects.'[144] Moreover, 'the composition of this belief is seldom altogether simple.' In the case of legal authority, Weber maintains, 'it is never purely legal.'[145] '[B]elief in legality' can help prop up traditional authority by virtue of habit, or it may co-mingle with charismatic elements.[146] In order for legal orders to secure success, 'consensual action' among the subjects of law is required.[147] Weber appears to admit that law's subjects typically will demand something more than procedural correctness. This is also appreciated by those having the power to rule over others. Weber acknowledges the 'generally observable need of any power, or even of any advantage of life, to justify itself.'[148]

This helps to explain why, for example, beliefs justifying superior wealth can deteriorate in the face of material inequality. When the disadvantages associated with inequality become 'openly visible to everyone as the factor determining every man's individual fate,' then the myth of a naturally privileged strata becomes 'one of the most passionately hated objects of attack.'[149] It is true that even the materially fortunate will look for legitimation—'[g]ood fortune has to be "legitimate",' Weber declares.[150] But it is at these moments that every form of rule 'always has the strongest need of self-justification.'[151] It is not sufficient, in other words, to leave subordinate strata with the impression that their fate is the product of arbitrariness.[152] In every system of domination, Weber concludes, there will be 'attempts to establish and to cultivate belief in its legitimacy.'[153] These clues about belief rub

143 Weber (1978) at 263.

144 Weber (1978) at 33. Subjective guarantees may be based upon emotional, value-rational, or religious grounds. It is possible, Weber adds, that 'ethically normative beliefs' (subjective elements) may 'have a profound influence on action in the absence of any sort of external guarantee' ([1978] at 36).

145 Weber (1978) at 263.

146 Weber (1978) at 263, 954 and Weber (1922) at 141.

147 Weber (1978) at 334, 213. Lassman (2000) at 88 declares that '[t]his definition [of legitimacy] is not concerned with … the question of the beliefs which justify acceptance.' This is hard to square with Weber's declaration that legitimacy rests upon belief.

148 Weber (1978) at 953.

149 Weber (1978) at 953.

150 Weber (1915) at 60 and in Weber (1978) at 491 ('Our everyday experience proves that there exists just such a need for psychic comfort about the legitimacy or deservedness of one's happiness'). See also discussion in Berger (1967) at 31 and Kronman (1983) at 41.

151 Weber (1978) at 954. Rulers must appeal to 'ultimate principles' expressed as one of the three ideal typical forms of rule—namely, tradition, charisma, and legality. See also Heller (1996) at 1148 ('Every political power is the more stable the more it succeeds in bringing to recognition the obligatory nature of its own orders of ideas and norms').

152 Kronman (1983) at 41. Weber (1915) at 60 and in Weber (1978) at 491 ('Our everyday experience proves that there exists just such a need for psychic comfort about the legitimacy or deservedness of one's happiness').

153 Weber (1978) at 213.

against the idea that Weber was not concerned with anything beyond the external force of the law. They underscore the need for legitimate forms of rule to justify themselves—to 'cultivate belief' among those who acquiesce to being ruled.[154] They offer credence to Weber's observation that there is an '(often hair-thin) line that separates science from belief.'[155]

This element is made most apparent in Weber's discussion of charismatic rule.[156] The successful charismatic ruler is entirely dependent on maintaining the belief among followers that the leader has the personal qualities to justify exercises of authority. Moreover, as charismatic rule becomes routinized, by designating successors and deploying bureaucratic-like staff to back up its authority, the community of followers 'is free to create, accept, and abolish laws just as it likes, whether in the general or in a particular case.'[157] The principle of election, in other words, emerges as an 'anti-authoritarian' check on 'charismatic judicial decisions.'[158] The subjects of legitimate rule, in other words, are active agents, as Fuller suggests, not merely passive subjects.

Weber's writings on parliamentary democracy and political education accentuate the element of tacit reciprocity present in functioning systems of democratic rule.[159] His ambition was to have Germany incorporate deliberative processes resembling idealized British ones, adapting to German circumstances functions performed by the English Parliament so as to provide a 'counterbalance' to rule by bureaucratic administration.[160] Parliamentary publicity was expected to generate responsive public opinion, establishing a 'medium of genuine if incomplete identity between rulers and ruled.'[161] Political education was likely to be enhanced as a consequence.[162] Not only would enfranchisement express the unity of the nation,[163] but it would also help 'mitigate' social and material inequalities.[164] With

[154] On justification, see Weber (1978) at 213 and Coutu (2018) at 83 (ethical rationalization 'is the key element') and Netelenbos (2016) at 11 (to achieve legitimacy, the ruled will 'value-rationally believe' in the right to rule). Legitimate rule is distinguished from rule by 'fear' or by motives of 'expediency' in Weber (1978) at 37. These conceivably are non-legitimate orders.

[155] Weber (1904) at 137.

[156] Hanke (2001) at 32 helpfully points to charismatic rule as forming the basis for Weber's thinking about legitimacy and its relationship to forms of domination.

[157] Weber (2019) at 406 and, alternatively, Weber (1978) at 267. Adair-Toteff (2017) at 82 notes that in his *Staatssoziologie* lectures, Weber emphasizes not choice but the 'duty' to obey charismatic leadership.

[158] Weber (2019) at 406 and Weber (1978) at 267. See discussion in Hanke (2025) at 263.

[159] Whimster (2007) at 235–40 emphasizes this element of participation 'from below.'

[160] Weber (1918b) at 185. See discussion in Palonen (2004).

[161] Cohen and Arato (1992) at 233.

[162] Scaff (1973) makes a key contribution here. Political education was a long-standing 'preoccupation,' according to Barbalet (2023) at 89, also Turner and Factor (1984) at 87. Both Hegel (1820) at paras. 315–16 and Mill (1861) at 216 argued that empowering citizens to participate in self-government advanced political education.

[163] Weber (1918b) at 268 associated 'national pride' with the 'degree to which the members of a nation, at least potentially, are *actively* involved in shaping the politics of the country' (emphasis in original).

[164] Weber (1917) at 103 and Weber (1918b) at 182. Weber (1918b) at 179–80 points to publicity associated with parliamentary commissions of inquiry as serving the aim of educating the public about political affairs, as it had in England. See discussion in Titunik (2005) at 158. On the constrained range of subjects available for political contestation, see Maley (2011) at 71.

experience, both ruler and ruled could secure responsible parliamentary self-government.[165] Education was required to instruct Germans 'about the harsh nature of political reality' and the 'chaos' engendered by value pluralism, Lassman observes.[166]

Turner and Factor's two-audience hypothesis helps to make sense of how legal legitimacy acts upon its subjects.[167] They treat the distinction between legality and legitimacy as being directed at two different audiences.[168] An emphasis on legality appeals to the sensibility of legally trained specialists. Professional lawyers are equipped to evaluate whether correct legal processes have been respected. The same cannot be said of non-professionals, namely, the preponderance of the law's addressees. This audience is 'concerned not merely with technical questions of legality but with legitimacy and they are forced to be so concerned with respect to the question of the status of the legal system as a whole.'[169] It reasonably follows that when Weber writes about 'belief' in his discussion of the legitimacy of legal rule, he is referring to a belief that authorities have done more than faithfully followed and applied what is required of them by law. We should expect that little effort will be made by non-lawyers to determine the correctness of the source of legal authority. Instead, as Weber emphasizes, law's subjects are more likely to yield to legal authority because of an influence exerted by other sources (habit, social convention, even pressure groups). In short, an extra-legal element, beyond formal legality, is added to generate belief.[170] Moreover, and this will be especially true for any newly established legal order, one can reasonably anticipate that some effort needs to be made to 'cultivate belief' in the legitimacy of that form of rule. Rulers are expected, in short, to offer something more, beyond the mere fact of technical legal correctness, for their rule over the governed.

[165] '[T]here is an immense work of political education to be done,' as regards both laborers and the propertied classes, in Weber (1895) at 27, though Turner and Factor (1984) at 89 suggest that this was for the purpose of promoting foreign, and not domestic, policy. Schmitt (1923) at 28 ridiculed this educative function, describing it as 'nothing else but that the educator identifies his will at least provisionally with that of the people, not to mention that the content of the education that the pupil will receive is also decided by the educator.' Villa (2001) at 91 misinterprets Weber as being 'curiously uninterested in deliberation' and 'public argument' being '*simply* [about] fighting' (emphasis in original). This is a better description of Schmitt rather than of Weber.

[166] Lassman (2023) at 377 and Weber (1895) at 20.

[167] Though they make no reference to this, Weber envisages four different audiences in Weber (1913b) at 300. Turner and Factor's reading appears to contemplate only two of them: (1) 'judges and lawyers' who are capable of understanding the 'meaning' behind an instituted legal order and (2) the 'mass' who habituate their behavior to conform with expectations though operating at a 'greater distance from the rational basis' of that order.

[168] Turner and Factor (1994) at 173.

[169] Turner and Factor (1994) at 173. I interpret 'not merely' to signify matters beyond the technically legal. Beetham (1985) at 115, in somewhat similar fashion, contrasts legality—which he associates with edicts that direct bureaucratic functions—with legitimacy which, for Weber, lay in conformity with society's 'moral standards' and 'operative ideals.'

[170] The 'civilized man,' Weber (1913b) at 301 writes, has 'generally accustomed himself to *believe* that the conditions of his everyday life, whether they are called trams, or lifts, or money, or law courts, or armed forces or medicine, are *in principal* rational in nature—that is to say: that they are human artefacts which can be rationally known, rationally created and rationally controlled' (emphasis in original).

In myriad ways, Weber signals that the assent of subjects is critical to the maintenance of legitimate legal rule. Technical legal formalities appear insufficient to instill the requisite belief. If religion offers a useful precedent for legitimating belief, perhaps investment law norm entrepreneurs should look to a religious 'recipe' for legitimation. Peter Berger offers just such a formula for institutional orders that are established from scratch. That recipe is composed of the following features:[171] first, all opponents are 'destroyed,' all appropriate 'means of coercion' are in one's hands, and 'reasonably safe provisions' are made for the 'transmission of power to one's designated successors.' Moreover, in order to solve legitimation problems, its 'institutional order' should be constructed so as to 'hide,' as much as possible, its constructed character. Let it appear that it has existed 'from the beginning of time' and '[l]et the people forget that this order was established by men and continues to be dependent' on their consent. 'Let them believe,' Berger writes, that, though imposed upon them, they are 'realizing their deepest aspirations' operating in 'harmony with the fundamental order of the universe.'

Contemporary rule under investment law has an uncanny affinity to some of Berger's strategies. As I explore in the next part, investment law professionals rely particularly on Berger's final technique: a deliberate forgetting of the political aims for which law serves as a vehicle.[172] This is because reliance on the mere power of law seems an inadequate response to legitimacy concerns.[173] Perhaps placing faith in successes associated with religion—a world where there is no need for legitimation beyond a 'sheer presence'—is what is called for.[174] Just as Weber's formally rational rule too often elides the values channeled by modern legal rule, so does international investment law strive to bury the values underpinning rule by investment law.[175]

II. Investment Law's Virtue?

Having drawn out the role belief plays in Weber's portrayal of legitimacy,[176] in this part, I turn to a principal way in which investment law's social carriers—its state officials, lawyers, and arbitrators—have sought to cultivate belief in this

[171] The quotes that follow in this paragraph are drawn from Berger (1967) at 33.

[172] In this way, as Behn, Fauchald, and Langford (2022) at 16 explain, 'sociological perspectives can sharpen normative claims.' They have made valuable contributions to the empirical evaluation of legitimacy claims in (2021), (2022a), and (2022b) also in Langford and Behn (2018) and Langford, Behn, and Fauchald (2018). I draw upon some of their findings in this chapter.

[173] Guizot (1861) at 63, 372, called for education, openness, and publicity, so that power could be subject to 'endless questioning' and its legitimacy rendered more secure.

[174] Berger (1967) at 47.

[175] Does this amount to a Bourdieusian 'misrecognition' which 'finds expression in the naïve illusion that things have always been as they are' in Bourdieu and Passeron (1990) at 9?

[176] The heading for this part is prompted by Garth (2018) at 156–57, fn. 1 who describes Dezalay and Garth (1996) as revealing 'how a particular community of commercial arbitrators succeeded in gaining enough identification with virtue—that is, making what they offered seen as virtuous—to be entrusted with and to profit from major business disputes.'

international regime. Among the modern law's principal features discussed in the first part and prized by both Weber and Fuller—generality, predictability, and reciprocity—the focus now turns to the 'generality' of investment law.[177] Having recourse to reasons to believe is unwarranted for some. Many investment law notables reject the idea that there is any sort of 'legitimacy crisis.' Judge Stephen Schwebel, for instance, claims that criticisms giving rise to legitimacy concerns are 'more colorful than they are cogent.'[178] Talk of a crisis of legitimacy 'misrepresents' the state of affairs and generates an 'unsuitable' basis for 'rational discourse.[179] Others acknowledge an existing public relations problem of some sort, but that this can be addressed through piecemeal reform or, simply, by weathering the storm. Brigitte Stern, for instance, diminishes the threat by describing a 'so-called crisis.' Given the regime's youthfulness, she likens this to 'teenage' growing pains.[180] Presumably, with maturity, the regime will emerge as a fully functioning adult. There is also some infighting among this group of legalists over what direction reform, if any, should take—over, for instance, the European-led initiative for a multilateral investment court.[181] Empirical studies suggest that the discourse of 'legitimacy crisis' has nudged arbitrators to issue results, in some circumstances, that are more favorable to respondent states.[182] It matters, however, which states are respondents in an investment dispute—more powerful and influential ones are more likely to benefit from curial deference.[183]

Other reasons are offered to short-circuit inquiries into investment law's merits. The reading of Weber that infers legitimacy out of legality can serve as a conversation stopper. This 'value-free' approach accepts the regime as a legal fact and so requires no further explanation. It is on this ground that Habermas accuses Weber of denouncing researchers who undertake 'independent evaluation' of the reasons that sustain belief in legitimacy.[184] This seems not to be an entirely accurate reading of Weber's methods. He does not foreclose inquiries into whether presuppositions are empirically verifiable.[185] If, according to Weber, social science cannot select among the conflicting ends that we chase after—that 'choice' is the

[177] Schultz (2014a) at 175–76 considers how well international arbitration comports with Fuller's principles of legality. His approach is entirely different from the one adopted here. Schultz subsumes the requirement of generality, together with publicity, prospectivity, and predictability under a rule of precedent. So long as the law's addressees, he writes, 'are able to infer general and foreseeable rules' from arbitral decisions, then arbitration can satisfy these principles of legality. If, in the field of investment arbitration, the rule of precedent is increasingly 'commonplace,' it lacks the publicity necessary to fully be called a system of law.

[178] Schwebel (2015). Denigrating critics of investment law seems to be a common reflex for this set of actors. For example, see Brower and Blanchard (2014) and Schneiderman (2016) for a discussion.

[179] Krishan (2011) at 113.

[180] Stern (2011) at 175.

[181] Compare the hyperbolic reaction of Born (2021) with Reinisch (2017).

[182] Langford, Behn, and Fauchauld (2018) at 99–100.

[183] Langford and Behn (2018) at 578. See also Behn, Berge, and Langford (2018).

[184] Habermas (1974) at 200.

[185] Weber (1907) at 189 associates unverifiable conceptual claims with 'scholastic mystification.'

researcher's 'own affair'—it can assist by offering '*knowledge* of the *meaning*' of what is being pursued. This involves highlighting the ideas in which one's chosen ends are 'rooted.'[186] Social science can even go beyond this task by 'judg[ing]' those goals and ideals and evaluating them 'critically.'[187] The mission is not to judge the validity of those 'beliefs' but 'uncovering the ideas underlying the value judgments' to ensure that ends are pursued responsibly.[188] It is, in short, entirely consonant with Weber's methods to evaluate the claims that are typically made by investment law professionals.[189]

In this part, I elucidate a principal virtue of investment law that is offered up to justify its power over states and citizens, namely, its generality.[190] In doing so, one learns how well this form of dispute resolution responds to legitimacy concerns. The regime's promoters tend to underscore the regime's prevalence—its mere facticity—as an indicator of its universal acceptance. All states, in both the North and the South, have voluntarily signed onto the regime's disciplines, it is said. There is 'no longer a choice for most States,' counsels Alvarez: '[p]articipation and compliance with them is, increasingly, the only option States have.'[191] It may well be a '*global* law, of universal application,' says another.[192] But as readers will have inferred, appeals to legal validity are insufficient to sustain belief in the legitimacy investment law's regime of legal constraint. We can surmise, even at this early stage of the discussion, that investment law professionals are not 'masters of the art of packaging.'[193]

Although Weber's methods offer up license to insist that individuals account for the 'ultimate meaning' of their conduct—'making things explicit' helps, after all[194]—no grammar is offered up to help critically guide this effort. For the most part, legal subjects are expected not to question, but to habitually orient, their behavior in accordance with legally valid directives.[195] With no mystical force to

[186] Weber (1904a) at 102.

[187] Weber (1904a) at 103 describes the task as one of testing goals against their 'internal *consistency*' (emphasis in original).

[188] Weber (1904a) at 103–04.

[189] Weber (1913a) at 312 ('the function of science is ... [to] see a *problem* in anything that is conventionally self-evident') (emphasis in original).

[190] Early in the life of the regime, Gus Van Harten identified five different justifications for investment treaty protections. See Van Harten (2010b) at 21 (encouraging investment, responding to bias and unreliability in domestic courts, advancing fairness and the rule of law, affirming sovereignty and bargaining strategies of states, and endorsed by the democratic process). Contrast Puig and Shaffer (2018) at 368 (choosing the goals of 'fairness, resource allocation efficiency, and peace').

[191] Alvarez (2011) at 438.

[192] Krishan (2011) at 140 (emphasis in original).

[193] Bourdieu (1984) at 464.

[194] Bourdieu (2000) at 172.

[195] This amounts to 'consensus-conditioned action' in Weber (1913b) at 293, whose validity we take for granted as 'when we make proper use of an electric tram, a hydraulic life or a gun' (Weber 1913b at 299). These 'general foundations of our orientation in this world' are 'the least problematical ones' in Weber (1919b) at 345.

guide us,[196] coupled with the irreversible fact of bureaucratic rule, few avenues are made available other than to act in 'piannisimo'—'in the smallest of circles, from one human being to another,' says Weber.[197] This is why it may be useful to have recourse to Bourdieu's sociology. He helps to uncover a field's 'genesis amnesia.'[198] Investment law professionals tend to want to forget the founding circumstances that inaugurated their universalizing predilections,[199] leaving the impression that these legal forms are 'non-political [in] character.'[200] They prefer to obscure the principal ambition of investment law's strictures—to protect foreign investors and their investments—and replace them with other, more appealing, virtues.[201] This is what Bourdieu calls 'misrecognition of the arbitrary,' having the effect of concealing the powerful interests served by the regime's edicts.[202] Legitimacy is better secured by means that promote 'the naïve illusion that things have always been as they are' or that they are naturally so.[203] This legitimation strategy asks subjects to neglect the originating conditions for the production of law tagged as 'legitimate' in the interests of demurring to the less-than-defensible status quo.

Weber Versus Fuller?

Before evaluating investment law's strategy of obfuscation, I wish to briefly explain why Weber's account of legitimately rational law is preferable to Fuller's. This is so simply because of Weber's attentiveness to class and to the power of the already privileged. Such elements are mostly absent from Fuller's account. He instead dismisses 'skeptics' (presumably American legal realists) who ascribe to reasoned justification a 'screen behind which [powerful interests] feather their nests.' Seeking to restore 'faith' in reason, Fuller aims to rebut the 'current prejudice against anything resembling natural law' or an 'inner aversion to what may look like a claim to oracular powers.'[204] Scholars, Fuller claims, should assume the role of 'priest' for when priests abdicate their power 'it is generally the warrior or spellbinder who takes over.'[205] Fuller understands that law confers power, but his preoccupation with generality, among other of law's features, veils how legal order is

[196] Other 'forces prevail than the opinions of university professors' in Weber (1919b) at 348.
[197] Weber (1919b) at 352.
[198] Bourdieu (2005) at 5. On Weber as his 'main source of inspiration,' see Bourdieu et al. (2011) at 116.
[199] Bourdieu and Wacquant (1999) at 41. The regime's Cold War origins are discussed in Chapter 4.
[200] Kennedy (2012) at 36. They 'restate their interests in universal terms' so as to 'present them as something more than "selfish",' in Kennedy (1997) at 41.
[201] For further discussion, see Schneiderman (2024a) at 199–200.
[202] Bourdieu (2023) at 168.
[203] Bourdieu and Passeron (1990) at 9.
[204] Fuller (1940) at 127.
[205] Fuller (1940) at 128.

meant to serve particular interests.[206] Such power dynamics are absent even from Fuller's understanding of international law. The product of voluntary 'contractual arrangements called treaties,' and tacit consent associated with customary international law, Fuller rejects a characterization of international law as being 'imposed from above.' The assumption that there is an equality of bargaining power in international society, something Fuller takes for granted (in his contract law case book[207]), is belied by the reality of 'legalized hegemons.'[208]

This is why Weber's account is superior to Fuller's. Fuller does not address how the rule of law empowers the already powerful. Fuller's emphasis on 'purpose' elides the contestable nature of what passes as law in capitalist societies. For Fuller, these will be in the pursuit of 'apolitical' purposes.[209] Weber, by contrast, is attentive to the partiality of formally rational law. If he insists that modern legal forms are neutral as to substance, he well understands that, as constructed, they serve the interests of some over others. They represent, after all, 'value compromises.'[210] This is because what passes for law in the modern West is the product of inevitable political struggle.[211] This is an insight not lost on some of Weber's readers, such as Llewellyn. He understood the 'bulk' of the law to be the product of 'clashing interests, of antagonistic persons or groups.'[212] Hence, Llewellyn writes, one can observe 'the eternal fight for control over the machinery of law, and of law making.'[213]

The Virtue of Generality?

As discussed above, the requirement that laws be addressed to all, generally, comprises one of the principal features of Fuller's internal morality of law. It has the practical advantage of expressing the 'power of law' to all at once, setting

[206] Following Neumann (1936) at 257, who asserts that the 'generality of law and independence of judges veil the power of one stratum of society.'

[207] Fuller and Eisenberg (1972) at 93.

[208] Simpson (2004) at 68.

[209] Kennedy (2000) at 171 accuses Fuller of promoting an 'apolitical' core to contact law that resolves conflicts by having recourse to moral reasoning rather than by acknowledging that they involve political choices. Kennedy claims Fuller's represents a 'center-right' politics that was 'aggressively ideological' in the context of the Cold War era ([2000] at 99, 171). Consider Fuller's review of Hale's *Freedom Through Law*, in Fuller (1954b) at 75–76, where he accentuates the virtue and indispensability of markets.

[210] Weber (1978) at 887.

[211] Weber (1919b) at 350. Old natural law conceptions have been 'unmasked,' Weber (1978) at 985 writes, 'as the technical means of compromise between conflicting interests.' Legislation is best understood, just as Kennedy describes the common law, as 'the outcome of ideological struggles' in Kennedy (1997) at 239.

[212] Llewellyn (1930) at 185, also Trubek and Galanter (1974) at 1083 ('[t]he tendency for formal equality to be compatible with domination did not escape [Weber's] notice'). On Weber's influence on Llewellyn, see Ansladi (1992).

[213] Llewellyn (1930) at 185 ('whereby highly interested As can hope partially to force their will upon the equally but adversely interested Bs, and to put behind that control the passive approval and support of the great body of Cs—who happen to be disinterested, or, what is equally to the point, uninterested').

'baselines' with which to order one's life.[214] 'It is ancient wisdom,' declares Fuller, that laws be general, 'addressed not to particular persons but to persons generally.'[215] We are also aware that Weber is like minded, attributing to rationally formal law the characteristics of a 'body of abstract, general legal norms'[216] under which is subsumed the particular case.[217] It offers a generalized means that 'indiscriminately facilitates the purposeful pursuit of all substantive ends.'[218] In Shil's formulation, Weber describes a process that gives rise to 'the reduction of all individual instances, whatever their diversity, to the status of general classes.'[219] Neoliberal thought leaders, like Hayek, laud the generality of law as an essential ingredient to the rule of law. It entails 'the enforcement of general rules, laid down irrespective of the particular case, and equally applicable to all.'[220] General rules are treated not as means but as 'ultimate values' that are 'common to all.' This enables individuals to be guided by general ends in the pursuit of their own, unknown-in-advance, particular ends.[221] Generality is a virtue for thinkers across the political spectrum. The historian E. P. Thompson was prompted to portray the rule of law as 'an unqualified human good' and a 'cultural achievement of universal significance' because it entitled subordinate classes to make claims against those whom laws were meant to inscribe advantages.[222] It comes as no surprise that legal theorists treat generality as the 'central idea of liberal legal systems' and as 'the essence of the rule of law.'[223] It is considered a vehicle for not only respecting equality but also stability and predictability.[224] It is obvious why investment law professionals would want to cloak themselves in this form of legitimate legal rule.

Yet we know that the generality of formal law does not serve all equally. Generally formulated legal rules often will generate outcomes that favor some interests over others.[225] 'The propertyless masses,' Weber admits, especially are not aided by formal 'equality before the law and the "calculable" adjudication

214 Fuller (1969b) at 234.

215 Fuller (1969b) at 163.

216 Brubaker (1984) at 18.

217 Mannheim (1927) at 214.

218 Brubaker (1984) at 37. Rather than permitting 'all' ends, Brubaker should say only 'some' ends.

219 Shils (1981) at 291 (the 'elimination of particular judgments which cannot be subsumed under a more general judgment').

220 Hayek (1960) at 156. This resembles the reading of Weber in Parsons (1964) at 80, 82. Parsons claims that Weber promotes an 'ethical universalism,' underscored by the laws of property and contract, that universalizes 'equality of opportunity.'

221 Hayek (1982) at 15–17 and Hayek (1973) at 137.

222 Thompson (1975) at 266, 267. This resembles Weber's claim, in (1978) at 667–68, that '[e]very right is thus a source of power of which even a hitherto entirely powerless person may become possessed.'

223 Neumann (1936) at 212 and Raz (1979) at 215. Both acknowledge that particular laws may be warranted to introduce some 'flexibility,' so long as they are 'stable and clear,' per Raz (1979) at 216, and, for Neumann (1937) at 127, when the state is confronted, not with 'equally strong competitors but with monopolies which reverse the principle of the free market.'

224 Schauer (2003) at 275.

225 Weber (1978) at 698.

and administration demanded by bourgeois interests.'[226] Such laws, abstract and seemingly general in their application, often do not serve the interests of the unpropertied classes. As such, generality is less defensible when it gives rise to an inequality in the availability of legal protections.

In the section of *Economy and Society* entitled 'Freedom and Coercion,' Weber queries the degree to which it could be said that formally rational law has increased the degree of freedom available to the subjects of law. This evaluation cannot be undertaken, Weber warns, 'simply by studying the development of formal legal institutions.'[227] Considering contracts for wage labor, for instance, the 'more powerful party' gets to lay down the terms and conditions on a 'take it or leave it' basis.[228] Though legal protections are 'officially available to all,' Weber continues, actually 'they are accessible only to the owners of property and thus in effect support' their superior authority. The law, as such, is a means for securing the 'exercise of power over others.'[229] The degree to which 'coercion' is more easily available in market economies in contrast to 'socialistic' ones, Weber chooses not to say. Formally speaking, freedom of contract can be said to represent a 'decrease of coercion.' 'But it is also obvious,' he adds, 'how advantageous this state of affairs is to those who are economically in the position to make use of their empowerments.'[230]

In the three sections that follow, I highlight how an emphasis on investment law's generality, first, elides its underlying politics, second, projects a false universality and, third, promotes freedom for only a privileged few. So as to illustrate these regime effects, I turn, fourth, to an investment dispute of grave concern to the Indigenous and Afro-Caribbean communities of La Guajira, Colombia. The proceedings in this dispute—its means of dispute resolution—expose the regime's ends—its particularistic ambitions that treat the interests of others, outside of the formal parties to the dispute, as peripheral.[231] The Wayúu are the regime's unprivileged other, undeserving of the solicitude that is owed by the lawyerly class to the investors that make investment law machinery hum.

Veiled Politics

If modern law instantiates the application of 'highly abstract rules' that diminish the 'significance' of 'elements' extrinsic to formally rational law,[232] then investor

[226] Weber (1978) at 980.
[227] Weber (1978) at 729.
[228] Weber (1978) at 730 (quotations in the original).
[229] Weber (1978) at 730.
[230] Weber (1978) at 730. Kennedy (2004) at 1049 describes these passages as presenting a 'tragic' choice as between modes of coercion, with different distributive outcomes.
[231] Schneiderman (2022) at 134 characterizes international investment law as not only 'indifferent' to Indigenous rights but 'complicit' in their violation.
[232] Weber (1978) at 657.

protections line up well with Weber's formulation. According to Wälde, international economic treaties enumerate goals that are 'multiple, general, ambiguous and open to widely different interpretation.'[233] Indeed, admits Salacuse, 'for a lawyer trained only in the domestic law governing investment transactions, the stated norms of the regime seem breathtaking in their generality, vagueness, and lack of specificity.'[234] With a focus only on means, formal legality renders illegible the 'social framework of interests'[235] out of which legal obligations are produced.[236] Whatever the content of formally rational law, it is kept at a safe distance from discussions about the values that motivate it. According to this reading, Weber's account can be treated as offering an argument for investment law.[237]

Those acquired rights, however, are in the pursuit of very substantive ends.[238] Weber accepts that the content of those rules did not fundamentally change with the demise of natural law. On this basis, Weber can characterize modern freedom of contract as serving primarily propertied interests, even if formally available to all equally.[239] Not only do business interests inherit advantageous general laws, but they also are entitled to 'special' laws and even to specialized courts. Weber acknowledges that 'bourgeois interests' justify access to specialized courts (in the case of commercial disputes, for instance) 'because compelling and clearly defined economic needs' required it.[240] Natural law influences could not be entirely eradicated, nor did it seem desirable to erase them.[241]

Weber also understands that substantive ends served by legal forms are the outcome of political struggle. The 'essence of all politics, as we shall emphasize repeatedly, is *conflict*,' he declares.[242] It cannot be the case that disagreement over ends simply disappears once they take the form of legal rules. All that can be expected of politics is 'irresolvable *conflict*, and consequently, the necessity of constant

[233] Wälde (2000) at 182, 200. The echoes of Hayek (1944) at 75 can be heard throughout Wälde's lengthy exposition.

[234] Salacuse (2010) at 453.

[235] Synonymous with politics, in Wolin (1991) at 201 (for Weber 'values functioned as the symbolic equivalent of politics').

[236] Habermas (1971b) at 82.

[237] Weber (1978) at 653–54, where he distinguishes between 'lawmaking' (norm creation) and 'lawfinding' (application of established norms).

[238] In Kennedy's formulation, Weber's assault on 'anti-formal tendencies' concerns legal interpretation (lawfinding), and not 'after law declaration has been politicized' (lawmaking) in Kennedy (2004) at 1064.

[239] Weber (1978) at 730.

[240] Weber (1978) at 858, as discussed in Chapter 1. He also notes that courts overseen by justices of the peace in England, dealing with 'daily troubles and misdemeanors of the masses,' serve similar substantive functions in Weber (1978) at 814. Gephart (2015) at 143 argues that, in this light, the legal particularism of international economic law underscores its deficient universality.

[241] Bendix (1962) at 432.

[242] Weber (1918b) at 173 (emphasis in original). He adds to this '*the recruitment of allies and a voluntary following*.' Strong (1994) at 118 contrasts the endemic conflict associated with politics to the depoliticization of legal order associated with bureaucratic rule. The latter 'effaces or disguises the fact that there is rule going on at all . . . Rules replace ruling.'

compromises.'[243] Compromise is the basis upon which '*economic* conflicts are settled,' Weber notes, and also the 'specific function performed by parliament: to make the "best" solution (relatively speaking) by a process of negotiation and compromise.'[244] Even if Weber brands modern law as a form of legitimate rule, it cannot be said to have been emptied of politics. Instead, politics is baked into modern law.[245]

Those promoting legal protections for foreign investors seem unaware of these findings. Or, if they are aware, dismiss them as extraneous to investment law's systemic logic. Investment law is neutral and impartial as to the status of states and of claimants.[246] Its standards of treatment for investors are formulated in general and neutral terms not only because all national legal institutions are suspect and, therefore, candidates to be disciplined by international norms. It is also neutral, as revealed by its preferred enforcement mechanism (ISDS), as to politics.[247] Vandevelde offers up two versions of this depoliticization argument in a 1992 address to the American Society of International Law. First, investment arbitration 'extricate[s]' home states from '*private* investment disputes'[248] and, second, this provides a 'fully legal, nonpoliticized remedy' for investors.[249] Vandevelde assumes that this legal order is not replete with 'submerged' value choices.[250]

Reading Weber against investment law's tropes, it would be more accurate to characterize the regime as not depoliticized but decentralized. Power is conveyed to investors and ultimately to a coterie of investment lawyers and arbitrators that populate its institutions and pronounce on the meaning of its rules. It follows that those seeking to promote the system would be well advised to find some other way of describing their political objective of keeping home states and their politics at bay.[251]

The generality of formally rational law serves, as Weber reveals, only to empower the already powerful. In his reading of Weber, Kronman offers an apology for this outcome.[252] It would be a morally acceptable result if we place a 'high value

[243] Weber (1913c).
[244] Weber (1917) at 102, 128.
[245] Hayek (1944) at 75 claims otherwise: 'that we do *not* know what particular ends these laws will further' (emphasis in original). Outside of purely procedural matters, this is an implausible claim, especially for laws enforcing classical liberal rights, such as those concerning property and contract.
[246] Jackson (1997) at 109–11. As Weber acknowledges, though the threat of force is available to enforce rule following, this is as likely to be the product of material self-interest, fear, or social norms.
[247] I document many of the sources for this claim in Schneiderman (2011). The claim, typically, is loosely made. See, for example, Krishan (2011) at 142 ('Investment is insulated from politics through the means of a BIT').
[248] Vandevelde (1992) at 535.
[249] Vandevelde (1992) at 540.
[250] Rittich (2002) at 13.
[251] I return to the depoliticization claim in Chapter 4 in text associated with notes 141–45.
[252] Kronman (1983) at 94 speaks here of 'a legal order composed of general, abstract rules' that emphasizes 'calculability,' all of which is assimilated here under the rubric of generality.

on individual freedom and legal calculability.'[253] But this excuse is hard to swallow given that the revealed benefits flowing from investment treaty commitments are so slender. Desperate for capital to finance important infrastructure projects, whether they be water, sewerage, or road projects, poorer states are still deprived of funds to finance development. The regime simply has not succeeded in delivering on its promise. The gap between new inward investment and developmental needs continues to widen.[254] This is despite the spread of a 'culture of commitment' associated with international investment law. Drowning in accumulated debt obligations, combined with shrinking sources from which to encourage economic development, outcomes almost inevitably result in the sacrifice of public services, even ones that states are constitutionally obliged to provide. Are there, then, real benefits to this trade-off: between waiting for doubtful inward investment and guaranteeing profits for the most powerful?

False Universalism

Among Fuller's criteria of legal excellence, it is said that the consequences of adhering to a principle of generality are 'profound.'[255] This capacity for generality, uniquely associated with formal law, can give rise to a 'practical universality.'[256] Though Weber eschews universalizing tendencies—he rejects transforming an 'image of the world' into 'a world view'[257]—generality can get converted into a 'source' of 'universal applicability.'[258] Presenting generality as a universal phenomenon is how, Neumann writes, 'the competitive economic system is invested with the dignity of a moral value.'[259] It amounts to, he says, 'secularized natural law.'[260] It bears a resemblance to those salvation religions that emphasize an openness to all who accept the 'universalism' of a divine grace.[261] Because 'suffering' is common to all who believe, salvation religions tilt in the direction of a 'universalist

[253] Kronman (1983) at 94.

[254] The annual investment gap required to meet 2030 sustainable development goals was US $4 trillion in 2022. See UNCTAD (2023c).

[255] Winston (1999) at 55.

[256] Bourdieu (1987) at 842, fn. 59. Generality and universality are considered synonymous in Hayek (1982) at 28.

[257] Weber (1909) at 253.

[258] Bourdieu (1987) at 844. It is the tendency of modern rationality to 'generalize' and 'equalize' which, Mannheim (1927) at 207 argues, precipitated the rise of conservative thought in Germany as a response to the threat posed by 'bourgeois rationalism.'

[259] Neumann (1936) at 213. Neumann argues that generality, along with judicial independence and the separation of powers, serve 'functions transcending the needs of competitive capitalism, since they secure personal liberty and personal equality' (Neumann [1936] at 257).

[260] Neumann (1953) at 199. Weber (1907) at 201 similarly accuses Stammler of designating as formal 'the unitary, the General, the "fundamentally universal".' Parsons' usage is telling. He describes Protestant 'universalism' as exhibiting 'generalized impersonal standards' in Parsons (1964) at 80.

[261] Weber (1963) at 272.

brotherhood.'[262] 'The "universalism" of the "churches",' declares Weber, 'allows their light to shine on both the righteous and unrighteous.'[263] 'Few,' however, 'are chosen to pass through the narrow gate,' adds Weber.[264]

This same presumed openness to all—a generality in the service of universality—is at work in international investment law.[265] The regime, however, is erected to benefit only the small stratum of foreign economic actors. Host states are meant to be held strictly to the terms of bargains they enter with foreign investors.[266] Investment arbitration serves as the regime's backstop and as a 'device' to narrow the law applied to investment disputes to those that are in the service of foreign ownership.[267] These privileges—heightened legal protections coupled with the rarified venue of investment treaty arbitration—are not meant to be available to national economic actors. Locals may even be competing with foreign firms operating within the same sector. But locals are not entitled to equal treatment. Instead, the reverse holds true. Not only are foreign investors required to be treated no worse than locals, but investment law also ensures that foreign investors receive treatment *better* than that received by locals. The panoply of protections available to foreign investors under investment treaty law, in the aggregate, imposes not equal but vastly unequal treatment.[268] It confers, one could say, a 'most favored position' on foreign investors.[269]

The generality associated with the rule of law may feature in some investment treaty reforms, to be sure, but their effects are at best modest. In their evaluation of whether the investment law regime can be considered to enhance global public welfare (as a 'global public good'), Behn, Fauchauld, and Langford conclude that the regime, as it currently operates, 'appears to provide no or few benefits to low income states while providing significant economic benefits to private actors from high income states,' including foreign investors and to the 'arbitrators, counsel experts, secretaries' engaged in investment treaty arbitration.[270] As for enhancing

[262] Weber (1915b) at 221.

[263] Weber (1906c) at 9. 'There is no such thing as Jew and Greek, slave and freeman, male and female, for you are all one person in Christ Jesus' (Letter of Paul to the Galatians 3:28). This was in contrast to what Weber designated as 'sects,' religious associations more selective in their tests for religious qualification and who viewed themselves as a religious 'elite' in Weber (1906c) at 9–10.

[264] Weber (1963) at 272.

[265] Gardner (2012) at 199 ('Stability and generality in law are also none other than stability and generality in the law's content').

[266] Boue (2022) at 33.

[267] Boue (2022) at 9. It was meant to provide 'a means to permit disputes to be judged outside the contracting nation and by the nationals of other countries' (Boue [2022] at 9, quoting Frank C. Hendryx).

[268] I make the more fulsome argument, in the context of the national treatment standard, in Schneiderman (2023).

[269] Simmel (1950) at 275, having affinities with the 'most favored nation' standard of treatment found in most international investment agreements.

[270] Behn, Fauchauld, and Langford (2021) at 111.

the rule of law, these authors describe the claim as 'weak' and the 'benefits vague and contradictory at times.'[271]

Freedom for the Few

Generality amplifies freedom, according to Fuller. Freedom is enhanced by a legal order of general rules that offers 'baselines' against which subjects of law can organize their lives.[272] The requirement of generality occupies a 'central part' of Fuller's understanding of 'the place of the legal subject.'[273] Similarly, for Jhering, a decisive influence on Weber, law serves as an 'objective organism' of 'human freedom' and is confined to areas where freedom needs to be delimited in the interests of the community.[274] Freedom becomes a determinant of the 'level of civilization gained by a people and its political institutions.'[275] Weber's account of the rise of modern law is like-minded, placing emphasis on the spread of the law of freedom of contract, which he associates with 'formal market freedom.'[276] The regulation of the purchase and sale 'of goods through free, purely economically rational exchange,' writes Weber, 'is the very constitutive element of the political community.'[277] 'There exists,' Weber admits, 'an intimate connection between the expansion of the market and the expanding measure of contractual freedom.'[278] In modern contract law, this freedom is attenuated whenever the interests of third parties require protection or in order to defend 'good morals.'[279]

Under the heading of 'Freedom and Coercion' in *Economy and Society*, Weber discusses how the features of formally rational legal orders are most interested in the spread and maintenance of freedom. But this is attenuated by freedom's limited reach. The extent to which the rise of freedom of contract 'has brought about an actual increase of the individual's freedom to shape the conditions of his own life or the extent to which, on the contrary, life has become more stereotyped in spite, or, perhaps, just because of this trend, cannot be determined simply by studying

[271] Behn, Fauchauld, and Langford (2021) at 114.
[272] Fuller (1969b) at 234, also Fuller (1969a) at 210.
[273] Rundle (2012) at 181.
[274] Belvisi (2023) at 184, quoting Jhering (1907) at 25. On Jhering's influence, see Turner and Factor (1994) (rendered as Ihering).
[275] Belvisi (2023) at 184.
[276] Weber (1978) at 639. Weber (1906a) at 146 considers freedom as synonymous with acting rationally. See discussion in Brubaker (1984) at 18–19, 93–94.
[277] Weber (1978) at 261.
[278] Weber (1978) at 668. Weber remains ambiguous about the influence of economic needs on the development of law ('economic influences have played their part … [in addressing complex conflicts associated with] the market economy or freedom of contract' and 'have influenced the systematization of the law' [1978] at 655). He continues to maintain that '[e]conomic situations do not automatically give birth to new legal forms; they merely provide the opportunity for the actual spread of a legal technique if it is invented' ([1978] at 687).
[279] Weber (1978) at 684–87.

the development of formal legal institutions,' insists Weber.[280] For example, he continues, the 'formal right of a worker to enter into any contract whatsoever with any employer whatsoever does not in practice represent for the employment seeker even the slightest freedom in the determination of his own conditions of work, and it does not guarantee him any influence on this process.'[281] Instead, freedom of contract in conditions of inequality empowers the already privileged, what he labels 'legal empowerment rules.'[282]

Unprivileged Others

Foreign investors already exercise outsized influence over states desirous for new capital inflows.[283] Local communities, directly confronting resource exploitation practices by multinational mining companies, have to combat not only the policy of state capitals, eager for new resource revenue, but also an international regime that serves as a backstop for foreign investments.[284] Leaders from the Colombian community of La Guajira, 50 percent of whom are Indigenous or Afro-descendant, describe the numerous harms they have encountered due to one of the world's largest open-pit mines.[285] The community has been portrayed as a barrier to development by the local investor, Carbones de Cerrejón Limited, a subsidiary of Glencore of Switzerland. If agriculture was a vibrant sector before the company's mining operations commenced—some 40 percent of income in 1960—it shrunk to an unviable 4.6 percent by 2010. In addition to acquiring 'food vulnerability,' infant mortality rates rose to an intolerable six times the national average.[286] Scarce water resources are being diverted and made more difficult to access—numerous streams have simply disappeared. The role of the state, for these communities, is not to protect them from the deleterious effects of resource extraction but to 'make things easier for the company.' 'They are killing us,' laments one community representative.

The Colombian Constitutional Court declared the systemic violation of human rights in La Guajira as giving rise to an 'unconstitutional state of affairs.'[287] In a pivotal 2017 Constitutional Court ruling, the investor was prohibited from diverting

[280] Weber (1978) at 729.
[281] Weber (1978) at 729.
[282] Weber (1978) at 730. Hayek (1960) at 79 acknowledges that the rule of law 'produces economic inequality,' only that it is 'not designed to affect particular people in a particular way.'
[283] Aisbett, McAusland, and Poulson (2025).
[284] I have previously addressed the marginalization of local communities in Schneiderman (2022e).
[285] I draw here upon my own notes from the 'Local Communities and Extractive Industries Workshop,' Externado University, Bogotá, Colombia (August 1, 2018). For details about the workshop and the impact of foreign investment in the area, see Perrone (2022) and Suárez Ricaurte (2022).
[286] Glencore International A.G. v. Republic of Colombia, 'Republic of Colombia's Summary of its Rebuttal to Claimant's Claim' ICSID Case No. ARB/21/30 (August 15, 2024) at para. 4.
[287] Colombian Constitutional Court T-302-2017.

the Arroyo Bruno creek in order to exploit coal underneath the riverbed.[288] According to the Court, the potential impact of the company's diversion of the waterway, in order to exploit the coal deposits beneath, 'constitutes a concrete, certain and direct threat to the rights to water, health, and food security and sovereignty of the communities dependent on the Bruno Creek.'[289] The Court ordered that an Inter-Institutional Working Group, composed of governmental and non-governmental actors including Carbones de Cerrojón, continue to do its work of consulting with civil society members and academics so as to determine whether the stream diversion project was 'environmentally viable.' The Court also ordered restoration of the creek's water flow in observance of the Constitution's incorporation of the precautionary principle.[290] While the Constitutional Court continues to monitor compliance with its 2017 ruling,[291] the Colombian Ombudsman's Office reports that six of the seven affected communities are still without drinking water.[292]

Suárez Ricaurte reports that there have been at least nine landmark rulings issued by the Court, responding to violations of air, noise, and water pollution, forced resettlement, denial of human rights to consultation, and to the Indigenous rights of the Wayúu community of La Guajira.[293] The project's foreign investor, Glencore, launched four separate investment claims against Colombia for violating a bilateral investment treaty with Switzerland as a consequence of these rulings. Glencore first was awarded US$ 19.1 million to compensate for a decision by Colombia's fiscal authority to reduce royalties paid to the investor.[294] A second claim secured US$ 9.4 million from Colombia for having inequitably burdened the investor with expenses associated with financing a port facility to transport the company's coal.[295] Currently pending is a third claim, seeking damages for the Colombian Constitutional Court ruling that blocked diversion of the Arroyo

288 Colombian Constitutional Court SU-698-2017.

289 Colombian Constitutional Court SU-698-2017 at para. 5.7.4 (translation by DeepL), also available in Censat Agua Viva (2023b).

290 See partial translation of 'Sentence SU698/17 (Arroyo Bruno case), Constitutional Court of Colombia' (November 28, 2017) at https://elaw.org/resource/cerrejon_arroyobruno (last accessed May 12, 2025).

291 Going so far as to hold a compliance hearing in the coastal city of Riohacha in March 2025. See Torres Lasso (2025).

292 La Defensoría del Pueblo de Colombia (2025).

293 Suárez Ricaurte (2022) at 858. Also see Censat Agua Viva (2023a) and Glencore International A.G. v. Republic of Colombia, 'Republic of Colombia's Summary of its Rebuttal to Claimant's Claim' ICSID Case No. ARB/21/30 (August 15, 2024) at para. 7.

294 Glencore International A.G. v. Republic of Colombia (I), 'Award' ICSID Case No. ARB/16/6 (August 27, 2019) at para. 1618. Colombia's application for annulment failed in Glencore International A.G. v. Republic of Colombia (I), 'Decision on Annulment' ICSID Case No. ARB/16/6 (September 22, 2021).

295 Glencore International A.G. v. Republic of Colombia (II), 'Award' ICSID Case No. ARB/19/22 (April 19, 2024) at para. 348. Specifically, the investor claimed that Colombia's conduct was 'arbitrary, inconsistent and lacking transparency, lacking due process, discriminatory, and contrary to Claimants' reasonable and legitimate expectations' (at para. 131).

Bruno creek to allow for expansion of the company's mining operations at its La Puente pit. The Court's order, the investor claims, added a 'layer of environmental review' that was not authorized by law.[296] Because the mining activity was initially authorized prior to environmental assessment legislation coming into force, the operator was relieved of the obligation of undergoing environmental scrutiny.[297] However, nothing in legislation could exempt the project from constitutional review. The investor, nevertheless, alleges that this amounts to a denial of fair and equitable treatment, a denial of justice, and an unreasonable measure under the terms of the Colombia-Swiss investment treaty.[298] The company seeks US$489 million in damages.[299] The grounds upon which the investor has launched its fourth claim against Colombia remain under wraps.[300]

These proceedings are, for the most part, kept confidential. The tribunal tasked with adjudicating the claim against Colombia granted permission, to the Wayúu communities of La Gran Parada and Paradero, to file a written submission as non-disputing parties because of their interest in the Creek and in the expansion of the La Puente pit. The tribunal, however, is less than open to hearing from other interested and affected third parties. The Colectivo de Abogados y Abogadas José Alvear Restrepo, a human rights organization that represented the affected communities in their successful *tutela* action before the Constitutional Court, was denied similar permission to file a written submission.[301] Because the tribunal ordered that the proceedings remain confidential (in the interests of ensuring their 'integrity'),[302] no intervenors will have access to the pleadings, expert opinions,

[296] Glencore International A.G. v. Republic of Colombia, 'Summary of the Claimant's Position' ICSID Case No. ARB/21/30 (August 15, 2024) at para. 10.

[297] Colombian Constitutional Court SU-698-2017 at paras. 1.4.1.1–1.4.1.3, 5.1.3 and Glencore International A.G. v. Republic of Colombia, 'Republic of Colombia's Summary of Its Rebuttal to Claimant's Claim' ICSID Case No. ARB/21/30 (August 15, 2024) at para. 14.

[298] Glencore International A.G. v. Republic of Colombia, 'Summary of the Claimant's Position' ICSID Case No. ARB/21/30 (August 15, 2024) at paras. 18ff.

[299] Despite having earned US$5.6 billion in revenue in 2022, according to Glencore International A.G. v. Republic of Colombia, 'Republic of Colombia's Summary of Its Rebuttal to Claimant's Claim' ICSID Case No. ARB/21/30 (August 15, 2024) at para. 33.

[300] Glencore International A.G. & others v. Republic of Colombia, ICSID Case No. ARB/23/50 (November 16, 2023).

[301] Glencore International A.G. v. Republic of Colombia (III), 'Procedural Order No. 3' ICSID Case No. ARB/21/30 (October 10, 2024) at para. 50. The tribunal wrote that '[e]very environmental or human rights organization has an interest in ensuring compliance with human rights and environmental law in the areas in which it operates; something more is needed to show a "significant interest" in this proceeding beyond this general interest' (Glencore International A.G. v. Republic of Colombia (III), 'Procedural Order No. 3' ICSID Case No. ARB/21/30 at para. 68). As is typically the case, the claimant opposed the application, arguing that they simply would duplicate the respondent State's arguments.

[302] Glencore International A.G. v. Republic of Colombia (III), 'Procedural Order No. 2' ICSID Case No. ARB/21/30 (January 26, 2024). See, for example, the six-page 'Summary of Claimant's Position' (August 15, 2024) at https://www.italaw.com/sites/default/files/case-documents/italaw182216.pdf (last accessed March 29, 2025) and the ten-page 'Republic of Colombia's Summary of Its Rebuttal to Claimant's Claims' (August 15, 2024) at https://www.italaw.com/sites/default/files/case-documents/italaw182215.pdf (last accessed March 29, 2025).

and witness statements filed by the parties to the dispute. Only summaries of these documents will be made available. Remarkably, the tribunal, staffed by lawyers whose daily work is to parse detailed legal argument, ruled that access to the principal arbitral documents 'would not help the Communities in preparing their submission.'[303] This is despite the fact that, among the narrow range of issues they are permitted to address, they are expected to join issue with the investor on some complex legal questions. Among them are the lack of investor 'compliance with the regulatory framework [for operating] the La Puente pit' and the 'consistency' of the Court's orders with 'the guarantees for investors contained in the Treaty.'[304] The investor's legal arguments regarding both of these matters surely would inform, and improve, any intervenor's argument.

Investment tribunals have proven to be not that interested in receiving third-party submissions. Even when granted standing, affected communities are often handicapped in their ability to effectively convey their knowledge and interests, including legal knowledge.[305] It is for this reason that the UN Special Rapporteur on the Rights of Indigenous Peoples described input by way of legal briefs in investment disputes as a 'grossly inadequate' means of participation.[306]

As Weber reminds us, the freedom offered by formal and generalized laws is enjoyed principally by those with economic power. Weber notes that the degree to which freedom is 'actually increased depends entirely upon the concrete economic order and especially upon the property distribution.' In 'no case,' he adds, 'can it be simply deduced from the content of the law.'[307] The freedom of disempowered local communities impacted by bad development is much less enhanced by investment treaty disciplines. Indeed, the kind of solicitude granted to foreign investors by investment law protections, authored and endorsed by states, offers Indigenous and Afro-Caribbean communities of Colombia little but oppression and less than hope.

If only a snapshot, we are led to the conclusion investment law instantiates what Weber labeled 'modern particularism'—distinct laws handled by 'specialized experts.'[308] It is a regime, nevertheless, couched in general terms that has the pretension of being universal. 'Professionals of the universal,' such as jurists, 'are virtuosi in the art of universalizing their particular interests,' says Bourdieu.[309] The end game of investment law professionals has long been to incorporate investment

[303] Glencore International A.G. v. Republic of Colombia (III), 'Procedural Order No. 3' ICSID Case No. ARB/21/30 (October 10, 2024) at para. 81.
[304] Glencore International A.G. v. Republic of Colombia (III), 'Procedural Order No. 3' ICSID Case No. ARB/21/30 (October 10, 2024) at para. 55 (b).
[305] Bernasconi, Brauch, and Mann (2020), Lin (2017), and Schadendorf (2009). Compare Born and Forrest (2019).
[306] United Nations (2016) at 15, para. 67.
[307] Weber (1978) at 730.
[308] Weber (1978) at 880, 882. One could say, along with Weber, 'specialists without heart.'
[309] Bourdieu (2014) at 343.

law strictures into the domestic law of every state.[310] After all, why shouldn't citizens all over the world not wish to adopt 'enlightened legal and constitutional principles' associated with highly developed capital-exporting states?[311]

III. Conclusion

Legitimacy is aptly described as an 'invisible institution.'[312] It is both hard to describe and difficult to establish, if not to maintain. It is particularly tricky to gauge in the case of international investment law. The regime is of relatively new vintage, one that took off only after the fall of the Soviet Union, and which is still undergoing construction. It continues to generate contestation by states, regional entities, and civil society in locales in both the Global North and South.

Weber warns that 'the continued exercise' of rule over others 'always has the strongest need of self-justification' by 'appealing to the principles of its legitimation.' These 'ultimate principles' are confined to 'only three.' They will be premised upon 'consciously made *rational* rules,'[313] sacred traditional authority, or extraordinary charismatic authority.[314] In Chapter 4, there will be an occasion to consider the degree to which arbitrators display characteristics associated with routinized charismatic authority. To whatever degree they exhibit charismatic qualities, those character traits are of an insufficient magnitude to serve as a legitimating principle for investment law. We are left to consider the first, more modern, form of legitimacy: the promulgation of rational rules enforced by public authority.

If most interpreters understand Weber as saying that modern legitimacy is derived solely from formal legality, then investment law should be considered an easy case. It appears to tick the requisite boxes to render this regime lawful and, therefore, legitimate. Yet it is not considered as such by its numerous audiences. It is with good reason, then, that Weber declared that legitimate rule must justify itself to those who are its subjects. Like Fuller, Guizot furnishes modest procedural criteria for securing and maintaining legitimacy: they include publicity, transparency, and openness.[315] Yet the investment treaty regime has had some difficulty satisfying even these few criteria. Investment law carriers have not been deeply interested in generating conditions to enhance its credibility. It is, after all, a regime structured

310 For example, Hart and Dymond (2002) at 168 and Vandevelde (1998b) at 639.

311 Vandevelde (2017) at 24–25.

312 The quoted phrase is from Rosanvallon (2011) at 8–9.

313 These 'may be either agreed upon or imposed from above ... In that case, every single bearer of powers of command is legitimated by that system of rational norms, and his power is legitimate insofar as it corresponds with the norm' in Weber (1978) at 954. These will typically be administered by a bureaucracy.

314 Weber (1978) at 954 (emphasis in original).

315 Guizot (1861) at 63, 296. See discussion in Schneiderman (2018b).

around confidentiality, convened in boardrooms of foreign capitals, and far removed from the locales in which investment disputes arise. Not a lot can be done while operating within the confines of the regime's logic other than, for instance, establishing an investment court or advisory centers to assist states in defusing investment disputes.[316]

Even though institutional efforts have been made, at ICSID for instance to enhance openness, the regime continues to operate at unacceptable levels of secrecy with enigmatic initial claims, privileged memorials, confidential proceedings, and undisclosed awards. These problems are compounded by the field's arcane discourse, protracted reasons, secret settlements, difficult-to-access scholarship, and pricey subscriptions to its specialized news outlets. Access to information, in other words, remains a problem. With little likelihood of such machinery materializing any time soon, shared belief in legitimacy is not likely to arise out of investment law's domains.

Having interrogated some of the ways in which regime legitimacy can be secured—with a focus on disguising its false universalism—investment law begins to look, in Beetham's memorable phrase, more 'like an extortion racket than a public service.'[317] Is it time to rethink the foundations of international investment law with a view to rendering it more fit for the role it is expected to play in the public life of citizens and states? Is it time to 'act differently'?[318] It is a task, given the investment regime's continuing instability and long-term legitimation difficulties, that will need attending to sooner or later. Having disputes resolved within national legal systems would help to alleviate some of these problems, but that is a goal that investment law's notables fiercely resist.[319] Instead, they have a different end game in sight: having states everywhere internalize investment law standards of treatment so that every economic actor within host states can benefit from similar protections, not just foreigners.[320] This is an unrealistic, if dystopic, scenario. Even if such a consensus was secured and a monolithic empire of economic rights installed, it is unlikely to result in stable outcomes. Disagreement about the proper relationship between politics and markets is endemic—it will always engender disagreement, particularly in an age of heightened economic inequality.[321] The search for a common good as a means of justifying relations of power will always attract contestation and resistance. To believe otherwise is to overestimate the legal profession's ability to generate legitimate authority to rule over others.

316 See the critique of advisory center proposals by UNCITRAL Working Group III in Fyock (2025) at 18–21.

317 Beetham (1991) at 83.

318 Weber (1919b) at 353.

319 The rationale for such a proposal, prompted by thoughts about the Latin maxim *audi alteram partem*, is developed in Schneiderman (2017b).

320 Wälde (2005) at 188.

321 Organization for Economic Co-Operation and Development (2017).

3

Proportionality and the Ethic of Conviction

How might we resolve deeply divisive legal questions that continually vex pluralistic polities? A device commonly deployed by high courts in constitutional democracies around the world is to focus on the relationship between means and ends associated with proportionality analysis.[1] Formal legal rationality, focused on the connection between means and ends, is described by Max Weber as the principal form of bureaucratic rule. Weber observes that accompanying the decline of magic and gods—and the spread of modern disenchantment—was the rise of bureaucratic rationality. Modern administration conducted along these lines rendered law calculable and predictable, the necessary handmaiden for the spread of both democracy and capitalism.[2] Tendencies toward the bureaucratization of power via this 'living machine' were 'inescapable.'[3] Weber bemoaned the absence of political leadership in Germany to counteract these tendencies.[4] 'The future belongs to bureaucratization,' he grudgingly admits.[5] Though Weber associates means-ends rationalizing with bureaucratic administration, rather than with courts,[6] the nearly worldwide embrace of proportionality review among apex courts around the world validates, in some measure, Weber's insight.[7]

It is precisely this tactic that is proposed for investment tribunals by investment law norm entrepreneurs to solve the field's nagging legitimacy concerns. A focus on means-ends scrutiny is described as the 'tailor-made solution' for resolving disputes 'with very high political stakes.'[8] Proportionality offers the 'best available' method 'with which to meet the present challenges to' the investment treaty system, writes Stone Sweet—it would be 'suicidal' to proceed otherwise.[9] Kingsbury and Schill claim that investment arbitrators have 'little choice' but to adopt proportionality

[1] Proportionality, writes Möller, 'has become *the* central concept in contemporary constitutional rights law' in Möller (2012) at 13 (emphasis in original).
[2] Weber (1918b) at 147–48.
[3] Weber (1918b) at 158.
[4] Weber (1919a) at 309.
[5] Weber (1918b) at 156.
[6] Weber (1978) at 979 ('general norms' play less of a role in 'administrative activity proper,' that is, outside the 'field of law creation and court procedure').
[7] It is 'a central structural feature of rights adjudication in liberal democracies worldwide' in Kumm (2010) at 142.
[8] Stone Sweet and Mathews (2009) at 89 and Stone Sweet (2010) at 75.
[9] Stone Sweet (2010) at 76, 47.

A Sociology of International Investment Law. David Schneiderman, Oxford University Press.
 DOI: 10.1093/9780198982739.003.0004

analysis if they wish to 'enhance' their legitimacy.[10] Tribunals thereby will have adopted standards 'congruent with an emerging set of public law principles for global regulatory governance.'[11] This is a revealing admission. High courts have had recourse to proportionality as a means of lending legitimacy to the exercise of judicial review in circumstances where there is a great deal of controversy over the content of constitutional fundamentals. We can reasonably surmise that the investment law field is as fraught as that of constitutional adjudication.

One problem is that, on those occasions where tribunals have sought to adopt proportionality's methods, they have not performed this task so well. This chapter evaluates the success of proportionality in light of the imperatives that drive investment arbitration. These are imperatives that I associate with, in Weber's terms, an 'ethic of conviction.' This is an ethical ambition that prefers to secure the attainment of chosen ideal ends—namely, the protection of foreign investors and their investments—irrespective of the means chosen. Proportionality is less likely to succeed, I argue, when arbitrators strive to secure the regime's ambitious ends despite its consequences for diminishing state policy capacity in the pursuit of the public interest. This is contrasted with an 'ethic of responsibility,' which encompasses the consequences of decision making, particularly having regard to the interests of all those affected by investment arbitration. Arbitrators, I argue, perform proportionality less well because their goal-oriented ethic of conviction overwhelms their analysis.

The chapter proceeds as follows. In Section II, I discuss Weber's well-known distinction between the ethic of conviction and the ethic of responsibility. In Section III, the familiar outlines of proportionality analysis are presented, and then, in Section IV, its application in investment arbitration is explored, with an emphasis on solar energy disputes against Spain under the European Energy Charter Treaty (ECT) (among the disputes that helped precipitate the demise of that treaty).[12] Finally, in Section V, an explanation for the flawed arbitral record is suggested. I turn first, in Section I, to a discussion of Weber's sociology of law and his ideal-typical version of bureaucratic rationality.

I. Rational Rule

Max Weber's diagnosis of our disenchanted world is explained with reference to means-ends analyses. We now have access, Weber declares, to 'technical means

[10] Kingsbury and Schill (2010) at 104 (citing Stone Sweet and Matthews [2009] in support at fn. 114).

[11] Kingsbury and Schill (2009) at 78.

[12] The European Council gave notice of withdrawal of the European Union from the Energy Charter Treaty in July 2024. On available mechanisms for exiting from the treaty while evading its sunset clause in Article 47(3) (investments made during the life of the treaty continue to be protected for a 20-year period), see EESC (2024) and Braoudakis, Craveia, and Baldon (2024).

and calculations' to solve modern problems. There is no longer a need to have recourse to 'magical means' so as 'to dominate or solicit the spirits.'[13] In this part, I turn to Weber's formulation of modern rationality and bureaucracy, outlined in *Economy and Society*, in order to identify mechanisms for resolving disagreement that many high courts now favor. Weber anticipates by almost a century the turn to proportionality on a nearly global scale.

Weber initially distinguishes between different ideal types of social action, two of which mostly concern us here and which serve as place holders for a discussion of the ethics of responsibility and conviction: 'instrumentally rational' action and 'value-rational' action.[14] Value rational action consciously puts into practice convictions generated by ethical, religious, or some other value or 'cause.'[15] Such convictions will be, in the opinion of the acting agent, 'binding' irrespective of 'possible cost.'[16] Instrumentally rational action, conversely, is guided by 'expectations' of human behavior; these expectations are the 'means' used 'for the attainment of the actor's own rationally pursued and calculated ends.'[17] 'Action is instrumentally rational when the end, the means, and the secondary results [side-effects] are all rationally taken into account and weighed,' declares Weber.[18] Value rational action, where the choice of means is determined solely by unqualified ends, will 'always [be] irrational.'[19] By contrast, instrumentally rational action always weighs ends, means, and side effects. Weber admits that it is 'unusual' to find these pure ideal types driving rational action in most 'concrete cases,' nor do these types exhaust the field of possibilities.[20] Here, in short, lies one of Weber's principal contributions to the history of ideas: 'the long trend of secularization, in which instrumental means-ends analysis is the core.'[21]

Weber conscripts these ideal types into his discussion of the economy, where he compares the 'formal rationality' of economic action (in which needs are satisfied based on impersonal technical calculation) with 'substantive rationality' (in which the provisioning of goods is shaped by the pursuit of some ultimate value).[22] The formal and the substantive are also foundational to his discussion of law and bureaucracy, where they undergo further refinement.[23] The focus, however, remains on the relationship between ends and means. Researchers can never be certain about ends—a focus on ends 'often cannot be understood completely' while a focus

[13] Weber (1919b) at 342.
[14] Weber (1978) at 24. Not discussed here is social action determined by 'affectual' or 'traditional' motivations (at 25). See Swedberg and Agevall (2016) at 165–67, 366.
[15] Weber (1978) at 25.
[16] Weber (1978) at 25.
[17] Weber (1978) at 24.
[18] Weber (1978) at 26.
[19] Weber (1978) at 26.
[20] Weber (1978) at 26.
[21] Eliaeson (2002) at 54.
[22] Weber (1978) at 85.
[23] Rheinstein (1954) at l.

on means generates 'the highest degree of verifiable certainty,' Weber writes.[24] In the latter case, the relation of means and ends will be intelligible on grounds of experience, 'particularly where the choice of means was inevitable.'[25] The bureaucratization of legality, in so far as it is intended to promote purposeful rational action, increasingly looks to assessments of means in light of antecedent ends.

Weber does not distinguish too sharply between the judicial and bureaucratic administration of justice. He did not view it as his task to 'specify differences' between discrete organizations. The task, instead, is to trace the outlines of an ideal typical bureaucracy that now dominates the West.[26] Therefore, subsumed under 'bureaucracy' were all of the state's 'administrative staff' who uphold 'the claim to the *monopoly* of the *legitimate* use of physical force in the enforcement of its order.'[27] Weber, for this reason, does not talk very much about judges—the 'lawfinders,' he called them, as opposed to the 'lawmaking' (legislators).[28] Instead, he preferred to assimilate under his discussion of bureaucratic rationality all forms of state administration, including the administration of justice.[29] Which is not to say that bureaucrats are precisely like judges,[30] only that judges (particularly civilian-trained judges on the Continent) bear many of the hallmarks Weber associated with professionalized bureaucracy. The predominant characteristics of modern bureaucratic administration included rule by a professional staff, with clear jurisdictional responsibilities, operating under a hierarchical order, managing written documents (files), and following depersonalized, general rules previously laid down.[31] The officeholder is appointed to serve a 'vocation' for which she is professionally trained (typically requiring some form of higher education) and for which she receives a salary and security of tenure (for life or with good behavior).[32]

What does the 'bureaucratization of justice' look like? A 'system of rationally debatable "reasons" stands behind every act of bureaucratic administration, namely,' Weber writes, 'either subsumption under norms, or a weighing of ends and means.'[33] By norms, Weber appears to be referring to conventional understandings about law and justice.[34] These will be determined by logical application of formally rational rules associated with legal reasoning. Decision making subsumed under general norms is meant to disrupt discretionary (Weber calls it 'creative') authority

[24] Weber (1978) at 5.
[25] Weber (1978) at 18.
[26] See Wrong (1970) at 35–36 ('Weber was chiefly concerned with drawing a sharp contrast between bureaucratic and nonbureaucratic forms of organization rather than with developing a model to employ in the comparative study of particular, concrete bureaucratic organizations') (at 36).
[27] Weber (1978) at 54 (emphasis in original).
[28] Sahni (2006) at 177.
[29] Kennedy (2004) at 1040, discussed further in Chapter 5.
[30] Kumm (2007) at 140, fn. 21.
[31] Weber (1978) at 957–59.
[32] Weber (1978) at 960*ff.*
[33] Weber (1978) at 979.
[34] Schluchter (1981) at 44.

that is delegated to public administration. By contrast, ends-means rationality confers some room to maneuver on the part of administrative staff.[35] The rationally debatable reasons issuing out of public administration, then, tend be focused on ends-means rationality. This has the advantage of precluding administration from ranking its own preferred ends.

As mentioned, Weber does not stipulate that judicial functions are better served under means-ends rationalizations. But he does liken the machinery of justice to actual machinery. Weber anticipates objections to his characterization of the 'modern judge as an automaton into which legal documents and fees are stuffed at the top in order that it may spill forth the verdict at the bottom, along with reasons, read mechanically from codified paragraphs.'[36] Such a conception would angrily be rejected, he admits, even though 'a certain approximation of this type would precisely be implied by a consistent bureaucratization of justice.'[37] Weber confines these disparaging remarks to German and continental judges. Weber characterizes common law judging based on precedent, however, in not much more favorable terms. Common law judging is an 'empirical art' associated with discretionary (associated with the derisive term 'khadi'[38]) justice, he writes, and therefore 'less rational and less bureaucratic' because it is focused on the individual case.[39]

A more sympathetic appreciation for the common law method is suggested elsewhere, however.[40] As mentioned in Chapter 1, in his essay on '"Roman and "Germanic" Law,' Weber appears to admire the penchant, among common law judges, of not 'avoid[ing] (in certain cases) the ethical consideration of economic events.'[41] That is, Weber acknowledges that taking into account the consequences of judicial decision making can be vital to judicial functions. This will have an affinity with the 'ethic of responsibility,' discussed next. By contrast, the 'German judge throws the executioner's sword far away and cries out for formal characteristics.'[42] This will ensure, he observes, that the 'social importance of the administration of civil law will remain relatively modest.'[43] Expressions of admiration for the system of English justice suggest that the common law was not 'deviant' but sufficiently formal, rational, and calculable to

[35] Weber (1978) at 979.

[36] Bureaucracy, Weber worries, is likely to issue decisions that 'maintain' its power. This often will be 'fused' with abstract and general norms associated with 'reason of state' in Weber (1978) at 979. Chapter 5 provides a more fulsome discussion of the judicial branch as bureaucracy.

[37] Weber (1978) at 979. Weber derisively describes the churning of a judicial 'slot machine into which one just drops the facts (plus the fee) in order to have it spew out the decision (plus opinion)' (at 886).

[38] Weber (1978) at 656, 976.

[39] Weber (1978) at 890, 976. Also see Schluchter (1981) at 90–91. 'Quite definitely,' Weber writes, 'English law-finding is not, like that of the Continent, 'application' of 'legal propositions logically derived from statutory texts' in Weber (1978) at 317.

[40] See Sahni (2009) at 215 who argues that Weber 'implicitly extols the English administration of justice.'

[41] Weber (1895b) at 244.

[42] Weber (1895b) at 245.

[43] Weber (1895b) at 245.

facilitate the rise of capitalism.[44] Nevertheless, even common law judges, Weber warns, cannot resist the spread of bureaucratized justice. He foresees that 'the traditional position of the English judge is also likely to be transformed permanently and profoundly' by these same forces.[45]

II. Conviction and Responsibility

Law, for Weber, is the means for achieving certain ends. Jurisprudence is preoccupied with whether law was valid in accordance with the 'rules of legal thought'—norms and forms that are accepted 'as binding.' The field cannot 'tell us *whether* particular legal rules should be established,' however. It can 'only indicate that, if one wants a certain result, then this [or that] particular legal rule is, according to the norms of legal thinking, the appropriate means of achieving it.'[46] Jurists, therefore, are well situated to evaluate the relationship between ends and means. They can forge the development of formal law 'in the direction of the rational state.'[47] Though, as mentioned, Weber at times singles out rule under jurists from public administration, he also subsumes judicial 'lawfinding' under bureaucratic rule. Even English common law judging could not escape the inevitable tendency toward machine-like bureaucratic justice.

In this part, I turn to Weber's 'politics as a vocation' lecture delivered in Munich at the invitation of a group of university students in January 1919.[48] It is in this lecture that Weber distinguishes between two ethics that are 'specific to politics': first, an ethics of conviction and, second, an ethics of responsibility.[49] The first corresponds to what Weber, in his sociology of law, portrays as contributing to anti-formalist tendencies in modern law. The ethic of conviction chooses means only with reference to values, irrespective of consequences. The second is compatible with what Weber contemplates as the jurist's role (recall his portrayal of the common law judge), that of evaluating the relationship between ends and means. This is because the ethic of responsibility accounts for 'the (foreseeable)

[44] Ewing (1987) at 499. The 'problem' of England is formulated in Trubek (1972a) at 746–48.

[45] Weber (1978) at 894. This appears to contradict an observation Weber makes elsewhere, that there is no 'visible tendency towards a transformation of the English legal system in the direction of the continental under the impetus of the capitalist economy.' He notes that where the two systems 'compete with one another, as in Canada, the Common Law has come out on top and has overcome the continental alternative rather quickly' (at 318). The contradiction can be resolved: Weber anticipates convergence not by reason of capitalism's inexorable force but due to an increase in the 'bureaucratization of formal legislation.' See Weber (1978) at 894. Weber's sociological reading of the Canadian experience—the only such reference I have found—seems hard to reconcile with the fact of Canadian bijuralism.

[46] Weber (1919b) at 345.

[47] Weber (1919a) at 328.

[48] Translation of '*Politics als Beruf.*' See Weber (1919a).

[49] Weber (1919a) at 357. This same binary is relied upon in an earlier essay on 'Intermediate Reflections' in Weber (2015b) at 229.

consequences of one's actions.'[50] Though Weber describes these two ethics as 'fundamentally opposed' ideal types, in practice, they cannot be absolute opposites. '[O]nly in combination do they produce the true human being who is *capable* of having a "vocation for politics"' he declared.[51] This is the type of political beast that does not 'live from' politics but 'lives for' politics.[52]

What is expected of a politician who recognizes an ethic of responsibility in the pursuit of political tasks? '[P]re-eminently decisive,' writes Weber, are 'passion, a sense of responsibility,' and a 'sense of proportion.'[53] As to the first, it turns out that responsible politicians also will have convictions—substantive ends that motivate political tasks. They will not simply exhibit '[e]mbitterment, philistinism' or a 'dull acceptance of the world.'[54] Instead, responsible politicians will have a passionate commitment to a cause, whether it be 'god or demon.'[55] Responsibility 'for that cause becomes the decisive lode-star of all action,' Weber acknowledges.[56]

Responsibility means attention to the vexing choices that accompany human affairs. It entails having an eye for proportion or good judgment. This calls for a sense of '*distance*' from political affairs. Reason and passion are each given their due, but a responsible politician will attain 'powerful control over the soul.'[57] This includes avoiding 'vanity,' the scourge of the power politician.[58] Because power is the means common to political action, those obsessed merely with attaining and retaining power exhibit 'a most wretched and superficial lack of concern for the *meaning* of human action, a blasé attitude that knows nothing of the tragedy in which all action, but quite particularly political action, is in truth enmeshed.'[59] It is at this juncture that the 'sense of responsibility' becomes apparent in the contrast drawn between politicians who live from and those who live for politics. Only the latter are attuned to the consequences of their actions.

Constitutionalists cannot help but notice the strong affinity between the ethic of responsibility and British Parliamentary practice.[60] In his political writings, Weber

[50] Weber (1919a) at 360 (emphasis in original).

[51] Weber (1919a) at 359, 360 (emphasis in original). Schluchter (1979) at 87–88 considers Weber's treatment as 'two diametrically opposed political ethics ... the absolute and the critical political ethic' (at 88).

[52] Weber (1919a) at 318.

[53] Weber (1946b) at 115 and Weber (1919a) at 352 where proportion (*augenmaß*) is translated as 'judgement.' Translations are mostly consistent regarding the first two features, *leidenschaft* and *verantwortungsgefühl*. See also Palonen (2010b) at 89 and Palonen (2017) at 182.

[54] Weber (1919a) at 368.

[55] Weber 1919a) at 353 and 355 (it is a 'question of faith') and (1919b) at 348 ('each individual must decide which one is God and which one of the Devil *for him*').

[56] Weber (1919a) at 353.

[57] Weber (1919a) at 353.

[58] Weber (1919a) at 354. This also is an 'occupational disease in academic and scholarly circles' (Weber 1919a).

[59] Weber (1919a) at 354–55.

[60] Its double meaning is described by Dicey (1908) at 321–22 (meaning, first, the responsibility of Ministers to 'retain the confidence of the House of Commons' and, second, being held 'responsible' for illegal acts though representing the Crown's will). Also see Amery (1947) at 30–31 (in the British

extolled the virtues of an ideal type of parliamentary rule, bemoaning the inability of German politicians to behave responsibly. Weber condemned political actors for acting like bureaucrats, sacrificing convictions to a '*duty of obedience*.'[61] These are politicians who hold office '*without responsibility*,' who 'have *refused* ... to accept material responsibility' for their actions.[62] Instead, he urged those holding political office to 'weigh the potential significance of public statements' and to, 'above all, ... have the *leading politician's* sense of responsibility.'[63] It was particularly via parliamentary committee systems that officialdom could be interrogated and held accountable. Only then would 'qualified, professional politicians who have been through the school of intensive committee work in a *working* parliament' produce 'responsible leaders as opposed to mere demagogues and amateurs.'[64]

Danger lurks even here, warns Weber, as the specific means available to political action is violence.[65] There is no getting around the fact that, having a monopoly on the use of force, political action reinforced by the state will cause certain, perhaps regrettable, effects. Weber insists that responsible politicians be attuned to these intended and unintended effects. It is this relationship between ends and means that Weber stresses in his lecture on politics as a vocation. For one thing, there are almost always unintended consequences. It is a 'fundamental fact,' Weber writes, that 'the eventual outcome of political action frequently, indeed regularly, stands in a quite inadequate, even paradoxical relation to its original, intended meaning and purpose.'[66] And these consequences might prove to be regrettable, if not injurious. 'No ethics in the world,' Weber continues, 'can get round the fact that the achievement of "good" ends is in many cases tied to the necessity of employing morally suspect or at least morally dangerous means.'[67] One must, for this reason, 'reckon with the possibility or even likelihood of evil side-effects.' Those 'who get involved in politics,' Weber warned his audience, will be implicated in the mechanics of 'power and violence.' They will be 'making a pact with diabolical powers' and confronting the dangerous ethical terrain 'that lurk[s] in all violence.'[68]

constitutional system responsibility operates in two senses: 'accountability to an outside or final authority' and also as 'a state of mind') and Jennings (1961) at 277ff, 497–98 (on collective ministerial responsibility) and 112–13 (on individual ministerial responsibility).

61 Weber (1918b) at 204 (emphasis in original).

62 Weber (1918b) at 205, 204 (emphasis in original). Palonen (2010) at 89 likens the role of 'officials' to those of scholars who, similarly, bear no responsibility for the consequences of their actions. But this interpretation undervalues the role of the teacher to compel an individual to 'give an account to himself of the ultimate meaning of his own conduct' in terms of chosen ends and 'unavoidable' means. Educators thereby assume 'the duty of creating clarity and a sense of responsibility' in Weber (1919b) at 350.

63 Weber (1918b) at 204 (emphasis in original). They should 'publicly *refuse* to accept responsibility for political actions if they conflict with his own convictions.' This has 'never happened here,' Weber unhappily adds (Weber 1918b).

64 Weber (1918b) at 191 (emphasis in original). See Loewenstein (1966) at 41–42.

65 Weber (1919a) at 357 also 310, 360.

66 Weber (1919a) at 355.

67 Weber (1919a) at 360.

68 Weber (1919a) at 362, 365.

This is why an ethic of conviction is so inadequate to the task of weighing ends against 'ethically dangerous means.'[69] 'The ethics of conviction is bound to founder hopelessly on this problem of how the end is to sanctify the means,' he warns.[70] The upshot is that those driven by religious or revolutionary convictions should stay out of politics. Those who have sought other-worldly 'goodness and love for mankind' (he mostly has in mind Jesus Christ), 'did not employ the means of politics, force.' Wars of faith fought purely out of ethical conviction have been discredited, he adds, because 'responsibility for *consequences* is lacking.'[71] It is attending to the consequences of one's actions and being held accountable for those effects that distinguishes a responsible politician from an irresponsible one. Even where responsible political action is motivated by some faith or conviction,[72] the weighing of ends versus means is required, and all consequences, direct or indirect, intended or unintended, are to be accounted for. Only those who subscribe to the ethic of responsibility, Weber declares in resounding fashion, will say: 'These consequences are to be attributed to my actions.'[73] Does proportionality analysis serve as a suitable vehicle for promoting an ethic of responsibility?

III. Balancing Proportionality

When a legal dispute arises, the administration of justice requires that decisions are made, and rulings issued. Adjudicators, in short, are called upon to take a stand. They have the capacity and obligation to be decisive. Having been allocated the task of resolving disputes, judges have the power to produce their own effects—the power to create the very 'things named,' according to Bourdieu.[74] Proportionality review is meant to facilitate these functions by isolating the relationship between ends and means, determining whether state objectives bear a reasonable relationship to means employed. In constitutional cases, apex courts typically address a preliminary question: Is the legislative objective sufficiently important to limit

69 Weber (1919a) at 360.

70 Weber (1919a) at 361.

71 Weber (1919a) at 366 (emphasis in original).

72 It is genuinely moving, Weber concludes, when a political actor declares, as did the Calvinist Martin Luther, 'Here I stand, I can do no other' in Weber (1919a) at 367. See the 'Conclusion' for a more contemporary example.

73 Weber (1919a) at 360 (the responsible politician will answer for the '(foreseeable) *consequences* of one's actions' [emphasis in original]). Also see Brown (2023) at 39 ('Not calculative reason, then, but a distinctive ethic of responsibility for *all* effects of an action, especially collateral and unintended ones, is required to guide and temporize without choking political passion') (emphasis in original). It is an ethic that is 'value-relational' in so far as it accounts for the pluralistic nature of modern polities. See Schluchter (1979) at 91.

74 Bourdieu (1987) at 838 ('[t]he law is the quintessential form of "active" discourse, able by its own operation to produce its effects' at 839). But having 'no influence over either the sword or the purse,' adds Alexander Hamilton in Hamilton, Jay, and Madison (1961) at 465 (No. 78).

constitutional rights and freedoms?[75] Characterization of the objective—the choice of the end being pursued—is critical to the inquiry as it sets the parameters against which chosen means will be evaluated. A number of sub-inquiries, focused on ends-means relations, comprise the proportionality inquiry.[76] First, are the means adopted *suitable* for advancing the objective, second, do the means infringe on those rights as little as *necessary* and, third, is the benefit gained by the legislative scheme *proportionate* to the deleterious effect on rights (this is proportionality *stricto sensu* or in the narrow sense).

The contemporary literature on the rise of proportionality review has mostly missed any connection with Weber.[77] Yet many of the critiques of proportionality review today were anticipated in sociological debates over means-ends rationality. Quarrels over, for instance, whether proportionality review elides the complexity of rights or whether there are requisite moral evaluations in determining the content and scope of rights have affinities with some of Weber's mid-twentieth-century critics.[78] Defenders of proportionality review seek to appease critics by rejecting the claim that proportionality is devoid of moral reasoning.[79] At the same time, advocates of proportionality applaud its structure of reasoning as it generates 'more rationality towards the whole process' of weighing rights.[80] Indeed, the scholarly literature today is replete with claims about improving the 'rationality' of judicial decision making.

More striking is the prevalence of mathematical or mechanical imagery.[81] This, for Weber, is a mark of modern rational thought. According to Robert Alexy's influential account, generalizing from the work of the German Constitutional Court, the greater the intensity of the infringement, the greater must be satisfaction of some countervailing constitutional principle.[82] This is reduced to a 'law of balancing'[83] and the generation of a mathematical model Alexy calls the 'weight formula.'[84] Others deny that answers to constitutional rights problems are always answerable by having recourse to the logic of numbers. Devices such as Alexy's 'weight

[75] Grimm (2007) at 388 and Barak (2007) at 371. Barak (2012) at 249 maintains that discussions of proportionality are premature without determining whether a proper purpose is being pursued. Alexy (2017) at 14, 19 describes this initial inquiry as 'superfluous,' as the public purpose will get weighed against limits on rights at the last stage (proportionality in the narrow sense). The only initial determination to be made is whether the purpose is constitutionally permissible.

[76] Following the German practice outlined in Alexy (2002) at 66ff.

[77] I have found only a handful of such references in the English-language literature, largely subsidiary to the main argument, in Urbina (2012) at 77–79; Cohen-Ilaya and Porat (2010) at 274; and Bomhoff (2008) at 575.

[78] The complaints by Tsakyrakis (2009) at 475 and Webber (2009) of proportionality resemble complaints by Marcuse (1971) and Habermas (1971a) of Weber.

[79] See Kumm (2007), Klatt and Meister (2012), and Stacey (2019).

[80] Klatt and Meister (2012).

[81] Klatt and Meister (2012) at 699.

[82] Alexy (2002) at 47–48. Alexy's formulation is dependent upon a distinction between rules and principles.

[83] Alexy (2010) at 28.

[84] Alexy (2007).

formula' help, however, to make the process more 'rational.' Acknowledging that proportionality aspires to have the precision of mathematics, the 'model works fine without any use of numbers,' admit Klatt and Meister.[85]

The seemingly neutral and mathematical merit of proportionality has not been lost on judges in many high courts around the world. It also has not been lost on agents promoting new transnational legal institutions that perform judicial functions. In the field of international investment law, for instance, investment tribunals have been wading into controversial policy domains, limiting state capacity to protect the interests of foreign investors. Some scholars have responded by advocating the adoption of proportionality as a means of resolving legitimacy concerns that continue to plague the system. These '[i]ntense concerns about legitimacy in the system,' it is said, 'should drive a rapid adoption of proportionality analysis as a standard technique.'[86] Others question whether proportionality is an apt technique for resolving every investment dispute, expressing doubts on numerous grounds. Among them are claims that proportionality is not yet a general principle of international law;[87] investment arbitration is unpredictable and decentralized;[88] proportionality is unsuitable for resolving expropriation disputes but a better fit for fair and equitable treatment claims;[89] states have not provided consent to its adoption;[90] or that it calls upon arbitrators to weigh incommensurable interests, or to second-guess state policy in the pursuit of public interest objectives, tasks for which arbitrators are not well equipped.[91] In light of this last objection (having to do with second-guessing policy priorities), some have endorsed incorporation of only the first two steps of the proportionality inquiry (suitability and necessity) but not proportionality in the strict sense.[92] The worry is that this last step grants license to arbitrators to balance restrictions on investor rights (means) against public interest goals (ends), which is well beyond arbitral expertise.[93] Some of the Spanish solar energy disputes, which I review in some detail below, reveal that as much caution should be placed on arbitrators' applying the second step (necessity). Before turning to a discussion of those cases, I first

[85] Klatt and Meister (2012) at 700.
[86] Kingsbury and Schill (2010) at 104.
[87] Titi (2018) at 113–15; Sornarajah (2015) at 366–67; and Vadi (2018) at 120. Kulick (2012) at 168–69 describes it as an emerging general principle of international law.
[88] De Brabandere and Miranda da Cruz (2020) at 491. Vadi (2018) at 56 describes it as lacking 'constitutional density.' Vadi's meaning is unclear, but it seems likely that centralizing adjudication in a multilateral investment court will remedy this deficit.
[89] Bücheler (2015) at 302. Or, as Henckels (2015) at 190 argues, it is more appropriate for standards of protection than for exceptions.
[90] Sornarajah (2015) at 366 and Ranjan (2014) at 866.
[91] Davitti (2021) at 87–88.
[92] See Ortino (2017) at 89, Henckels (2015) at 28–29, 168 and Ranjan (2014) at 882. Kürtz (2010) at 368 appears to rely exclusively on the test of necessity (the inquiry into less restrictive means).
[93] The concern is that arbitrators are not embedded within local legal and cultural contexts. However, this is oft claimed to be the presumed advantage of investment arbitration over local legal adjudication.

evaluate whether investment arbitrators have embraced proportionality and, to the extent that they have, whether they have performed that function well. Driven by their ethic of conviction, I argue that when arbitrators undertake the task of weighing ends versus means, their values cloud the performance of proportionality review.

IV. Occluding Proportionality

In spite of pleas that proportionality analysis be rapidly adopted so as to lend legitimacy to the investor–state dispute settlement (ISDS) enterprise,[94] there appears to be a marked reluctance on the part of investment arbitrators to do so. This is so even in the face of new textual signals, in treaty annexes on expropriation, for instance, that direct tribunals to determine whether means are excessive in light of ends sought.[95] To be sure, the occasions where this method of reasoning has been applied are on the rise. For the most part, however, the widespread adoption of this adjudicative style has been resisted. In this part, I briefly review examples of this diffidence and, in the next part, try to understand why the enterprise appears to be so flawed.

A small empirical study that I undertook a decade ago indicated that tribunals are hearing more about proportionality from legal counsel and that tribunals are exhibiting openness to applying these considerations in the context of resolving investment disputes.[96] Then, as now, the numbers remain low, and a significant amount of learning has yet to occur. The trendline is tentative, resembling an awkward, often flawed, embrace.[97] Given the low frequency with which proportionality is undertaken by investment tribunals, what helps to explain its infrequent admission into investment law's domains? It may be that, for reasons previously mentioned (e.g., the absence of references to proportionality in earlier generations of investment treaties or its weak candidacy as a general principle of international law), this outcome can reasonably be explained. On the other hand, tribunals have eagerly reached beyond text, general principles, and customary international law to identify legal content (consider, for instance, legitimate expectations doctrine)[98]

[94] Stone Sweet (2010) at 75.

[95] See, for example, Canada-EU Comprehensive Economic Trade Agreement (CETA) 'Annex 8-A Expropriation,' s. 3 ('For greater certainty, except in the rare circumstance where the impact of the measure or series of measures is so severe in light of its purpose that it appears manifestly excessive . . . .').

[96] In the period 1994–2010, I identified a total of 23 decisions (out of 210) where proportionality was mentioned expressly or impliedly in tribunal decisions. Of these, in only 13 decisions did tribunals approvingly invoke proportionality analysis in discussing the law and, of these, only 8 tribunals applied some semblance of proportionality analysis. See Schneiderman (2011). Van Harten turned up forty documents where proportionality was relevant in his study of disputes from 1899 to 2012 in Van Harten (2013) at 62, fn. 78.

[97] Stone Sweet (2011) at 15 accurately describes the trendline as 'timid.'

[98] Referring to investor expectations that have been prompted by host state behavior. See Ostřanský (2023) at 127–37.

that constrains state capacity. Why the hesitation in the case of a technique that purports to lend predictability and transparency to the process by which states can defend alleged treaty violations? It is a technique that requires judgment, it is true, but not too much erudition. It offers a method with distinct steps that are easily grasped, even by the lay public.[99]

Most scholars point to the Tecmed ruling as illustrative of how proportionality doctrine has been conscripted into the resolution of investment disputes.[100] It is even singled out by some as exhibiting good technique.[101] The dispute arose under a Spain-Mexico Bilateral Investment Treaty (BIT) and concerned a failure to renew a permit to operate the Cytrar hazardous waste facility site at Los Víboras, eight kilometers from Hermosillo, the Sonora state capital. The Madrid-based company Técnicas Medioambientales S.A. purchased the site at auction from the municipality in the expectation that it would continue to operate the facility for years to come under a newly formed Mexican subsidiary.[102] The facility operated for two years (from 1996 to 1998) mostly without incident. Civil society opposition began to mobilize against Cytrar; however, once reports began circulating that soil contaminated with toxic waste was being imported from out of state. Hermosillo citizens organized petitions and protests, blocking access to the site. Eventually, the Mexican authority declined to renew the operating permit.[103]

The investor claimed that this was a compensable event tantamount to expropriation and that there was a denial of fair and equitable treatment. The tribunal's proportionality discussion arises in the context of the first expropriation claim. Regulatory takings (the analogous US constitutional law construct)[104] fall within the terms of the Spain-Mexico BIT as a sub-set of indirect expropriations. According to the tribunal, these are regulations that are 'irreversible and permanent' such that the ability to profit from an investment 'has disappeared; i.e. the economic value of the use, enjoyment or disposition of the assets or rights affected by the administrative action or decision have been neutralized or destroyed,' requiring the payment of compensation.[105] Even where measures are 'beneficial to society as a whole—such as environmental protection,' the obligation to pay compensation remains, the tribunal declared.[106] The 'government's intention,' the

[99] On its global appeal, see Beatty (2004).
[100] Técnicas Medioambientales (2003).
[101] For example, Cottier et al. (2017) at 658 (lauding the tribunal's 'two-step analysis'), Kingsbury and Schill (2010) at 91 ('illustrates well the use of a proportionality analysis'), and Krommendijk and Morijn (2009) at 444.
[102] Tecmed (2003) at para. 88.
[103] I have drawn upon an earlier discussion of the Tecmed dispute in Schneiderman (2013b) at 81–83. The dispute is discussed further in Chapter 4.
[104] Referring to host state regulations that, in whole or in part, are tantamount to depriving an investment of value. See Perrone (2023) at 79–87 (described as giving rise to 'the most controversial indirect expropriation cases').
[105] Tecmed (2003) at para. 116.
[106] Tecmed (2003) at para. 121.

tribunal wrote, 'is less important than the effects of the measure' on the investor.[107] In this instance, the government's actions 'fully and irrevocably destroyed' the investment and so amounted to an expropriation.[108]

The tribunal was not content with examining only the effects of a measure on the investor, however. In order to determine whether the government's action was expropriatory, and not merely a defensible exercise of the state regulatory capacity (an exercise of state police powers jurisdiction), the tribunal sought to determine whether such a measure was proportionate in its effects in light of the government's objective. This conceivably would have the effect of mitigating an emphasis solely on the impact of a measure on an investor. Even here, the tribunal admitted, 'the significance of such impact [on the investor] has a key role' in determining whether there has been proportionality.[109]

The question, as framed by the tribunal, was 'whether such measures are reasonable with respect to their goals, the deprivation of economic rights and the legitimate expectations of [those] who suffered such deprivation.'[110] Though having already found the measure to have risen to the level of a compensable taking, the analysis began with the 'due deference' that is owed to the state when it takes measures in the public interest. Among the factors to be considered in assessing proportionality, the tribunal added, was the 'size of the ownership deprivation' and whether compensation was offered. Also weighing into the proportionality analysis is 'that the foreign investor has a reduced or nil participation in the taking of the decisions that affect it, partly because investors are not entitle[d] to exercise political rights reserved to the nationals of the state, such as voting for the authorities that will issue the decisions that affect such investors.'[111] Defects in the political process, in other words, lend support to the investor's sense of being wronged.[112] In light of these considerations, the tribunal concluded that Mexico had failed to satisfy the tribunal that its failure to renew the hazardous waste license was not disproportionate.

The proportionality exercise at work here seems confused. First, the tribunal fails to distinguish between proportionality's place not in determining whether a treaty breach has occurred but whether it is justifiable (or non-compensable). Proportionality typically addresses justifiable limitations, not determinations about whether a limitation of rights has occurred.[113] Second, the tribunal appears to have skipped over earlier elements of proportionality to settle upon proportionality in the strict sense (the last step).[114] It is not clear, however, the degree

[107] Tecmed (2003) at para. 116.
[108] Tecmed (2003) at para. 117.
[109] Tecmed (2003) at para. 122.
[110] Tecmed (2003) at para. 122.
[111] Tecmed (2003) at para. 122.
[112] I have addressed the weak empirical support for this political process argument in Schneiderman (2010b).
[113] Cohen-Eliya and Porat (2004). See Leonhardsen (2012) at 124.
[114] Leonhardsen (2012) at 124.

of strictness that the tribunal applied. Was it a strict 'necessity' test or something looser? The tribunal paid lip service to something it labeled 'due deference.' Was this akin to the European formulation of 'margin of appreciation' (a measure of deference familiar to European human rights law)?[115] Calamita is equally confused by Tecmed's reasoning.[116] He assumes a stricter approach was applied, though the tribunal spoke in the language of deference. For this reason, he characterizes the Tecmed tribunal's discussion of proportionality as amounting to a 'rhetorical flourish[] about deference' rather than its 'actual *application*.'[117] That methodological problems arise suggests that there are hints of confusion, if not reluctance, in integrating proportionality into ISDS.[118] In other awards that address alleged expropriations, police powers doctrine, an analytically distinct categorical rule that excuses the obligation to pay compensation, is wrapped up in discussions of proportionality.[119]

Even then, the application of proportionality analysis in expropriation cases remains fleeting. Though imprecise, a search in mid-2023 revealed twenty-six hits, among ninety expropriation disputes, which included a proportionality analysis.[120] Only twelve were revealed to encompass a nominal discussion of proportionality's method. The data as regards fair and equitable treatment reveals a more robust number of hits: among sixty-five awards, forty-one include an analysis of the proportionality of impugned measures. A large proportion of these awards concern disputes against Spain and Italy, lodged under the ECT, for altering the regime for state support of solar energy investments. The largest number of these arises in awards against Spain.[121] Of the fifty-one disputes lodged against Spain, as of December 2022, thirty-two awards were issued, of which Spain lost twenty-six (an 81 percent win rate for investors). At that time, more than €1.4 billion in compensation was due to be paid to investors for upsetting the solar energy regime, in addition to €116 million in legal and tribunal fees.[122]

By taking up a selection of these Spanish cases, we learn more about how an ethic of conviction drives proportionality analysis in investment arbitration.[123]

[115] On the margin of appreciation as a device for prompting deference in investment law, see Leonhardsen (2021). For a critique, see Born, Morris, and Forrest (2020).

[116] Calamita (2015).

[117] Calamita (2015) at 187.

[118] On occasion, police powers doctrine, an analytically distinct categorical rule, is wrapped up in the discussion of proportionality. See, for example, *Mohamed Abdel Raouf Bahgat* (2019) at para. 232.

[119] Philip Morris (2003) at paras. 305–6.

[120] This data was generated using Investment Arbitration Reporter's Topic Tool on June 9, 2023.

[121] Claims were initiated under ECT Article 10(1) which provides: 'Each Contracting Party shall, in accordance with the provisions of this Treaty, encourage and create stable, equitable, favourable and transparent conditions for Investors of other Contracting Parties to make Investments in its Area. Such conditions shall include a commitment to accord at all times to Investments of Investors of other Contracting Parties fair and equitable treatment....'

[122] The win–loss and compensation data are from Mehranvar and Sachs (2023) at 9. Also see Mehranvar and Sasmal (2022) at 11.

[123] This requires taking a deeper dive into the legal dogmatics of investment arbitration than some readers may prefer.

Though this discussion is not meant to be exhaustive, it does call for a close analysis of tribunal reasoning. Spain employed a 'feed-in' tariffs (FIT) regime in order to attract investment in solar energy production. These schemes ensured that energy produced would be purchased by the state at rates guaranteed for fixed periods. After the global economic recession of 2008, and a subsequent reduction in electricity consumption, promised rates proved to be unsustainable. Between 2007 and 2009, subsidies paid to solar energy producers skyrocketed from €194 million to €2.6 billion. As declared by the government in the preamble to its Royal Decree 9/2013, 'the Spanish electricity system has generated a tariff deficit which, over time, has become structural due to the fact that the real costs associated with ... the operation of the electricity sector are higher than the revenues collected from the fees set by the government and paid by consumers.'[124] Accumulated debt grew by leaps and deficits proved untenable.[125] By means of a series of ministerial decrees (between 2010 and 2014),[126] the Spanish government took steps to reduce its commitment to solar energy providers, going so far as to claw back funds already paid out. Each decree nevertheless 'guaranteed' that producers would be provided with a 'reasonable return on their investments.' This reduced commitment was balanced against the interests of consumers, who were ensured that costs for the purchase of electricity would be 'reasonable.'[127]

Spanish courts repeatedly held that rolling back of subsidies to solar energy producers was consistent with Spanish law. There was no constitutional requirement to provide additional compensation. Yet most investors were able to secure additional compensation via claims made pursuant to legitimate expectations doctrine under the ECT.[128] In many of these tribunal awards, proportionality was not a consideration. These awards are described by arbitrator Douglas as imposing 'strict liability' on respondent states, where no 'public interest or proportionality defence can be raised.'[129] The commitment by Spain to provide FIT for fixed periods of time amounted, for these tribunals, to 'stabilization' commitments—meaning no substantial change to the regulatory environment would be tolerated—frozen by legitimate expectations doctrine under fair and equitable treatment. Concurring and dissenting Arbitrator Brower, in *PV Investors*, describes these awards (fifteen of eighteen at the time) as properly guaranteeing the investors' 'primary' expectations.[130] The *Eiser* award illustrates well this line of cases. No discussion of proportionality arises; instead, the tribunal is concerned solely with the impact of reducing tariffs on the foreign investor.[131]

[124] RWE Innogy (2019) at para. 555.
[125] RWE Innogy (2019) at para. 556.
[126] These measures are outlined in PV Investors (2020) at paras. 590–97.
[127] In Royal Decree 661/2007. See discussion in Mathis Kruck (2022) at para. 67.
[128] Mehranvar and Sachs (2023) at 8, 14. For example, STS/6317/2006 (discussed in Mehranvar and Sachs 2023 at 14–15).
[129] In his Dissenting Opinion in Mathis Kruck (2022) at para. 11.
[130] PV Investors (2020) in 'Concurring and Dissenting Opinion of Charles N. Brower.'
[131] Eiser (2017) at para. 418.

When discussions of proportionality analysis arise, they do so in a set of tribunal rulings that evaluate what is called an investors' 'secondary' claim.[132] In these disputes, tribunals have rejected the primary claim, namely, that expected profits are guaranteed. Having rejected guaranteed profits at *promised* rates of return, tribunals turn to an alternative claim, asking whether an investor has received a *reasonable* rate of return on their investment. They answer this question by having recourse to the three steps of a typical proportionality inquiry. However, even here, when turning to the last step in the analysis, asking whether Spain has placed a disproportionate burden on investors in light of the objective sought, tribunals typically have answered with reference to mathematical formulations. Illustrative of this development is the *Sevilla Beheer* award, where both reasonableness (typically a separate consideration) and proportionality merge into a single inquiry. The tribunal acknowledged that the Spanish economy faced 'serious problems that called for immediate action' and that Spain sought to find a 'middle ground' in which investors could maintain a reasonable rate of return.[133] Purporting to adopt a margin of appreciation, the tribunal described a deferential proportionality inquiry as the 'most appropriate.'[134] The tribunal concluded, therefore, that abolishing a special regime providing subsidies to producers was not 'unreasonable or disproportionate.' However, the claw back of subsidies already received, if depriving an investor of a 'reasonable return,' upset legitimate expectations. The focus of the tribunal turned, therefore, to the 'economic impact' of the measures on the investment.[135] Disproportionality would be determined solely with reference to the rate of return, which the tribunal deemed 'reasonable' at a rate of 7 percent. Compensation would be awarded to the investor to the degree the return on the investment fell below this rate, in addition to whatever monies were owing due to the retroactive claw back.[136] The public interest that typically gets weighed into proportionality analysis goes mostly unmentioned.

The *RWE Innogy* award also began by adopting a margin of appreciation in its proportionality analysis, signaling that a measure of deference was appropriate 'in terms of balancing the differing public and private interests that may be in play.'[137] The first step of suitability was easily satisfied, the tribunal concluded.[138] The claimant also failed to show that other less restrictive alternatives were available at the second, necessity, step.[139] This burden was misplaced, however.[140] It is the

[132] I am mindful that Schmidl (2021) divides the Spanish solar energy cases into more than two categories.
[133] Sevilla Beheer (2022) at para. 928.
[134] Sevilla Beheer (2022) at paras. 929–30.
[135] Sevilla Beheer (2022) at para. 934.
[136] Sevilla Beheer (2022) at para. 1021.
[137] RWE Innogy (2019) at para. 553.
[138] RWE Innogy (2019) at para. 560.
[139] RWE Innogy (2019) at paras. 567, 572.
[140] Barak (2012) at 412, 444. In constitutional rights cases, the burden of proof shifts to the party seeking to justify the limitation.

respondent state that has knowledge of all reasonably available options. Turning, finally, to proportionality in the strict sense, the tribunal likened its task to striking a 'balance.' Though this task generally should be approached with some caution,[141] there was less reason to be deferential, the tribunal ruled, when a state deploys incentives to lure investors to invest and purports to 'guarantee' rates of return. Therefore, the tribunal did 'not consider it appropriate to allow a particularly wide margin' of appreciation to apply. Proportionality, instead, would be applied strictly.[142] Was the burden passed on to investors disproportionate to the objectives sought? Refusing to pass the full costs on to consumers in order to pay out foreign investors did not give rise to disproportionality.[143] Instead, the inquiry was resolved, again, with reference to rates of return on the investment. The tribunal found that reducing that rate imposed an 'excessive and disproportionate' burden on the claimants.[144] Once again, there is little discussion of the public interest benefit gained by reducing the rate of return below 7 percent.

Finally, consider the award in *PV Investors*. The tribunal rejected the investors' primary claim that any reduction in tariffs violated the treaty by 'drastically' reducing the investor's 'cash flows.'[145] The tribunal accepted that Spain should enjoy a margin of appreciation in making economic policy choices.[146] As for the secondary claim, that the PV Investors had a legitimate expectation that they would receive a reasonable rate of return, the tribunal appeared to focus exclusively on proportionality in the strict sense without considering the prior two steps. The tribunal asked whether there was an 'appropriate correlation between the policy sought by the state and the measure.'[147] This question would be answered only with reference to whether the investor was afforded a reasonable rate of return.[148] The tribunal acknowledged that, unlike most disputes where liability is distinct from the quantum claimed, the 'quantification of the harm' would inform 'the finding of liability.' In the tribunal's words, 'reasonableness, non-arbitrariness, proportionality, etc.' would be determined by an 'assessment of the [monetary] harm suffered by the Claimants.'[149] Having reduced the rate of return for these investors to a rate below 7 percent, Spain acted 'unreasonably and disproportionately and hence violated FET.'[150]

[141] A 'tribunal will have no wish to replace its own subjective appreciations for those of the State' in RWE Innogy (2019) at para. 571.
[142] RWE Innogy (2019) at para. 571.
[143] Indeed, some of the costs had been passed onto consumers, as acknowledged in PV Investors (2020) at para. 627.
[144] RWE Innogy (2019) at para. 599.
[145] PV Investors (2020) at paras. 314, 620.
[146] PV Investors (2020) at para. 583.
[147] PV Investors (2020) at para. 625, quoting Electrabel (2015) at para. 180.
[148] PV Investors (2020) at para. 630.
[149] PV Investors (2020) at para. 648 ('It is *only if* the alteration of the regulatory framework called into question the guarantee of reasonable return that the Claimants would be entitled to compensation' [emphasis added]).
[150] PV Investors (2020) at para. 847.

In addition to intermingling proportionality with inquiries into reasonableness,[151] these awards exhibit a flawed application of proportionality doctrine. Putting to one side awards where the primary claim was accepted and strict liability for reduced tariffs imposed upon Spain, on those occasions where tribunals arrived at the last stage of proportionality in the strict sense, they seem to have adopted, instead, what looks like a second-stage inquiry into necessity. Recall that at the second step of proportionality, adjudicators typically ask, in disputes where economic policy is at issue, whether the means adopted were chosen from among a range of reasonable alternatives. In other words, tribunals ask whether the same objective could reasonably be achieved by using alternative means that are less restrictive of the claimed right. The purpose is taken as given—only means chosen are scrutinized. Juxtapose this inquiry with the last stage of proportionality in the strict sense, where adjudicators weigh the harmful effects on rights against the benefits to the public interest gained by the state action. In the awards just discussed, where liability turns on whether the rate of return to investors was reasonable, there is no evaluation of the benefits gained by reducing the rate of return below levels determined by tribunals to be 'reasonable.' Tribunals are not evaluating whether benefits to the public interest outweigh harms suffered by the rights claimant.[152] Instead, the inquiry resembles the second step of proportionality, where means are tested solely against given ends. There simply is no discussion by tribunals of the societal benefits to be gained by reducing profits below what tribunals deem to be 'reasonable' to alleviate pressure on the public purse, in addition to the burden on consumers. There is no weighing of state benefits against the injury to investor rights. Instead, state objectives get buried under the weight of a calculation into reasonable rates of return. But rates of return do not represent the state's objective. It is, instead, a measure intended to fulfill obligations the state feels it owes to foreign investors.

The inquiry turns out to be heavily weighted in favor of economic impact on investors. Not weighed into the equation are the advantages secured by reducing public subsidies to, and therefore profits of, foreign investors in the renewable energy sector.[153] For this reason, Ortino can conclude that the tribunals in these awards 'fail to recognize appropriately the legal relevance of the public interest in determining whether a legitimate expectation deserves legal protection.'[154] Similarly, Mehranvar and Sachs conclude that, 'in most (if not all)' of the awards

[151] As observed by Ortino (2023). Discussions of 'arbitrariness,' which would seem to be caught by the first suitability requirement, are also wrapped into some of these inquiries.

[152] Barak (2012) at 415.

[153] It is helpful to recall Michelman's (1967) advice: 'What fairness (or the utilitarian test) demands is assurance that society will not act deliberately so as to inflict painful burdens on some of its members unless such action is 'unavoidable' in the interest of long run, general well-being.... Society violates that assurance [when it proceeds] with measures which seem certain to cause painful individual losses *while not clearly promising any net social improvement*' (emphasis added).

[154] Ortino (2023) at 19.

against Spain, tribunals 'did not consider Spain's public policy justification for the contested measures.'[155]

V. Eclipsing Proportionality

What helps to explain this outcome? We return to Weber to draw the outlines of an answer. Recall the distinction between an ethics of conviction and an ethic of responsibility. Those faithful to an ethic of conviction pursue ends without regard to consequences. Those exercising responsibility—Weber's preferred ethic for those seeking to exercise political leadership—will consider all of the effects of their actions. That is, they will have regard to their preferred ends but also keep in mind the consequences of pursuing those ends. Responsible leadership weighs means and their relation to ends, so that all consequences, intended or unintended, are accounted for. Those subscribing to an ethic of responsibility are mindful of the consequences of their actions and accountable for those consequences.[156] Responsibility calls for both judgment and patience, what Weber calls the 'slow, strong drilling through hard boards.'[157]

Arbitrators are not truly accountable for the decisions that they make. Only their reputational capital is at stake. They become accountable only at some distant *future* point in time—at the moment when parties contemplate whether an arbitrator is welcomed as a repeat player and invited to sit on a newly constituted tribunal. This seems insufficient to induce *present* responsibility. Should arbitrators wish to act responsibly as regards the dispute before them, when they arrive at the strict proportionality stage, they should weigh ends and means and arrive at an all-things-considered evaluation. Arbitrators act irresponsibly when they drop the public interest out of their discussion (even as they pay lip service to it) and become overly preoccupied with ensuring that investors are reasonably compensated. Means are closely scrutinized to ensure that fixed ends are achieved. Conviction clouds the proportionality inquiry.

If the primary concern of tribunals is whether the means employed by states serve the end of investor protection—something that looks like a reasonable rate of return for investors—then it turns out that, in the Spanish energy disputes, tribunals never genuinely address the last stage of the proportionality analysis. Rather, tribunals appear to be stuck at the second stage of proportionality, where means are scrutinized with respect to certain unyielding ends. Arbitrators thereby are inattentive to the consequences of their actions, especially when tribunals issue compensation awards that cripple the public fisc.[158] It seems of little consequence

[155] Mehranvar and Sachs (2023) at 20.
[156] Weber (1919a) at 360.
[157] Weber (1919a) at 369.
[158] Paparinskis (2020) and Schneiderman (2022b), chap. 4.

to tribunals in the Spanish energy cases that their awards cumulatively amount to a payout of more than €1.4 billion to investors.[159]

The ethic of conviction so impairs proportionality analysis that the inquiry, which is meant to be more open-ended, is eclipsed by solicitude for investor interests. Scholarly unease has been expressed at having tribunals second-guess whether public policy ends outweigh deleterious effects on rights at the last stage of proportionality.[160] The worry, as stated by Henckels, is that, even with a margin of appreciation, this last step places too much discretion in the hands of tribunals. 'By its very nature,' she writes, proportionality in the strict sense 'can only operate to reduce the regulatory autonomy of states compared to the application of the necessity test, as it can result in a tribunal ruling unlawful the only way that the government has of achieving its aim.'[161] It is therefore preferred, Henckels and others suggest, that tribunals forego this last stage of proportionality. Given the manner in which the Spanish solar disputes were resolved, there should be similar worry expressed about tribunals undertaking only the second stage of the analysis.

It is instructive that, at the Supreme Court of Canada, most laws stand or fall under scrutiny at the second stage of proportionality.[162] In contrast to other apex courts, where much work gets done at the final (proportionality in the strict sense) stage, the Supreme Court of Canada has decisively ruled on constitutional questions when inquiring into 'necessity': whether the means used minimally impair the claimed right. Dieter Grimm surmises that the Supreme Court of Canada avoids relying on proportionality in the strict sense for similar reasons identified by Henckels, 'out of fear that a court might make policy decisions at this stage rather than legal decisions.' Yet, Grimm adds, the Court's record at this second step 'looks more value laden than that of the German Court.'[163] The Court, he concludes, 'risks self-deception when all the value-oriented considerations have been made under the guise of a seemingly value-neutral category.'[164] It turns out, then, that scholarly anxiety about tribunals second-guessing policy decisions is misplaced. It is the second stage where much damage can be done to the public interest. Those interests simply never get weighed into the equation.

[159] Mehranvar and Sachs (2023) at 9.

[160] Henckels (2015) at 168, Ortino (2017) at 88–89, and Paine (2021) at 726.

[161] Henckels (2015) at 168. Henckels's formula raises the burden on states to show that their action was 'only way' to achieve the end sought. The question at this step is, typically, whether the end sought could be achieved using means less restrictive of the claimed right. Henckels seems to be incorporating standards associated with the test of 'necessity' under customary international law as defined by the International Law Commission (ILC) Articles on State Responsibility, Art. 25. 1(a) (the defense of necessity is available if it is 'the only way for the State to safeguard an essential interest against a grave and imminent peril').

[162] See *Alberta* v. *Hutterian Brethren* (2009) at para. 75 (the third step 'has not often been used'), referring to Hogg (2019) vol. 2, at section 38.12, who argues that this step has turned out to be 'actually redundant.' A comparable result issues out of the US Supreme Court when it requires 'narrow tailoring' under strict scrutiny. This, too, is a 'difficult test' for governments to meet, per Barak (2012) at 541.

[163] Grimm (2007) at 395.

[164] Grimm (2007) at 395.

So it seems that arbitrators do perform their functions as if they were bureaucratic machines without responsibility other than a duty to evaluate means-ends relations. Recall Weber's characterization of bureaucratic administration as being guided by either predetermined norms or 'weighing of ends and means.'[165] Pursuing their convictions is not a part of that remit. Instead, bureaucracies are expected to carry out tasks without regard to consequences—without regard to an ethic of responsibility. This explains why Weber emphasized the role of responsible political leadership in serving as a check on bureaucratic power.

Arbitrators, in this ideal typical light, are performing functions in the service of an ethic of conviction by having regard only to scrutinizing the relation between ends and means. In a later chapter, I address in more detail how investment arbitration functions as an international bureaucracy. What is emphasized here is the role of arbitrators in fulfilling an ideal typical function that serves an ethic of conviction regardless of the consequences. This approach to adjudication should comfort those who have bemoaned the global spread of proportionality. Webber, for instance, complains that proportionality 'provides no strict demarcation against unacceptable State action.'[166] He laments a state of affairs in which 'rights lose any sense of certainty.' He prefers, instead, that '[w]hen a right is defined' then infringements should be 'resolutely resisted.'[167] Webber can take solace that investment tribunals interpret investor rights mostly in this fashion.

What are the values that drive proportionality analysis? Typically, arbitrators will have recourse to Article 31 of the Vienna Convention on the Law of Treaties.[168] Treaties are to be interpreted in good faith, given 'ordinary meaning' in 'context,' and 'in light of its object and purpose.' The prevailing view is that treaty standards have as their object and purpose the protection and promotion of foreign investment.[169] If that is their object and purpose, priority must be given to the strict enforcement of investor protections, lest these goals be undermined. Anything less than providing a stable legal order to investors is inconsistent with that rationale. This, after all, is the arbitrator's task: to give effect to the object and purpose of treaty text, not to frustrate it.[170]

There is a countervailing view about object and purpose that would have the practical effect of widening the circle of concern beyond those of foreign investors. Kürtz argues that there is a multiplicity of values expressed in 'preambular recitals' beyond merely that of protecting investors.[171] These textual signals suggest that

[165] Weber (1978) at 979.
[166] Webber (2009) at 102.
[167] Webber (2009) at 103.
[168] 'Vienna Convention on the Law of Treaties,' U.N.T.S. Vol. 1155 (January 27, 1980) at 331.
[169] The investment need not genuinely be cross-border. According to Bárcena and Flues (2022) at 13, ten of the eleven supposed Dutch investors are Spanish-controlled entities.
[170] Dolzer and Schreur (2008) at 32 observe that frequent references to treaty preambles for discerning object and purpose 'typically' lead to an interpretation that is 'favorable to the investor.'
[171] Kürtz (2010) at 351 (he describes the dominant view as a 'key, untested assumption' at 350).

there are several purposes being served by investment treaty law and arbitration. Ortino similarly maintains that investment treaties advance no single overarching purpose but channel conflicting objects and purposes.[172] Adopting an evolutionary approach to treaty interpretation, Ortino maintains that sustainable development is now one of the main purposes of the investment treaty regime, even though it may not have been so at earlier periods of time.[173] If the intention of these authors is to widen the policy space available to states, this multiplication of values promoted by the regime has not taken hold among investment treaty arbitrators. With a focus solely upon economic impact, what the dominant approach reveals is that arbitrators' ethic of conviction supersedes their ethic of responsibility.

VI. Conclusion

Things, of course, could change. If arbitral reluctance to embrace proportionality imperils the future of investment law, it may be that states will demand that tribunals address proportionality more forthrightly. New treaty text appears to direct tribunals to consider at least the necessity of a measure restricting investment treaty protections. There are numerous examples of annexes to expropriation clauses directing tribunals, in the case of indirect expropriations, to consider whether a measure 'is so severe in light of its purpose that it appears manifestly excessive.'[174] The 2015 EU-Vietnam Free Trade Agreement investment chapter provides that deviations from the principle of national treatment will be permitted, so long as measures are 'necessary to protect public security, public morals or to maintain public order ... or necessary to protect human, animal or plant life or health,' among other things.[175] These look like invitations to tribunals to consider perhaps only the second stage of the proportionality inquiry. But, considering the track record to date, one can safely predict that these clauses are unlikely to result in any 'rapid adoption' of robust proportionality analysis.

The Eco Oro award, discussed in Chapter 1, reveals how tribunals do not respond well to directives in treaty text that are intended to widen the scope for the right to regulate. The Eco Oro tribunal concluded that there was an obligation to provide compensation to the investor for cancellation of a mining license, even though Colombia had sought to preserve an ecologically sensitive páramo that

[172] Ortino (2017) at 77. Ortino distinguishes between object, as concerning the substance of the treaty, and purpose, which concerns the reason for the treaty (at 76). I don't find this distinction all that helpful. It appears to render 'object' redundant for the purpose of treaty interpretation.

[173] Ortino (2021) at 81. Not only 'economic growth' but 'environmental protection and social equity' are values advanced by investment treaties (at 91). This deserves a more fulsome response than can be given here. One need only observe that, if this were the case, investment treaties seem inapt vehicles for advancing those interests.

[174] CETA, Annex X.11: Expropriation, para. 3.

[175] Art. 9.3.

provided fresh water to Colombian citizens.[176] The treaty text presumed to absolve the state of liability under the treaty in cases when it adopted measures 'necessary' to protect the environment. The tribunal, however, concluded that this 'general exceptions' clause could not absolve the state of liability for violating investor standards of protection. The state offered no 'justification as to why it is necessary for the protection of the environment not to offer compensation to an investor for any loss suffered.'[177] It goes without saying that there was no proportionality inquiry undertaken in this award, though the treaty text invited such an inquiry.

Instead of new treaty text, what may be called for is bringing a semblance of proportionality to the system as a whole. If the object has been to signal openness to foreign direct investment, the signing of over 3,000 BITs with muscular and enforceable disciplines seems disproportionate to this objective. There are a number of less drastic measures that could indicate to investors that they will be treated fairly.[178] In other words, being attentive to all the consequences of the investment treaty regime calls for an ethic of responsibility that would guide reform efforts. It means attending to the 'diabolical powers' that are being put to work in investment treaty law and arbitration.[179]

[176] Eco Oro (2021) at paras. 822–37, discussing Art. 2201(3) of the Canada–Colombia FTA, which provides that 'nothing in this Agreement shall be construed to prevent a Party from adopting or enforcing measures necessary [t]o protect human, animal or plant life or health, which the Parties understand to include environmental measures necessary to protect human, animal or plant life and health . . . [and for] the conservation of living or non-living exhaustible natural resources.'

[177] Eco Oro (2021) at paras. 830, 832. The tribunal in Montauk Metals (2024) at para. 982 agreed with this interpretation but found no violation of the FTA's standards of protection.

[178] Consider, for instance, Schneiderman (2017b).

[179] Weber (1919a) at 366–67.

4
Investment Law's Ideal Types

This chapter is framed by one methodological move and one insight drawn from the work of Max Weber. The first utilizes the heuristic of the 'ideal type.' This is an imagined set of relationships that 'clarify the *distinctive character* of that interrelation'[1] by drawing upon 'patterns of social action' in addition to 'systems of belief.'[2] It is a 'one-sided accentuation of *one* or a *number* of viewpoints'—it is a 'utopia,' Weber insists.[3] The task, he advises, is to test 'how close to reality' that ideal is. The ideal type offers an opportunity to hypothesize about selected 'empirical regularities.' These will help to 'guide the formulation of hypotheses' about what motivates social actors.[4] The rational, self-maximizing individual that Weber associates with the ideal of 'capitalist culture,' for instance, is one such ideal type. There are as likely to be more than one kind of type at play in any given case.[5] None are likely to predominate; rather, each may claim to represent partially of what is in view. To the extent, however, that an ideal type corresponds to features of social life, it deepens understanding of that reality.[6]

The second is an insight drawn from Weber's studies on the role of 'carriers' in the rise of rational law, already mentioned in Chapter 1. Weber placed emphasis on the role that groups of persons played when they carried forward styles of thinking.[7] Various modes of knowledge, from this angle, are spread and promoted by expert social carriers. Training in legal knowledge, in particular, provided by universities and legal mentors proved to be central to his account of the spread of formally rational law.[8] Accompanying the increasing rationalization of law, Weber

[1] Weber (1904a) at 125.
[2] Kalberg (2008) at 275 and Runciman (1972) at 33.
[3] Weber (1904) at 124–25. Also see Kalberg (2008) at 275 (The 'patterned social action' that is captured by an ideal image will, it is hoped, reveal causal probabilities).
[4] Swedberg (2018) at 188 (referring to 'causal adequacy') and Turner and Factor (1994) at 154 (referring to a 'kind of causal knowledge').
[5] Multiple candidates can serve as ideal types. Jenks (1993) at 53–54 acknowledges 'the non-contradictory possibility of having a proliferation of "ideal types" concerning what common sense might regard as the same phenomenon' while Strong (1994) at 125 insists that the formulation of ideal types 'compels the acknowledgment of one's own stance and status and thus keeps one from pretending to a transcendence to which one is not entitled.'
[6] Weber (1904) at 125.
[7] Weber (1920c) at 74.
[8] Weber (1920a) at 207. See discussion in Gephart (2015) chap. VIII.

A Sociology of International Investment Law. David Schneiderman, Oxford University Press.
 DOI: 10.1093/9780198982739.003.0005

observed, is an increasing professionalization for which 'specialized, i.e. rational, training is an ineluctable requirement.'[9] Weber, in contrast to Marx, insists that such developments could not be reduced to merely the product of economic and social conditions. Such forces only indirectly influenced the direction law would take. Instead, Weber claims that rationalization develops 'intrajuristically,' and so placed emphasis on the 'prevailing' type of legal education and professional training in any given period.[10] Members of the legal profession were the principal agents in the proliferation of rational law in the West.[11] For this reason, professional legal training, by both academics and practitioners, in both institutions of higher learning and in professional settings, serves as carrier for the success of Western legal institutions and norms.[12] The development of formally rational law requires, then, the agency of legally trained specialists.[13]

Conjoining ideal types with carriers of legal instruction can help to deepen understanding of the role played by education investment law,[14] opening up new channels for observation and critique.[15] Legal training is provided by both practitioners and scholars (who sometimes serve in a professional capacity as well[16]), working within and outside of institutions of higher learning.[17] They promote the field and cultivate their own professional reputation within it by training new generations of lawyers who will not only fill its ranks but also work to defend the field.[18] They are, in this sense, 'double agents' of investment law.[19] This chapter is prompted, then, by the intuition that legal training is complicit in securing the spread and arguable success of international investment law. Though a young field in law schools to which most students will have little exposure,[20] these professionals write, cajole, argue, fight, and contribute to the content of international investment law not only by teaching but by their writings in articles, chapters, and books.

[9] Weber (1978) at 775.
[10] Weber (1978) at 776.
[11] Weber (1920) at 215.
[12] Weber (2009) at 152 and Bendix (1962) at 85–87.
[13] Weber (1978) at 775.
[14] Kalberg (2008) at 276 maintains that 'patterned social action,' associated with ideal types, occurs primarily 'within carrier groupings.' See also Kalberg (2017) at 63 ('each ideal type implies the possibility of an empirical causal thrust' that is carried forward by 'demarcated groups').
[15] *Contra* Wolin (1991) at 211 who argues that ideal types hinder criticism as they offer no 'theoretical counterparadigm' or 'alternative vision.'
[16] 'Specific' and 'general academic standing,' for instance, are secondary factors in the appointment of arbitrators, according to Schultz and Kovacs (2012) at 167.
[17] The discussion intermingles professional training ('vocational preparation' to attain 'mastery of a subject') with education (schooling for the purpose of presenting knowledge 'on the basis of a consciously planned programme'), discussed in Mannheim and Stewart (1962) at 12–18. Their boundaries, as Weber (1978) at 1143 maintains, are fluid.
[18] Garth (2018) at 158. This 'investment arbitration community' is considered a 'fairly close knit' one according to Hirsch (2020) at 719–20.
[19] Dezalay and Garth (1996) at 119 (speaking of business lawyers serving both their own interests and those of their merchant clients).
[20] Cottier (2017) at 579 (international economic law 'is not a mainstream topic in legal education, and relatively few students' are exposed to the subject).

Their published products are candidates for 'teachings of the most highly qualified publicists' that serve as a subsidiary source of international law, according to the statute governing the International Court of Justice.[21] International law educators can 'relish' the thought that their writings are 'capable of influencing or determining' the content of international investment law.[22] In this fashion, they have privileged access to defining the attributes of what constitutes the 'universal.'[23]

The discussion that follows is not, specifically, about Weber's legal sociology, though at least one ideal type (charisma) is inspired by his categories of domination. At other points, Weber's sociology of law helps to illuminate a particular argument. The principal object, instead, is to uncover suppositions and blind spots that are shared by major players in this international legal field. As in the rest of this book, I assume that there are aspects of Weber's sociological thought that can inform thinking about investment law that has escaped scholarly commentary. Here, the role that legal training plays in the upkeep of investment law's machinery is stressed. If the premise of this chapter is correct, it turns out that these mentors, who serve as critical carriers of investment law thinking, play a key role in the regime's upkeep.

The 'generic concepts'[24] emphasized here are caricatures, to be sure, and highlight only certain aspects of the roles played by norm entrepreneurs who cultivate the field of investment law. In this chapter, I emphasize three overlapping roles that these instructors inhabit: as cold warriors, charismatics, and moralists. These three archetypes may seem atypical, but they have the advantage of assimilating, within them, more obvious types such as liberal institutionalists and neoliberals. I turn first to those who insist that investment law disciplines serve to forestall the revival of non-capitalist alternatives.

I. Cold Warriors

The 'cold warriors' of international investment law are those who conceive of their field as a prophylactic to the rise of socialism or communism within states that went through processes of political decolonization. These are states, principally in the Global South, whose retreat from deregulated market forms would be intolerable or would threaten the future of global capitalism. Investment law, in this sense, serves as a bulwark against the spread of an anti-capitalist threat, reminiscent of the Cold War conflict between Russia and the West. From this angle, investment law can be viewed as a Marshall Plan for the post-colonial world but with a

[21] See the Statute of the International Court of Justice, Article 38(d).
[22] Ridi and Schultz (2021) at 213.
[23] Bourdieu (2000) at 123.
[24] Salomon (1934) at 161.

sharper bite, comprised of constitution-like commitments that ensure there will be no departure from mythical developmental trajectories.[25] This can be one, among others, of the principal messages delivered to novices in the course of their legal training.

At the height of the post–World War II environment, it was assumed to be the responsibility of the United States—as global avatar for the developed world—along with its allies, to prevent slippage of states in the newly decolonized Global South from allying with the Soviet Union and its satellite states. Fear of a Communist threat enveloping the world-at-large was the specter that drove foreign policy, including international economic relations. The watchword was 'development' that purportedly mimicked pathways to economic success in the developed world. A specific trajectory was mapped out by thinkers like Rostow, who fashioned 'stages' to economic growth as laid down in his book bearing the sub-title 'A Non-Communist Manifesto.'[26] 'Foreign economic policy,' announced National Security Council report 68 of 1950, would emerge as a 'major instrument in the conduct of United States foreign relations.'[27] The path forward was to remain steadfastly anti-communist and to yield no ground to the weak kneed. Chronicler of the Vietnam War, David Halberstam described the cold warrior caste as 'hardnosed' and 'rigid,' where 'little real criticism was permitted.'[28]

So as to lock-in states to Western-style development plans, local conditions required adjustment.[29] First, direct colonialism would have to be abandoned by those European states still desirous of maintaining political control over subordinated states in the Global South.[30] Emerging in its stead were congeries of newly independent states labeled the Third World. Deviation from orthodox paths, however, would not be tolerated. States that resisted joining this US-led alliance would be labeled as Communist. There would be no ground given to accommodating new and alternative paths to economic improvement, even when this strategy undermined economic development, as in Indonesia, or ensured military, rather than civilian, rule as in much of Latin America.[31]

International legal norms conjured up by the Global North promoted adherence to this same set of values. As Pahuja explains, international law was

[25] Gerstle (2022) at 11 is correct to claim, then, that the 'fall of communism ... forms a central part of the story of neoliberalism's triumph.'

[26] Rostow (1960). On Rostow's influence on successive presidents of the United States, see Lawrence (2021) at 30–31, 293–94.

[27] United States (1950). On the strategy's achievements, see Kapstein (2020). Foreign policy still motivates US investment law policy, according to Chilton (2016).

[28] Halberstam (1983) at 33.

[29] Westad (2005) at 111.

[30] Westad (2005) at 112.

[31] Westad (2005) at 119. On Indonesia, see Westad (2005) at 128–31 and on Latin America, Westad (2005) at 143–52. On the Asian strategy, which departed from the hegemonic model, see World Bank (1993) at 355 (Japan, Korea, Taiwan, and China 'selectively promot[ed] capital- and knowledge-intensive industries').

duplicitous, offering pathways to liberation while preserving some imperial functions.[32] That is, the divide between political and economic power would come to be 'juridified.'[33] If newly decolonized states could take advantage of the principle of sovereign equality under international law, they also would be expected to have their newly won political power yield to the exigencies of 'development' as defined by powerful capital-exporting states. This was a powerful discourse 'no less pervasive and effective' than colonialism, Escobar adds.[34] It reflected a policy authored by an 'exclusive club,' complained Bedjaoui, who 'make and proclaim the law for all.'[35] The international legal fiction of independence yielded to 'inegalitarian relations of domination.'[36]

State-driven economic policy also was unwelcome, even as economists like Myrdal acknowledged that all those who 'have taken the time and trouble to acquaint themselves with the problems' of undeveloped areas 'assume a greater role for the state.'[37] International financial institutions promoted private credit and investment in the place of state-led planning. Then, as now, poorer states were encouraged to improve their 'investment climate' so as to attract new private investment.[38] Eisenhower administration officials were directed to encourage states to 'adopt investor-friendly policies.'[39] Natural resource extraction for export, attracting unpredictable price fluctuations, environmental degradation, widening inequality, and political instability, was the product of this developmentalist recipe. The investment gap—reflecting the less than adequate amounts of foreign direct investment flowing to poorer states as compared to wealthier ones—continued to widen.[40] This prompted Third World responses, such as a plea for more aid,[41] policies of import substitution,[42] declarations of permanent sovereignty over natural resources (PSNR), and the writing-off of public debt.[43] US foreign economic policy contributed, then, not so much to economic improvement but to the production of an intransigent Third World citizenry 'determined to maintain a unified bargaining front.'[44]

It was in direct response to these plans that proposals for a New International Economic Order (NIEO) were authored by Southern states, culminating in the

[32] Pahuja (2011) at 5.
[33] Pahuja (2011) at 22.
[34] Escobar (1995) at 15.
[35] Bedjaoui (1979) at 157.
[36] Bedjaoui (1979) at 255.
[37] Myrdal (1956) at 201.
[38] Kapstein (2020) at 122–23.
[39] Kapstein (2020) at 132.
[40] Kapstein (2020) at 136.
[41] World Bank (1969).
[42] Promoted by economic thinkers such as Raul Prebisch at the United Nations Economic Commission for Latin America and the Caribbean (ECLAC). See Prebisch (1986).
[43] South Commission (1990) at 228.
[44] Independent Commission on International Development Issues, (1980) at 39; Westad (2005) at 157.

1974 Charter of Rights and Economic Duties of States (CERDS). Among other instruments, investment arbitration was the preferred legal hardware endorsed by richer states.[45] A turning point were the elections of Thatcher in Great Britain (1979) and Reagan in the United States (1980) and their promotion of a 'messy' neoliberal agenda that called for the retreat of the state in all facets of social and economic life and the institutionalization of an 'unforgiving economy.'[46] UN Declarations in the pursuance of the NIEO were labeled as non-binding resolutions by powerful Northern states, denying that they made any contribution to the content of international law.[47] The hope, articulated by Charles N. Brower (who would go on to become a prominent investment arbitrator), was that the 'tide of rhetorical unrealism may abate' and be replaced by 'the principles of Jefferson and Lincoln, [that] respects the precepts of our own [US] constitutional tradition.'[48] The subsequent 'tsunami' of thousands of BITs would eventually replace these '"soapbox" Resolutions of the General Assembly,' Brower triumphantly declared some forty years later.[49]

The argument, so far, is not that there is a straight line between the Cold War era and today, only that there are observable discursive continuities. By pushing this analogy a little further, one could say that investment law professionals defend investment law disciplines, in part, because they can forestall a return to a divided capitalist and non-capitalist world. This is underscored by the fact that a number of the investment law notables cut their teeth in debates over the rise of the NIEO.[50] Brower, already mentioned, described negotiations with the Soviet Union, while serving in the Nixon administration, as revealing the 'challenges that made international arbitration increasingly necessary.'[51] Proposals to reform international law along the lines contained in the 1974 CERDS were required to be 'vanquished,' he explains, and replaced with 'reliable mechanisms' for dispute resolution.[52] Judge and investment arbitrator Stephen Schwebel describes heated debates with the Mexican delegation over CERDs while serving as Chairman of the US delegation. Having thwarted this initiative, 'things have veered off in another and much healthier direction,' Schwebel contends, namely in the direction of 'very progressive Treaties which promote the flow of foreign investment.'[53] Evidence that such

[45] Via the Convention on the Settlement of Investment Disputes Between States and Nationals of Other States (the ICSID Convention) and bilateral investment treaties (BITs), accompanied by investor–state dispute settlement (ISDS).

[46] Schlegel (2008) at 594. On its messiness, see Peck (2010) at 7.

[47] Brownlie (1979) at 542–43, also Brower and Tepe, Jr (1975) at 297, 302. Their 'high hopes came to nothing,' boasts Wälde (1999) at 169.

[48] Brower (1976) at 708–9. The minimum standard of treatment in BITs was 'invented by the United States,' Brower explains in (2023) at 168, to replace less robust investor protections under customary international law.

[49] Brower and Melikian (2015) at 22.

[50] The NIEO debates are discussed in Perrone and Schneiderman (2024).

[51] Brower (2023) at 41.

[52] Brower (2023) at 165–66.

[53] Dingle and Bates (2009) at Q19.

benefits 'flow' to host states from economically developed ones continues to be elusive. Cold warriors have not been dissuaded from believing that joining their team is beneficial to less wealthy states. The point is that many of those who would go on to become the first generation of investment arbitrators 'were deeply shaped (or even scarred) by their experience with the NIEO and Charter of Economic Rights and Duties of States and that era's wave of expropriations.'[54]

Scholars, too, have acknowledged this Cold War legacy. Cottier, Gehn, and Schultheiss, for instance, maintain that modern investment treaty commitments check 'communist or socialist approach[es] to property [that] carries risks for foreign investors ... mainly an issue during the Cold War, but still exists today.'[55] The late Thomas Wälde repeatedly exhibits this orientation, candidly invoking this argument in support of investment law disciplines. Only slightly less polemical than Brower, he was one not to pull his punches. He admits, for instance, that the universe of BITs signed since the 1980s was 'intentionally developed into an instrument to counter ... NIEO positions.'[56] Wälde explains the transition from the customary law for the protection of alien property to international investment law as prompted by the 'State-oriented and socialist colours of economic development theory' at the time of the Cold War and the NIEO.[57] The basic intention behind the rise of BITs, declares Wälde, was 'to create a counterweight' to NIEO principles.[58] The 'State-centred socialist dirigiste-approach to development ... [had by this time] manifestly failed, both in developing and Communist countries.' It is this 'Fabian socialist' approach that 'remains stuck in the 1960s, with the NIEO United Nations General Assembly Resolutions of 1974 as the last authoritative statement of that position.' It is noteworthy that Wälde conflates Fabian socialism in early twentieth-century Britain as analogous to Soviet Communism, an equivalency he continually insisted upon. Though there was some ground for treating them as equivalent—the leading Fabians of the day (Sidney and Beatrice Webb), after all, published a book-length tribute to Stalinist Russia[59]—the Fabians, thought leaders of the British Labour party, promoted *social democracy* as the means by which nationalization of the forces of production could be achieved, not totalitarian rule.[60] But with the 'collapse of Communism, this game [was] over,' Wälde declares.[61]

[54] Quote from an arbitrator who reviewed an earlier version of Garth (2018) at 161.
[55] Cottier, Gehne, and Schultheiss (2012) at 371.
[56] Wälde (2005) at 199.
[57] Wälde (2007) at 74.
[58] Wälde (1999) at 182.
[59] Webb and Webb (1935). But see fellow Labour Party socialist Laski (1927) at 238 ('It is, of course, a dangerous doctrine'). What the Fabians had in mind was 'piecemeal collectivist social engineering, inspired, directed, and administered from on high than with any version of Marxism' in Miliband (1977) at 160. According to Sydney Webb, their program was 'not the sub-division of property ... but the control and administration of it by the representatives of the community' quoted in Webb (1948) at 106.
[60] Though they did share a belief in the inevitability of the collapse of capitalism and the rise socialism. See Shklar (1957) at 256–57.
[61] Waelde (1998) at 782.

Along with 'the withering of the NIEO,' the 'Third World as a separate, block-type identity' lost out 'to international institutions controlled by the West—The World Bank, the IMF, the OECD, GATT and ... European Energy Charter institutions.'[62]

It might be thought that polarization associated with the Cold War has since been overtaken by the division between supporters and critics of the investment law regime. There appears little in the way of détente, however. Instead, critics are vilified.[63] An enthusiastic supporter of the regime describes the premises of even modest reformers as 'often flawed, half-cooked, and misinformed.'[64] 'Marxist worldview[s],' one lawyer exclaims, have the potential 'to dismantle what represents, with the benefit of hindsight, the greatest achievement of humankind.'[65] It is now the environmental movement that 'inherits the mantle of the socialist and statist philosophy,' allege Wälde and Kolo.[66]

These norm entrepreneurs, in turn, are accused of serving their own financial self-interest by promoting a regime from which they personally profit. We can make 'piles of money,' Brower admits.[67] It is true that regime enthusiasts will offer multiple other reasons for supporting this legal order other than maximization of their own profits—in so far as they are liberal institutionalists, they will react negatively to the shrinking of international law strictures. Yet it is curious that, while eagerly accusing almost every other relevant actor of acting in their own self-interest, they deny that this is a motivating factor for their own conduct.

A cold war mindset, nevertheless, has been the inheritance of those who participated in international legal debates in the 1970s and 1980s. Indeed, we can expect these intellectual leaders to not only stand guard against a revival of statist socialism, as they put it, but to ensure that a new generation of norm entrepreneurs will continue to fight their fight. In this way, cold warriors also serve as the founding fathers of a charismatic form of domination, an ideal type to which I turn next.

II. Charismatics

This type offers justifications for the regime by having recourse to their own authority and expertise. Charismatics offer leadership via legal education as a means of training and recruiting newer generations who will fight on behalf of investment law's ideals. This is a category familiar to readers of Weber. Charisma is described as a form of authority that has been overtaken by rational bureaucratic

[62] Waelde (1998) at 786.
[63] See Schneiderman (2016a).
[64] Dautaj (2021) at 299. The author does not explicate the Calvo doctrine nor cite the critical literature which is the target of his polemic.
[65] Dautaj (2021) at 319.
[66] Wälde and Kolo (2001) at 823.
[67] Brower (2023) at 207.

administration. As Weber was inspired to think about charisma in the leadership of religious movements, it might seem an inapt category for investment law instructors.[68] Weber maintains, however, that features associated with charisma were in principle 'universal' and, therefore, generalizable.[69] I want to suggest that this category, conjoined with bureaucratic 'routinization'—an evolutionary process Weber associates with charismatic authority—captures this tendency, particularly through the guise of 'charismatic education.'

Drawing upon the model of the religious charismatic, Weber emphasized the personal relationship between a 'leader' and his 'followers' who see within him/her 'extraordinary' powers or properties. If originally applied to prophetic figures, like Jesus,[70] Weber would also apply it to 'individuals thought to have special therapeutic powers' or those possessing 'legal wisdom.'[71] Weber mentions former Bavarian President Kurt Eisner as a demagogue who ruled in this personalist fashion.[72] Neo-Weberians extended the logic of charismatic rule to twentieth-century totalitarians such as Adolf Hitler[73] and Mao Tse-tung,[74] evolving into an 'academic cottage industry of sorts.'[75] One historian links charismatic leadership in the eighteenth and early nineteenth centuries to revolutionary moments that provide a foundation for modern democratic rule.[76]

At its origins, charisma is not bound by any external law or precedent and is 'disconnected from the economy.'[77] Instead, followers are governed by the charismatic ruler's declarations. Such arbitrariness renders this form of leadership, in Weber's parlance, 'irrational' and at some distance from the features associated with formally rational rule that govern modern-day life.[78] Weber's explanation for the origins of charismatic rule is of less consequence for this discussion, however. These early instantiations, in any event, are treated by Weber in 'too hasty [a manner] and [are] even unclear,' complains Cavalli.[79] Of more interest is Weber's

[68] Weber (1978) at 216 credits Rudolf Sohm for having worked out charisma in early Christianity. Others credit Eduard Meyer for having a more sustained influence on Weber. On Sohm, see Ghosh (2014) at 307 and, on Meyer, see Tenbruck (1987).

[69] Weber (1978) at 1112. On the generalizability of charisma beyond the original case, see Ghosh (2014) at 305–17 and Smith (2013) at 28 (charisma is 'socially constructed' and so encompasses 'socialists, swindlers, or loquacious National Socialist sadists').

[70] Schmitt (1970) at 66–67 claims that the 'Apostle Paul in the New Testament remains the theological source for all that Max Weber has said sociologically about *charisma*' (emphasis in original).

[71] Weber (2019) at 374.

[72] Weber (2019) at 374.

[73] Cavalli (2006) at 326–30.

[74] Bendix and Roth (1971) at 183–86.

[75] Bell (2020) at 238.

[76] Bell (2020).

[77] Weber (2019) at 377.

[78] Charisma hardly wins in a contest with rationally formal rule, maintains Anter (2014) at 66 ('legal-rational rule has proved itself to be incomparably stronger').

[79] Cavalli (2006) at 319. Also see Geertz (1983) at 121 on the concept of 'uncertainty.'

turn to the 'routinization of charisma.'[80] At some stage, the community of believers organize themselves and charismatic rule evolves into something 'more traditional or more rational (more legal).'[81] Modes of succession, together with methods of recruitment, need to be devised. This may entail both 'education' and 'tests of eligibility.'[82] Processes of routinization connect up with economic concerns—an interest in the 'fixed share of revenue' via fees, for instance—and the establishment of an administrative staff to oversee the maintenance of this mode of leadership.[83] The process resembles the bureaucratization of rationally formal law. 'In all cases,' Weber observes, the routinization of charisma is impelled by a 'striving for security,' the 'legitimization of positions of social rule,' and economic opportunity for its followers.[84] This reading of Weber accentuates the training of disciples by charismatic leadership so that this form of rule can reproduce itself.[85]

How well does Weber's account of charismatic rule, beyond the moment of its genesis, fit training in investment law? Note that Weber contemplates forms of *legal* rule that exhibit charismatic leadership. Because all rule, he writes, is founded on 'belief'—for instance, legal rule is 'never purely legal'—so is charismatic rule 'acquired' and 'conditioned by tradition.'[86] Democratic legitimacy can be attached to charismatic rule, where followers are 'free' to 'select' or 'depose' leaders. Even judicial functions can develop 'into the idea that the community is free to create, accept, and abolish laws just as it likes, whether in the general or in a particular case.'[87]

Critical legal scholars have extended notions of charismatic rule to judicial functions. Kennedy repeatedly invokes the image of the charismatic judge. The 'prestige of the judge,' he observes, 'is professional and technical, as well as charismatic and arcane.'[88] Kennedy associates judging as deploying 'mana, the charisma, the concentrated authority that derives from our cultural understanding of the Judge.'[89] This is a force more vigorous in the United States than in Europe

[80] On 'pure charisma' in contrast 'legitimate charisma' or 'charisma of office,' see Bensman and Givant (1975) at 577. If pressed, one could point to elder statesmen in the arbitration field as its original charismatic leaders (e.g., Charles N. Brower, Emmanuel Gaillard, Jan Paulsson, Stephen Schwebel). Investment arbitrators were not primarily recruited from the legal academy, at least not initially. See Dezalay and Dezalay (2017) at 330.

[81] Weber (2019) at 379.

[82] Weber (2019) at 383.

[83] Weber (2019) at 384–85.

[84] Weber (2019) at 387. Among commentators there is disagreement about whether Weber placed emphasis on personalized leadership or whether his approach is better described as stressing the consent and activities of the followers. Compare Friedrich (1961) with Smith (2013).

[85] Smith (2013) at 34 resists the proposition that charismatic leadership actively 'produces' its followers while admitting that leaders 'may greatly spur charismatic faith' (at 35). Smith is mostly silent about routinization by which charismatic rule sustains itself. This, by definition, requires the production (and reproduction) of this form of legitimate rule.

[86] Weber (2019) at 401. This is consistent with the observation that charismatic rule rarely appears in 'pure' form in Weber (2019) at 402.

[87] Weber (2019) at 406 (emphasis in original).

[88] Kennedy (1976) at 1775.

[89] Kennedy (1997) at 227.

and Britain: 'His (or her) resonance, mythic and daily companionship, and charismatic power are real but notably less than here [in the US].'[90] Others, less familiar with Weber, have attributed this same power to judges. Hendriato's work on 'heroic' judges in the Indonesian context describes them as serving as the 'savior of society from social wrongs by discovering rights in the law.'[91] Work on 'Towering Judges' similarly underscores the singular role played by judicial leadership: they will 'be individually distinguished from their colleagues and they should have a substantial influence on their constitutional systems.'[92]

Charismatic adjudication has even been extended to dispute resolution by arbitral tribunals. In their innovative socio-legal study of commercial arbitration, Dezalay and Garth describe how the 'grand old men,' who inaugurated the field, exhibit an 'aura of charisma.' In the 'glorious past,' arbitrators were discouraged from entering the field solely to 'make a living.'[93] In contrast to the early period, when a small group of 'impeccable, outstanding professionals—characters known around the world'—monopolized this market for legal services, there is now a crowded field. One of their interviewees—later described as one of the 'stars of the next generation'[94]—even declared that the 'time has come' for Weber's 'routinization of charisma.'[95] They go so far as to describe elite lawyers working for the US foreign policy establishment as exhibiting charisma, which gets routinized via 'bureaucratic institutions' operating under a 'combination of "hard" and "soft" law.'[96]

Sahni links judging to charisma in an explicit Weberian fashion.[97] If bureaucratic rationality, according to Weber, is value-free and concerned only with ensuring that means are in the service of ends chosen by political leadership, judicial authority combines these two functions. These will be performed, typically, by a single *fonctionnaire* implementing rational systems of rule.[98] The intractable disputes calling for adjudication by the judiciary necessarily demand authoritative interpretations that attract charisma. Sahni maintains that this is how Weber understands English administration of justice, which incorporates ethical ends into adjudicative functions,[99] allowing judges to take on a 'larger and more

[90] Kennedy (1997) at 4.

[91] Hendrianto (2018) at 15.

[92] Abeyratne and Porat (2021) at 3. See also Gava (2001) (complaining about Australian judges who 'emancipate[] themselves as they see it from the straightjacket of law as authority' at 747) and Sunstein (2014) (identifying 'heroic' judges who 'believe in an imperial and potentially transformative role for the federal judiciary in the Constitution's name' at 436).

[93] Dezalay and Garth (1996) at 34.

[94] Dezalay and Garth (2012) at 2335.

[95] Dezalay and Garth (1996) at 36–37.

[96] Dezalay and Garth (2008) at 720.

[97] Sahni (2009).

[98] Weber (1978) at 645. Distinguishing between 'adjudication' and impersonal 'government,' Weber acknowledges that judges are 'frequently instructed, either by positive law or by legal theory, to render his decision on the basis of ethics, equity, or expediency.'

[99] Sahni (2009) at 215. Weber attributes the description of the English judge as 'living oracle' to Blackstone in Weber (1978) at 767 quoting Blackstone Vol. 1 at 172, 173. He also ascribes the 'charismatic character of lawfinding' functions to 'new countries,' such as the United States, in Weber (1978) at 890. This renders legal rationality 'essentially lower' than that found in Europe (Weber 1978).

honourable role' than judges on the continent.[100] 'Characteristics of the charismatic epoch ... have persisted to a considerable extent,' Weber writes, 'in many of the institutions of the period of rational enactment and application of the law.' The principal difference from charismatic rule is the necessity for judges to deliver reasons (that is, to offer 'rational grounds').[101] According to Sahni, the 'charismatic politician is singled out as the archetypal mediator of irreconcilable dichotomies who, alone, manages the grave and subjective endpoint of decision making.'[102] It turns out that it is not only politicians with conviction but also judges who integrate choice of ends with the scrutiny of means.

This is no less the case in international investment arbitration.[103] It has been characterized as an 'art and not a science,' 'partly depend[ing] on intuition' and operating in a 'largely indeterminate setting.'[104] The investment arbitration community has been described as dominated by a small 'club' of eighteen arbitrators (a number that has grown larger with time[105]) who are repeat players, mostly drawn from capital-exporting states of the North Atlantic.[106] Those with distinctively different career paths are shut out of these fora. 'Once arbitrators become central' figures in the arbitration industry, Puig observes, policies that suit 'their political preferences will probably become more dominant.'[107] These investment law notables dominate legal production in the field and thereby influence legal training both inside and outside of universities. If the sensibility of arbitration is, generally, one of 'right-wing laissez-faire politics,'[108] united by a 'common ethos of investor protection,'[109] one might expect to see this value system transmitted to those who seek out instruction in the field.

Consider, then, the term that Weber originated to describe instruction for the purposes of regenerating this class of notables: 'charismatic education.' The personal gifts held by the original charismatics are presumed to be capable of being 'taught and learned.'[110] The production of new generations of disciples turns out to be a central preoccupation for this form of rule.[111] Weber admits that the borders between charismatic education and 'rationalized specialized training is of course

[100] In his 1895 essay on '"Roman" and "Germanic" Law,' Weber expressed admiration for English judges in the final paragraphs. They were a no mere 'paragraph and precedent machine' crying out for 'formal characteristics,' as on the Continent. See Weber (1895b) at 244. This is the interpretation of Weber's so-called English problem in Sahni (2009) and suggested by Piers Beirne's introduction to Weber's essay (expressing a 'veiled preference for the importance of natural law or "socio-ethical" principles' in Weber [1895b] at 239).

[101] Weber (1978) at 767.

[102] Sahni (2009) at 221.

[103] I elaborate on this connection in Chapter 3.

[104] Koskeniemmi (2005) at 340.

[105] Gaillard (2015) at 201.

[106] Puig (2014) at 416, 419.

[107] Puig (2014) at 422.

[108] Schultz (2020) at 257.

[109] Waibel (2015) at 164.

[110] Weber (1978) at 1143.

[111] On the role of disciples in charismatic regeneration and the rise of capitalism, see Smith (2016).

fluid.' Education in professional fields—'often treated as secret know-how for the sake of prestige and monopolization'[112]—calls for specialist knowledge that will be transmitted by insiders who are members of 'secret priestly fraternities or aristocratic clubs.'[113] In order to cement the place of arbitration in legal practice, the introduction of international law courses into law school curricula was a principal strategy adopted by international lawyers in the early twentieth century.[114] The case method was ill suited for international law courses, complained one instructor at Bryn Mawr, as this body of law hardly ever 'came before courts.'[115] This has turned out to be less of a problem for investment law educators. If law school instructors typically offer training by drawing upon the reason-giving of judges published in official law reports, investment law educators can achieve similar effects with arbitral rulings.[116] As in other courses that are organized around judicial rulings, where investment law teachers adopt the case method, students will be asked to mimic the reason-giving of arbitral tribunals in the cases assigned to them.[117] Students are, thereby, expected to absorb the ethical lessons associated with investment law reasoning into their legal training.[118]

By examining the research and teaching profiles of leading investment law teachers in top English-speaking law schools,[119] one can learn something about the routinized charisma at work in this field. I chose to focus on the top twenty-five law schools because, as Koskeniemmi maintains, 'the culture of international law has grown around a limited number of academic centers' and that one cannot be expected to enter an international legal profession 'without an LLM or doctorate from one of a handful of law schools in Anglophone world, or maybe Paris.'[120] As is said about international law, generally, so it can be said of investment law: there is only the 'well-known, but narrow academic pathway.'[121] Roberts confirms this influence in her empirical study of international lawyering. Not only do graduate students congregate in few academic locales at high financial cost,[122] but this also means that 'legal academics at elite schools in core states are prone to be highly

[112] Weber (1978) at 1143.
[113] Weber (1978) at 1145.
[114] Coates (2016) at 78.
[115] Coates (2016) at 79.
[116] On the eminence of case law method in contract law teaching, see Sandomierski (2020) at 254–55.
[117] By way of example, see Bishop, Crawford, and Reisman (2005) and Lim, Ho, and Paparinskis (2021).
[118] Schultz (2020) at 257 describes the ethos as one 'where greed is good, where being poor is a failure and . . . your fault.'
[119] English is increasingly becoming the lingua franca for international law scholarship and practice, claims Roberts (2017) at 260. Citation counts other than in the English language are almost impossible to calculate, report Ridi and Schultz (2021) at 222.
[120] Koskeniemmi (2017b) at xiii.
[121] Koskeniemmi (2017b) at xiii.
[122] Given the costs, these students 'disproportionately represent the elite of their states' in Roberts (2017) at 217.

influential in constituting the transnational field of international law.'[123] To sum up, law schools remain the 'chief delivery vehicle' for information about investment law.[124]

It should be noted, first, that teaching of investment law in law schools is a relatively recent phenomenon.[125] These course offerings also do not typically attract large numbers of students. The subject, for this reason, will often be assimilated into larger courses in international economic law or confined to more intimate settings like seminars. One expects to find, among those teaching the subject, both 'insider' and 'outsider' perspectives.[126] According to David Kennedy, these 'ideal-typical positions' represent the divide between those who welcome rule by global technocrats and those who worry that global governance entrenches rule by the already powerful. The professional aim of the former is 'reform;' for the latter, 'rupture.' Kennedy admits that these two positions in international lawyering are more often on a 'continuum.'[127]

In the politically fraught field of investment law, I surmise that there is much less overlap or movement between insiders and outsiders. Outsiders mostly are unwelcome—they are not invited to big international conferences or asked to contribute to *festschrifts* dedicated to its notables. Speaking from personal experience, outsiders are likely to be subject to hostile peer review in scholarship and funding applications. There are, for these reasons, professional disadvantages to being labeled an outsider and many inducements to joining the insider club, including the chance to benefit not only reputationally, but financially. The knowledge production of outsiders mostly is 'non-marketable'—those who can make use of it 'cannot imagine having to pay for it' nor can they hardly afford to.[128] This helps to explain why one will find many more insiders than outsiders making their homes at leading English-speaking law schools. Add to this the predominant role of adjunct (non-full-time) professors teaching the subject, who likely have careers in the arbitration industry, the insider perspective emerges as more prominent in legal education.

An examination of the top twenty-five QS (Quacquarelli Symonds) ranked law schools (complemented by Times Higher Education rankings) in 2022 reveals, in Table 4.1, the following:

[123] Roberts (2017) at 68.
[124] Schultz and Ridi (2020) at 12.
[125] McRae (2014) at 628.
[126] Roberts and St. John (2023) describe state officials participating in reform of ISDS at UNCITRAL Working Group III as being either insiders or outsiders. While there is here some overlap with their account, we part ways when they characterize EU officials, promoting a multilateral investment court, as outsiders (at 1164).
[127] Kennedy (2016) at 106, table 3.1.
[128] Santos (2018) at 120–21.

Table 4.1 Top 25 Law School Rankings[a]

Law School	Full-Time	Adjunct	Arbitration Industry	Professional Association	Teaches WTO Law	Publication Record
Harvard	1	6	6	2	3	Insider
Oxford	2		2	2	0	Insider
Cambridge	1	1	1	1	0	Insider/Outsider
Yale	1	1	2	2	0	Insider
Stanford	1				1	Insider
LSE	1	1	1	1	1	Insider/Outsider
Columbia	1	2	3	3	0	Insider
NYU	2	2	4	2	1	Insider
UC Berkeley	0	1	1	1		Insider (Commercial Arbitration)
NUS	2		2	1	0	Insider/Outsider
Melbourne	2		1	2	0	Insider
Chicago	1	1	1	1	0	Insider (Commercial Arbitration)
UNSW	1	1	1	0	0	Insider/Outsider
Sydney	1		1	1	0	Insider
UCL	1	2	3	3	0	Insider
King's College	2		0	1	1	Insider/Outsider
ANU	2	0	2	2	0	Insider/Outsider
Toronto	1	3	3	3	0	Insider/Outsider
Georgetown	0	5	5	5	0	Insider
Paris I	2	0	2	1	0	Insider
Duke	0	1	0	0	1	Insider
Edinburgh		2	0	2	1	Insider
McGill	1		1	1	1	Insider
Michigan	2	1	1	1	1	Inside/Outside
Cornell	1		0	1	0	Insider

[a]I am grateful to Emily Rand for generating this table.

First, adjunct teaching fills in for full-time lecturing in many of these institutions (in addition to visiting faculty appointments at some top US law schools). Second, a large majority of full-time instructors have some professional association with the arbitration industry. We can assume that, in each case, they earn revenue, in addition to teaching income, by participating in this regime. Being in alliance with the arbitration industry, they mostly will be investment law insiders. Third, about half of the investment law instructors also teach other international economic law subjects.[129] One would expect that those teaching the law of the World Trade Organization, for instance, will color their teaching by framing investment law as normatively in the pursuit of efficiency and competitiveness. Finally, the scholarship of full-time teachers is directed mostly at an audience of other insiders (scholars, practitioners, and arbitrators). Scholarship will be tilted in the direction of descriptive, doctrinal, and perhaps reformist scholarship rather than critical or interdisciplinary scholarship that invites less conventional perspectives.

Other empirical work confirms that the most influential scholars—leaders in the field of investment law—write doctrinal scholarship. If '[s]cholarly publication is one of the key criteria for admission to the field,' observes Garth, 'the publications themselves rarely take strong stands on major issues for fear that the writer will scare some potential appointing parties or even lead to disqualification for bias.'[130] It is 'virtually impossible to spot,' among the most cited scholarship in investment arbitration, 'any work with a systemic or critical ambition,' report Ridi and Schultz.[131] If you want to be an authority, they conclude, '[w]rite doctrinal scholarship.'[132]

What does this data set reveal about charismatic education? It suggests that legal educators play a substantial role in the upkeep of investment law's machinery while maintaining an intimate relationship to its practice. This is partly because there is 'significant' overlap between the academic- and practitioner-based communities.[133] It is true that the scholarly profiles of the personnel delivering this training increasingly adopt more interdisciplinary styles and approaches. But until that relationship is mostly severed, there is little prospect that the investment law professoriate will not continue to attack opponents, fight for the spread and maintenance of the regime, and that this will continue to be the main message that is passed on to disciples.

[129] See also Cottier (2017) at 579 ('an increasing number of leadings law professors teach trade and investment classes in law schools around the world').

[130] Garth (2018) at 158.

[131] Ridi and Schultz (2021) at 234. International law teaching and scholarship produces 'surprisingly little' that sheds light on the unequal 'global distribution of authority,' per Kennedy (2016) at 106, table 3.1.

[132] Ridi and Schultz (2021) at 237.

[133] Schultz and Ridi (2021) at 15.

III. Moralists

One of the important distinguishing characteristics between pure charismatic rule and its routinization is the obligation to provide reasons. As Weber elsewhere admits, power always is obliged to 'justify itself.'[134] Those whom I cast as moralists in this field behave more like charismatics when they issue verdicts about the morality of international investment law. That is, no fact-based empirical evaluation is undertaken; instead, the system is appraised in universalizable and self-evident terms. Moralists mark out 'righteous divisions' meant to exclude or neglect that which does not easily fit within their moral economy.[135] In investment law, this is made manifest in claims to objectivity that are purportedly unavailable to judges in national courts.[136] Arbitrators performing adjudicative functions have an advantage, it is said, over compromised dispute resolution processes available within states.[137] Investor–state dispute resolution processes offer investors impartial and neutral adjudication. Investment law, from this Weberian angle, promotes a regime of 'dispassionate' legality[138] by enforcing 'calculable' legal rules.[139]

This sort of legal embellishment, often espoused by those participating in investment arbitration legal training, has affinities with what I have elsewhere called the extravagant depoliticization thesis: that adjudication of investor–state disputes is emptied of all politics. Arbitrators might not be 'celebrities,' Paulsson admits, but they 'have the requisite insight and impartiality' to be adjudicators.[140] Defending the idea that there should be an 'elite' corps of arbitrators who are repeat players, Paulsson describes them as exhibiting, 'above all[,] absolute impartiality.'[141] Schreuer declares that investor–state arbitration is 'depoliticized and subject[s disputes] to objective legal criteria.'[142] This is in contrast to the more modest thesis that 'depoliticization' means the removal of home states from investment disputes—only investors are entitled to initiate disputes without screening by their home states.[143] It is of passing interest that Alvarez describes the US government as having become 'disenchanted' with the narrative of depoliticization: that

[134] Weber (1978) at 953.
[135] Connolly (1993) at 132.
[136] Koskeniemmi (2017a) at 64.
[137] Clayton (2015) at para. 439. At the ICSID Convention's origins, Bachand and Gélinas (2020) at 387 write, courts in host states and the laws they enforced were 'widely viewed as falling short of the expected standards of neutrality and predictability.'
[138] Weber (1920c) at 147.
[139] Weber (1920a) at 215.
[140] Paulsson (2005) at 238.
[141] Paulsson (2013) at 171.
[142] Schreuer (2009) at 416. Schreuer might be understood to be making only the more modest claim, but he couples depoliticization with objectivity, as if investment law standards of treatment are devoid of political value. This sort of slippage occurs repeatedly in the literature, for example, Kriebaum (2018).
[143] Discussed further in Schneiderman (2012).

'politics continue to play a role even when we resort to arbitration and get the U.S. State Department out of the claims espousal business.'[144]

Unsubstantiated assertions about the benefits of investor–state arbitration are too numerous to mention. Two of them already have been flagged in this book.[145] First, the exorbitant claim that signing treaties attracts new inward investment continues to be made despite the equivocal evidence that has been generated to date. Meta-studies confirm that treaty effects are 'economically negligible.'[146] Also frequently alleged is the claim that treaties have the effect of instilling practices of good governance.[147] Yet there is virtually no empirical evidence to support the proposition that treaties enhance stability and predictability, due process, transparency, and legitimate expectations in states that do not already exhibit these virtues.[148] The relationship between investment law and good governance, like that between attracting inward investment by signing BITs, turns out to be mostly rhetorical.

Critics, in turn, are accused by these same authors of mostly making stuff up. The notables of investment law are quick to accuse critics of offering baseless and empirically vacuous complaints. Attracting particular indignation is the report entitled 'Profiting from Injustice' by Eberhardt and Olivet, published by the Corporate Europe Observatory and the Transnational Institute. The report, empirically driven and supported by original data, addresses such things as the costs of arbitration, third-party funding, and editorial control of academic publishing by industry insiders. Even if controversial, these certainly are subjects worthy of debate. Yet Brower and Blanchard do not hesitate to condemn the authors, and their allies, for issuing a 'propagandistic screed,' being based on 'nothing more than empty rhetoric.'[149] Brower and Blanchard purport to 'destroy' arguments that investment law is one-sided or serves to chill regulatory action by referring to uncertain data and ambivalent arbitral rulings.[150] But they also are quick to claim that treaties attract new investment[151] and deride the 'one critic,' who has been vindicated by the accumulated evidence, for being 'unreliable.'[152] They seize on the early work of Franck who, with impeachable data to back up her claim,

144 Alvarez (2010) at 147. See Gertz, Jandhylala, and Poulsen (2018) on the United States engaging in political retaliation, including economic sanctions, in the face of ongoing investment claims.

145 See the 'Introduction.'

146 Bellak (2015) at 19 and the evidence summarized in Bauerle Danzman (2019) at 26 and Pohl (2018) This data is discussed in more detail in Chapter 6.

147 Schill (2010).

148 For example, Calamita and Berman (2022).

149 Brower and Blanchard (2014) at 691, 717.

150 Brower and Blanchard (2014) at 700 describe having 'reference to the most recent and sophisticated empirical research.'

151 Brower and Blanchard (2014) at 708. Yet Paulsson characterizes this claim as 'dubious' and 'wrong' in Paulsson (2010) at 346.

152 Brower and Blanchard (2014) at 703, 704 referring to Jason Yackee, at 703, fn. 50 and 704, fn. 56.

concludes that there is no 'bias' in investment treaty arbitration.[153] They allege, finally, without supporting evidence, that investment treaties improve governance in capital-importing states.[154]

This kind of hyperbolic attack on critics of the system displays more than a tone of mere disagreement. It is a moralizing posture, a sanctimonious stance that promotes a contestable truth. Why else would the investment treaty system have spread so far and so wide, they ask? The regime, after all, is preoccupied with the preserving morals associated with market civilization premised on free competition. Anything else, that which Hayek contemptuously labeled 'social justice,' has no place in market-based economic orders.[155] Weber, by contrast, purported to abjure moralizing in legal thought.[156] Yet Weber could never succeed in separating formal law from substantive values, as argued in Chapter 2. Schluchter observes that Weber posited an ethical minimum in his formalist conception of law, rather than an empty legality.[157] Weber's exalted form of rational law, in both its procedural and substantive dimensions, could not be 'without some elements of substantive rationality'[158]—a rationality congenial to market-based legal orders.[159]

Rooting out the moral values at work in investment law has been a signal contribution made by Steven Ratner. His claim is that, despite denials to the contrary, a rigorous philosophical approach to the subject reveals the necessarily implicit presence of morals within investment law.[160] Ratner pulls the rug out from under those who claim that the field is 'objective' and 'neutral'—in Weberian parlance, that it is 'value free.' He acknowledges that, from an international lawyer's 'standard of justice,' everything may seem fine but, from a moral point of view, the system is replete with defects.[161] To this end, Ratner calls for more empirically driven work to inform both critics and supporters of the system.[162] The problem with Ratner's own work is that his evaluations of the morality of investment law are often divorced from the very empiricism that he calls for. Rather than isolating

[153] Brower and Blanchard (2014) at 711, referring to Franck (2009). Her results are questioned in Van Harten (2012). Schultz and Ridi (2020) at 28 report that the arbitration literature 'seems to lack serious engagement' with critical scholarship.

[154] Brower and Blanchard (2014) at 755.

[155] Hayek (1982) at 68. Hayek criticized Weber for not recognizing the possibility of spontaneous ordering rather than commands issuing as binding law in at 170, fn. 50. For a discussion of Hayek's theory of morals, see Whyte (2019), chap. 1.

[156] Ghosh (2019) at 104.

[157] Schluchter (1981) at 114.

[158] Schluchter (1981) at 117. Habermas (1984) at 309, by contrast, described modern law as 'uncoupled from ethical motives.'

[159] Weber (1920b) at 275. '[I]nhumanity is hidden in the rationality of the balance sheet,' observes Marcuse (1971) at 140. See also Mannheim (1927) at 145 (describing the 'falsity' of a 'one-sided emphasis upon rationalism').

[160] Ratner (2017) at 747.

[161] Ratner (2017) at 772.

[162] For example, Ratner (2017) at 762.

the values that predominate the field, and targeting them for critique, his work has smoothed over controversial readings of that experience.

The moral calculation that Ratner proposes is that investment law's norms 'should not, nor be interpreted to, interfere with basic human rights.'[163] It should not be too costly, in other words, to protect basic human rights.[164] This is one of two pillars that constitute what he calls 'thin' global justice.[165] Evaluating the arbitral record regarding two important standards of treatment commonly found in investment treaties—fair and equitable treatment (FET) and expropriation—Ratner concludes that their interpretation, 'at least provisionally,' meets the standard of thin justice.[166] Which is to say that the arbitral archive, 'when read closely,'[167] does not reveal what the usual critiques that are leveled at the regime allege. Instead, Ratner's diagnosis is that neither 'body of law' (referring to tribunal interpretations of these two standards of treatment) 'is unjust under the standard of thin justice.'[168]

Ratner's 'close' reading of some of the leading cases, however, leaves much to be desired. His evaluations are heavily reliant on the tribunal's reasons and not much else. As a consequence, his readings do not deviate from dominant accounts offered by others. He singles out interpretations that I have offered, in other work, as affording a 'starkly different view.' He maintains that the cases—'as I [Ratner] read them,' 'as I interpret them,' and 'interpreted my way'[169]—did not produce the outcomes that have been described as problematic.[170]

This is not the occasion to take up every one of the seven or so cases that Ratner discusses under these two related standards of treatment. For my purposes, two things can be said. First, he misses the relationship between these two protections for foreign investors. FET has swallowed up expropriation by pulling out one strand of the expropriation inquiry—whether an investor's expectation has been upset—and elevating it to a stand-alone element of FET under 'legitimate expectations' doctrine. The resulting burden on investors in the case of FET will be lower than for proving the occurrence of an expropriation. This lower burden of proof helps to explain why many tribunals decline to find an expropriation while

[163] Ratner (2017) at 773. He adds, 'in particular economic rights.' I assume Ratner is referring to obligations arising out of the International Covenant on Economic, Social, and Cultural Rights, mentioned in Ratner (2017) at 757–78.

[164] Elaborated upon in Ratner (2015) at 73–77 (generally those that guarantee a life free of external intrusion on the *fundamental freedom of the individual* ... coupled with the *basic material goods and conditions* necessary to a minimally flourishing life' (Ratner (2015) at 76–77, emphasis in original). There are numerous problems with employing this standard, among them, the 'undue abstractness' of human rights and their often-contradictory directives. See Kennedy (2004) chap. 1.

[165] See Ratner (2015) chap. 3. The other pillar is the standard of peace promotion.

[166] Ratner (2015) at 364 and Ratner (2017) at 772 (treaties have not been interpreted 'so as to truly prevent a host state from protecting basic human rights').

[167] Ratner (2015) at 364.

[168] Ratner (2015) at 378. Ratner's view has evolved to allow for a more robust protection of human rights in Ratner (2022).

[169] Ratner (2017) at 763 and Ratner (2018) at 124.

[170] A number of the cases are discussed in Schneiderman (2013).

concluding that there has been a denial of FET requiring the payment of a sum of damages.[171]

Second, there is a recurring methodological problem that Ratner exhibits in his evaluation of the record; he does not disclose any new facts nor contradict those others have relied upon. The *Tecmed* case illustrates the point well.[172] The account that Ratner provides is in lock step with the tribunal's reasons. Everything said by the tribunal is accepted as fact: the investor, whose renewal of a license to operate a hazardous waste site, eight kilometers from the municipality of Hermosillo, Mexico, had not been 'warned of any [environmental] irregularities that could be remedied' in a timely fashion. Moreover, the Mexican regulator was covering up, under the guise of public health, its politically motivated behavior.[173] Ratner's 'reading' adds little to the official account while disregarding facts that lend doubt to his human rights–friendly reading. Brower and Blanchard's virulent attack on critics of the investment law regime offers up a virtually identical account of the dispute: the regulator responded to 'purely political pressure' while the investor operated the site with 'only minor infractions.'[174]

After having examined the public record a little more 'closely,' one learns that public opposition to the site grew due to numerous reports of toxic waste being shipped in from out of state. Hazardous waste lying exposed and uncontained at the site prompted blockades, petitions, human rights complaints, access to information requests, and filings to the (toothless) NAFTA Commission for Environmental Cooperation.[175] Public protest was prompted by genuine concerns about public health, a fact that was not admitted by the tribunal nor acknowledged by many commentators. That there were no genuine environmental or public health concerns prompting the decision not to renew the license to operate the site is simply inaccurate. The grounds for refusal addressed these concerns: the operator had exceeded landfill limits, temporarily stored waste outside of the landfill, and received 'liquid and biological-infectious waste' that was not authorized by the permit.[176] Remarkably, though these environmental transgressions are documented in the tribunal's reasons, the tribunal concluded that the decision failed to 'specify any reasons of public interest' to justify it.[177] It is true that Mexican authorities mishandled the investor's investment, overlooked earlier environmental transgressions and, if they had been more patient, might have renegotiated

[171] He acknowledges that, even in 'arbitrations where the government is found to have violated FET, tribunals have typically not found an expropriation' in Ratner (2015) at 361. See Eco Oro (2021), for example.

[172] Técnicas Medioambientales (2003) at 133–95. I discuss this dispute in detail in Schneiderman (2013) at 119–23.

[173] Ratner (2015) at 355.

[174] Brower and Blanchard (2014) at 737. For a similar reading, see Newcombe and Paradell (2009).

[175] Schneiderman (2013) at 120–21.

[176] Tecmed (2003) at para. 99.

[177] Tecmed (2003) at para. 125.

an alternative site. But to expect otherwise is to hold politically accountable authorities to standards of perfection, benchmarks that can hardly be met by even fully developed states.[178]

What is revealing of the four FET cases from which Ratner derives his verdict that they satisfy 'thin justice' is that, in each instance, the states were accused of behaving politically rather than in accordance with their contractual obligations. In each instance, the state was accused of colorably invoking legitimate grounds, such as those regarding public health or environmental protection, to provide cover for their politically motivated behavior. This, too, Ratner accepts without hesitation. As I have argued elsewhere, these awards reveal a predilection to punish state behavior that is not in the service of market logic.[179] Behavior that is far removed from that expected of profit-seeking market actors, namely, protecting the legitimate interests of campesinos, consumers, or vulnerable citizens, is considered to be out of bounds. It is protection of these latter interests that attracts the pejorative label of 'political' and, consequently, liability under investment treaty law.

This is not to say that moral theory is unwelcome, as both a heuristic for understanding and a salve for resolving many of investment law's flaws. Rather, the problem with Ratner's moralizing is that he is not faithful to the advice he eagerly provides to the rest of us: to check our interpretations against the available empirical evidence. With heavy reliance upon tribunal findings, his readings hardly deviate from orthodox interpretations while, at the same time, taking issue with discordant accounts (including my own) with little else to offer to his readers. Moreover, he does so without providing a detailed exposition of those facts that drive him in the direction of the dominant view (other than by deferring to arbitral reasons). It is revealing that his version of international legal morality leaves things pretty much intact. The morality he promotes is encased within parameters laid down by a field that prefers to forget or neglect voices from outside of the system.[180] It turns out to serve as an excuse for the field's morally deficient status quo.[181]

[178] Douglas (2006) at 28.

[179] The argument is made in Schneiderman (2022d).

[180] Connolly (1993) at 132 describes such a moral economy as involving a 'certain forgetting' of its own 'arbitrary impositions.'

[181] Ratner has since elevated the place of human rights in investment arbitration so that it takes priority over FET violations when state action is 'reasonably related' to obligations owed to citizens under human rights treaties in Ratner (2022) at 569. FET will not have been violated, Ratner says, when state action is 'rationally related' to carrying out a human rights duty, consequently, tribunals should interpret FET so as to grant to states 'substantial flexibility' when taking action to protect human rights (at 581). An investor should only succeed if there is a 'significant disconnect between ends and means' (at 590). This more 'morally convincing position' is intended to lend 'legitimacy' to the embattled regime (at 569). He has not revisited, however, his reading of Tecmed (2003) or the other three FET cases discussed in Ratner (2018).

IV. Conclusion

This chapter conjoined the heuristic of ideal types with the concept of social carriers of legal instruction. Ideal types 'accentuate' select features of social reality and so emphasize only certain observable attributes. They serve, nevertheless, as heuristics for ascertaining the value orientation of investment law's carriers.[182] All three ideal types are meant to illustrate features of investment law training that are mostly neglected. Inspired by charismatic cold warriors, recruited to join the investment arbitration industry via the routinization of charisma, so as to promote a value orientation that perpetuates professional success—each contributes to investment law's endurance. Insisting on a moral value structure that is oriented toward promoting free trade and investment, while condemning strategies that threaten the spread and maintenance of free markets, is meant to ensure that investment law continues to persevere even as citizens in many locales remain doubtful about its benefits.

Ideal types aid in understanding not only value orientations but also the means by which the field is reproduced. Instruction in investment law exhibits, in Weber's terms, a tension between openness and closedness.[183] The profession is open to new members so long as they satisfy 'qualifying tests' exhibiting the values that advance the interests of the investment law profession.[184] Not only do new entrants exercise power and influence in the production of legal norms, if successful, but they also get invited to serve at the apex of the system as arbitrator—a 'judge' of sorts. The field is otherwise closed to those who do not share in this commitment to the group's value structure.[185] Those who reject a preference for markets over all else are relegated to being outsiders. As in the Cold War era, 'little real criticism' is 'permitted.'[186] Outsiders are not welcomed at conferences convened at fancy hotels. Nor are they invited to contribute to the texts that define the field. By policing the boundaries of acceptable critique, investment law professionals exercise a form of power. This authority facilitates the persistence of insider hegemony within the halls of the academy. It becomes difficult to dislodge the taken-for-granted narratives that they repeat. Their accounts echo in lecture halls, seminars, and scholarly publications.

It is undoubtedly seductive to join this club. Serving both the material and ideological interests of the profession, in addition to the clients that they serve, the appeal of this system becomes difficult to resist for budding lawyers. According to

[182] Bruun (2007) at 220.

[183] See the invaluable discussion in Parkin (1979), chap. 4. The relationship to Luhmann's autopoiesis—systems open or closed to communication from other sub-systems—should be apparent. See Luhmann (2004) at 105.

[184] Weber (1978) at 45.

[185] Weber (1978) at 44. Following Parkin (1979) at 48, they exhibit a 'form of closure designed to control and monitor entry' to this professional class.

[186] Halberstam (1983) at 33.

Garth, unlike earlier generations that emerged to challenge the content of norms that inform international law, there is 'no vocal generation playing the role that the younger generation played in the 1980s when developing countries became disillusioned with their strings of losses.'[187] Training in investment law turns out to be, then, in a regrettably calcified and lamentable state. It will remain, for the most part, dominated by the regime's defenders—its norm entrepreneurs—rather than those who have no stake in perpetuating the regime's market logic. By focusing on the various ideal types operating in investment law, we might better 'grasp the contradictions, dissimulations, disturbances, sublimations, tensions and values' that these social carriers exhibit.[188] Rather than offering, as Wolin maintains, 'a small purchase point' for critique, ideal typical analysis can raise awareness, allowing one to become more open to rethinking the field's presuppositions.[189]

[187] Garth (2018) at 164.
[188] Freund (1968) at 110.
[189] Wolin (1991) at 211.

5
An International Bureaucracy?

Weber characterized bureaucratic power as one of the most 'fateful' forces in modern life. 'The future belongs to bureaucratisation,' he proclaimed.[1] Accompanying the rise of formally rational law was a staff of well-trained and independent bureaucrats who administer and enforce it. Bureaucratic authority epitomized rational rule. It offered a technically efficient means of impersonally achieving ends that are generalizable for the administration of both public and private affairs.[2]

Weber did not distinguish sharply between figures who administered justice and other bureaucrats.[3] The official, for Weber, comprises 'many occupational categories' than might, at first glance, be the case.[4] These officials were central to his conception of domination under formally rational rules administered by 'lawyer-bureaucrats.'[5] By subsuming judicial machinery under the larger body of public officials administering state law, he could characterize the modern judge as an 'automaton' who produces judgments in mechanical fashion.[6] 'Juridical formalism,' Weber declares, 'enables the legal system to operate like a technically rational machine.'[7] The system 'works in a more or less *calculable* way.'[8]

Yet bureaucracy is deeply enmeshed in politics, having its own 'concealed normativity,' observes Koskenniemi. It is a mechanism 'that privileges values and actors occupying dominant positions in international institutions and who therefore

[1] Weber (1918b) at 156.

[2] Beetham (1985) at 64.

[3] In contrast to models that envisage the judiciary serving as a check on bureaucracy. See discussion in Frug (1984) at 1283, 1334ff.

[4] Albrow (1970) at 42.

[5] Ghosh (2014) at 169. Bureaucracy, writes Freund (1968) at 234, is 'the most typical example of legal authority' and, according to Bendix (1968) at 130, 'establishes a relation between legally instated authorities and their subordinate officials which is characterized by defined rights and duties.' Raz (1994) at 370–73 associates 'a bureaucratic model argument for the rule of law' with 'formal justice,' which requires fairness, publicity, impartiality, and predictability. This is contrasted with a 'tradition-oriented approach' rooted in vindicating 'community' values, best suited to homogenous societies. Raz prefers a third approach which 'facilitate[s] the integration of particular pieces of legislation with the underlying doctrines of the legal system,' which ensures both coherence and respect for tradition (at 375–77).

[6] Weber (1978) at 979. Bell (1987) at 44 resists this characterization, in the case of common law judging, which creates 'greater freedom from hierarchical control' even if there are 'many similarities.' The fact that 'greater responsibility' is accorded to common law judges makes characterization of the judiciary as 'bureaucratic ... inadequate' (at 55).

[7] Weber (1978) at 811.

[8] Weber (1918b) at 149 (emphasis in original).

A Sociology of International Investment Law. David Schneiderman, Oxford University Press.
 DOI: 10.1093/9780198982739.003.0006

have no reason to take a critical attitude to those institutions.' All that remains for these mandarins, he adds, are 'technical questions, questions about how to smooth the prince's path.'[9] Not only the prince but the career path to professional success for the mandarin, looking no further than 'the prospects for the next promotion: *my* success,' Koskenniemi writes, serves 'as the criterion of the world's happiness.'[10]

It is perilous, for this reason, to empty bureaucratic power of its politics.[11] Though emphasizing detached and impersonal rule by officials, even Weber had doubts about the neutrality of public administration. Particularly alarming were those circumstances where bureaucrats escaped political oversight. Absent the presence of control mechanisms—for Weber, these would include parliamentary committees staffed with responsible politicians—technocrats can 'acquire partial or total autonomy vis-à-vis majoritarian institutions [even] while remaining formally subordinate to the latter.'[12] This endows bureaucracy with the 'appearance of "rationality,"' according to Bourdieu, even as it is 'invested with the most mysterious properties of magical efficacy.'[13]

Weber famously characterized modern rational rule as 'disenchanted,' bereft of magic and superstition. Magic served as the proxy for a 'miscellany of non-rational behaviour.'[14] If magical, does bureaucratic authority give rise to a species of re-enchantment?[15] Does bureaucracy, in short, successfully conceal the power it wields? Jean d'Aspremont complains that the dominant Weberian account moves in this direction. He accuses Weber of attributing to bureaucratic power only the 'knowledge they use,' overlooking that 'the knowledge they use is controlled by them.' D'Aspremont insists that we acknowledge the 'power of bureaucracies to shape the very problems that they ought to address.' We ignore at our peril 'the extent to which bureaucracies influence the construction of the social reality in which they intervene.'[16] International courts, from this angle, exercise power not just '*through* knowledge but by virtue of their control *over* knowledge.'[17]

[9] Koskenniemi (1989) at 73. Legal formalism 'has a strong status-quo bias' allowing for little deviation from established order, writes Steffek (2017) at 135.

[10] Koskenniemi (2006) at 30.

[11] Bourdieu (1991) at 131 labels this 'depoliticized political discourse.' To this effect, Thomas (2006) at 418 describes Talcott Parsons's early translations as 'bowdlerizing' of Weber.

[12] Tortola (2020) at 68 and Anter (2014) at 171. In addition to political institutional checks, Ghosh (2014) at 333 adds the 'capitalist entrepreneur.'

[13] Bourdieu (1997) at 48.

[14] Ghosh (2014) at 264.

[15] Drawing upon Weber (1978) at 448, does rule by officialdom amount to rule validated by magic and superstition, like an emperor who is able to summon the rains to ensure a bountiful harvest? Weber never really elaborates on what constitutes magic. Instead, as Ghosh (2014) at 264 argues, it serves to exemplify non-rational behavior. On the demise of magic, see Weber (1919b) at 342 and (1920c) at 107 and further discussion in the 'Conclusion.'

[16] d'Aspremont (2020) at 333.

[17] d'Aspremont (2020) at 333.

This element of concealed power did worry Weber.[18] First, as Beetham puts it, bureaucracy has a tendency to 'exceed' its institutional authority and 'to become a separate force within society.' This slippage into an autonomous authority is aberrant, Weber insists, as it amounts to occupying a role for which civil servants are entirely 'unsuited.'[19] Second, bureaucracy has a tendency to ally itself to 'the outlook of the social classes from which it is recruited and to which it is allied.'[20] This endows administration with a 'capacity to influence' the political branches in ways that are not entirely independent of the balance of class forces in society.[21]

Bureaucracy can unduly influence not only the political branches but also other branches of public administration. If we approach questions of bureaucratic power with the knowledge that states are not homogenous unified wholes but, instead, are fragmented and influence within them unevenly distributed, then some fractions of the civil service will wield more authority than others.[22] Lawyers within departments of state and foreign affairs influence international economic policy and have been critical to both the construction and maintenance of the investment law regime—'the lawyers told us,' it is often said.[23] This phenomenon, too, was not lost on Weber. What Weber called the 'monocratic variety of bureaucracy'—a hierarchical form of supervisory authority exercised over subordinates—is the most efficient form of rule and 'indispensable' to the rise of the modern Western state.[24] This is in contrast to 'collegial' forms of bureaucratic administration, where there exists a multiplicity of monocratic officials or where voting or consultation of peers is required.[25] Relations of domination can 'exist reciprocally ... among officials of different departments.' Insofar as some branches have power over others, each can 'be subject to the others' powers of command.'[26]

No more influential are those whose authority can, practically speaking, veto state policy.[27] Arbitrators have the power to 'create' their preferred social world,[28] actualizing their desired approaches to law, economic development, in addition to managing threats to their supremacy. Having been assigned a virtual monopoly

[18] See Weber (1978) at 225 and text associated with fns. 80–83, below.

[19] Beetham (1985) at 65.

[20] Beetham (1985) at 66.

[21] Beetham (1985) at 67.

[22] The 'relative dominance of departments or ministries'—say, finance or treasury departments—'can underwrite the hegemony of specific material and ideal interests,' writes Jessop (2016) at 68.

[23] See the evidence gathered in Van Harten and Scott (2016). In the case of South Africa, a single legal advisor triggered changes to investment treaty policy resulting, ultimately, to the withdrawal of South Africa from the regime. Williams (2009) at 2 explains that he was 'quite horrified to read the content of a BIT' when he first took over as the lead investment treaty negotiator for South Africa's Department of Trade and Industry in 2001. On subsequent reforms in South Africa, see Carim (2016).

[24] Weber (1978) at 223.

[25] Weber (1978) at 272–74.

[26] Weber (1978) at 947.

[27] See Tsebelis (2002) at 226 on judicial veto points. I elaborate on this point in Schneiderman (2020).

[28] Bourdieu (1987) at 839.

on interpretation,[29] irrespective of textual directives or 'subsequent agreement between the parties,'[30] they almost always win the battle over 'control' of legal text.[31]

This chapter inquires into whether investment arbitration should be characterized as an international bureaucracy, first, by summarizing Weber's worry about bureaucracy and, second, by examining scholarship that considers the means by which the authority of international adjudicators, operating in a wide variety of settings, can be reined in. Finally, in the third part, I consider ways in which investment arbitration fits into the machinery for international justice for foreign investors, serving at the apex of investment law's bureaucracy. My aim is to restore politics at the center of bureaucratic rule, portraying investment arbitration as bureaucratic in style and political in substance.

I. Weber's Worry

For Weber, modern legal authority calls for an administrative staff to impersonally apply abstract rules to particular cases.[32] This was a development, as regards other features of modernity, which he 'simultaneously welcomed and opposed.'[33] The 'purest type' of legal authority relies on (i) a specialized administrative staff, (ii) organized into a 'clearly defined hierarchy,' (iii) operating under an 'established system of rules and regulations,' (iv) providing for continuity or 'routinization,' (v) adopting an 'impersonal orientation,' and (vi) appointed with fixed salaries enabling a professional career in public service.[34] These organizational features are confined not only to public administration, Weber reminds us, but equally are applicable to charitable and profit-making enterprises.[35]

Their specialized functions ensure the 'objective' administration of affairs and entail the 'discharge of business according to *calculable* rules and "without regard for persons."'[36] This accounts for the 'dehumanization' of professional

[29] Weber (1978) at 947 describes the 'popular American view' of 'the judge simply [as] a man who has been granted the monopoly to give a person a decision.'

[30] Referring to provisions in the Vienna Convention of the Law of Treaties, U.N.T.S. Vol. 1155, p. 331, Art. 31.

[31] Bourdieu (1987) at 818.

[32] Weber (1978) at 217.

[33] Mommsen (1989) at 111.

[34] Many of these features are identified in Weber (1978) at 220–21, also at 958–63. See Blau (1968) at 141–42 and Beetham (1987) at 11–12 for a summary. Otto Hintze identified many of the same features of bureaucratic administration several years before Weber. See discussion in Kocka (1978) at 285. Hintze did not, however, observe any deep division between officials and their political masters in Kocka (1987) at 286.

[35] Weber (1978) 221 (these are private enterprises 'serving ideal or material ends'). See Kocka (1981) for a revealing discussion of the bureaucratization of the Berlin-based Siemens electrical manufacturing company in the mid-late nineteenth centuries that had a 'direct contribution to the success of the business' (at 458).

[36] Weber (1978) at 975 (emphasis in original).

administration, 'eliminating from official business love, hatred, and all purely personal, irrational, and emotional elements which escape calculation.'[37] Capitalist enterprise also relies upon this disinterestedness in public administration—that it 'be discharged precisely, unambiguously, continuously and with as much speed as possible.'[38] Sacrificing their own convictions for a 'duty of obedience,' administrators have the upper hand but 'without responsibility.'[39] Administrative staff are expected not to be responsible in the sense, for instance, that members of the executive branch are responsible to Parliament.[40] Weber complained about the inverse phenomenon he observed in Germany: of politicians behaving like bureaucratic staff by sacrificing their convictions for a '*duty of obedience*.'[41] The impartial and rational official who functions without conviction represents, in Weber's thinking, the ideal typical bureaucrat.[42]

Without authority to follow through one's own convictions, bureaucratic power administers formal law seemingly at a distance from substantive values. Yet it is difficult to maintain the illusion of remoteness when bureaucrats are enmeshed in the everyday administration of legal code. They serve as *maître d'hôtel* for the enforcement of the political choices that are inscribed in law[43]—they are the 'organizational embodiment of values.'[44] Acknowledging, as he must, that ideal types do not necessarily mirror empirical reality, what the 'experience of the last few decades show[s is] that formal and substantive rationality coincide to a relatively high degree.'[45] As Steffek notes, bureaucratization

[37] Weber (1978) at 975, also 973 ('Precision, speed, unambiguity, knowledge of the files, continuity discretion, unity, strict subordination, reduction of friction and of material and personal costs—these are raised to the optimum point in the strictly bureaucratic administration, especially in its monocratic form').

[38] Weber (1978) at 974.

[39] Weber (1918b) at 204, 205. Weber's 'ethic of responsibility' entails having a sense of proportion between ends sought and means used. See Weber (1919a) at 360 and discussion in Chapter 3.

[40] Officials are accountable to their supervisors only to the extent that they faithfully apply laws and execute directives duly enacted.

[41] Weber (1918b) at 204 (emphasis in original).

[42] Page (2024) re-evaluates Weber's account of the rise of bureaucracy in Europe and concludes that he mischaracterizes the development of bureaucratic power. For instance, the emergence of law- and rule-bound decision making opened the door for a 'huge range of activities—creating, amending, modifying, monitoring, and updating policy regimes ... in which officials, even at a relatively junior level ... could be routinely and legitimately involved' (at 205). These findings underscore Weber's worry about the rise of independent bureaucratic authority, discussed below. Page admits that he is not interested in addressing, what he calls, Weber's 'nuanced and paradoxical arguments.' Rather, he is interested only in the dominant understandings of Weber that have shaped the empirical literature (at 13).

[43] Bell (1987) at 54 (courts are 'front-line institutions').

[44] Sezlnick (1992) at 275 (emphasis removed) and Bell (1987) at 42 (courts are in 'the service of substantive values which grounds' their legitimacy). Also Kennedy (2004) at 1064, 1066 (because 'legislative politics' defines the 'ethical substance of the legal order,' this renders Weber's claims about the coherence of legal formalism 'false in fact').

[45] Weber (1978) at 108–9. Weber admits, for example, that rational capital accounting in a money economy is the 'most general presupposition' for the 'existence of present-day capitalism' in Weber (1920b) at 276. Though the 'full development of the money economy' is not a 'precondition for bureaucratization,' a permanent bureaucracy is 'knit to the one presupposition of the availability of continuous revenues to maintain it' in Weber (1978) at 968.

exhibits both formal and material rationality, even if formalism is the dominant element.[46]

Consequently, in contrast to the formalistic account, where the administration of justice calls for impersonal application of general rules previously laid down, Weber acknowledges those instances where bureaucracy wields power independently.[47] For instance, bureaucracy is described as a 'precision instrument' that can be put at the service of 'varied interests' including the masses.[48] They can, on occasion, consider their official functions from a 'utilitarian point of view in the interest of the welfare of those under their authority.'[49] This is the 'tendency' toward substantive rationality' present in bureaucratic administration, which works to the benefit of those (the masses) who are not advantaged by protections 'already secured.'[50] This will be most present when relying upon 'expertise.' For instance, the 'bureaucratic judge,' when performing 'law-finding' functions, will be directed to more 'individualized' outcomes.[51]

Officialdom's 'creative' opportunities can also give rise to a different phenomenon, one that works to the advantage of the self-interest of bureaucratic power. 'General norms,' which are meant to serve as a barrier to administrative discretion,[52] can be fused with the goal of maintaining 'its own power' by 'intensifying the system of patronage,' for instance, or '"gratuities" for delivery.'[53] This renders 'any control of the administration illusory.'[54] All else being equal, it is always these interests 'which tip the balance.'[55] For instance, changes to the census, under the control of state bureaucracy, could be manipulated so as to produce suffrage reform preferred by officialdom, complains Weber.[56] The 'spirit of bureaucracy,' he declares in his final lectures, exhibits a tendency toward 'plutocracy.'[57]

Public administration can also serve the interests of the most powerful interests in society. They might preserve the status quo and work to maintain the supremacy of dominant forces that influence, if not control, bureaucratic machinery. Bureaucracy is more likely to serve the class interests of those from whose ranks its staff are recruited. Just as propertied classes can pull 'thousands of strings' in order to get their way,[58] so can they influence bureaucratic outcomes to benefit

[46] Steffek (2017) at 134.
[47] Wehler (1985) at 65 describes the bureaucracy in Wilhelmine Germany as being 'in a position to prepare and formulate decisions in advance, taking them directly or—what was equally significant—delaying, obstructing or rejecting them.'
[48] Weber (1978) at 990.
[49] Weber (1978) at 226.
[50] Weber (1978) at 226.
[51] Weber (1978) at 979.
[52] Weber (1978) at 970.
[53] Weber (1918b) at 151.
[54] Weber (1918b) at 151.
[55] Weber (1978) at 979.
[56] Beetham (1985) at 74.
[57] Weber (2009) at 82–83 (translation by Bjorn Wagenpfeil).
[58] Weber (1917) at 93.

their interests.[59] Weber alleges that 'juridico-technical improvement favours the economically stronger.'[60] This was particularly the case for the legal profession, whose 'members are inclined to stand on the side of "order".'[61] This was the lesson that Weber drew from Junker control of German state bureaucracy.[62] It would be a mistake, his brother Alfred Weber declared, to deny that bureaucracy has a 'social basis' in 'those power groups which control the organisation of society.'[63]

Despite these concessions, Weber's ideal typical monocratic bureaucracy, he tells us, offers the most superior form of 'exercising authority over human beings.'[64] Bureaucracies are ubiquitous and 'cut to fit' the framework of patterns of 'everyday life.'[65] As are machines when compared to 'non-mechanical modes of production,' the 'fully developed bureaucratic apparatus' is superior to all else.[66] Its superiority resides in expertise—the 'technical knowledge' garnered under modern technology and modes of production, whether capitalist or socialist.[67] This superior power is a fateful one, however. It 'stands unshaken.'[68] The only way to escape the 'idolization of bureaucracy'[69] is by creating yet other organizations, which are then susceptible to the same bureaucratization phenomenon.[70] It amounts to the 'housing' of a 'future serfdom.' If individuals 'consider that the ultimate and only value by which the conduct of their affairs is to be decided is good administration and provision for their needs by officials,' then bureaucracy achieves this 'incomparably better than any structure of rule.'[71] It gives rise to a form of servitude, 'just like the slaves in the ancient state of Egypt.' The bureaucrat, once appointed,

[59] Or stand in the way of other interests. In Russia, for instance, peasants sought to remove the Tsar's layer of bureaucracy insulating him from the people in Weber (1906b) at 56–57.

[60] Weber (1895b) at 242. Wehler (1985) at 65 describes Wilhelmine bureaucracy as cooperating 'closely with ruling elites, particularly the aristocracy,' exerting influence as an 'obedient executive.' Compare Von Mises (1944) at 9ff who polemically describes bureaucracies as tending toward totalitarianism. This is a view that is closer to Alfred Weber than to Max. See discussion in Whimster (2023) at 89 and text of note 64, infra.

[61] Weber (1978) at 876. Elsewhere, Weber associated the desire for order with political 'timidity,' 'as if we were to become men who need "order" and nothing but order,' quoted in Mayer (1955) at 128.

[62] Scaff (1984) at 33, Bendix (1962) at 465, and Kocka (1987) at 287–88. Mommsen (1984) at 26 concludes that Weber admired this landed aristocracy for their political leadership skills, foreshadowing 'significant elements in Weber's legal and political theory.'

[63] Beetham (1985) at 66, who assumes that Max's brother Alfred spoke for both of them in these circumstances. Max admitted that '[a]lthough our opinions differ in many things,' the brothers agreed that 'the forward progress of bureaucratic mechanization was irresistible' in Mayer (1955) at 125. Also see Radkau (2011) at 323 who characterizes Alfred Weber's antipathy to bureaucratic rule as amounting to a 'hatred' and discussion in Whimster (2023) at 89.

[64] Weber (1978) at 223.

[65] Weber (1978) at 223.

[66] Weber (1978) at 973 and Weber (1918b) at 158. Also see Weber quoted in Mayer (1955) at 126 ('official hierarchy does these things ... as objectively, precisely, and "soullessly" as any machine').

[67] Weber (1978) at 223.

[68] Quoted in Mayer (1955) at 126.

[69] Quoted in Mayer (1955) at 129.

[70] Weber (1978) at 224. Only business expertise is superior to bureaucratic knowledge in Weber (1978) at 224, 994. Economic enterprises, unlike bureaucracies, are disciplined by the prospect of losses.

[71] Weber (1918b) at 158 (emphasis in original removed).

is 'chained' to his desk, merely 'a small cog in a ceaselessly moving mechanism.' The subjects of domination, on the other hand, are dependent on functions being performed competently, as the 'material fate of the masses depends upon the continuous and correct functioning' of bureaucratic machinery.[72]

Moreover, once established, Weber warns, bureaucracy is the 'hardest to destroy'[73]—it is 'unstoppable.'[74] Where administration is bureaucratized, 'the resulting system of domination is practically indestructible.'[75] The 'idea of eliminating them becomes more and more utopian.'[76] '[A]ll order' is 'dependent on the system of files and the disciplines of officialdom.'[77] In which case, the forward march of bureaucratization appears to be both irresistible and irreversible.[78] Weber laments that it is enough to 'drive one to despair.'[79]

At bottom, the 'question is always who controls the existing bureaucratic machinery.' '[S]uch control is possible only to a very limited degree to persons who are not technically specialists,' warns Weber.[80] There certainly will be no parity as between the bureaucrat and his political masters. The former's 'power position' is 'always great,' even 'overtowering.' Politicians will always find themselves 'in the position of a dilettante facing the expert.'[81] 'Bureaucratic administration,' Weber concludes, 'means fundamentally domination through knowledge.'[82] What 'can we oppose to this machinery,' Weber asks, 'in order to keep a portion of mankind free from this parcelling out of the soul, from this supreme mastery'?[83]

Weber's skepticism about universals, together with his probabilistic sensibilities, suggested modes by which to control bureaucracies that sought to manipulate or otherwise stall political authority.[84] He envisaged, for instance, a powerful executive branch serving as a check on bureaucratic administration conjoined with legislative committees having the authority to investigate and control their activities.[85]

[72] Weber (1978) at 988.
[73] Weber (1978) at 987.
[74] Weber (1918b) at 159.
[75] Weber (1978) at 987.
[76] Weber (1978) at 988.
[77] Weber (1978) at 988.
[78] Weber (1978) at 1002. But see Bendix (1968) at 135.
[79] Quoted in Mayer (1955) at 127.
[80] Weber (1978) at 224–25 and 988–89 ('the mechanism ... is easily made to work for anybody who knows how to gain control over it'). See also Weber (1978) at 990 ('The bureaucracy is a precision instrument which can put itself at the disposal of quite varied interests, purely political as well as purely economic ones, or any other sort').
[81] Weber (1978) at 991.
[82] Weber (1978) at 225.
[83] Quoted in Mayer (1955) at 128.
[84] Douglass (2018) at 21, 134–35.
[85] Breiner (1996) at 139 maintains that, for Weber, only 'charismatic domination' can check bureaucratic power. Weber admits that mass democracies inevitably will be ruled by 'small numbers,' which he associates with 'Caesarism,' in Weber (1918b) at 174. Earlier, Weber had envisaged that a working parliament and responsible leadership offered sufficient control. On parliamentary control as a check on bureaucracy, see Palonen (2004) and Palonen (2010).

Both of these checking functions offered up a means, for Weber, of curbing administrative power.[86]

Mommsen is less convinced by Weber's conviction that openness and 'public moral exposure' would check public administration. If Weber was 'an ethical man of conviction,' Mommsen declares, he also was filled with 'illusions.'[87] The problem of 'control' is a question that preoccupied not only Weber but also many others, including scholars thinking about national and international courts. What are the means, they ask, by which the political branches can check judicial branches at both national and international levels?

II. Losing Control?

The sociology of bureaucracy is preoccupied with 'one basic dilemma,' declares Eisenstadt, 'namely, whether the bureaucracy is master or servant, an independent body or a tool.'[88] Any bureaucracy, he adds, must have some degree of autonomy in so far as officials perform mediative or regulative functions and serve, consequently, in a 'power position.' Autonomy is, therefore, 'inherent' in the 'very genesis and nature' of bureaucratic power.[89] Eisenstadt analytically distinguishes between bureaucracy—the establishment of organized authority that fulfills designated functions—and bureaucratization—the 'acquisition of unregulated power.'[90] It is the worry about power let loose by bureaucratization that animates this analysis.

Autonomy and degrees of unregulated power have been a preoccupation among scholars of judicial politics too. Two associated strategies, drawing upon legal relationships in company law and the common law,[91] have been offered to conceptualize the control of judicial functions by political branches. In the first, courts are analogized to 'agents' and the political branches to their 'principals.' According to this Principal-Agent (P-A) model, courts are delegated responsibility to generate answers to controversial legal questions, all the while remaining under the 'control' of their principal. Yackee describes the virtue of this framework by highlighting how agents 'effectively serve the interests of their legitimate political masters.'[92] This is akin to Veeder's portrayal of arbitral functions: the arbitrator serves as 'master of the arbitration but not the parties' master.'[93] Political mastery, however,

[86] These mechanisms would, by 1918, give way to the felt need for plebiscitary leadership, notes Mommsen (1984) at 184.

[87] Mommsen (1984) at 170.

[88] Eisenstadt (1958) at 100.

[89] Eisenstadt (1958) at 102.

[90] Eisenstadt (1958) at 103.

[91] Frug (1984) at 1307.

[92] Yackee (2012) at 399. He admits, however, that it is not 'fully accurate as a descriptive matter or exclusively useful' (at 400).

[93] Veeder (2014) at 93.

appears illusory. In national contexts where apex courts have autonomy and independence, courts behave more freely, even if operating under constraints of judicial propriety. Posner has observed that in constitutional cases, a high court's freedom of action is as capacious as that of a legislature's.[94] If judges are agents, writes Fuller, 'they are agents who habitually talk as if they were principals.'[95] Given ineffectual control mechanisms, Alter considers the 're-contracting tools' available to principals as being 'weak.'[96] Courts, in particular, are in a 'hierarchically privileged position compared to any other actor'—their rulings are taken as 'legally authoritative.'[97] For these, and associated reasons, P-A theory, she concludes, 'is simply unhelpful.'[98] As Frug describes the relationship between shareholders and company executives in the company law context, it fails to grasp the 'realities' of the judicial form.[99]

Despite the weakness of those constraints, the P-A model has been conscripted into accounts of how states control international courts. This is how Pavel describes the model operating at international levels:[100]

> The *principal-agent model* as a modified consent model can address some of the worries related to the legitimate authority of international institutions to make rules for states. According to this model, coercive international institutions should be conceived as agents of people living in separate states, whose task is to keep those states within acceptable bounds of legitimate behavior by filling in governance gaps in the state system. Supranational authorities should function as an insurance scheme against the possibility that states may fail to fulfill their duties.

This account, too, not only discounts the difficulty of controlling international courts but also misrecognizes the politics that are at stake.[101] Focused on the struggle between degrees of autonomy principals grant to agents, the political authority gained by agents is obscured. Instead, delegation to international courts staffed by judicial *functionnaires* is treated as unproblematic.

The authority that they do command, moreover, can evolve into narrow-minded agendas of not much benefit to their principals. Barnett and Finnemore's

[94] Posner (2008) at 82.
[95] Fuller (1940) at 24. Or agents without principals, according to Lindseth (2020) at 44.
[96] Alter (2006) at 327.
[97] Alter (2008) at 47.
[98] Alter (2006) at 337.
[99] Frug (1984) at 1307.
[100] Pavel (2015) at 26–27 (emphasis in original). One is here reminded of the good governance rationale for binding investment treaty obligations discussed further in Chapter 6.
[101] Bourdieu (2000) at 108 attributes 'misrecognition' to Weber who 'pointed out long ago, there is no greater threat to a worker's movement, or any other, than "objectives rooted in misrecognition of real relationships".'

qualitative studies of international organizations reveal that the impersonal and generalized rules that are assigned to international courts for enforcement can render them 'unresponsive to their environments, obsessed with their own rules at the expense of primary missions,' resulting in 'inefficient, self-defeating behavior.'[102] Even if international organizations are understood as 'reasonably responsive to state interests,' they are as likely to undermine their principal's objectives by developing 'distinctive internal cultures' that create a 'cultural disposition toward undesirable' outcomes.[103]

Another model conceives of courts as trustees, but does not fare much better. Trustee theory acknowledges that international courts have authority to exercise independent discretion but, in addition, owe '[c]ore obligations of loyalty, accountability and deliberative engagement' to the beneficiaries of the trust relationship.[104] Courts owe duties to these fiduciaries, whom we might imagine to be states but are as often described as 'the people.' Courts act not as mere agents, but as 'super-agents' of the people who authorize the exercise of authority over them, say Stone Sweet and Matthews.[105] Neither executive branches nor political parties are the principals in the trustee model; instead, the people are presumed to control the trust relationship.

This model, too, is an ill-fitting one. The people hardly play a role in the establishment of international agencies or courts. Instead, they delegate their authority to elected officials who vote in representative assemblies which, particularly in the realm of foreign affairs, often are under the control of the executive branch.[106] Supervision of trustee authority is acute in international arenas due to the absence of adequate oversight and limited public scrutiny.[107] As in the corporate law field, where the trustee model is ubiquitous, the beneficiaries to whom a fiduciary duty is owed are a 'fully objectified abstraction.'[108] As applied to judicial power, 'decision rules heavily favour the continuous dominance of constitutional judges over the interpretation of the constitutional law,' Stone Sweet admits.[109] The people remain mostly powerless in this trust relationship.

Sweet's concession about domination is welcome, seeing as much of this literature tends to downplay international judicial power. Recall that, in Weber's

[102] Barnett and Finnemore (2004) at 700.

[103] Barnett and Finnemore (2004) at 715–18.

[104] Stone Sweet and Grisel (2017) at 116, also Stone Sweet and Brunell (2013).

[105] Stone Sweet and Matthews (2019) at 21 and fn. 63, also Stone Sweet and Brunell (2013) at 62.

[106] For a discussion of how authority in international economic affairs is concentrated in selected countries, see Schneiderman (2024). For treaty making in the common law world, see McLachlan (2014).

[107] Venzke (2008) at 1426. If, as Weber (1978) at 992 puts it, '[b]ureaucratic administration always tends to exclude the public,' there is very little public knowledge, or even awareness, of investment arbitration (outside of those host states where disputes have become politicized).

[108] Frug (1984) at 1308.

[109] Stone Sweet (2000) at 25. He concedes, as well, that the judiciary is implicated in what is a 'profoundly political process' (at 150).

formulation, bureaucratic expertise gives rise to a power imbalance and domination over citizens. It is precisely this Weberian worry that animates Barnett and Finnemore's study. They identify five 'pathologies' that are recurring features in the ways such international organizations function.[110] These include the 'irrationality of rationalization' (i), where mandates are taken to extremes so that the means used ultimately come to determine the ends sought.[111] A pathology of universalism (ii) 'flattens diversity' and offers standardized formulae for complex problems.[112] They chronicle a 'normalization of deviance' (iii), where rules become routinized and exceptions become the rule,[113] in addition to 'organizational insulation' (iv) that gives rise to 'parochial' professionalism and the 'absence of [an] effective feedback loop.'[114] Organizations also produce 'cultural contestation' (v) that produces division and dissensus 'linked to normative contradictions' that are available to be exploited by insiders.[115]

Many of the pathologies identified by Barnett and Finnemore will be familiar to observers of international investment arbitration. What is meant to be a system that rationalizes expectations as between investors and states turns out to be less predictable, giving rise to expansionary trends that tailor investor protections to unexpected outcomes for states (i).[116] These trendlines get taken up by an array of disparate arbitration tribunals, giving rise to the application of relatively uniform standards despite the varying contexts in which investment disputes arise. Arbitrators choose to downplay diversity and, instead, impose their own empire of uniformity (ii).[117] These interpretations may have the effect of deviating significantly from text and practice while insulating arbitral decision making from outside influences, such as those generated by non-governmental organization (NGOs) or local communities (iii).[118] Even where a shift in investment treaty standards of protection may be desired, as evinced in the newer generation of model treaties, changes are slow to take hold, and so principals/beneficiaries will, consequently, have little influence (iv).[119] Finally, cultural contestation is tolerated to a degree, given the frequency of dissenting opinions in arbitral decision making.[120] Nevertheless, the dominant consensus among investment arbitrators,

[110] Barnett and Finnemore (2004) at 39–40.
[111] Barnett and Finnemore (1999) at 720.
[112] Barnett and Finnemore (1999) at 721. Thomas (2008) at 65ff labels this the 'one-size-fits-all' model.
[113] Barnett and Finnemore (1999) at 721–22.
[114] Barnett and Finnemore (1999) at 723.
[115] Barnett and Finnemore (1999) at 724–25.
[116] Sornarajah (2008). Consider, for example, legitimate expectations doctrine.
[117] Tully (1995) at 25.
[118] See Hobér (2014) at 943. This will be familiar to a system-theoretical account of investment arbitration explored in Schneiderman (2011).
[119] Alschner (2022). Even here, there is hesitation to relax those standards any further, as evinced by the priority powerful states have placed on procedural, and not substantive, reform of ISDS at UNCITRAL Working Group III negotiations. See discussion in Polonskaya (2020).
[120] Dissents are tolerated but not always welcome. See Van den Berg (2010) who exhorts tribunal members to come to unanimous agreement ('investment arbitration would function better and be

lawyers, and academics renders contestation difficult (v).[121] '[I]nconsistencies of principle are relatively rare,' declares arbitrator Paulsson, revealing the near unanimity among investment law professionals.[122] Garth is prompted to observe that investment lawyers generally keep 'their criticisms within bounds, arguing in favour of the basic tenets of the system.'[123]

Barnett and Finnemore are informed by detailed case studies of various international organizations, including the International Monetary Fund (on the rise of conditionality), the United Nations High Commissioner for Refugees (on the definition of a refugee), and the United Nations Security Council (on peacekeeping in Rwanda). There is, regrettably, no comparable study of investment arbitration, though some scholars have applied the P-A model to propose modest reforms.[124] Yackee, for example, describes the agents at work in this system as a coterie of government representatives, delegates to intergovernmental organizations, lawyers, and academics.[125] This seems too diffuse a group to be described as agents in the sense in which this model typically operates. Arbitrators are situated, nonetheless, in a complex and dispersed supportive environment to which these other actors provide support for their endeavors, which I discuss in more detail later in this chapter.

Kulick merges both P-A and trusteeship accounts into a hybrid model.[126] If the principals in the P-A model are contracting State parties and investors, the trusteeship model implies a more modest range of control. Perhaps beneficiaries can only interpret treaties after the fact—by amending, terminating, or by issuing subsequent binding interpretations—he cautions. But states cannot control the

more credible if party-appointed arbitrators observe the principle: *nemine dissentiente*'). I reported, in Schneiderman (2010c), that Van den Berg had not issued dissenting reasons in any cases in a 2008 database.

[121] On the dominant consensus around the standard of national treatment, see Schneiderman (2024b).

[122] Paulsson (2005) at 243. Some issues 'remain controversial,' Paulsson acknowledges, but only 'some time is needed to achieve a settled jurisprudence.' Crystallization of the law may, in practice, be 'more rapid' as compared to other international regimes.

[123] Garth (2018) at 164.

[124] See van Aaken (2014) and Yackee (2012). Alter (2014) at 228–34 provides a modest discussion of the Metalclad (2000) dispute. She claims (at 238), though without much evidence, that the ICSID system 'casts less of a shadow over administrative decision making' and that, to the extent it has influenced bargaining, 'it has been to encourage firms to obtain all the required permits *before* purchasing a local enterprise or undertaking construction' (emphasis in original). It has been most 'helpful,' she says, when states and investors 'want a clear determination of "fair compensation" for an investment gone wrong' (at 229). But these determinations are fraught with conflict and unreliable. It is 'never just about quantum,' explains Boué (2023) at 219.

[125] Yackee (2012) at 404–5. But, Yackee insists, they do not constitute a 'mafia' (at 406), the derogatory term Dezalay and Garth (1996) at 10 use to describe lawyers participating in commercial arbitration. This very same group, however, is described as an 'old boys' club' in Swigart and Terris (2014) at 635.

[126] This also is the approach adopted by Stone Sweet and Brunell (2013) at 62, who adopt a theory of trusteeship 'from within the standard principal-agent framework.'

outcome of dispute resolution.[127] There are direct implications, too, for arbitral roles depending on which model (P-A or trustee) is adopted—in P-A, no duties are owed to non-disputants while, in the trustee frame, strategies to legitimate arbitral functions are more justifiable, permitting, for instance, submissions by non-disputing parties.[128] Pollack prefers not to rely on either model, emphasizing that control in any instance is an empirical and not a theoretical question.[129]

In the context of investor–state dispute resolution, such accounts almost invariably downplay the power relations that are at work. Yet, investment arbitration seems the most obvious candidate for interrogation along these lines, given the politics embedded within the norms and structures of its system. The regime seeks to achieve, in short, material rationalization and not merely along procedural lines. The 'close connection' between material and formal rationality in bureaucratized systems 'tend to expand jointly,' observe Morcillo Laiz and Schlichte.[130] Steffek places emphasis on how this tendency contributes to the depoliticization of those subjects under the control of international organizations.[131] Even if the dominant 'spirit' of bureaucracy, according to Weber, is 'formalism,' officials will adopt 'utilitarian' perspectives in order to best reach their stated purposes, exhibiting a tendency toward substantive rationality.[132] However we characterize them, bureaucracies 'are not apolitical,' write Morcillo Laiz and Schlichte: '[t]heir means are means of domination, forms of wielding institutionalized power; the attempts to rationalize are themselves political acts.'[133] In accounts that emphasize agency or trusteeship models, the politics embedded within international institutions mostly get suppressed. The literature tends to, in Mannheim's apt phrasing, turn 'problems of politics into problems of administration.'[134]

By re-centering politics, newer institutional imaginaries are available. Characterizing the investment law system as a 'policymaking agency,' Yackee offers up one such proposal. States can have restored to them the last word on 'how society's complex set of values and priorities should ultimately be balanced.'[135] Yackee proposes that state principals exercise more control over investment law agents by imposing US administrative law practices of 'notice and comment' (soliciting input from the public-at-large) and legislative veto (correcting undesirable agency outputs).[136] Investment law's agents are analogized to common law

[127] Kulick (2017) at 17–20.
[128] Elaborated upon in Alvarez (2014) at 161, 165–66.
[129] Pollack (2014) at 381.
[130] Morcillo Laiz and Schlichte (2016) at 176.
[131] Steffek (2017) at 134–35.
[132] Weber (1978) at 226 (material and formal rationality are 'apparently, and in part genuinely, in contradiction'). This is a tension that Steffek claims Weber 'never really resolved,' in Steffek (2017) at 135. A fuller discussion can be found in Chapter 1.
[133] Morcillo Laiz and Schlichte (2016) at 180.
[134] Mannheim (1959) at 118.
[135] Yackee (2012) at 394.
[136] Yackee (2012) at 434–45.

courts in which their rule pronouncements are 'policy-like because it is expertise based, and not purely law based, and is intended to advance in instrumental fashion the state-defined goal of promoting investment.'[137] To this end, Yackee calls upon us to be a 'bit less "romantic" about the inherent value' of arbitral awards and so to be open to the reassertion of more control.[138] This turns out to be anathema to investment law professionals, as discussed next.

III. Investment Law's *Fonctionnaires*

Just as Weber understood that his portrayal of judges as 'automatons' would attract fierce resistance so, I imagine, will this discussion. 'Surely there can be no valid comparison,' writes arbitrator Jan Paulsson, 'between "faceless bureaucrats" *imposed* upon parties and the arbitrators *selected* by the disputants in international arbitration involving states.'[139] Note the emphasis on selection processes available to parties as opposed to the infliction of bureaucratic power upon unwilling supplicants. It is telling that Paulsson at least entertains the analogy between arbitral functions and bureaucratic power. Elsewhere, he takes up the image of the P-A model. The arbitrator, he maintains, is asked only to perform a 'task'—'[h]e is, one might think, their agent.'[140] They are not, however, machines: '[i]nternational adjudicators are not robots,' Paulsson insists.[141] Public servants, on the other hand, even in the 'best of societies, blessed with mature institutions,' have a tendency toward 'corruption, lethargy, and the simple lack of resources.'[142] An antipathy toward bureaucratic rule is palpable in Paulsson's writings, describing an 'avalanche of legislation' and regulation that 'cannot sensibly be called "law",' even if hedged by reference to Weber's conclusion that a 'well-functioning and incorruptible bureaucracy' is one of modernity's achievements.[143] Certainly, ordinary judges, particularly in an 'institutionally immature state,' are not competent to resolve disputes between investors and host states. It is 'hard to take seriously' the idea that international arbitration stifles the development of national courts, Paulsson claims.[144]

137 Yackee (2012) at 413.

138 Yackee (2012) at 440. This proposal, he claims, serves as a corrective to a constitutional frame, something I have proposed in Schneiderman (2008) and Schneiderman (2020). I argue that the constitutional analogy—which likens investment arbitration to the judicial function in the interpretation of constitutional rights—has the advantage of highlighting the power that investment arbitrators hold over state policy making capacity. The constitutional frame is meant to place these in the foreground, not in order to 'make them' constitutional, per Yackee (2012) at 399.

139 Paulsson (2005) at 242 (emphasis in original). We are also told that '[a]rbitrators do not operate as judges' in Rodríguez (2023) at 387.

140 Paulsson (2013) at 106.

141 Paulsson (2005) at 252.

142 Paulsson (2013) at 300.

143 Paulsson (2013) at 102.

144 Paulsson (2013) at 258. He does not even deign to provide scholarly authority for this proposition!

Those judges are simply too juvenile to develop their own law independently of international tribunals. Paulsson speaks for many investment law professionals when he declares that local judges cannot be 'taken seriously' as a replacement for the institutionalized expertise offered by investment arbitration.

Arbitral Environment

Even if, for the moment, one accepts Paulsson's assertion that arbitrators are not bureaucrats, investment arbitration cannot function without a bureaucratic apparatus on which it is wholly reliant. Investment arbitration is heavily 'dependent on the outside world for its resources.'[145] Hirsch, for this reason, describes the 'community' of investment arbitration as being 'fairly close knit,' 'comprised of lawyers, arbitrators, arbitral institutions, and scholars.'[146] Soave similarly argues that a 'supporting legal bureaucracy' is 'inseparable' from the 'international judicial community' which they serve.[147] International courts, add Caserta and Rask Madsen, 'are complex organizations with many categories of employees, each of whom contribute to the formation of judgments.' For these reasons, it makes more sense, they argue, to reject the 'conventional distinction between institutions and their context—as well as between the external and internal dimensions of law—and instead,' recognize the 'broader field' in which international courts operate.[148] Both Kronman and Fiss associate the delegation of such responsibilities with 'bureaucratization' of the judiciary.[149]

We should view the supportive environment for investment arbitration as serving multiple functions, not just administrative ones. As investment treaty arbitration offers privatized dispute resolution processes, states do not provide the administrative scaffolds for decision making as they do for local judiciaries. Arbitration, for this reason, is 'highly dependent' on the institutional support generated by international organizations in addition to professional support provided by a cadre of lawyers and scholars who 'authenticate' the arbitration industry's 'legal accomplishments, act as vigilant custodians, and defend its authority against a variety of external criticisms,' observes Vauchez. In addition, '[i]n the absence of a feed court from which to recruit new members, these legal networks are also key in providing a transnational breeding ground of judges (of former students, research assistants, law clerks, or interns) already socialized in [arbitration's] core beliefs and therefore willing to perpetuate' investment arbitration's legacy.[150] They,

[145] Eisenstadt (1958) at 111.
[146] Hirsch (2020) at 719, 720, having affinities with the mapping of the investment law network by Puig (2014) and Ridi and Schultz (2021).
[147] Soave (2022) at 36–39.
[148] Caserta and Rask Madsen (2022) at 932, 933.
[149] Kronman (1993) at 325 and Fiss (1983).
[150] Vauchez (2014) at 659–60 and discussed further in Chapter 4.

in short, serve to routinize the administration of investment arbitration and police the boundaries of legitimate critique.

The authority exercised by various actors operating within this larger context is not evenly distributed, to be sure.[151] Functioning in a hierarchical power environment, adjudicators performing judicial functions will sit at the top of the food chain. Nevertheless, the legal outputs upon which international lawyers place much emphasis elide the 'invisible army' that operates 'deep [in] the bowels of the system.'[152] For instance, a multitude of arbitral facilities around the world compete for the provision of arbitral services in both commercial and investment arbitration. These facilities provide board rooms, case management staff, information and communication technology, in addition to other administrative support, for the conduct of investment arbitration. They also channel payments to arbitrators[153] and are regarded as a 'social hub for arbitral communities.'[154] They serve as the infrastructure that states otherwise provide to their home state courts. I first sketch this supportive institutional architecture before turning, in the next section, to a discussion of the arbitration industry itself.

Arbitral institutions—facilities that host investor–state dispute resolution—are characterized as 'ancillary entities' that can take on roles that can 'assume a decisional character.'[155] Consider, for example, the Stockholm Chamber of Commerce Centre for Arbitration, established in 1917, which has operated as an investment arbitration facility since 1993. The Center boasts playing a 'prominent role' in resolving investment disputes, serving as host to the 'second largest' number of cases. By ensuring confidentiality in proceedings, the Centre's rules are described as the 'third most widely used' for the resolution of investment disputes.[156] The Singapore Investment Arbitration Centre is a relative newcomer to the world of arbitration. Established in 1991, it is touted as a 'respected neutral arbitral institution with a record of enforcement.' It is 'ranked 2nd among the world's top 5 arbitral institutions' by the Queen Mary University of London School of International Arbitration.[157]

At the apex of arbitral institutions is the International Centre for the Settlement of Investment Disputes (ICSID). It is described by its former Deputy Secretary-General as the 'premier international investment arbitration facility in the world.'[158]

151 Cole, Ortolani, and Wright (2020) at 934 ('international commercial arbitration operates as a tiered structure').
152 Soave (2022) at 114.
153 Onwuamaegbu (2017) at 313.
154 Cole, Ortolani, and Wright (2020) at 945.
155 Mistelis (2020) at 370.
156 See https://sccarbitrationinstitute.se/en/our-services/investment-disputes (last accessed September 19, 2023). It is second only to ICSID, discussed below.
157 See https://siac.org.sg/about-us/why-siac (last accessed September 19, 2023). The data is from White and Case (2021) at 6. They report that the top five 'most preferred seats for arbitration' are London, Singapore, Hong Kong, Paris, and Geneva. These 'cities have cemented a dominant position as seats of choice.'
158 Parra (2017) at 268.

Though operating under the auspices of the World Bank, it is described as 'almost independent.'[159] However, ICSID's success, according to three practitioners, is due to it being constituted as an organ of the World Bank. Failure to comply with ICSID awards, they write, 'would have indirect political consequences in terms of credibility with the World Bank.'[160] The Bank seems to agree, reporting in 1997 that the 'threat of international censure makes countries less likely to reverse course' in terms of international economic policy.[161] ICSID offers a suite of case management support, including a 'case team' comprised of 'an ICSID legal counsel, paralegal, legal assistant and hearings organizer, who assist the parties and the Tribunal throughout the process,' in addition to a 'financial team [which] ... manages the finances of the case.' In addition, a network of translators, technicians, and logistical support is on hand. The Centre offers 'first class hearing facilities' at World Bank offices in Washington, Paris, and other global capitals. Where state parties are signatories to the International Convention on the Settlement of Investment Disputes, ICSID has the advantage of enabling the enforcement of tribunal awards within host state legal space. In other instances, either ICSID's Additional Facility Rules apply (where one of the states is not a party to the Convention) or, alternatively, rules produced in other locales, such as those authored by UNCITRAL, are also available.

ICSID does more than all of these things, however. Its staff assist states in 'formulating' dispute settlement clauses in their model treaties and advise on new legislation to promote inward investment.[162] Its house organ, ICSID Review—Foreign Investment Law Journal, is meant to be the premiere locale for scholarly publications regarding investment arbitration. In 2023, the journal launched its 'Practice Notes' section, meant 'to provide legal practitioners with user-friendly guidance on practical issues related to international arbitration.'[163] Overall, writes Puig, ICSID has 'cemented the promotion of a particular understanding of the role of FDI in national economic development.'[164] It is a particular view of investor rights, one that 'construct[s] a credible narrative around the need for international investment protection.'[165] ICSID contributes, in short, to enlarging the market for investment arbitration from which the professional class of scholars, lawyers, and arbitrators all benefit. In many ways, ICSID's success is their success.

There are a myriad of arbitration facilities around the world available to host both investment and commercial arbitration. They all seek to provide a suite of services seeking to accrue the 'financial benefits' that can be derived 'from the

[159] Puig (2013) at 583.
[160] Reed, Paulsson, and Blackaby (2004) at 9.
[161] World Bank (1997) at 101.
[162] Puig (2013) at 544, 576.
[163] International Centre for the Settlement of Investment Disputes (2023) at 44.
[164] Puig (2013) at 597.
[165] Puig (2013) at 606.

fees they charge and the publicity they gain from involvement' in the cases.[166] These costs are by no means meager. This is a relatively big business.[167] Though there is not a lot of transparency around tribunal-related costs and administrative expenses, Franck advises that facility fees typically amount to about US$ 1 million.[168]

If the World Bank serves as a backstop for the enforcement of ICSID awards, other branches of the Bank offer support that promotes the spread of investment treaty arbitration. The Bank, alongside the International Monetary Fund, touts deregulation and privatization of public enterprise as best bets for successful economic development.[169] Shrinking the state and transferring the delivery of public services to private hands are viewed as more efficient and welfare enhancing.[170] Once privatized, investors require legal safeguards to ensure that reversals are too costly to realize. Offering up expertise in statecraft, the Bank maintains that markets 'cannot develop without effective property rights,' which prevent what it calls 'arbitrary government actions,' including 'unpredictable' or 'ad hoc regulations and taxes . . . that disrupt business activity.' Without the rule of law support for property rights, a 'lawlessness syndrome' results.[171] This support need not only be available within national legal spaces but also without. Having recourse to 'external mechanisms' operates to forestall 'lawlessness,' serving as a 'substitute for limitations on the ability of national institutions to enforce rules or to signal credibly that the rules will remain reasonably stable over time.' The threat of 'extraterritorial adjudication,' the Bank advises, can make it more costly to 'reverse course.'[172] Legal security turns out to be a top priority for business but not for citizens impacted negatively by World Bank structural adjustment programs. 'It all depends on where you stand,' Rittich reminds us.[173]

Other international bureaucracies provide different supports for the spread of investment arbitration. Consider the role played by the United Nations Conference on Trade and Development (UNCTAD), whose mandate is to 'lay the foundations of a better world economic order.'[174] Under the direction of political economist Raul Prebisch, UNCTAD was prepared early on to promote alternative models for economic development, such as import substitution. This pathway gave way to the orthodoxy now promoted by powerful capital-exporting states with UNCTAD in lock step, one that insists upon opening of borders to trade and investment to

[166] Onwuamaegbu (2017) at 313.

[167] ICSID identifies as a non-profit but seeks cost recovery for its services via facility fees.

[168] Franck (2019) at 206. She reports that 'less than 40% of tribunals provided full fiscal details about their own costs and administrative expenses.'

[169] Sarfaty (2012) at 68.

[170] Feigenbaum, Henig, and Hamnett (1999) at 50.

[171] World Bank (1997) at 41. For a discussion of the World Bank's rule of law discourse, see Santos (2006) at 269–77.

[172] World Bank (1997) at 101.

[173] Rittich (2002) at 67.

[174] Finger and Ruchat (2000) at 7.

allow for the free flow of capital unencumbered by state-led models of development. This policy toolkit includes not only privatization but also the adoption of investment treaty commitments. To this end, UNCTAD famously 'facilitated' rounds of signing ceremonies where multiple countries would commit to investor protections by way of treaty. UNCTAD, Poulsen reports, 'promoted the process by bearing the costs of travel, full board, and lodging for developing country officials as well as organizing the necessary facilities and substantive support.'[175] No 'real negotiations' took place—these were offered to poorer countries on a take it or leave it basis.[176]

UNCTAD's role in promoting investment treaty practice throughout the 1990s is fully on display in its annually published World Investment Reports. Their main message, Perrone documents, is to let markets do their work and reduce obstacles to the entry of foreign direct investment.[177] This would be secured by having states 'lock-in' to investment treaty commitments so that they would, per UNCTAD, 'bind themselves with respect to actions and measures that they do not wish to take, with the twin purpose of creating a favorable investment climate that will attract FDI and make it more difficult for such measures to be taken in the future.'[178] While evidence about the alleged benefits of signing investment treaties has failed to materialize, UNCTAD continues to tout their benefits, even as the organization has officially expressed doubt. In its 2015 World Investment Report, UNCTAD reassured its audience that the 'key function' of investment disciplines was to ensure 'predictability, stability, and transparency' and aid in the facilitation of cross-border investment flows. Having recited these benefits, UNCTAD acknowledges that investment treaties might 'bite' as 'they limit the regulatory space' of host states, giving rise to a 'legitimacy crisis.'[179] The task ahead is to ensure that states 'retain their right to regulate for pursuing public policy interests.' But 'policymakers' are warned that this does not provide 'legal cover for investment protection or unjustified discrimination.'[180] Given the 'significant drawbacks' to ISDS in its 'present incarnation,'[181] a suite of treaty and dispute settlement reforms are mapped out by UNCTAD.[182] Even the benefits of 'locking-in' investment treaty commitments were placed in doubt by UNCTAD in 2018, as it could inhibit the introduction of new industrial policy.[183]

[175] Poulsen (2015) at 92.
[176] Poulsen (2015) at 96.
[177] Perrone (2018) at 19.
[178] World Investment Report 1996 at 194, quoted in Perrone (2018) at 20.
[179] UNCTAD (2015a) at 125, 128. A similar account can be provided about UNICTRAL Working Group III tasked with proposing reform to investor–state dispute settlement.
[180] UNCTAD (2015a) at 128.
[181] UNCTAD (2015a) at 154.
[182] UNCTAD (2015b).
[183] UNCTAD (2018) at 163–64.

UNCTAD continues to track changes in national investment policies that liberalize foreign investment policy at national levels, seeming to celebrate (as in its 2015 Report) that the 'share of liberalization and promotion increased significantly.'[184] A less favorable trend was identified in 2018, when it was reported that the 'overall share of restrictive' investment policy measures 'significantly increased' (of 126 measures in 65 states, 18 were more restrictive, and 15 neutral).[185] Restrictive measures rose precipitously during the COVID-19 pandemic, prompted by states wishing to protect critical technology and production facilities, but these have since been restored to pre-pandemic levels. UNCTAD seems gratified by this uptick as it reflects 'recognition by policymakers of the need to stimulate investment and promote economic growth.'[186] Has UNCTAD changed course? Does the organization regret having aggressively promoted investment treaty law and arbitration? Even if the organization has finally acknowledged that there are flaws in the regime's design, the message to states, desperate for new inward investment, continues to be 'if you build it, they will come':[187] sign new and improved treaties and then investment flows will be unleashed.[188]

There is a final element of investment law's infrastructure worthy of mention that helps to thrust its machinery into motion. Third-party funders emerged as financiers of investor–state dispute settlement in the 2010s. As Dafe and Williams explain it, institutional investors were seeking out sources for profit making in the aftermath of the 2008 financial crisis.[189] With few investment opportunities available, returns on litigation could be 'large,' outperforming other investment vehicles reports one of their interviewees.[190]

According to Omni Bridgeway, a third-party financier of investment arbitration, a major advantage of offloading responsibility for the conduct of litigation is that the funder bears all legal costs and, if successful, shares the proceeds of any ISDS victory with the foreign investor. If unsuccessful, costs awards become the funders' responsibility.[191] All of which has the advantage of '[m]oving arbitration

[184] UNCTAD (2015a) at 102.

[185] UNCTAD (2018) at 80.

[186] UNCTAD (2023b) at 58. If private investment is 'crucial to achieve' Sustainable Development Goals (SDGs), as UNCTAD (2015a) at 105 concludes, results to date have been woeful. The annual 'gap' between amounts of investment needed to meet SDGs in developing countries by 2030 has grown to US$4 trillion, as reported in UNCTAD (2023c).

[187] These are words spoken by farmer Ray Kinsella in the film 'Field of Dreams' (1989), originally from W. P. Kinsella (1980) at 39 ('if you build it, he will come').

[188] I do not mean to imply that there is not a myriad of shifting rationales on offer in support of ISDS. Some of these are canvassed in Chapter 5 and others in Schneiderman (2022a). As Zarbiyev (2023) sardonically declares in the title to his article: 'These are my principles. If you don't like them I have others.'

[189] Dafe and Williams (2021) at 1374, referring to ICCA (2018) at 19.

[190] Dafe and Williams (2021) at 1373.

[191] Though recovery of costs awards from third parties has, on occasion, proven to be difficult for winning party states. UNCITRAL Working Group III, for this reason, has discussed proposals to ensure security for costs.

costs off company financial statements.'[192] This is a valuable maneuver, not only for investors in financial straits but also for companies seeking to improve their overall financial position—an increasing audience for litigation finance.[193] For Omni Bridgeway, the principal criteria are:[194]

- Strong prospects of the funded party achieving successful results in the dispute
- Clear ability for the opposing party to pay (enforcement services available from our team)
- Anticipated awards exceeding 10× the requested funding amount for the funded party.

The potential financial rewards for the third-party funder are required to be substantial. This renders the argument that third-party financing enhances 'access to justice' a pretty weak rationale as funding is confined to only the most lucrative claims.

According to Favro of Cleary Gottlieb Steen & Hamilton LLP, the availability of financing 'can even the playing field between David and Goliath by providing the less pecunious Davids with the financial means to pursue meritorious claims against well financed Goliaths.'[195] Omni Bridgeway purports to be doing just this: 'As access to justice is becoming increasingly cost-prohibitive, courts recognize the need for litigation finance ... [b]y relieving these financial pressures, equal justice under the law can be achieved, as legal disputes will truly be decided on the merits.'[196] Singapore, in its submission to UNCITRAL Working Group III, insists that third-party finding 'can promote access to justice,' especially for those 'with more limited resources.'[197] This is not truly their motivation.[198] Funders are not altruistic businesses in search of 'justice' but financiers in search of profits.[199] For this reason, funders increasingly may prefer to finance a portfolio of investment claims, rather than a single case, in order to spread the risk of loss across multiple claimants.[200]

Funders do their 'due diligence' before agreeing to take on an investment claim. This likely will entail obtaining legal advice about the validity of the claim and

[192] Omni Bridgeway (2024). Double-entry bookkeeping, as Weber maintained, ensures predictable business rationality.
[193] Dafe and Williams (2021) at 1372.
[194] Omni Bridgeway (2024).
[195] Favro (2022).
[196] Omni Bridgeway (2024).
[197] UNCITRAL (2023b),
[198] Dafe and Williams (2021) at 1372.
[199] Dafe and Williams (2021) at 1372.
[200] Omni Bridgeway (2024), Dafe and Williams (2021) at 1377, and Stothard (2023) ('Funders are more attracted to, and offer more competitive pricing for, a portfolio of claims by which they can spread their risk over multiple different claims').

prospects for success. The practice varies according to each firm but typically, firms use in-house legal teams or 'engage trusted outside diligence counsel and economic advisors to provide a second opinion about the likelihood of a favorable outcome.'[201] Lawyers, in other words, are intimately involved in the surge of third-party funding in investor–state dispute settlement. Dafe and Williams, for this reason, liken its rise to 'earlier efforts by ... commercial arbitration lawyers and arbitrators, to promote the use of' private dispute resolution.[202] In this fashion, legal advisors can be said to be critical to the growth of third-party funding in investment arbitration, though operating semi-autonomously from the apparatus financing litigation.

While there is 'interdependence' and symbiosis with legal practitioners, investment dispute facilities have amended procedural rules to accommodate this emerging practice. Beginning with the Singapore Investment Arbitration Centre in 2017, most facilities hosting investment arbitration have adopted modest disclosure rules, including in ICSID's recent rules amendments.[203] In addition, new treaty text increasingly incorporates disclosure requirements.[204] For this reason, we can treat the machinery by which investment arbitration is increasingly funded as a part of the environment supporting the spread and maintenance of investment arbitration.

Arbitrators

How well does the characterization of investment arbitrators as *fonctionnaires* hold up? They have evolved from what Dezalay and Garth describe (in their study of commercial arbitration) as a small group of 'grand notables'—who rely upon reputation and feel—to 'technocrats'—masters of process and substance—who market their services to business firms.[205] In this pathbreaking study, Dezalay and Garth describe a transition away from the 'Continental model of legal artisan' to the ascendance of Anglo-American style business law practice.[206] If, early on, arbitrators were discouraged from entering the profession to 'make a living,'[207] they

[201] Omni Bridgeway (2024).

[202] Dafe and Williams (2021) at 1375.

[203] Rule 14. See discussion in Davitti and Vargiu (2023) at 499. UNICITRAL Working Group III is discussing proposals that would allow investment tribunals to 'limit' funding when, for instance, the funder's return is expected to exceed a 'reasonable amount' in UNCITRAL (2023a) at 'Draft Provision 21: Third Party Funding,' s. 6(a) at 10. See UNCITRAL (2019) for a survey of the proposals under discussion.

[204] CETA, Arts. 8.1, 8.26.

[205] Dezalay and Garth (1996) at 36–37. Bourdieu did not write much about 'technocracy' but see Bourdieu (1992) at 214–15 (contrasting the technocracy with 'neucleocracy'—'members of state nobility' who enjoy 'almost unconditional delegation'). Also see Habermas (2015) at 6 (on the 'lure of technocracy' who aspire to 'strengthen' European executive power).

[206] Dezalay and Garth (1996) at 39.

[207] Dezalay and Garth (1996) at 34.

now were encouraged to expand the market for their legal services 'because it is essential for their business.'[208] 'They labor,' admits Paulsson, 'but not for love.'[209]

Among arbitrators' ideal functions will be having a technical grasp of the relevant 'materials'—displaying both the legal expertise and capacity to organize these materials into digestible and coherent narratives—in addition to the managerial skills necessary for administration of both the tribunal's 'internal affairs' and its relationship to the outside world.[210] It is this latter set of managerial skills that seems to have risen in prominence in recent accounts. Schultz and Kovacs document how arbitrators, since Garth and Dezalay's study, have evolved from technocrats to managers.[211] Their survey of fifty-eight lawyers and arbitrators from twenty-three countries reveals that 'management abilities' are among the three most important attributes for appointment.[212] These are cited by some participants as the 'single most important attribute to consider.' Today's arbitrators, one claims, are 'professional dispute managers.'[213] The manager turns out to be one of the three ideal types of arbitral chairpersons identified by Tucker.[214] The manager, he writes, 'runs hearings and deliberations as they were board meetings' and seeks compromise only to the extent necessary to secure a majority.[215] This 'sad indictment' of arbitrators may be 'going too far,' laments Crawford.[216] Yet the 'efficient management' of the case, including 'planning, organizing, and structuring the conduct of the [arbitration] process' is described as being of overriding value to the corporate 'users' of arbitration.[217] Moreno Rodríguez endorses the view that an arbitrator's skill lies in 'procedural fairness, forensic and witness skills, effective case management and, above all else' the production of a 'timely enforceable decision.'[218] Albert Jan van den Berg details the requisite organizational skills at length in his chapter in *The Leading Arbitrators' Guide to International Arbitration*. Among the chief attributes that 'any chairperson' should exhibit, he writes, are 'speed,' 'cost effectiveness,' and the 'rendering of services.'[219] There is no avoiding the fact that

[208] Paulsson quoted in Crawford (2017) at 1012.

[209] Paulsson quoted in Crawford (2017) at 1012.

[210] Eisenstadt (1958) at 114 ('bureaucratic organization is in a constant state of interaction with its environment' at 123).

[211] They have evolved from 'being "oracles dealing in virtue" to being "service providers dealing in efficiency"' in Cole, Ortolani, and Wright (2020) at 924.

[212] Schultz and Kovacs (2012) at 166. Among the management skills mentioned by participants included a 'firm hand,' 'natural authority,' 'ability to run a proceeding,' 'ability to manage the proceedings efficiently and fairly,' and 'balance between flexibility and control' (at 166). Chairpersons of arbitral tribunals were expected to have an 'ability to manage the proceedings,' 'good back-office' skills, 'management capabilities,' and 'administrative experience' (at 169).

[213] Schultz and Kovacs (2012) at 170.

[214] Tucker (2018) at 97–101 identifies social, managerial, and dictatorial chairpersons.

[215] Tucker (2018) at 98, 106, 110.

[216] Crawford (2017) at 1017. He acknowledged that commercial arbitrators were better at managing certain aspects of the proceedings, including cross-examination of quantum experts (at 1018).

[217] Mistelis (2020) at 359, 354.

[218] Quoted in Rodríguez (2023) at 387.

[219] van den Berg (2014) at 417–18.

managerial skills and technocratic style are demanded by those paying fees for arbitral services.

This is expected not only from presiding arbitrators but also from party-appointed tribunal members. They are required to apply 'case management skills' so that they 'work the file,' insist Brekoulakis and Howard.[220] We are 'service providers,' one interviewee reports. Tribunal members are expected to 'do the work' and 'perform promptly.'[221] In the course of their interviews with ninety-six key actors in ISDS, the authors report that a 'hard-working disposition was the internal characteristic most consistently identified' as likely to influence arbitral outcomes.[222]

The task resembles the amassing of dossiers described by Latour in his study of France's *Conseil d'État*.[223] The circulation of gray and dusty files dominates Latour's account of how this apex administrative legal body operates. Absent an ethnographic study such as Latour's, or by an 'observer participant' such as Dominique Schnapper who was appointed to the *Conseil constitutionnel*,[224] we are left to imagine the manner in which tribunals both ruminate and produce their protracted decisions. Any 'inside-the-room' account likely will elide the ongoing and mostly unchecked exercises of authority by international investment tribunals. Sociological accounts of legal decision making distract us from the quandary of control that plagues international courts. An emphasis on technocracy, managerialism, and on the physicality of files conceals the exercise of domination that goes largely unchecked. Responsibility, in the Weberian sense, for investment law outcomes proves to be elusive. Responsibility becomes 'shifting,' even 'free floating.'[225] Investment arbitration is marked by 'organized irresponsibility.'[226] Its institutional 'organization as a whole' is designed as 'an instrument to obliterate responsibility.'[227] Even if formally subordinate to their clienteles, an excessive delegation of authority to tribunals entails surrendering political choices to the logic of markets.[228]

Rising prominently to the surface is the need to justify the supervision of state policy space. This speaks to the role of the arbitrator interacting with the

[220] Brekoulakis and Howard (2023) at 656.
[221] Brekoulakis and Howard (2023) at 656.
[222] Cahill-O'Callaghan, Howard, and Brekoulakis (2023) at 29.
[223] Latour (2010) at 70.
[224] Schnapper (2010).
[225] Bauman (1989) at 162–63.
[226] Beck's term in (1999) at 6, 149 (referring to the 'global market' as an 'institutional form so impersonal as to have no responsibilities, even to itself,' where 'no individual or institution seems to be held specifically accountable for anything'). Decisions about our collective future become 'unimputable,' according to Beck (2009) at 139, 194. Lash explains that by 'organized irresponsibility' Beck refers to a coalition of 'business firms, policy makers and experts who create the dangers of contemporary society and then construct a set of discourses of disavowal of such responsibility,' in Beck, Giddens, and Lash (1994) at 201.
[227] Bauman (1989) at 163 (describing collective authority to perpetrate 'cruel acts').
[228] See discussion in Tortola (2020) at 68–69.

world-at-large. Pauwelyn perhaps specifies what is required of the next generation of investment arbitrators that can rise to this challenge. If what previously was needed was 'technical expertise and experience to fill gaps in domestic court systems' what is now required is 'representativeness, inclusiveness, and trust by governments and other stakeholders so as to justify ISDS' intrusion into domestic legal processes.'[229] In short, what is desired are better legitimating strategies for rule by investment arbitration.[230] At present, this is provided not by investment arbitration institutions themselves but by the 'individual characteristics' of 'repeatedly appointed star arbitrators.'[231] Reliance on 'bureaucratic charisma,' however, seems to be an untested and risky strategy.[232]

What do leading investment arbitrators think will work better? They seem mostly opposed to the establishment of a standing investment tribunal and appellate mechanism that is being promoted by the European Commission. One leading practitioner has likened this departure from party-appointed arbitration to National Socialism.[233] Others admit that the 'processes' of investment arbitration can be improved. Schwebel, for instance, proposes that orders of 'security for costs' be imposed and annulment proceedings available under ICSID be abolished because they are 'time-consuming and expensive.'[234] The UNCITRAL Working Group III, tasked with proposing reforms to ISDS, similarly has prioritized procedural questions over controversies precipitated by the substantive limits posed by investment treaty law and arbitration on policy choices.[235] Modest proposals for change reveal the sort of stinginess that Weber observed when English lawyers opposed reforms that would diminish the market for their services.[236] Investment law professionals, too, can be expected to fight to preserve their privileges.

IV. Conclusion

I have argued in this chapter that, following Weber, we might conjoin judicial functions served by investment arbitration with the rise of bureaucratic expertise that served the spread of capitalism. Weber, on the one hand, applauded the diffusion of formal rationality that accompanied bureaucratic administration. But he

229 Pauwelyn (2015) at 764.
230 Pauwelyn (2015) at 797, 803.
231 Pauwelyn (2015) at 803.
232 A term introduced in Bourdieu (2005) at 132 and inaugurated in Weber (1978) at 219. Zürn, Binder, and Ecker-Ehrardt (2012) at 92–94 suggest that international bodies that issue interpretive rulings require more legitimacy and that this need is heightened when interpretation is combined with binding and enforceable outcomes. The investment law context provides an opportunity to test the cogency of this hypothesis.
233 Born (2021) and, for a reply, Živković (2022).
234 Schwebel (2015) at 10.
235 See Guntrip, Paine, and Titi (2025).
236 Weber (1978) at 788.

also worried about the ways in which technocrats can impede responsible political leadership by employing secrecy, discretion, and juridico-technical obstacles. Checking bureaucratic power was a central preoccupation for Weber, as it is for social scientists exploring the power of international courts today. It turns out that the models on offer—the P-A and trusteeship models—are benign frames that mostly approve of international judicial functions. What is elided is the fact that investment arbitration confronts states and citizens with what Weber labeled 'negative politics.' Outsiders are treated as a 'hostile power' that is 'fobbed off ... with the irreducible minimum of information, ... regarded as a mere hindrance, an assembly of impotent grumblers and know-alls.'[237] It turns out that there are few checks available to states today with which to contain the spread of arbitral authority other than, perhaps, exiting the regime.

We are then confronted with one of the principal questions in the field under study: why do states empower tribunals to rule over them? Why tolerate having tribunals determine the limits to their ability to enact laws and regulations in the public interest? Numerous explanations are offered, including a competition for capital among states desperate for new inward investment.[238] As the promoters of the ICSID Convention promised, joining the regime would help to create an investment climate friendly to foreign investors.[239] But there is another motivation that often goes unmentioned, having to do with surreptitiously limiting state authority to intervene in markets. This is an aspect of the depoliticization story that is often passed over in silence. Typically, depoliticization in the investment context refers to the removal of home states from investment disputes—they are not party to these disputes and, pursuant to the ICSID Convention, are disentitled from playing any role in the dispute once the requisite notice of intent to launch a dispute is filed.[240] The form of depoliticization that gets mostly elided is one that removes instruments from state policy toolkits.[241] The object of entering into investment treaties, according to this narrative, is to tie the hands of future governments. This was the motivation mentioned by an Egyptian government representative in 2005 when entering into negotiations for a free trade and investment agreement with the United States: it would prevent 'anybody in the future from going backwards,' explained the Egyptian finance minister.[242] A similar motivation prompted Polish leadership to commence negotiations that would culminate in a BIT with the United States. This would be the backdoor by which austerity measures could be imposed on Polish citizens.[243] The record suggests that the depoliticization of

[237] Weber (1918b) at 165, 166, 177.

[238] Elkins, Guzman, and Simmons (2006).

[239] Parra (2017) at 11 refers to the signing onto Convention on the Settlement of Investment Disputes Between States and Nationals of Other States, UNTS 575, No. 8359 (1966).

[240] But see Gertz, Jandhyala, and Poulsen (2018) and Schneiderman (2012).

[241] These two conceptions of depoliticization are discussed in Schneiderman (2012).

[242] Alden (2005).

[243] The US trade representative used the opportunity to promote a strict version of intellectual property rights protection. See discussion in St. John (2018) at 222–26.

contestable economic matters is an 'achievement' that gets buried by the rhetorical weight of improved cross-border investment flows.

Is it not a singular feature of democratic regimes to choose to change course? Weber reminds us that bureaucratic power is difficult, if not impossible to reverse. Investment treaty protections, administered by a bureaucratic appsaratus of investment law professionals, help to ensure there is no turning back. The regime offers only a steel-hard casing—an 'iron cage'—with which to contain the conduct of democratic life. It was Weber's task, as it is in our time, to imagine pathways forward out of this dead end.

6
The Façade of Development

Can law contribute to economic development?[1] Many assume that Weber espoused the view that it could.[2] They assume that he embraced the Whig view of history: a history whose direction is preordained and lands 'beautifully upon the present.'[3] The assumption is on display in a handful investment arbitration awards[4] in addition to a range of investment law scholarship. Investment law exemplifies, for Wälde, a 'growing attachment to "law" as a way to manage social relations domestically and disputes between states internationally.' Wälde analogizes the growth of investment arbitration to the 'professionalisation of the conduct by the modern bureaucratic nation state described by Max Weber.'[5] For Potesta, the source of the claim that 'legal certainty and the individuals' capability to foresee the consequences of their actions are prerequisites for rational enterprise in a capitalist economy no doubt is found in the work of the eminent scholar Max Weber.'[6] To similar effect, Salacuse attributes to Weber the insight that 'predictability ... facilitate[es] the kinds of long-term economic transactions necessary for productive investment.'[7]

We can fairly assume that these authors, toiling in this sub-field of public international law, do not self-identify as specialists in law and development. Yet the

[1] The kind of economic development envisaged by investment law proponents is that which has already been achieved by developed states. See Escobar (1995) at 83. Economic success requires mimicking mythical paths to development associated with the 'Washington consensus': privatization, deregulation, disciplining labor, market rates for utilities, etc. On the mythical nature of this path, see Chang (2002) at 127. It requires the kind of belt tightening that has historically been attached to IMF lending, as discussed in Schneiderman (2022a) at 106–11. Such planning contemplates, first, the denationalization of economic policy and, second, the concentration of oversight in supranational machinery, as discussed in Streeck (2024) at 44–47. Development, explains Dann (2023) at 36–37, 'is a standard mostly formulated by the West and to be achieved by the non-West.'

[2] Scholars like Dam (2006) at 3 and Golub (2006) at 110 refer to Weber as prompting causal connections between the rule of law and economic development. These authors associate themselves with as an 'internal' point of view to development, which emphasizes 'values, attitudes and motives' in 'isolation from any [external] global economic context' (see Turner [1981] at 236). This turns out to be a misreading of Weber as, according to Turner, he 'treats the problem of capitalist development as simultaneously a matter of internal social structures within the context of external restraints and opportunities' (Turner [1981] at 248–49).

[3] See Butterfield (1965) at 12. But see Butterfield (1981) at 215 (God, rather than progress, guides the hand of history).

[4] For example, Suez (2010) at para. 222, discussed in the Introduction. This was cited with approval in 'Dissenting Opinion of Mr. Gary Born' in Antaris (2018) at para. 32, fn. 46, p. 12.

[5] Wälde (2006) at 455.

[6] Potestà (2013) at 94 and fn. 30.

[7] Salacuse (2000) at 399.

A Sociology of International Investment Law. David Schneiderman, Oxford University Press.
 DOI: 10.1093/9780198982739.003.0007

causal claims that they make have affinities with the first 'movement' of law and development studies. Housed primarily in US law schools, these scholars shared presuppositions about the benefits associated with importing 'liberal legalism.' Legal innovation that mimicked the rules and institutions in the Global North, write Trubek and Galanter, were expected to promote 'rational, instrumental action' that secured 'greater material well-being and other developmental goals.'[8] Among the instrumentalities for achieving these ends was not only improving local law and the administration of justice but cultivating the legal profession and enhancing legal education.[9] In other words, 'rule of law' reforms would improve local legal conditions. The operating assumption of this band of 'legal optimists'[10] was that legal reform 'would change behaviour.'[11] It is only sometime later, after funding for law and development projects was exhausted, Trubek and Galanter confess, were these assumptions acknowledged to be 'naïve' and premised on 'ethnocentric' thinking. The 'cumulative weight of the evidence contradicting all aspects of the model has been too great to resist.'[12] The project was as good as a failure.[13]

The motivation for the spread of investment treaty arbitration is not, however, traceable to law and development. Its origins lie in an earlier movement, spurred on by lawyers and legal academics, to install private arbitration as a mechanism for resolving disputes between foreign nationals, who make their home in 'civilized' states and states serving as host to their economic activities.[14] St. John's account of the birth of the International Convention on the Settlement of Investment Disputes (ICSID) makes clear that these lawyer activists were critical to the spread of investment law's norms. Rather than placing responsibility at the foot of the legal profession, she prefers to characterize these players as 'international' or 'expert officials.'[15] These officials all shared a belief 'in the power of law.'[16] It is no coincidence that the 'defining trait' of officials who populated four consultative conferences establishing ICSID was 'legal training.'[17] Counsel for corporate interests, in particular, were

[8] Trubek and Galanter (1974) at 1074. Legal rule, they write, 'implied impersonal governance through universal rules,' resulting in more 'equal treatment of all citizens,' and the curbing of 'arbitrary government.'

[9] Trubek and Galanter (1974) at 1075.

[10] Davis and Trebilcock (2008) at 898ff.

[11] Trubek and Galanter (1974) at 1079.

[12] Trubek and Galanter (1974) at 1089. Trubek (2016) at 307, fn. 15 later would complain that Weber's idea of an elective affinity between 'law and historic capitalist accumulation … were insufficient' for this twentieth century movement.

[13] Davis and Trebilcock (2008) at 915.

[14] Coates (2016).

[15] St. John (2018) at 3, 199. They are the opposite of what Desai (2023) at 15 describes as 'ignorant experts,' those 'whose expertise is explicitly the inverse of authoritative and knowledgeable.' They instead exhibit confidence in an ability to foretell the future as a consequence of proposed legal reforms.

[16] St. John (2018) at 4 (a key figure was General Counsel to the World Bank and first ICSID Secretary General, Aaron Broches).

[17] St. John (2018) at 137.

a driving force behind the spread of the resolution of disputes via international arbitration. Perrone, for instance, emphasizes the role that industry lawyers, in addition to bankers and industrialists, played in the spread of investment treaty arbitration. The impetus was to enhance profitability and reduce 'excessive governmental influence' in host states.[18] Departments of foreign affairs within developed states, in addition to institutions within the World Bank, the United Nations, professional bar associations, and law firms, eagerly promoted investment treaty disciplines. It is apparent that, at its origins, the regime was intended to remove local law and institutions from the resolution of disputes and to hold states fast to their commitments to foreign investors.[19] This was not a regime that emerged spontaneously,[20] but one that was constructed 'very much by design, and with plenty of self-awareness.'[21]

The important distinction to be made, then, between the first movement in law and development and investment law's origins is that, in the former, states were the target for legal reform while, in the latter, national legal reform was abandoned in favor of utilizing international law as a disciplinary stick. This would be the aim even as states remained critical agents in the construction of a regime organized around binding treaty commitments. Rather than 'improving the rule of law *within* particular states,' as Kleinfeld puts it, the rule of law is deployed to achieve 'security for *other* states.'[22]

This chapter returns to a question that Weber did not precisely ask: can ideal typical formally rational law contribute to economic development? Even if there is much in Weber's account that lends support to investment law's suppositions, it is mistaken to expect legal reforms to trigger investment for economic development. Even if it is tempting to read Weber as mapping a pathway for development that others simply can mimic—like W. W. Rostow's rocket-like trajectory to economic success[23]—this constitutes an unfortunate misreading.[24] Weber's conclusions are more cautious and tentative. Only detailed historical studies could explain patterns of development arising out of unique locales. There are no universal pathways to development to be prescribed.[25] Indeed, it would be

[18] Perrone (2021) at 61–63.
[19] Boue (2022) at 9, 33.
[20] A claim made by Pauwelyn (2014) at 3–4 (a 'spontaneous order emerging from decentralized interactions').
[21] Boue (2022) at 39.
[22] Kleinfeld (2006) at 57 (emphasis in original).
[23] Rostow (1960). On Rostovian modernization theory see Thomas (2008) at 66–78.
[24] Bruun (2007) at 236 describes Weber's thesis as having 'wearisomely often been discussed as if he claimed the existence of an actual *relation of cause and effect* between two sections of historical reality in their entirety.'
[25] Modernity is not the 'result of a *project*,' explains Tribe (2005) at 151 (emphasis in original). Instead, Weber saw modernity 'as a contingent result of multiple processes … but it is the simple story of this "singular outcome" that sells.'

irresponsible for social scientists to so claim.[26] '[I]t can never be the task of a science of empirical experience to determine binding norms and ideals from which practical prescriptions may then be deduced,' Weber declares.[27] Economic stages of development made little sense other than as ideal types—as heuristics 'where their character as ideal theoretical constructs should be carefully maintained' and not 'confused with history.'[28] By contrast, investment law professionals are too quick to inflate their ideal—for instance, promoting the rule of law by signing investment treaties—with the real. They should instead be more tentative and careful about the expected benefits arising out of investment treaty commitments. They should be more forthright about the ethical stance that determines the object and purpose of investment treaty disciplines: to vindicate the economic interests of foreign investors.[29]

Weber envisages law as a field that is autonomous from, though intimately connected to, the economy, a discussion that gets taken up in the first part of the chapter. I subsequently ask whether investment law exhibits anti-formalist tendencies that undermine its capacity to contribute to economic improvement. Further along, Weber's methods are conscripted to interrogate investment law's suppositions that it contributes toward economic development. Finally, in the last part, Weber's liberal economic nationalism is interrogated. Do his early positions on agricultural production in East Elbia, support for imperialist endeavors abroad, and proposals for stock exchange reform belie his probabilistic stance as regards the relation between law and economic development?[30] Reluctant to offer up policy prescriptions, we learn from these episodes that Weber was incited by an irrepressible German nationalism. The chapter concludes with a reflection on how investment law professionals fail to hedge what reasonably is secured by the regime's disciplines. At most, they are directed at protecting foreign investors and not at ameliorating economic conditions in the poorest parts of the world.

[26] On an 'abstract level,' writes Collins (1980) at 935, 'Weber is at least implicitly proposing such a theory' of economic development. It is this implicit reading that has led many, including investment law professionals, astray.

[27] Weber (1904a) at 101–02.

[28] Weber (1904a) at 135 and Swedberg (1998) at 45–46. In a handwritten note, Weber warns that use of the term 'development' is to select from the 'chaos of causal interconnections' that which is 'significant and important … It is not some hidden agent behind the course of history' in Bruun and Whimster (2012) at 416.

[29] As I argue in the Conclusion, they must stop enchanting vulnerable populations with false promises of economic development. On disenchantment by means of calculation, see Weber (1946b) at 139 and Weber (1915b) at 238–39. Investment law professionals should also be more modest about the production of legal outcomes. Despite incorporating one-sided legal guarantees, intended to provide comfort to investors, the regime has produced high degrees of inconsistency and unpredictability (see discussion infra in text associated with notes 88–111).

[30] Freund (1968) at 75 and Strand and Lizardo (2022), associated with Weber's key word 'chance,' discussed in text associated with notes 132–37, below. On the continuities between his early research output and later contributions see Hennis (1987) at 63, 69, 71. Also see Coutu (2024).

I. Autonomy

Weber took care to create distance between legal and economic developments. Rather than being merely epiphenomenal of markets and serving only the interests of market actors, as Marx insisted,[31] Weber sought to carve out space for the autonomous development of law that was not designed merely to serve economic interests. He appreciated, nevertheless, that there was much to be gained by scrutinizing the 'socialist critique of bourgeois society.'[32] Weber was therefore preoccupied with offering a non-materialist account of society while acknowledging the utility of Marx's heuristic as an ideal type.[33] That view is summarized in his methodological essay of 1904:[34]

> While we have abandoned the outworn belief according to which the totality of cultural phenomena can be *deduced* as a product or a function of "material" constellation of interests, we for our part still believe that the *analysis of social phenomena and cultural processes*, from the particular perspective of their *economic* conditionality and implications, has been a creative fruitful scientific principle, and will continue to be so in the foreseeable future, provided it is applied carefully and without dogmatic prejudice.

Even if 'expressed crudely, but with genius' in *The Communist Manifesto*,[35] holistic or single causal explanations of historical events are eschewed in favor of more 'finite' inquiries.[36] This is how Weber conceptualizes the contribution that he made in *The Protestant Ethic and the Spirit of Capitalism*. That work revealed how religious beliefs significantly shaped the 'character' and 'organization of life.' It was not offered as a 'one-sided spiritualistic analysis of the causes of culture and history in place of an equally one-sided "materialistic" analysis.'[37] This is not how 'historical truth' can be represented, Weber maintains. Rather than claiming 'to be the conclusion of an investigation' it was, instead, laying down a "preparatory stage".'[38]

[31] Marx (1883) at 251 ('first there is *commerce*, and then a *legal order* develops out of it').

[32] Mommsen (1985) at 234.

[33] Weber (1904a) at 132. Hence, Weber (1915c) at 280, declared '[n]ot ideas, but material and ideal interests, directly govern men's conduct.' See also Weber (1915a) at 69.

[34] Weber (1904a) at 111 (emphasis in original).

[35] Weber (1918a) at 286–87 describes the Communist Manifesto as a 'scholarly achievement of the highest order' having 'fruitful effects on scholarship, more so than many a work of uninspired correctness.' Weber had both 'reservations about' and 'respect for' Marx, observes Abrams (1982) at 79.

[36] Weber (1904a) at 111, 114.

[37] Weber (1920c) at 159 ('Both,' he writes, are 'equally possible'). Elsewhere, he describes the Protestant ethic essays as investigating 'only one side of the causal relationship' in Weber (1920a) at 217. Earlier, in his reply to Stammler, Weber (1907) at 188 bemoans 'one-sided perspectives,' described as the 'hopeless attempt to present historical formations as being solely determined and qualified by one single component.'

[38] Weber (1920c) at 159. Abrams (1982) at 77 insists that this passage 'commands attention' as it overcomes one-sidedness by using a 'deliberately one-sided method of research.'

We might understand Weber's legal sociology as having similar purposes in mind: closely analyzing the rise of legal rationality in specific locales for the purpose of isolating its determinants. These might include, though not exclusively, material interests. Weber's method is, therefore, agnostic about whether the law serves economic interests. Answers will only be found in detailed studies. His method represents a 'scientific open-mindedness,' writes Löwith, 'especially *vis-à-vis* one's own prejudices, [which] characterizes for Weber the ethos of theory.'[39] For Jaspers, Weber was open to the 'acquisition of all accessible viewpoints for every reality,' serving to advance only the interests of 'impartial knowledge.'[40] As discussed below, though Weber claims a sphere of autonomy for legal development, he was compelled to acknowledge that its growth served even material interests, particularly powerful economic ones.[41] This admission reveals the ongoing two-sidedness of Weber that is often characterized as signaling ambivalence or oscillation.[42] It can also be characterized as evidence of Weber's unrelenting insistence on being open to myriad explanations for any particular social phenomena.

How, then, to explain, the spread of his ideal type of formally rational law? Its rise was a consequence, Weber explains, 'of the intrinsic intellectual needs of the legal theorists and their disciples, i.e., of a typical aristocracy of legal literati.'[43] These 'legal *honoratiores*' were comprised of 'university trained' judges, notaries and advocates.[44] The 'practical needs' of business for calculable law 'did not play any considerable role in this particular process,' Weber insists.[45] Describing the influence of Roman legal thought, the rise to prominence of formally rational law reflected a desire to construct 'abstract legal concepts' that served essentially theoretical interests rather than practical requirements' leading to, Weber writes, the 'results which we have before us now.'[46] Market forces had only an 'indirect influence' on legal developments—'they have nowhere been decisive alone and by themselves.'[47] If economic needs played a modest role in legal development, the influence of law on markets was much greater. Lawmaking (legislation) in the service of 'political factors' have exercised an even 'strong[er] influence' on markets.[48]

[39] Löwith (1982) at 33.
[40] Jaspers (1989) at 95.
[41] For such reasons, writes Lechner (2023) at 329, 'law becomes an institutional incubator of or support system for economic change.'
[42] Geertz (1983) at 121 describes this as Weber's 'chronic elusiveness' that was offset by 'his extraordinary ability to hold together warring ideas.'
[43] Weber (1978) at 855. 'Literati' was a term Weber used derisively.
[44] Weber (1978) at 855. 'Honoratiores' is an archaic term Weber used to describe law created by 'cautelary jurisprudence and adherence to precedent' (at 882).
[45] Weber (1978) at 855.
[46] Weber (1978) at 799.
[47] Weber (1978) at 883. Weber 'objected to' the 'law-as superstructure' paradigm advanced in Marxian accounts, in Mommsen (1977) at 378. It was this which he 'objected most strongly to' in Mommsen (2021) at 46. Yet Weber could be found using the term 'superstructure' in publications on the collapse of ancient Rome. See Weber (1896a) at 78, 86.
[48] Weber (1978) at 655.

Indeed, new legal forms need to get 'invented' before they can serve economic needs.[49]

Despite his insistence on the law's autonomy, Weber is also compelled to acknowledge the influence of the economy on legal development.[50] Much of what passes for formally rational law in the west functions in the service of markets, Weber concedes. 'Obviously,' he writes, 'legal guaranties are directly at the service of economic interests' and where this does not seem to be the case, 'economic interests are among the strongest factors influencing the creation of law.'[51] It remains the case, however, that markets need law more than law needs markets. The 'tempo of modern business communication requires a promptly and predictably functioning legal system, i.e., one which is guaranteed by the strongest coercive power' available.[52] Economic exchange relies 'overwhelmingly' on the 'threat of legal coercion' to ensure that 'legitimately acquired rights' are honored.[53] This guarantees the stability and predictability that markets need to thrive.[54]

These tendencies get reinforced by the legal profession's conservatism. Weber stipulates that lawyers 'remain cool to substantive postulates' emanating from 'below' ('in the name of the social').[55] Despite the potential for equanimity, 'the legal profession of the present day,' Weber observes, is more likely to side with those holding power. The 'typical ideological affinities' of 'its members are inclined to stand on the side of "order."' In practice, this 'means that they will take the side of the "legitimate" authoritarian political power that happens to predominate at the given moment.'[56] This is hardly a recipe for lawyers leading the charge for social change.

Investment law's promoters presuppose that, in so far as laws are predictable then legal forms can aid in the service of economic development. What of legal systems that are not so predictable or in which substantive values predominate? Here, Weber's discussion of the England 'problem' reveals that law can encourage economic development without exhibiting features associated with Weber's ideal typical model.[57] The English common law did not mimic the Continent's

[49] Weber (1978) at 687. See also Weber (1978) at 720 ('the development of the legal structure of organizations has by no means been predominantly determined by economic factors'). See discussion in Reisebrodt (1989) at 141 (legal changes create the 'preconditions for economic change').

[50] This ambivalence, Kronman (1983) at 125 observes, results in Weber making as 'many different claims about the influence of law on economic life ... that one could conceivably make.' Compare this observation with the characterization of Weber's earlier agrarian studies, in Reisebrodt (1986) at 154, as displaying an 'ability to integrate seemingly incompatible perspectives.'

[51] Weber (1978) at 334.

[52] Weber (1978) at 337.

[53] Weber (1978) at 329 (italics omitted) and 334.

[54] Weber (1978) at 337.

[55] Weber (1978) at 875. Weber adds, as well as from 'above ... in the name of patriarchal power or welfare policies.' For a discussion of the 'independent power position' of lawyers, preserving the law from 'either proletarian demands for social justice or patriarchal welfare-statism,' see Albrow (1975) at 24.

[56] Weber (1978) at 876.

[57] As discussed in Chapter 1. On Weber's England problem, see Trubek (1972a) at 746–48.

legal trajectory, Weber acknowledges. Rather than encouraging a logical and gapless system independent of substantive values, English law relies on case-by-case determinations of legal questions that are not necessarily logical or systematic. Even if exhibiting formal characteristics—in its rigid system of pleadings, for instance[58]—the common law is 'bound by precedent and analogies to precedent.'[59] No rational system of law can emerge under the influence of the 'craftlike specialization' of lawyers aiming at a 'practically useful scheme of contracts and actions, oriented towards the interests of clients in typically recurrent situations.'[60] This is what Weber calls, following Roman law, 'cautelary jurisprudence.'[61] However, proximity to the needs of their clientele assists in adjusting the common law to commercial expectations.[62] Rather than promoting abstract thinking and a 'blind desire for logical consistency,' the English common law adapted and conformed to the needs of the profession's patrons.[63] It did not even 'avoid (in certain cases) the ethical consideration of economic events.'[64] As Waddams admits, '[m]any extra-legal considerations have been influential' in the evolution of the common law of contract, but no single influence of an ethical, religious, or philosophical kind has been predominant.[65] Consequently, for Weber capitalism succeeded in England despite presumed deficiencies by producing a sufficiently predictable, if adaptable, legal 'framework for entrepreneurial activity.' So long as legal rules are 'framed and interpreted in a fashion that is consistent' with businessmen's extra-juristic expectations, then the law can successfully secure the needs of commercial interests.[66] Weber could then issue the verdict 'that England achieved capitalistic supremacy among the nations not because but rather in spite of its judicial system.'[67]

II. Causality?

The dominant view was that there is a correlation between signing treaties and attracting inward investment. Investment lawyers, arbitrators, and scholars were perennial believers in legal discipline having a 'significant causal role' in economic development.[68] If representatives of some capital-exporting states were careful

[58] Maitland (1913).
[59] Weber (1978) at 787.
[60] Weber (1978) at 787. According to Weber (1978)at 788, the self-interest of English lawyers also played a role. They resisted the introduction of 'a systematic and rational type of lawmaking and a rational legal education, such as exists in the Continental universities.'
[61] Weber (1978) at 787.
[62] Kronman (1983) at 121.
[63] Weber (1978) at 789.
[64] Weber (1895b) at 244.
[65] Waddams (2011) at 221. But see Atiyah (1979) at 388*ff* (formalism played a 'vital part' in development of the English law of contract from 1770–1878).
[66] Kronman (1983) at 122.
[67] Weber (1978) at 814.
[68] Davis and Trebilcock (2008) at 896 (they are 'legal optimists').

not to promise capital improvements, others were not so cautious. The United Nations Conference on Trade and Development (UNCTAD), for instance, kept indicating throughout the 1990s that if you signed Bilateral Investment Treaties (BITs), you would get more foreign direct investment (FDI). British diplomatic missions delivered letters intended to kickstart negotiations by sending the message that signing a BIT with the United Kingdom 'would encourage further substantial investment.' Yet, behind the scenes, Poulsen reports, the British Foreign and Commonwealth Office admitted that, if a BIT was 'very much in our interests, it might not serve the interests of developing countries very well.'[69] This was not the message that was sent to capital-importing states, however. It was, instead, that hoped-for economic improvements would be forthcoming if only states, desperate for capital, signed onto the investment treaty regime. This belief, unsubstantiated by empirical evidence, still resurfaces occasionally, even long after the data suggests otherwise.

Recent meta-studies confirm that the promised deluge of investment never arrived. According to one such summation, the 'fragility of this statistical relationship cautions observers against taking an overly optimistic view.'[70] Another analysis offers up the damning conclusion that treaty effects are 'economically negligible.'[71] In a study of twelve Central and Eastern European states, the authors conclude that BITs do not attract 'development-enhancing FDI.'[72] Their analysis challenges 'the idea that BITs are a desirable policy tool to enhance development.'[73] An apparent consensus has taken hold, that treaties have, at best, a marginal effect in attracting investment required for development. Yet, the myth continues to be proffered with indefensible insouciance. Hippolyte, for instance, prefers to characterize developing states' rebellious attitude toward foreign investment protection as 'tantamount to fiscal suicide.' Should they fall into line and embrace investment disciplines, they 'stand to benefit significantly from the foreign investment regime' he confidently announces.[74] Senior arbitrator Brower employs similar hyperbole in a recent memoir: exiting the regime for investor protection is 'tantamount to economic suicide,' he declares.[75] Without the security and stability that investment treaties are presumed to provide, investors will be disinclined 'to invest in the poorest countries that need these inflows the most.'[76] Yet, as Fauchauld observes, investment agreements do not generate flows of FDI to those who need it most.[77] One of the leading texts in the field, now in its third edition, embraces this same

[69] Poulsen (2015) at 68.
[70] Summarizing the social science evidence in Bauerle Danzman (2019) at 26, also Pohl (2018).
[71] Bellak (2015) at 19.
[72] Colen and Guariso (2013) at 156.
[73] Colen and Guariso (2013) at 156.
[74] Hippolyte (2019) at 73, 75.
[75] Brower (2023) at 251.
[76] Brower (2023).
[77] Fauchauld (2021) 192.

viewpoint, even as the authors hedge their bet. By signing onto investment treaty obligations, a host state, they write, 'deliberately renounces an element of its sovereignty in return for a new opportunity: the chance to improve its attractiveness for new foreign investments *which it would not be able to acquire in the absence of a treaty*.'[78]

As the weak evidence revealing little meaningful correlation between signing investment treaties and improving economic development began piling up, the ground underneath shifted. There emerged a new rationale offered up in support of the spread and maintenance of the investment treaty system. One that rose to prominence (already mentioned in the Introduction) was 'good governance.' A new correlation was assumed, that between signing treaties and internalizing investment disciplines, so that host states would begin to govern in accordance with the rules laid down in investment treaties framed by powerful capital-exporting states.[79] Wälde, who was skeptical about the utility of BITs in attracting foreign investment, reached for this rationale in the early 2000s.[80] The regime was a civilizing machine, he maintained, creating 'proto-constitutional rules for the global economy.' The countries that resist pressures to internalize these rules, he wrote with Weiler, behave as '"minors" without full legal capacity.'[81] Schill expanded upon the argument by focusing upon obligations imposed by fair and equitable treatment (FET). These strictures were expected to improve host state governance so that they would resemble capital-exporting state behavior. They could now be expected to respect the 'rule of law' including its associated features of stability and predictability, due process, transparency, and legitimate expectations. He even had recourse to the discredited argument that ISDS 'reduces risk ... necessary to attract foreign investment.'[82]

No empirical evidence was produced to support this shifting justificatory ground. Sattorova punctured the illusion by evaluating the relationship between investment law and features of good governance, undertaking fifty-four interviews with officials from five different developing countries. She revealed that states have not responded to investment disputes, actual or threatened, by internalizing good governance norms.[83] Instead, she concluded that there is little awareness

[78] Dolzer, Kriebaum, and Schreuer (2022) at 26 (emphasis added). This is a 'policy judgment,' they add, 'the nature of which escapes precise evaluation.' They admit that 'legal stability [and predictability] ... will be one of several factors in the decision to make a new investment but will not by itself serve as the decisive incentive for potential foreign investors' (Dolzer, Kriebaum, and Schreuer 2022 at 29–30).

[79] Alschner (2022). Not only do developed states get to have their preferences embodied within treaty text, it turns out that these BITs are less likely to be terminated by developed signatory states. See Jones and Rao (2022) at 284.

[80] For example, in Wälde and Dow (2000).

[81] Wälde and Weiler (2002) at 163.

[82] Schill (2010) at 180–81. Živković (2023) at 188–89 argues that FET aligns with the object and purpose of investment treaties, which is to protect investors and improve the domestic rule of law, the latter which 'should encourage economic development,' the 'ultimate objective of investment treaties.'

[83] Sattorova (2018).

of investment disputes across branches of government, beyond small cadres of officials. Where there is some knowledge, there is no felt need to revise laws or practices. The relationship between investment law and good governance, she reports, turned out to be mostly a rhetorical one.

Her findings have prompted a number of follow-up studies. Ostřanský and Perez Aznar indicate that, in India, actors do not necessarily internalize investment law disciplines so as to avoid liability. Instead, these coauthors report that BITs are used strategically within government to advance the agenda of particular officials.[84] Similarly, Bonnitcha advises that the effects of BITs on domestic governance in Myanmar are mediated mostly through the executive branch, are ad hoc and limited, having 'no discernible impact on the judicial system' and 'little impact on legislation or regulatory rule-making processes.'[85] Atanasova's study of Singapore similarly reveals no support for the good governance hypothesis. She warns that the causal links remain unclear and ambiguous, concluding that there is little evidence of any relationship between investment treaties and the rule of law.[86] This is not to say that some countries have not adopted processes to ensure compliance with investment treaty commitments,[87] only that it is not a widespread phenomenon.

III. Certainty?

As I have suggested in Chapter 1, investment law can reasonably be characterized as antiformal. The jurisprudence emerging out of investment law treaty and arbitration does not resemble codified Continental legal systems but, instead, exhibits characteristics familiar to the English common law. This renders investment law less calculable and predictable than is ordinarily assumed, despite claims by investment law professionals that the regime exhibits these very features. Indeed, one could say that the system of investment treaty law and arbitration renders the regime not only an unstable means of promoting economic development but a costly and protracted system for the administration of justice for foreign investors.[88]

The regime was not initially expected to be so unpredictable. Dezalay and Garth describe a struggle between the 'grand old men,' lawyers making Europe their home who championed the flexible, fluid, and academic 'law merchant' (*lex mercatoria*) in matters of commercial arbitration, and the 'young technocrats' who promoted US-style litigation techniques. Rather than offering answers to legal disputes by what 'feels right,' US practice emphasizes 'sufficient security and predictability.'[89]

[84] Ostřanský and Pérez Aznar (2021).
[85] Bonnitcha (2022) at 130.
[86] Atanasova (2022).
[87] For example, in Canada, see Van Harten and Scott (2016).
[88] Hodgson, Kryvoi, and Hrcka (2021).
[89] Dezalay and Garth (1996) at 38–39.

This was a battle won by large American law firms, a victory that would migrate from commercial to investment arbitration. The problem was that laconic treaty standards, which investment lawyers and arbitrators were asked to interpret, provided little in the way of certainty or predictability. Writing about the now ubiquitous treaty standard of FET, F. A. Mann, for instance, described this protection as 'very familiar' but 'hardly ever judicially considered.'[90] Its content could only be filled out later, once investment arbitrators began doing their interpretive work.[91] Even now, the standard, as construed, is so expansive and unwieldy a weapon that investors can, without much effort, impugn most state behavior.[92]

Yet, legal certainty is alleged to be the impetus—the 'central concern'—for the rise of investment treaty arbitration.[93] Economic development would be the hoped-for by-product. Host state courts are considered suspect—regarded as biased and 'politicized'—and so removal of investment disputes to international arbitration is considered the best means of ensuring 'neutrality and predictability.'[94] The International Convention for the Settlement of Investment Disputes, conjoined with a compendium of precise procedural rules, would provide a locus for the resolution of disputes. But what about the standards of treatment, that protect investors, themselves? The decentralized, revolving, and ad hoc nature of investment treaty arbitration—tribunals are disbanded after resolving claims—hardly addresses consistency concerns. Though there is occasional stability,[95] securing some of the legal certainty associated with the 'rule of law' through the rise of influential precedent (*jurisprudence constante*),[96] it is sufficiently serious a problem that United Nations Commission on International Trade Law (UNCITRAL) Working Group III, tasked with proposing reforms to ISDS, included among its priority agenda items a focus on 'consistency, coherence, [and] predictability.'[97] Academics affiliated with the UNCITRAL process conclude that inconsistency in 'standards'—such as the investment treaty standard of protection of FET—is less problematic than inconsistency in the application of rules—such as whether breach of contract gives rise to tribunal jurisdiction under international treaty.[98] Inconsistency has its benefits, the authors argue, by allowing for 'course corrections or progressive development of the law.'[99] Therefore, even though the system is

[90] Mann (1981) at 243.

[91] As Bachand and Gélinas (2020) at 391 admit, when the regime began to grow in the mid-1990s, it 'could hardly have been described as a fully developed body of substantive law.'

[92] Ostřanský (2023).

[93] Bachand and Gélinas (2020) at 387.

[94] Bachand and Gélinas (2020) at 387, 392.

[95] But see Ortino (2012).

[96] For an early statement, see Bjorklund (2008). There is by now a large literature on the subject.

[97] UNCITRAL (2018).

[98] See Arato, Brown, and Ortino (2020), building upon the thesis advanced in Ortino (2013). FET is described in Živković (2023) as 'the most important single standard of investment protection. The argument about tolerable inconsistency is filled out in Arato (2023).

[99] The authors cite Fuller (1969a) for this proposition but offer a very partial reading of *The Morality of Law*. Fuller, instead, identifies 'constancy' as an element of the internal morality of the law. Even if

'riven with inconsistent interpretation' and, FET in particular, with a 'troubling degree of inconsistency,' that degree of unpredictability is tolerable.[100] The extremely varied ways in which standards of treatment are interpreted is the product of a 'design choice,' they argue: 'A degree of inconsistency is in the nature of standards of this kind, and is indeed the trade-off for a degree of flexibility which, over the long term, may be desirable.'[101] The same does not hold true, these scholars say, for threshold rules that lay down alternative paths available for the adjudication of disputes. That degree of unpredictability, they argue, is intolerable.[102] Yet rules-based predictability and consistency in remedial avenues can be, and have been, addressed via investment treaty reform. No such treaty reform is recommended by these authors in respect of vague and unpredictable standards of treatment.[103] Academics advising the UNCITRAL process therefore see no need to ensure any more predictability as regards protections for foreign investors. Instead, it suffices that investment law is adopting something like common law methods though, arguably, it is still far from having achieved even this level of predictability.[104] There is no likelihood of a code of investment law emerging. Only 'soft codification' will arise via what Bjorklund and Reinisch characterize as the 'coherent interpretation of investment law instruments by investment tribunals.' This turns out to be nothing more than an expression of satisfaction with the status quo.[105]

Despite its shortcomings as a formally logical system, has investment law achieved the kind of predictability for investors that is associated with the common law tradition? The empirical evidence does not precisely answer this question, but there are suggestions that investment law fails according to a number of indicators. States and investors evenly win investment disputes,[106] but settlements (often requiring the payment of compensation to investors in amounts that are similar

he offers a non-absolutist formulation (deviations are permitted in the extreme case), he sees 'close affinities' between the problem of 'too frequent changes in the law' and retrospective legislation (another feature of law's inner morality) (at 80). Fuller is concerned with granting to subjects of law 'fair notice' about changes to it, per Sebok (2010) at 194.

[100] Arato, Brown, and Ortino (2020) at 342, 351. Behn, Langford, and Létourneau-Tremblay (2020) at 223, however, describe it as 'unjustified inconsistency.'

[101] Arato, Brown, and Ortino (2020) at 356.

[102] Compare this conclusion with the results of public opinion questionnaires in Marceddu and Ortolani (2020) at 426 who report that criticism amongst non-specialists was leveled not at 'the procedures whereby investor–state disputes are resolved but, rather, by the very nature of the substantive rights that international investment law confers upon investors.'

[103] Arato, Brown, and Ortino (2020) discuss a multilateral investment court (MIC) and appellate tribunal proposal (both advanced by the European Union either at UNCITRAL or in new treaties) as a means of addressing this problem (at 371). Abandoning ISDS is not recommended (it is 'complex and unpredictable') as it would remove disputes to local courts (at 372). On why a MIC may not solve the problem of predictability, see Yu (2022).

[104] Bjorklund and Reinisch (2012) at 311.

[105] Bjorklund and Reinisch (2012) at 318. They declare the 'end of the classical codification period' which has been replaced by soft law instruments: 'guidelines, draft articles or other softer forms of codification' (at 306).

[106] Behn, Langford, and Létourneau-Tremblay (2020) at 193.

to those awarded by investment tribunals) tilt outcomes in favor of investors.[107] The lengthy duration of and enormous costs associated with investment disputes, admittedly concerning complex litigation, also seem out of proportion compared to national judicial systems. Investor–state dispute settlement has been described as the 'Wild, Wild West.' Though it has the 'trappings of a legal system ... there really are no hard and fast rules,' according to investment lawyer George Kahale III.[108] If predictability is an appropriate yardstick for measuring systems of law, investment arbitration seems to fall short. Even assuming that ISDS—a mode of individualized decision making tailored to fit the dispute at hand—is a sound way to resolve disputes between states and foreign investors, Schultz concludes, 'we should not call it law' but a 'mode of governance' that is characterized by 'pre-legal communities.'[109] Weber had a derogatory term for this: kadi justice.[110]

IV. Modesty

As noted in the introduction to this chapter, a handful of investment law professionals are of the view that Weber prescribed binding legal rules on developing and less developed states in order to instigate economic development. Not only does this distort Weber's views, but it also erases the careful methodological distance Weber maintained from claims of this type. Weber, for example, did not purport to find the source for the rise of western capitalism in the spread of Calvinist Protestant doctrine. He maintained that he offered no such 'one-sided' account.[111] As Weber explained in his final course of lectures in Munich, modern capitalism was produced by myriad factors.[112] These included the introduction of modern bookkeeping methods (capital accounting), the private appropriation of property, free markets, free labor, advances in science and technology, calculable law, and the commercialization of economic life, including economic speculation.[113] Capitalist enterprises, Weber insisted, have been 'an enduring, highly universal and ancient organization' which was present 'in *all* the world's

[107] Ubilava (2020) at 548.
[108] Kahale, III (2018) at 2.
[109] Schultz (2014a) at 175, 178. Because it is a regime built to decide cases correctly on an ad hoc basis, Schultz surmises that consistency should not be a priority, particularly if the regime they are constructing produces bad law, as it may 'do more harm than good.' See Schultz (2014b) at 298.
[110] Defined as 'informal judgments rendered in terms of concrete ethical or other practical values' in Weber (1978) at 976. Weber associates it with the prophetic verdict: 'It is written ... but I say unto you' (at 978). This is contrasted with 'empirical justice' which relies upon analogical reasoning under the rule of precedent, as in England (at 976).
[111] Weber (1920c) at 159. Protestantism, instead, lay the groundwork for the modern pursuit of profits and accumulation of wealth.
[112] Collins (1980) at 934 ('Weber's constant theme is that the *pattern of relations among the various factors* is crucial in determining their effects upon economic rationalization') (emphasis in original).
[113] Weber (1920b) at 275–78. These factors are discussed in more depth in Weber (1920a) at 208–13 and in Collins (1980).

civilizations.'[114] '[R]ationalization paths have characteristically varied according to cultural and historical factors.'[115] Weber's research question—'why did the "Western pathway of development" not arise elsewhere'[116]—could be answered only partially, with a focus on religion as a causal force in his later comparative religious studies. The 'special characteristic features of Western rationalism,' were of unique origin. It was his task to 'identify this uniqueness and explain its origin.'[117]

Though it has been tempting to carriers of investment law to believe so, Weber does not map routes for development that others simply can follow.[118] Weber's conclusions are far more tentative. There are no law-like patterns or master narratives to be adopted and transplanted elsewhere.[119] He only identified trendlines, 'cumulative processes' taken from a birds-eye view.[120] History offered only a 'record of differences, contingencies, unanticipated consequences and paradoxical meanings,' observes Scaff, an illustration of his 'cautious nominalism.'[121] Development, it turned out, was not a linear process—there were no objectively necessary' or 'progressive stages' through which to proceed[122]—but a highly contextualized one.[123]

Weber is justifiably cautious about prescriptions that could be drawn from his comparative studies. 'When [we are] dealing with the "explanation" of concrete events,' Weber writes, 'the possibility of formulating judgments of causal *necessity* is by no means the rule but [rather] the exception, and such judgments always concern individual elements of the event.'[124] The factors that appear most important

[114] Weber (1920a) at 210 (emphasis in original).
[115] Weber (1920a) at 216.
[116] Weber (1920a) at 217.
[117] Weber (1920a) at 216.
[118] Cao (1997) at 548 makes this regrettable mistake, describing Weber as offering a 'prescriptive elaboration of the connection between predictable law and the capitalist market.' She attributes to Weber the merit of having identified 'sequences toward progressively higher stages of development' which looked toward the role of law ... as causally related to the development of a capitalist, industrial economy.'
[119] Tribe (2023) at 301 (there is 'no imputed "progress," no imperious cultural supremacy, no single impulse'), Hennis (1986) at 172, Swedberg (1998) at 88–89, and Thomas (2008) at 106. Gerth and Mills (1946) at 51 'feel justified in holding that a unilinear construction is clearly implied in Weber's idea of the bureaucratic trend.' I suggest, in Chapter 5, that even if this was a trendline that Weber chose to emphasize, he did not give up on the possibility of also checking bureaucratic domination. Mommsen (2021) at 15 suggests that Weber's later work moves beyond developing ideal types that arise out of 'specific historical forms of social conduct' to 'a much more generalized interpretation' relevant to more 'diverse historical contexts.'
[120] Ghosh (2014) at 59.
[121] Scaff (1984a) at 30 and Scaff (1984b) at 94.
[122] Schluchter (1989) at 41. Schluchter offers a subtle account of Weber's developmentalism, which is 'broken up' into a plurality of experiences rather than tracking the fate of 'one [single] humanity' (at 42).
[123] Weber (1895a) at 11 ('Human history contains examples both of the victory of less developed types of human being and the disappearance of fine flowers of intellectual and emotional life'). This is where Trebilcock (2016) ends up after a lengthy career contributing to this field. There is 'an emerging consensus,' he writes, 'that contextual factors are of overriding importance in defining both the ends of development and feasible strategies for attaining them' (at 333).
[124] Weber (1906d) at 43 (emphasis in original).

to us will be determined, in part, by our own preoccupations—our 'cognitive interest.'[125] For instance, a judge evaluating whether Brutus was the cause of Caesar's murder will seek out answers to questions different from a historian investigating why Brutus assassinated Caesar.[126] 'In history, as in law,' Weber postulates, the 'nature' of our 'interest' determines which factors are of casual significance and those which are of irrelevance.[127] Researchers will be focusing, inevitably, upon 'abstractions'—'imaginary pictures'—and 'judgments of possibility'[128] from among the 'chaos of causal interconnections.'[129] In all cases, 'what happens is simply that we isolate by abstraction some of the "conditions" present in the "material" [furnished by] events and make them the object of "judgements of possibility".' This is 'in order to gain, with the help of rules of experience, an insight into the causal "importance" of the individual components of events.' 'In order to grasp the real causal interconnections, he concludes this point, '*we construct unreal ones*.'[130]

If Weber's approach to causality in the social sciences looks complicated it was simplified somewhat by his adopting 'chance' as a key word in later works.[131] The notion of chance offered up the possibility that, for example, legal subjects would follow legal rules because of the probability that the state would step in and enforce its directives.[132] Weber's sociology was premised on such chances—that individuals will orient their behavior in ways expected of them—but this amounted only to an 'objective possibility.'[133] Expectations associated with lived experience drove Weber's understanding of causation: it 'refers to a sequence of events where it is known from experience that there is the chance that the sequence will always occur in exactly same manner.'[134] Palonen characterizes this as the element of 'radical contingency' at the bottom of Weber's thinking.[135] It seems less than radical as it relies on 'recurrence and repetition' and 'developmental tendencies'[136] but remains, nevertheless, uncertain.[137]

Nowhere was Weber's caution more evident than in his reluctance to suppose that there is a one-to-one relationship between legal reform and economic development. I have already mentioned Weber's doubts about attributing causal

[125] Weber (1904a) at 109.
[126] Weber (1904a) at 173. In his reply to Stammler, Weber elaborates on the distinctiveness of legal as compared to empirical inquiries in Weber (1907) at 218–19. He also famously describes how the game of skat (a three-player card game popular in Germany) can be the 'object of knowledge' in 'fundamentally different' ways: as policy, in relation to 'laws and jurisprudence,' and as empirical inquiry (at 215).
[127] Weber (1904a) at 173.
[128] Weber (1904a) at 175.
[129] Weber '7 Handwritten Note' in Bruun and Whimster (2012) at 416.
[130] Weber (1904a) at 182 (emphasis in original). He is referring to the construction of ideal types.
[131] Palonen (2017) at 1.
[132] Weber (1910a) at 366, also Weber (1978) at 312 ('law' is defined in this manner).
[133] Tribe (2019) at 57.
[134] Weber (2019) at 87.
[135] Palonen (2017) at 123.
[136] Weber (1894a) at 182.
[137] Strand and Lizardo (2022) at 140.

significance to legal ordering on the economy—what has been described as Weber's 'causal agnosticism.'[138] Guaranteed law, backed up by a coercive state apparatus, is 'not indispensable to any basic economic phenomenon,' writes Weber, from a 'purely theoretical point of view.'[139] The 'modern type' of economic system, however, 'could not exist without a legal order with very special features.'[140] But we are still left with the question of how to (re)produce paths to economic development outside of the West? Weber's conclusion is that there is no recipe book. Indeed, investment law professionals might have as much success (perhaps even more) by promoting a capitalist ethic amongst the populations of host states by encouraging the embrace of a doctrine of Calvinist predestination. Or perhaps by encouraging their home states to find overseas dependencies from whom they can extract natural resources, and which can also serve as markets for their manufactured goods? Or, more simply, permitting states to legally engage in behavior, like import substitution, which presently is prohibited under international economic law but which developed states were privileged historically to experiment with?[141]

Having failed to offer up a convincing account of how law influences the economy upon which investment law's carriers can rely—leaning, instead, on 'sloppy empirics'[142]—we might fairly conclude that Weber's sociology of law is mostly unhelpful to them. A preferable reading, one more consistent with Weber's methods, is suggested by Kronman, which is to avoid 'overgeneralization' and to confine claims about the causal relationship between law and economy to 'particular cases.'[143] More work, in short, needs to be done to explain paths to economic success. They turn out not to be the ones promoted by investment law professionals.

V. Nationalism and Imperialism

It remains to address whether Weber's liberal and economic nationalism betrayed his radical nominalist stance as regards economic development. Tensions arise due to Weber's interventions on agricultural production in East Elbia, his opposition to protectionist tariffs for agricultural production, his contributions to stock exchange reform, and his unalloyed imperialism. Do these episodes, arising early in his academic career, display a determinism—an 'appearance of exactitude'[144]—that belie Weber's resistance to universalist developmental pathways? I suggest resisting the

[138] Kronman (1983) at 124ff.
[139] Weber (1978) at 336.
[140] Weber (1978) at 336. On Weber's 'delicate balancing act' between rejecting 'simple economic reductionism' and granting too much autonomy to law from economics, see Turner (1981) at 323.
[141] Chang (2002).
[142] Desai (2023) at 40.
[143] Kronman (1983) at 130.
[144] Weber (1906d) at 37.

conclusion that Weber departs from his cautious approach to causality—that there are no 'abstract law-like regularities' that direct historical outcomes.[145] Rather, his diagnoses are a highly contextual 'set of policy prescriptions' appropriate (for Weber) to the circumstances of Wilhelmine Germany.[146] They also reveal a preference for state intervention to promote economic development, an anathema to investment law professionals.

Writing in 1893, Schmoller described Weber as exhibiting a 'moderate political standpoint' together with a 'Prussian patriotism' free of 'any socialist tinge.'[147] In addition to his liberal faith,[148] economic nationalism occupied a prominent place in Weber's thought.[149] This was coupled, early in his career, with regrettable stereotyping of Polish laborers. Weber attacked Prussian landowners in the East for importing seasonal workers, following the demise of the traditional seigneurial system,[150] and paying them the lowest of wages.[151] These workers, Weber declared, could not be expected to become Germans.[152] They were 'Polish animals'[153] who were stuck in a 'habitually low physical and intellectual standard of living.'[154] This

[145] Weber (1906a) at 172. For an elaboration, see Turner and Factor (1994), chap. 6.

[146] Trebilcock and Prado (2011) at 10.

[147] Gustav Schmoller to Friedrich Althoff (3 March 1893) quoted in Schön (1987) at 63. Yet, Schumpeter (1994) at 805 describes Weber (and Sombart) as being 'anything but exponents of capitalist interests.'

[148] Weber (1895a) at 23 ('I am a member of the bourgeois (*bürgerlich*) classes. I feel myself to be a bourgeois, and I have been brought up to share their views and ideals').

[149] Mommsen (1984) at 48 & 50 describes Weber's nationalism as a 'fundamental value' for him and so was 'confined ... by the national enthusiasm characteristic of the Wilhelmine epoch.' The 'national idea' was 'an ultimate norm that justified the exercise of power' (at 64). Bhambra and Holmwood (2021) at 129 also describe the 'nation' as a 'fundamental value' for Weber. Compare Palonen (2017) chap. 7.

[150] Weber (1894a) at 160–63 and see discussion in Riesebrodt (1989) at 134–36.

[151] Having moved to low paid wage agricultural production, German laborers abandoned eastern farms in favor of the cities. They were replaced by Polish laborers who would work for less. The 'foreigners came in unimpeded,' writes his wife M Weber (1975) at 129, 'occupying the eastern borderlands that the Germans had wrested from these people centuries before.'

[152] Mommsen (1984) at 24, Weber (1894a) at 173, and Ghosh (2005) at 343, on the rise of seasonal migrant labor. 'The Poles were loyal if passive "Prussians" but they were not "Germans" interested in the existence of the *Reich*' in Weber (1978) at 396.

[153] Weber quoted in Tribe (1983) at 114. Mommsen (2021) at 27 describes Weber's tone as an admixture of 'militant nationalism,' 'Social Darwinism,' and 'racialist notions.' On the social Darwinism prevalent among social scientists at this time, lending to 'German economic nationalism its life-or-death attitude,' see Suesse (2023) at 87. Weber repudiates the process of natural selection that is associated with Darwin, Barbalet (2023) at 51, reminds us. He is better described as 'Eurocentric' but non-'essentialist' in Löwy and Varikas (2021) at 70, 71 and as exhibiting a nationalism 'devoid of the ethnic nationalist obsession with primordiality that pervaded German nationalism' in Kim (2002) at 434. Compare with Boatcă (2013).

[154] Weber (1895a) at 10. Mommsen (1984) at 50, observes that, after this Freiburg address, Weber 'increasingly distanced himself from emotional national feelings based upon linguistic and ethnic particularities.' He moderated his hostility toward Poles and 'grew less directly concerned with the inroads of alien ethnic groups' (at 56). Instead, he turned toward concern for preserving Polish cultural autonomy for Poles under Russian imperialism (at 56–60). See also discussion in Bellamy (1992) at 505 and Mommsen (2021) at 30 (discussing how Weber eventually came to the Poles' 'assistance'). However, at a meeting with Heidelberg students, Weber was met with 'uncomprehending silence' when he asked that when 'the first Polish official to enter Danzig is hit by a bullet ... then *come to me*!' quoted in M Weber (1975) at 631–32 (emphasis in original).

amounted, in Beetham's summation, to 'the survival of the *un*fittest.'[155] Weber's proposals for reform entailed closing the Eastern border to 'Slav' labor and protecting the German nation by having the state intervene in order to 'defend' it.[156] Though he initially expressed an interest in its potential,[157] Weber came to eschew race as a heuristic in his research programme, describing racial theorizing from a sociological viewpoint as 'unfruitful'[158] and a 'scientific crime.'[159] He preferred to rely upon notions of 'ethnic affinity' based upon a bundle of factors such as 'common language' and 'shared religious beliefs.'[160] If Weber inaugurated his academic career by focusing on the Eastern agrarian question, he also continued to be fixated on the '"Polish question" ... throughout his adult life,' even coming to the defence of Polish areas against Russian incursion.[161] This would always be undertaken, however, with a view to buoying up German national interest.[162]

Weber consistently called upon the state to take steps to secure the future of economic development in East Elbia. It was time, he declared, for the state to realize its 'social vocation'[163] by transferring 'significant tracts of Eastern Germany' held by the landed aristocracy (the Junkers) 'into the hands of the state.'[164] These lands could then be distributed and cultivated by self-sustaining German peasant farmers.[165] This was not because peasant agricultural output would be more

155 Beetham (1985) at 38 (italics in original).

156 Weber (1895a) at 13 and discussion in Tribe (1983) at 108.

157 Weber (1920a) at 219. Weber 'confesses that he is inclined, personally and subjectively, to estimate highly the importance of biological heredity ... [though] the comparative study of racial neurology [must move] beyond its rudimentary beginnings of today (which are promising in many ways) ... [are] ... (at this time still) unknown factors' (at 219–20).

158 Weber (1910c) at 39, also see Weber (1910d) and discussion in Manasse (1947) at 210, subjecting his 'originally intuitive conception of race to an ever sharpening criticism' resulting in the 'almost complete destruction of his original conception' (at 221).

159 Quoted in Weber (1978) at 398, fn. 1.

160 Weber (1978) at 390. Weber maintained an interest in the social construction of race, the product of 'mass beliefs' in Weber (1910d) at 312. Barbalet (2024) at 15 describes Weber's concept of race as not 'based on innate characteristics' but by shared past and values, 'consolidated through and expressed in a national capacity.' On language as the glue for national culture, see discussion in Beetham (1985) at 122–23.

161 Barbalet (2023) at 42 and M Weber (1975) at 553.

162 Barbalet (2024) at 12.

163 Weber quoted in Tribe (1983) at 113 (on its 'own initiative ... put a spoke in the wheel of social development'). Weber's concept of development, according to Reisebrodt (1989) at 145, refers to the 'transformation of social conditions.'

164 Weber (1895a) at 12. This is described in the year earlier as a 'radical intervention' in Weber (1894a) at 183. This was a policy that had been pursued by the Settlement Commission and General Commission, Weber (1894a) at 184 acknowledges, settling some 7,500 peasants between them, but the policy was abandoned in the 1870s. It was taken up again in the 1880s, when 33,000 Poles were deported on short notice, per Roth (1993) at 158. Their 'success' prompted a 1908 Prussian law on expropriation, that was 'applied only sparingly' (at 159). For an argument that Weber's contempt for the Junkers was prompted by resentment toward his father, see Mitzman (1969) at 84 and, for skepticism about this claim, see Mommsen (1984) at 430.

165 Mommsen (1984) at 28. Because Weber feared the spread of a 'landowning *proletariat*,' he advocated the leasing of state-owned lands to 'wealthy farmers', rather than to rural peasants, together with 'loans for improvements' in Weber (1894a) at 184. They were meant to be a 'sustainable middle stratum of tenant farmers,' according to Strazerri (2022) at 205.

productive but because 'hunger' would be used 'to bind them to their homeland.'[166] These early texts display prescriptive tendencies, despite his reluctance to offer detailed plans for development.[167] Weber resisted the implication, however, that these 'developmental tendencies' had 'the character of ruling natural laws.'[168] Rather, the outcome he envisaged could 'only develop under specific conditions engendered by the distribution of landed property.'[169] The conjuncture of particular events in Germany's eastern frontier called for this sort of state intervention.[170]

Despite calls for nationalization of agrarian lands, Weber also advocated free trade and the integration of the Germany economy into international markets. Intervening in a debate over autarchy ('independence through self-sufficiency'), Weber exhorted his audience to understand that Germany could not achieve economic greatness without an open export policy.[171] He denied being one of 'those optimists of capitalism' who promoted 'integration [into] the international division of labour.' Instead, he preferred the placement of 'barriers ... in the way of natural development of the markets for German industry,' preferably through the negotiation of 'commercial treaties.'[172] If open borders entailed a 'massive *risk*' to the German economy, it is one that 'all great trading and industrial peoples of the past' have assumed.[173] But not all would be at risk. Weber, for instance, tolerated modest tariffs on agricultural exports.[174] The proper scientific question, Weber asked, is whether Germany could prevent export oriented 'capitalistic development.' It '*cannot be prevented*,' he declared: 'for us it is unavoidable.' It only was possible to 'economically influence the course which it takes.'[175] To both 'vigorous applause and hissing,' Weber proclaimed that 'those nations which today fail to mobilize their economic future for national greatness do not have a future.'[176]

Weber's intervention on reform of the stock exchange, like his stance on agricultural tariffs, aimed to expose German markets to international competition.

166 Weber in 1893, quoted in Tribe (1983) at 115. The 'cause of German survival,' Mommsen adds, required a self-sufficient economic system that did not produce for the market,' in (1984) at 37–38.

167 He did so, writes Mommsen (1984) at 28, with 'resignation' and 'not with positive political fervour.' Weber 'offered his proposals with mixed emotions' (at 29). It is worthy of note that Weber, though expressing 'regret' about agrarian policy, 'avoids taking any direct national-political position' in his lecture notes for students. See Aldenhoff-Hübinger (2009) at 199.

168 Weber (1894a) at 182. Tribe (1983) at 101 describes Weber's work on agrarian practices in Ancient Rome as revealing 'tendencies in development' which 'were no sense law-like.'

169 Weber (1894a) at 182.

170 Further nationalizations were anticipated after the War in Weber (1918c).

171 In a debate with Karl Oldenburg in 1897. See Roth (1993) at 153. Derman (2025) at 183, 194 reports that Oldenburg was not advocating 'strict autarky' but 'semi-autarky.' He objected to German reliance 'on the world economy to maintain full employment and feed its population.'

172 Weber (1897) at 213.

173 Weber (1897) at 213 (emphasis in original).

174 Mommsen (1984) at 30.

175 Weber (1897) at 214 (emphasis in original).

176 Weber (1897) at 219. Tribe (2010) at 66 reports that Weber was barred from participating in a Bundesrat committee on financial affairs because of his 'overly close connection to financial interests.' This was the impression left upon audiences by his vigorous endorsement of open markets in the grain trade (at 83, fn. 19). See also Roth (2002) at 515–16.

Given the 'casino-like quality' of the futures market, losses in speculative securities and commodities exchanges caused sufficient consternation that the Imperial Ministry of the Interior struck a Provisional Bourse Committee to advise the Bundesrat. Weber was one of two academics invited to sit on the provisional committee, though he was not asked to continue serving as a member of the permanent committee.[177] Weber threw himself into this work becoming, in short order, one of Germany's leading experts on stock and commodity exchanges (if not its youngest), contributing to both popular and academic publications regarding proposed reforms. At the behest of powerful agrarian interests, the Reichstag in 1896 enacted a ban on futures trading in grain. Weber opposed these restrictions for fear that it would weaken Germany's international leadership. He preferred that the state regulate the quality of the personnel entitled to trade on German markets by disqualifying 'unprofessional individuals.'[178] Only persons of 'economic means,' 'such as his own relatives,' Roth surmises, 'should trade on the exchange.'[179] Imposing legal restrictions on the capacity of the Berlin stock exchange, Weber later complained, for '*purely* theoretical and moral reasons,' would amount to unilateral disarmament in the struggle for international capital.[180] A 'strong stock exchange,' he declared, was not 'a club for "ethical culture"' but, rather, '*a medium of power*' in 'economic struggle.' The 'ultimate obligation' of state policy is to 'safeguard the nation from [economic] disarmament by fanatical self-interest, or by unworldly apostles of economic peace.'[181]

Not only did Weber promote the internal colonization of the East, he also served as exuberant promoter of an overseas empire, until Germany's defeat in the First World War.[182] Competition between states required that Germany take its place among European powers by expanding its navy and exercising economic dominion over weaker states abroad.[183] This would be achieved not by colonization

[177] Borchardt (2002) at 152, 160. See also Lestition (2000) and Kemple and Meyer-Stoll (2003). This was likely, as Tribe (2010) at 66 mentions, because Weber was perceived as being too close to financial interests, however faulty the impression. 'I seem to have met with the approval of the millionaires,' Weber sardonically remarked in a letter to his wife Marianne in M Weber (1975) at 198. 'One of them, 'always squeezes my hand so vigorously that I am surprised at not finding a check for 100,000 marks under my blotter' (at 198–99).

[178] Weber (1894b) at 331. As in the case of East Elbian agricultural production, Bendix (1962) at 36 observes, the problem was that the German middle class was 'not capitalist enough.'

[179] Roth (2002) at 514.

[180] Quoted in Mommsen (1984) at 74. See also Weber (1896b) at 369 and Tribe (2002) at 245.

[181] Quoted in Tribe (2002) at 245. See also Käsler (1988) at 65.

[182] Weber's 1895 Freiburg address, Mommsen (1984) at 71 writes, was 'the impetus for the rise of liberal imperialism in Wilhelmine Germany.' Weber (1918c) at 31 announced the 'renunciation of imperialist dreams' after the First World War. Mommsen (1981) at 77, 83 acknowledges that the 'driving force behind German imperialism' came from 'the rising middle classes and the intelligentsia' whose influence was 'quite disproportionate to the level of popular support that they actually were capable of mustering.' This may be why, in his 1895 address, Weber was interested in political education, not for the purpose of stimulating domestic political participation but to enhance the primacy of foreign policy, explain Turner and Factor (1984) at 89.

[183] Candidates for 'overseas imperialism' were those 'foreign areas that are politically weak' in Weber (1978) at 914.

through settlement but by economic and political coercion.[184] 'The safest way of monopolizing ... profit opportunities which are linked to the public economy of the foreign territory,' Weber declared, 'is to occupy it or at least to subject the foreign political power in the form of a "protectorate" or some such arrangement.' It was this 'imperialist' tendency that was displacing a '"pacifist" strategy of expansion which aims merely at freedom of trade,' which he also energetically promoted.[185] The exercise of imperial authority over colonies would secure 'for the broad masses of our people ... a permanent livelihood at home and the possibility of progressive improvement,' Weber pronounced to an 1896 congress on unemployment.[186] It was upon this basis that 'successors' would judge his generation: 'for the amount of elbow-room in the world which we conquer and bequeath to them.'[187] Germany would then take its place among those great European powers struggling for overseas outlets that enhanced economic prospects at home.[188] Only 'power, naked power, will count in the international market,' Weber admits, 'and in this mighty struggle, the strongest will be the victor.'[189] Weber was content, then, to have recourse to non-legitimate domination in order to colonize subaltern peoples.[190]

The future course of Germany's economy required steering by the state even as Weber sought to advance international economic integration. This is the dilemma faced by all economic nationalists: navigating between international economic engagement and isolation.[191] The interests of the nation state ('reason of state') were the 'ultimate criterion for economic policy,'[192] wrote Weber. Yet this was in tension with ideal typical economic theory, 'unequivocally directed to a single end, the maximization of economic advantage.'[193] Explaining that processes of 'economic development are power struggles too,' Weber sought to pilot these difficult shoals by seeking, for Germany, 'world equality' and a 'respectable colonial empire.'[194]

[184] Weber sought 'economic expansion and enlargement of the nation's living space,' observes Mommsen (1984) at 73.

[185] Weber (1978) at 919. With the qualifications already noted in text associated with notes 172–77, supra.

[186] Quoted in Beetham (1985) at 134. On the connections between the rural labor question and imperialism, see Strazzeri (2022) at 222.

[187] Weber (1895a) at 16. This also is the tenor of Weber (1916). On Weber's imperialism, generally, see Zimmerman (2006) and on the culture of imperialism in the Wilhemine foreign policy (*Weltpolitik*), see Marchand (2009) chap. 8.

[188] 'Every expansion of a country's power sphere increases the profit potential of the respective capitalist interests,' in Weber (1978) at 346 and Mommsen (1984) at 78.

[189] Letter from Weber to Mannheim (13 December 1897) quoted in Mommsen (1984) at 77 and Weber quoted in Radkau (2011) at 332–33 ('*only power* will decide each nation's share in the economic control of the planet and therefore the earnings of its population,' emphasis in original).

[190] Bhambra and Holmwood (2021) at 130, 138. Turner (2025) at 285 defines non-legitimate domination as encompassing 'every power that is not sanctioned by charisma, law or tradition.'

[191] Suesse (2023) at 5. Roth (1993) at 160–61 shrewdly describes Weber as 'uneasily' combining a 'cosmopolitan economic strategy oriented toward the world market and a narrow nationalist policy of ethnic exclusion.'

[192] Weber (1895a) at 17 (emphasis in original).

[193] Weber (1978) at 9. See Swedberg (1998) at 25–28.

[194] Mommsen (1984) at 158.

It was the 'prestige' associated with imperial expansion that was closely allied to Weber's nationalistic economic ambitions.[195] He was, in short, an economic nationalist throughout his intellectual life.[196] Although Weber offered prescriptions for economic success, they were proposals for German economic success. If they presupposed ethnic superiority, imperialism, and even deportation,[197] they were meant to be cautious, partial, and particular to German circumstances.

VI. Conclusion

Those promoting the spread of investment law are quick to inflate their ideal—whether it be the promotion of economic development, the rule of law, or good governance by signing investment treaties—with the real. Weber ridiculed this naïve view. Just as the lawyer is 'conceptually inclined' to view us as 'potential litigant[s]', he wrote, so does the shoemaker regard us as potential customers.[198] By entering into this relationship from the other end, one does 'not have to be a cobbler oneself in order to know whether a shoe made by the cobbler pinches.'[199] Imagined facts might, therefore, not correspond very well to real ones. Gephart summarizes Weber's view this way: 'Since the normative and causal spheres are completely heterogeneous, there can be no direct causal effect of the ideal content of a norm in the sphere of factual validity.'[200] By denying reality, we enter into the realm of magic.[201] If enchanting vulnerable populations with the promise of economic development has proven effective in the past, it can no longer be credibly claimed in light of the state of 'empirical knowledge.'[202] Investment law professionals need to be more careful, then, about expectations arising out of investment treaty commitments.

That they are not more careful reveals how an ethic of conviction—their value preferences—drives their claims.[203] Paradoxically, it is the investment lawyers who are quick to accuse their critics of being ideologically motivated. This stance, akin to a 'hermeneutic of suspicion,'[204] charges opponents with offering wrong answers to legal questions. 'My' side, bereft of politics, has all of

[195] Mommsen (1984) at 81. Derman (2025) at 195 describes Weber as having envisaged 'a world where economic interdependence and belligerence coexist.' For this reason, he concludes, 'Weber remains very much our contemporary.'

[196] Weber (1918c) at 31 called for the end of 'imperialist dreams' in favor of a 'purely *autonomous nationality ideal*' (emphasis in original). This reading of Weber is not inconsistent with Palonen (2017) at 100, who maintains that Weber's use of 'nation' reveals him as 'an apologist of the nation state within the concert of great powers.'

[197] Strazzeri (2022) at 323–25 calls these 'partisan gestures' of Weber's 'anti-utopia.'

[198] Or skat players viewing them as a potential 'third man.' Quoted in Gephart (2015) at 46.

[199] Weber (1918b) at 227.

[200] Gephart (2015) at 51.

[201] Koskenniemi (2005) at 555.

[202] Weber (1915b) at 238. See discussion in the Conclusion.

[203] I discuss this 'ethic of conviction' in Chapter 3.

[204] Kennedy (2014) and Kennedy (2020), also Orford (2021) at 310.

the correct answers, they will say.[205] This hermeneutic gives rise to a high stakes game, Orford notes.[206] If the future of international adjudication is dependent on a regime that is perceived as 'neutral, impartial and free of politics,'[207] it is a particularly acute problem for investment arbitration as it aims to aggressively reduce the policy space available to states and citizens. Given these stakes, it is no wonder that investment law elites view the opposition not only with suspicion but with hostility.

Their mindset exhibits a scholasticism that is hard to defend. Mannheim analogizes scholastic thinking to a religious 'sect'—communities of faith according to Weber[208]—that 'dogmatically' give 'binding force' to certain 'modes of thought.'[209] It is as if power is so concentrated that a 'uniformity of thought and experience can be imposed' upon others. It is a 'monopolistic type of thought' that is relatively 'remote from the open conflicts of everyday life.' It amounts to an arbitrariness that is dependent upon the success of the sect to make their 'own intellectual and experiential traditions the traditions for the entire' population.[210] The scholastic disposition, Bourdieu adds, 'implies more or less a triumphant ignorance' of the suppressed conditions giving rise to their rule and 'of the economic and political conditions that make it possible.'[211] Investment law professionals deny, in short, that that there may be more than one answer to investment law questions and, therefore, multiple paths to economic development.

Boosting their confidence is the invitation provided to investment law scholars by Article 38(4) of the Statute of the Permanent Court of International Justice. Serving as 'most highly qualified publicists,' according to the Statute's terminology, they are encouraged to generate, through their scholarship, subsidiary sources of international law. This enticement operates as a springboard for investment law scholars to contribute to regime maintenance via academic and professional writing.[212] Are they aware that their legal answers are susceptible to the charge of being ideologically motivated?[213] Though they will have recourse to

[205] Kennedy (2014) at 91. For an elaboration of this argument, see Schneiderman (2022c).

[206] Orford (2021) at 312–14.

[207] Orford (2021) at 312.

[208] In contrast to a church as an institution, a sect is a 'voluntary association of only those who, according to the principle, are religiously and morally qualified' in Weber (1922b) at 306, also in Weber (1906c) at 9.

[209] Mannheim (1959) at 11.

[210] Mannheim (1959) at 11.

[211] Bourdieu (2000) at 11.

[212] On 'double hatting' (performing various roles in different disputes), see Langford, Behn, and Lie, (2017).

[213] Kennedy (2020) at 91. Mannheim (1959) at 74 describes the 'expansion and diffusion' of ideology as a 'weapon' such that 'it is no longer possible for one point of view and interpretation to assail all others as ideological without itself being placed in the position of having to meet that challenge.'

forms of argument associated with classical legal thought,[214] they do not appear to be 'chastened' by the charge of ideologically motivated formalism. Moreover, they do not appear willing to accept any outcomes that do not align with their convictions.[215] The fury directed at critics who argue otherwise is, I believe, evidence that they are not willing even to give an inch.

[214] See Horwitz (1992). Classical legal thought is discussed in Chapter 1.
[215] Kennedy (2020) at 111 describes chastened legal elites as 'hoping that this will not happen in too many or too horrible cases.'

Conclusion

Do Weber's themes aid in understanding the contemporary world? Martin Albrow is of the view that Weber's account of domination (*Herrschaft*) is tied 'so closely to tendencies of his time that he has made them unusable for the present.'[1] It is a 'historic relic'—a 'world away' from our own.[2] It is in the realm of developments associated with 'global governance,' Albrow maintains, where intergovernmental relations, interacting with transnational NGOs and global media, produce conditions for which Weber's ideal type of leadership has no place. Albrow concedes, however, that other of Weber's 'fundamental concepts' remain vital,[3] such as individuals as the basic unit of analysis or 'order' backed by 'legitimacy.'[4]

Whimster insists that Weber remains relevant to understanding these same global forces. He explains that neoliberalism 'has returned us to the contours of capitalism that were familiar to Weber in his day.'[5] Whimster alleges that Weber's ideal typical characteristics associated with markets is 'more or less [an] exact specification of neoliberalism'[6] and its allied institutions of global governance. Whimster mentions the structures of the European Union, including the European Court of Justice, as exemplars that foreclose national economies from interrupting the free movement of goods, services, and capital. Structures that appear to 'work in theory' by relying on formal rationality, Whimster maintains, translate into institutions that promote a 'substantive rationality' in alignment with the limited state.[7]

By now, readers will have appreciated that this project falls comfortably within the parameters of Whimster's account. By testing presuppositions that underlie the muscular international legal order to protect foreign investors with reference to themes from Weber, we learn a fair amount about the regime's flaws, weak links, and prevailing values. By examining how formally rational law aspires to shield the regime from ethical imperatives beyond investor protection (Chapter 1), devises weak legitimation strategies for continued regime maintenance (Chapter 2), purports to be focused on means when overcome by ends-based reasoning (Chapter 3), erects a bureaucratic apparatus that routinizes professional charisma (Chapters 4 and 5), or continues to make extravagant claims

1 Albrow (2017) at 534.
2 Albrow (2017) at 536.
3 Albrow (2017) at 534.
4 Albrow (2017) at 537.
5 Whimster (2019b) at 30 (though neoliberalism 'immediately fails the Weberian test of clarity of concept and definition' at 26).
6 Whimster (2019b) at 32. His discussion is not confined to Weber's *Herrschaft*.
7 Whimster (2019b) at 32.

A Sociology of International Investment Law. David Schneiderman, Oxford University Press.
 DOI: 10.1093/9780198982739.003.0008

about the correlation between signing treaties and improving conditions of life for many people in the world (Chapter 6), readers will have a deeper understanding of a legal regime that was quickly established, without many moments for deep self-reflection on the part of its social carriers. It should also prompt rethinking about the utility of many of the reform efforts presently on offer.

What helps to explain the durability of the regime? By way of conclusion, I propose revisiting Weber's concept of 'enchantment' so as to contend with the ways in which investment law's edicts remain a formidable obstacle to reviving or expanding political possibilities. Lawyers, state officials, and even citizens continue to be enchanted by international investment law. This dampens the possibility for re-politicizing those spheres of social and economic life that are meant to be barricaded off from its version of formally rational law.

Weber famously described the contemporary world as having entered into a place of disenchantment (*Entzauberung*).[8] By this he meant to say that, rather than being ruled by magic and spirits, we are now governed by 'technology and calculation.' Weber described a process by which 'consensus' derived from religious beliefs was replaced by a spirit of accumulation and contestation,[9] embroiling citizens in unceasing market activity.[10] There are no longer mysterious forces at work in our lives. We instead, have 'the knowledge, or the belief, that *if we wished to*, we *could* at any time learn about' controlling our lived conditions.[11] When 'we can—in principle—*dominate* everything by means of *calculation* ... the world has lost its magic.'[12]

Neither magic nor prophets can be relied upon to direct the conduct of our everyday lives. Instead, in the modern age, individuals are forced to choose the 'ultimate standpoints' that they prefer to adopt.[13] These 'numerous gods of former times ... have lost their magic,' Weber writes. Individuals now must assume responsibility for selecting from among various 'ultimate positions' that 'dominate our

[8] Swedburg and Agevall (2016) at 86 describe 'disenchantment of the world' (*Entzauberung der Welt*) as a 'world no longer explained by magic but by science and rationality.' Bruun and Whimster (2012) at 481 prefer to translate the term as 'loss of magic.'

[9] Colliot-Thélène (1992) at 149. Whereas Weber typically undertakes close studies of historically contingent developments, Colliot-Thélène describes this deviation as an 'idealist inflection'—imposing a unity upon European history—influenced by Nietzsche (at 150–51). Tenbruck's reading, she says, underscores this 'universal historical perspective,' in Tenbruck (1980) at 344.

[10] Weber (1915b) at 238–89 (where 'rational empirical knowledge has consistently carried through the disenchantment of the world and its transformation into a causal mechanism, there emerges a tension with the claim of ethical postulates—that the world, for religion, is ultimately willed and ordained by God').

[11] Weber (1919b) at 342.

[12] Weber (1919b) at 342 (emphasis in original).

[13] One 'has to choose which of these gods he will serve ... at all times he will find himself engaged in a fight against one or other of the gods of this world, and above all he will always find that he is far from the God of Christianity' in Weber (1916) at 79. Also see Weber (1895a) at 18 (emphasis in original) (there is 'a *chaos* of different evaluative criteria').

lives.'[14] We are forced to choose from among those Gods who 'have risen out of their graves' and at whose altar we pray.[15] It is the 'weakness' of our age, Weber maintained, to 'be unable to face up to [this] grave fate.'[16]

Is Weber insistent that magic and Gods have been excised from the world or might he admit that they persist in modern rationalized forms?[17] As Josephson-Storm explains, disenchantment entails 'not the end of belief in magic.'[18] What Weber has in mind is not 'an accomplished state of affairs' but a 'program' that is 'in place' but not yet 'complete.'[19] We are not yet at a point where enchantment is eradicated.[20] Instead, enchantment takes on different, more modern, guises. Magic is cut off from religious belief—no longer does Calvinist predestination determine how some live their lives—but relocated to spheres controlled by 'diverse types of professionals,' Josephson-Storm observes.[21] If disenchantment is associated with the rise of rationality, it does not necessarily correspond to the decline of magical thinking. Just as Weber views modern music, which could not exist '[w]ithout the tensions motivated by the irrationality of melody,' so does modern rationality coexist with irrational systems of value.[22] If we have 'broken away from religion,' adds Gauchet, this condition has been achieved 'only by finding substitutes for it at every level.'[23] There remains a desire, in Schluchter's words, for 'ethical guidance' to steer the actions of believers.[24]

Where can such guidance be found? Today, it is often acquired from those promoting an economic orthodoxy associated with neoliberal tenets. It is believed that, by being faithful to these pronouncements, economic success in the modern world can be secured. In Davies formulation, it amounts to the 'disenchantment of politics by economics.'[25] The subsumption of politics to economics rests on a

[14] Weber (1919b) at 348. Taylor (2007) at 300 calls this the 'nova effect': 'we are now living in a spiritual super-nova, a kind of galloping pluralism on the spiritual plane.'

[15] Weber (1919a) at 348.

[16] Weber (1919b) at 348.

[17] Josephson-Storm (2021) at 31. Disenchantment, for this reason, should not be confused with secularization. As Taylor (2007) at 553 insists, 'we cannot just equate the two.' '[R]eligious forms reconstitute themselves,' in which case, 'the religious dimension is inescapable' (at 708). See also Schluchter (2017) at 46, Kippenberg (2021) and De Vriese and Vanheeswijk (2024). Cornel West regrettably misreads Weber when he accuses Weber of excising 'worship and faith' from modernity in Butler and West (2011) at 105.

[18] Josephson-Storm (2017) at 280.

[19] Josephson-Storm (2017) at 300.

[20] Taylor (2024) at 47 claims that it is 'not clear that all facets of human life can be understood within the terms set by natural science ... it is far from being established that animate beings can be exhaustively understood in such reductive terms.'

[21] Josephson-Storm (2021) at 46. In addition to professionalization, bureaucratization and technological changes also contribute to disenchantment (at 46). On re-enchantment in law's domains, see Blank (2011).

[22] Weber (1921) at 10 ('Chordal rationalization also conceals in itself an irrationality ...'). Josephson-Storm (2021) at 46–47 notes affinities between the rise of rationality in music to the 'rationalization of modern magic in a disenchanting world.'

[23] Gauchet (1997) at 6.

[24] Schluchter (1981) at 168.

[25] Davies (2017) at xx.

particular kind of 'moral agenda,' Davies observes, by which 'certain vocational commitments and intrinsic notions of the common good,' even if unarticulated, reign supreme.[26] The paradox is that in a world where all can be 'dominated' by 'means of calculation,' neoliberal thought has emerged as a predominant ethos that, instead of being calculable, promotes a programmatic agenda that is difficult to pin down.[27] For instance, as I have argued in Chapter 6, though we have available to us the means by which to evaluate the investment treaty program's success in promoting economic well-being—having 'knowledge of the techniques for controlling life ... by calculation'[28]—rationality has been abandoned in favor of wishful thinking. The indefensible but continual insistence on the correlation between signing treaties and securing a myriad of side effects (whether attracting foreign investment, promoting the rule of law, or encouraging good governance) removes foreign investment law from the realm of the calculable to the mythical. It turns out, writes Davies, that our 'wholly calculable, measurable world is only possible on the basis of particular non-calculable, immeasurable values or vocations.'[29] A presumably superior economic rationality offered by the social carriers of investment law amounts only to empty scholarly prophecy. Removing markets from political realms—depriving citizens of those subjects that continue to preoccupy democratic self-rule—amounts to much more than mere subordination to bureaucratic rationality and double entry bookkeeping. It calls upon us to rely upon magical thinking, summoning an enchanted world of economic grace that empties out our capacity for political debate and struggle.[30] Rather than enhancing social and economic improvement, the regime tends to generate, in Weber's words, 'only fanatical sects, but never a genuine community.'[31]

How can we pull away from the lure of investment law's neoliberal logic? There remains an antidote that Weber himself prescribed: that of taking responsibility.[32] Values, Weber insists, cannot be scrubbed out of existence. No social science can assist us in choosing sides in the conflict over values.[33] We can, instead (as discussed in Chapter 3), evaluate the means we choose to employ in order to put those ends into practice.[34] The assessment of means encourages one to be '*conscious* of the fact that *any* action ... will have consequences that imply *taking*

[26] Davies (2017) at 10.
[27] On the pliability of neoliberal reason, see Peck (2010).
[28] Weber (1919b) at 349.
[29] Davies (2017) at 10.
[30] Brown (2023) at 33 ('political life' should serve as the 'theatre for [debating and] renewing' values). This is an ethic, she says, that 'entails a sacrifice of self but not others to a vision, and steadfastly refuses nihilistic reductions of political life to individual interest, advantage, power, or security' (at 47).
[31] Weber (1919b) at 352, quoted in Davies (2017) at 145.
[32] Kennedy (2004) at 1069.
[33] Weber (1919b) at 344 (science 'does not furnish an answer to the only question of importance to us: 'What should we do? How should we live?"') (quoting Tolstoy).
[34] Taylor (1989) at 149 goes so far as to charge the disenchanted world as setting ends in mechanistic and instrumental terms so that they serve as a 'domain of possible means.'

sides.'[35] The social scientist, Weber declares, assumes the 'duty of creating clarity and a sense of responsibility' about the consequences that follow from certain action.[36] There will be no prophetic voice to provide us with ethical guidance.[37] The choice of ends, Wendy Brown reminds us, 'carry our distinctly political capacity to craft the world according to chosen purposes.' That sense of responsibility is particularly acute when our capacity to choose 'seems nearly extinguished' by the forces of neoliberalism.[38]

This sense of responsibility is perhaps best illustrated, in the age of international investment law, by Carlos Gaviria Díaz, former President of the Constitutional Court of Colombia.[39] Gaviria Díaz was appointed in 2013 by former Ecuadorian President Rafael Correa to serve as chair of CAITISA, tasked with conducting an audit of investment treaties and arbitration.[40] The audit was composed of experts in economics and law who were to advise President Correa on the constitutionality and utility of investment treaties signed by Ecuador.[41] As President Correa continued to court foreign investment in resource development, over the objections of indigenous communities and social movements, even going so far as to enter into a new trade and investment agreement with the European Union, Gaviria Díaz served notice of his resignation.[42] He began his letter of resignation by expressing his shared 'conviction [for] the purposes that inform [t]his political project,'[43] recognizing the difficult bind in which Ecuadorians find themselves. They are '[c]onfronting the rampant global market economy' where '[t]oo many adverse circumstances have to be overcome, and these have been magnified as if by *magic*.'[44]

By entering into a new free trade agreement with Europe—in the pursuit of the same neoliberal logic that frames the investment treaty regime—it was now clear to Gaviria Díaz the path the Government wished to pursue. The 'scope of sovereign action has been reduced so much that it has almost become extinct,' he observed, compelling even 'the deepest political will [to] surrender to the infinite

[35] Weber (1904a) at 102 (emphasis in original).
[36] Weber (1919b) at 360.
[37] Weber (1919b) at 351.
[38] Brown (2023) at 109.
[39] Gaviria Díaz served on the Constitutional Court from 1993–2001. I am grateful to Federico Suárez Ricaurte, who served as an assistant to the President of the Commission, for informing this sequence of events. See his account at Suárez Ricaurte (2015). The following translations were generated by Google Translate.
[40] Polodemocratico (2013). CAITISA is the acronym for Comisión para la Auditoría Integral Ciudadana de los Tratados de Protección Recíproca de Inversiones y del Sistema de Arbitraje Internacional en Materia de Inversiones.
[41] Suárez Ricaurte (2015) attributes Gaviria Díaz's thinking to the influence of Alf Ross and Scandinavian legal realism.
[42] Suárez Ricaurte (2015). The escalating conflict between President Correa and Indigenous Peoples in Ecuador is chronicled in Santos (2023) at 400–05.
[43] Gaviria Díaz (2015).
[44] Gaviria Díaz (2015) (emphasis added).

stubbornness of the facts.' This inevitably would result in CAITISA's report being filed in the garbage bin. Gaviria Díaz concluded his letter of resignation with the following:[45]

> I perfectly understand the situation you face, Mr. President, but mine is different: appealing to the Weberian dichotomy, you must act in accordance with an ethic of responsibility, which is the responsibility of the ruler. I, on the other hand, who do not have those functions, can continue to act according to the ethics of conviction, which is what has guided my behavior for so many years, and it tells me that I should not defer to factual situations that are no less worthy of censure because they are irresistible.

In truth, Gaviria Díaz chose to flatter the President. Correa had yielded to the forces of neoliberal globalization. If a politics of responsibility impelled Correa to sign a new Free Trade Agreement (FTA) with Europe, it was in the pursuit of a conviction that there was no alternative but to ally with forces he had previously declared to be contemptible.[46] This was an ethic of responsibility in alignment with investment law's ends. Gaviria Díaz, by contrast, portrayed himself as the intellectual, relying upon an ethic of principled conviction.[47] Gaviria Díaz, by the force of his resignation, would help to 'clarify' the stakes involved in Correa's yielding to the force of neoliberal logic.[48] In Weber's terms, Correa would be forced to answer for the foreseeable consequences of his actions before the Ecuadorian public.

Gaviria Díaz's letter of resignation suggests that the ethical poles of conviction and responsibility are opposed to each other. This would be a mistaken reading of Weber's ideal typical politician. At the conclusion of his lecture on the 'Profession and Vocation of Politics,' Weber admits that they are not 'absolute opposites.' Rather, they are 'complementary to one another, and only in combination do they produce the true human being who is *capable* of having a "vocation for politics".'[49] It is the unelected Gaviria Díaz, rather than Correa, who acts responsibly. He takes into account all of the effects of his action—keeping both ends and means in mind, even as they remain analytically distinct.[50] Gaviria Díaz could say, as Weber's ideal typical politician could declare: 'Here I stand, I can do no other.'[51]

[45] Gaviria Díaz (2015).
[46] I discuss Correa's inimical stance vis-à-vis BITs in Schneiderman (2013a) 148–50.
[47] Weber (1919a) at 359.
[48] Weber (1919b) at 349.
[49] Weber (1919a) at 368 (emphasis in original). Elsewhere in the lecture, Weber insists that it is 'not possible to unite the ethic of conviction with the ethic of responsibility' in (1919a) at 362.
[50] Brown (2023) at 43.
[51] Weber (1919a) at 367. The quote is attributed to Martin Luther at the Diet of Worms by the editors of Weber (1919a) at 367, fn. 60.

Bibliography

Abeyratne, Rehan and Iddo Porat (2021) 'Introduction: Towering Judges – A Conceptual and Comparative Analysis' in Rehan Abeyratne and Iddo Porat (eds) *Towering Judges: A Comparative Study of Constitutional Judges* (Cambridge UP) 1–20

Abrams, Philip (1982) *Historical Sociology* (Cornell UP)

Adair-Toteff, Christopher (2013) '"Sinn Der Welt": Max Weber and the Problem of Theodicy' *Max Weber Studies* 13: 87–107

Adair-Toteff, Christopher (2017) 'Max Weber's Legal Thinking: Why Read his Recht (Law and Legitimacy)' in Werner Gephart and Daniel Witte (eds) *Recht als Kultur? Beiträge zu Max Webers Soziologie des Rechts* (Vittorio Klostermann) 75–85

Adair-Toteff, Christopher (2018) 'Weber's "Use and Abuse" of Calvin's Doctrine of Predestination' *Journal of Religious and Political Practice* 4: 336–53

Aisbett, Emma, Carol McAusland, and Lauge Poulsen (2025) 'Relative Treatment of Aliens: How Level Is the Playing Field for Foreign Firms in Developing Countries?' *Socio-Economic Review* 23: 1975–2006

Akhavam, Payam et al. (2015) 'An open letter about investor-state dispute settlement' (20 April 2015) at https://www.opnlttr.com/letter/open-letter-about-investor-state-dispute-settlement-april-2015 (last accessed 28 January 2026)

Albrow, Martin (1970) *Bureaucracy* (Macmillan)

Albrow, Martin (1975) 'Legal Positivism and Bourgeois Materialism: Max Weber's View of the Sociology of Law' *British Journal of Law and Society* 2: 14–31

Albrow, Martin (2017) 'From Max Weber's Sociology of Law to a Sociology of Global Governance' in Werner Gephart and Daniel Witte (eds) *Recht als Kultur? Beiträge zu Max Webers Soziologie des Rechts* (Vittorio Klostermann) 527–39

Alden, Edward (2005) 'US Faces Tough Talks with Egypt in its Push for Regional Trade Accords' *The Financial Post* (September 29) 6

Aldenhoff-Hübinger, Rita (2009) 'The Editing of Max Weber's Lectures from 1894-1900: An Interim Report' *Max Weber Studies* 9: 189–99

Alexander, Gregory S. (2005) *The Global Debate Over Constitutional Property: Lessons for American Takings Jurisprudence* (U Chicago Press)

Alexander, Jeffrey C. (1983) *Theoretical Logic in Sociology, Volume Three – The Classical Attempt at Theoretical Synthesis: Max Weber* (U California Press)

Alexy, Robert (2002) *A Theory of Constitutional Rights*, translated by Julian Rivers (Oxford UP)

Alexy, Robert (2007) 'The Weight Formula' in Jerzy Stelmach, Bartosz Brozek, and Wojciech Zaluski (eds) *Studies in the Philosophy of Law III: Frontiers of the Economic Analysis of Law* (Jagiellonian UP)

Alexy, Robert (2010) 'The Construction of Constitutional Rights' *Law & Ethics of Human Rights* 4: 21–32

Alexy, Robert (2017) 'Proportionality and Rationality' in Vicki C. Jackson and Mark Tushnet (eds) *Proportionality: New Frontiers, New Challenges* (Cambridge UP) 13–29

Alschner, Wolfgang (2020) 'Correctness of Investment Awards: Why Wrong Decisions Don't Die' *The Law and Practice of International Courts and Tribunals* 18: 345–68

Alschner, Wolfgang (2022) *Investment Arbitration and State-Driven Reform: New Treaties, Old Outcomes* (Oxford UP)

Alter, Karen J. (2006) 'Delegation to International Courts and the Limits of Re-Contracting Political Power' in Darren G. Hawkins, David A. Lake, Daniel L. Nielson, and Michael J. Tierney (eds) *Delegation and Agency in International Organizations* (Cambridge UP) 312–38

Alter, Karen J. (2008) 'Agents or Trustees? International Courts in their Political Context' *European Journal of International Relations* 14: 33–63

Alter, Karen J. (2014) *The New Terrain of International Law: Courts, Politics, Rights* (Princeton UP)

Alvarez, José E. (2009) 'Contemporary Foreign Investment Law: An "Empire of Law" or the "Law of Empire"?' *Alabama Law Review* 60: 943–75

Alvarez, José E. (2010) 'What and Why are we "Re-Calibrating"?' *World Arbitration & Mediation Review* 4: 143–61

Alvarez, José E. (2011) *The Public International Law Regime Governing International Investment* (Brill)

Alvarez, José E. (2014) 'What are International Judges For? The Main Functions of International Adjudication' in Cesare P. R. Romano, Karen J. Alter, and Yuval Shany, *The Oxford Handbook of International Adjudication* (Oxford UP) 158–78

Alvarez, José E. (2016) 'Beware Border Crossings' in Tsvi Kahana and Anat Scolnicov (eds) *Boundaries of States, Boundaries of Rights: Human Rights, Private Actors And Positive Obligations* (Cambridge UP) 43–93

Alvarez, José E. and Tegan Brink (2012) 'The Argentine Crisis and Foreign Investors: A Glimpse into the Heart of the Investment Regime' *Yearbook on International Investment Law and Policy, 2010-2011*: 319–62

Álvaro, Morcillo Laiz and Klaus Schlichte (2016) 'Rationality and International Domination: Revisiting Max Weber' *International Political Sociology* 10: 168–184

American Bar Association (2016) Investment Treaty Working Group, 'Task Force Report on the Investment Court System Proposal' (14 October)

Amery, Rt. Hon. L. S. (1947) *Thoughts on the Constitution* (Oxford UP)

Ansaldi, Michael (1992) 'The German Llewellyn' *Brooklyn Law Review* 58: 705–77

Anter, Andreas (2014) *Max Weber's Theory of The Modern State: Origins, Structure and Significance* (Palgrave Macmillan)

Arato, Julian (2023) 'Two Moralities of Consistency' in August Reinisch and Stephan W. Schill (eds) *Investment Protection Standards and the Rule of Law* (Oxford UP) 235–57

Arato, Julian, Chester Brown, and Federico Ortino (2020) 'Parsing and Managing Inconsistency in Investor-State Dispute Settlement' *The Journal of World Investment & Trade* 21: 336–373

Arcuri, Alessandra and Frederica Violi (2021) 'Public Interest and International Investment Law: A Critical Perspective on Three Mainstream Narratives' in Julian Chaisse, Leïla Choukroune, and Sufian Jusoh (eds) *Handbook of International Investment Law and Policy* (Springer) 2185–2210

Arendt, Hannah (1972) *'On Violence'* in Hannah Arendt, *Crises of the Republic* (Harcourt, Brace and Company) 103–85

Aron, Raymond (1970) *Main Currents in Sociological Thought, Volume II: Durkheim, Pareto, Weber*, translated by Richard Howard and Helen Weaver (Anchor Books)

Atanasova, Dafina (2022) 'The Impact of Investment Treaties on the Rule of Law in Singapore' in N. Jansen Calamita and Ayelet Berman (eds) *Investment Treaties and the Rule of Law Promise: The Internalisation of International Commitments in Asia* (Cambridge UP) 166–203

Atiyah, P. S. (1979) *The Rise and Fall of Freedom of Contract* (Oxford UP)

Atiyah, P. S. and Robert S. Summers (1987) *Form and Substance in Anglo-American Law: A Comparative Study of Legal Reasoning, Legal Theory, and Legal Institutions* (Clarendon Press)

Bachand, Frédéric and Fabien Gélinas (2020) 'Legal Certainty and Arbitration' in Thomas Schultz and Federico Ortino (eds) *The Oxford Handbook of International Arbitration* (Oxford UP) 377–97

Baier, Horst M., Rainer Lepsius, Wolfgang J. Mommsen, and Wolfgang Schluchter (2000) 'Overview of the Text of Economy and Society by the Editors of the Max Weber Gesamtausgabe' *Max Weber Studies* 1: 104–14

Ballantyne, Jack (2023) 'A New Damages Model for an Uncertain World' *Global Arbitration Review* (14 February)

Barak, Aharon (2007) 'Proportionate Effect: The Israeli Experience' (2007) *University of Toronto Law Journal* 57: 369–82

Barak, Aharon (2012) *Proportionality, Constitutional Rights and Their Limitations*, translated by Doron Kalir (Cambridge UP)
Barbalet, Jack (2023) *Nation and State in Max Weber* (Routledge)
Barbalet, Jack (2024) 'Race and its Reformulation in Max Weber: Cultural Germanism as Political Imperialism' *Journal of Classical Sociology* 24: 3–18
Bárcena, Lucía and Fabian Flues (2022) 'From Solar Dream to Legal Nightmare: How Financial Investors, Law Firms and Arbitrators Are Profiting From the Investment Arbitration Boom in Spain' (May) (Transnational Institute and PowerShift) at https://www.tni.org/en/publication/from-solar-dream-to-legal-nightmare (last accessed 15 June 2023)
Barnett, Michael N. and Martha Finnemore (1999) 'The Politics, Power, and Pathologies of International Organizations' *International Organization* 53: 699–732
Barnett, Michael and Martha Finnemore (2004) *Rules for the World: International Organizations in Global Politics* (Cornell UP)
Barry, Brian (1995) *Justice as Impartiality* (Oxford UP)
Bauerle Danzman, Sarah (2019) 'The Political Economy of Bilateral Investment Treaties' in Markus Krajewski and Rhea Tamara Hoffman (eds) *Research Handbook on Foreign Direct Investment* (Edward Elgar) 11–38
Bauman, Zygmunt (1989) *Modernity and the Holocaust* (Cornell UP)
Beatty, David M. (2004) *The Ultimate Rule of Law* (Oxford UP)
Beck, Ulrich (1999) *World Risk Society* (Polity)
Beck, Ulrich (2009) *World at Risk*, translated by Ciarin Cronin (Polity)
Beck, Ulrich, Anthony Giddens, and Scott Lash (1994) *Reflexive Modernization: Politics, Tradition and Aesthetics in the Modern Social Order* (Stanford UP)
Bedjaoui, Mohammed (1979) *Towards a New International Economic Order* (Holmes & Meier)
Beetham, David (1985) *Max Weber and the Theory of Modern Politics* (Polity)
Beetham, David (1987) *Bureaucracy* (U of Minnesota Press)
Beetham, David (1989) 'Max Weber and the Liberal Political Tradition' *European Journal of Sociology/Archives Européennes de Sociologie* 30: 311–23
Beetham, David (1991) *The Legitimation of Power* (Macmillan)
Behn, Daniel, Malcolm Langford, and Laura Létourneau-Tremblay (2020) 'Empirical Perspectives on Investment Arbitration: What Do We Know? Does it Matter?' *Journal of World Investment & Trade* 21: 188–250
Behn, Daniel, Tarald Laudal Berge, and Malcolm Langford (2018) 'Poor states or Poor Governance? Explaining Outcomes in Investment Treaty Arbitration' *Northwestern Journal of International Law & Business* 38: 333–389
Behn, Daniel, Ole Kristian Fauchald, and Malcolm Langford (2021) A Global Public Good? An Empirical Perspective on International Investment Law and Arbitration' in Massimo Iovane, Fulvio M. Palombino, Daniele Amoroso, and Giovanni Zarra (eds) *The Protection of General Interests in Contemporary International Law: A Theoretical and Empirical Inquiry* (Oxford UP) 91–118
Behn, Daniel, Ole Kristian Fauchald, and Malcolm Langford (2022a) 'Introduction: The Legitimacy of Investment Arbitration' in Daniel Behn, Ole Kristian Fauchald, and Malcolm Langford (eds) *The Legitimacy of Investment Arbitration: Empirical Perspectives* (Cambridge UP) 1–38
Behn, Daniel, Ole Kristian Fauchald, and Malcolm Langford (2022b) 'The International Investment Law Regime and its Discontents' in Daniel Behn, Ole Kristian Fauchald, and Malcolm Langford (eds) *The Legitimacy of Investment Arbitration: Empirical Perspectives* (Cambridge UP) 39–82
Beirne, Piers (1979) 'Ideology and Rationality in Max Weber's Sociology of Law' *Research in Law and Sociology* 2: 103–31
Bell, Catherine (2014) 'Belief: A Classificatory Lacuna and Disciplinary "Problem"' in Willi Braun and Russell T. McCutcheon (eds) *Introducing Religion: Essays in Honour of Jonathan Z. Smith* (Routledge) 85–99
Bell, David A. (2020) *Men on Horseback: The Power of Charisma in the Age of Revolution* (Farrar, Straus and Giroux)

Bell, John (1987) 'The Judge as Bureaucrat' in John Eekalaar and John Bell (eds) *Oxford Essays in Jurisprudence*, 3rd Series (Clarendon Press)

Bellak, Christian (2015) *Economic Impact of Investment Agreements' Department of Economics*, Vienna University of Economics and Business, Working Paper No. 200 (August) https://epub.wu.ac.at/4625/1/wp200.pdf (last accessed 12 August 2023)

Bellak, Christian and Lorenz Reiter (2020) 'Effects of BITs on FDI: The Role of Publication Bias' in Julien Chaisse, Leïla Choukroune, and Sufian Jusoh (eds) *Handbook of International Investment Law and Policy* (Springer) 1–28

Bellamy, Richard (1992) 'Liberalism and Nationalism in the Thought of Max Weber' *History of European Ideas* 14: 499–507

Belvisi, Francesco (2023) 'Jhering, Rudolf von' in Gianfrancesco Zanetti, Mortimer Sellers, and Stephane Kirst (eds) *Handbook of the History of the Philosophy of Law and Social Philosophy, Volume 2: From Kant to Nietszche* (Springer) 181–92

Bendix, Reinhard (1962) *Max Weber: An Intellectual Portrait* (Anchor Books)

Bendix, Reinhard (1968) 'Bureaucracy' in Reinhard Bendix and Guenther Roth, *Scholarship and Partisanship: Essays on Max Weber* (U California Press, 1971) 129–55

Bendix, Reinhard and Guenther Roth (1971) *Scholarship and Partisanship: Essays on Max Weber* (U California Press)

Bensman, Joseph and Michael Givant (1975) 'Charisma and Modernity: The Use and Abuse of a Concept' *Social Research* 42: 570–614

Berge, Tarald Laudal and Axel Berger (2021) 'Do Investor-State Dispute Settlement Cases Influence Domestic Environmental Regulation? The Role of Respondent State Bureaucratic Capacity' *Journal of International Dispute Settlement* 12: 1–41

Berger, Peter L. (1967) *The Sacred Canopy: Elements of a Sociological Theory of Religion* (Random House)

Berman, Harold J. (1983) *Law and Revolution: The Formation of the Western Legal Tradition* (Harvard UP)

Berman, Harold J. (1985) 'The Religious Sources of General Contract Law: An Historical Perspective' *Journal of Law and Religion* 4: 103–24

Berman, Harold J. (2003) *Law and Revolution II: The Impact of the Protestant Reformations on the Western Legal Tradition* (Harvard UP)

Bernasconi, Nathalie, Martin Dietrich Brauch, and Howard Mann (2020) 'Civil Society and International Investment Arbitration: Tracing the Evolution of Concern' in Frederico Ortino and Thomas Schultz (eds) *Oxford Handbook of International Arbitration* (Oxford UP) 304–27

Bhambra, Gurminder K. and John Holmwood (2021) *Colonialism and Modern Social Theory* (Polity)

Bishop, R. Doak, James Crawford, and W. Michael Reisman (2005) *Foreign Investment Disputes: Cases, Materials And Commentary* (Kluwer Law)

Bjorklund, Andrea (2008) 'Investment Treaty Arbitral Decisions as Jurisprudence Constante' in Colin Picker, Isabella Bunn, and Douglas Arner (eds) *International Economic Law: The State and Future of the Discipline* (British Institute of International and Comparative Law) 265

Bjorklund, Andrea (2023) 'The Road(s) Not Taken—the Past, Present, and Future of International Investment Law Reform' *Arbitration International* 39: 455–68

Bjorklund, Andrea and August Reinisch (2012) 'Soft Codification of International Investment Law' in Andrea Bjorklund and August Reinisch (eds) *International Investment Law and Soft Law* (Edward Elgar) 305–18

Blank, Yishai (2011) 'The Reenchantment of Law' *Cornell Law Review* 96: 633–70

Blau, Peter M. (1968) 'Weber's Theory of Bureaucracy' in Dennis Wrong (ed) *Max Weber* (Prentice Hall, Inc., 1970) 141–45

Boatcă, Manuela (2013) '"From the Standpoint of Germanism": A Postcolonial Critique of Weber's Theory of Race and Ethnicity' *Political Power and Social Theory* 24: 55–80

Bodansky, Daniel (2013) 'Legitimacy in International Law and International Relations' in Jeffrey L. Dunoff and Mark A. Pollack (eds) *Interdisciplinary Perspectives on International Law and International Relations: The State of the Art* (Cambridge UP) 321–42

Bomhoff, Jacco (2008) 'Balancing, the Global and the Local: Judicial Balancing as a Problematic Topic in Comparative (Constitutional) Law' *Hastings International and Comparative Law Review* 31: 555–86

Bonnitcha, Jonathan (2022) 'The Impact of Investment Treaties on the Rule of Law in Myanmar' in N. Jansen Calamita and Ayelet Berman (eds) *Investment Treaties and the Rule of Law Promise: The Internalisation of International Commitments in Asia* (Cambridge UP) 127–65

Book of General Lawes and Libertyes (1648) (Harvard UP, 1929)

Borchardt, Knut (2002) 'Max Weber's Writings on the Bourse: Puzzling Out a Forgotten Corpus' *Max Weber Studies* 2: 139–62

Born, Gary (2021) 'The 1933 Directives on Arbitration of the German Reich: Echoes of the Past?' *Journal of International Arbitration* 38: 417–56

Born, Gary and Stephanie Forrest (2019) 'Amicus Curiae Participation in Investment Arbitration' *ICSID Review* 34: 626–65

Born, Gary, Danielle Morris, and Stephanie Forrest (2020) '"A Margin of Appreciation": Appreciating Its Irrelevance in International Law' *Harvard International Law Journal* 61: 65–134

Bottomore, Tom (1984) *The Frankfurt School* (Ellis Horwood Limited and Tavistock Publications)

Boué, Juan Carlos (2022) 'Much More than a Footnote (or Three): Frank C. Hendryx and an Untold Story of Petroleum Concessions and the Genesis of ICSID' *Journal of International Dispute Settlement* 13: 1–40

Boué, Juan Carlos (2023) 'The Determination of Quantum and Claim Inflation' in David Schneiderman and Gus Van Harten (eds) *Rethinking Investment Law: Perspectives and Prospects* (Oxford UP) 200–21

Bourdieu, Pierre (1984) *Distinction: A Social Critique of the Judgement of Taste*, translated by Richard Nice (Harvard UP)

Bourdieu, Pierre (1987) 'The Force of Law: Toward a Sociology of the Juridical Field' *Hastings Law Journal* 38: 805–53

Bourdieu, Pierre (1991) *Language and Symbolic Power*, translated by Gino Raymond and Matthew Adamson (Harvard UP)

Bourdieu, Pierre (1992) 'For an International of Intellectuals' in Pierre Bourdieu, *Political Interventions: Social Science and Political Action*, translated by David Fernbach (Verso) 209–17

Bourdieu, Pierre (1996) *The State Nobility*, translated by Lauretta C. Clough (Stanford UP)

Bourdieu, Pierre (1997) 'From the King's House to Reason of State: A Model of the Genesis of the Bureaucratic Field' in Loïc Wacquant (ed) *Pierre Bourdieu and Democratic Politics* (Polity, 2005) 29–54

Bourdieu, Pierre (2000) *Pascalian Meditations*, translated by Richard Nice (Stanford UP)

Bourdieu, Pierre (2005) *The Social Structures of the Economy*, translated by Chris Turner (Polity)

Bourdieu, Pierre (2014) *On the State: Lectures at the Collège de France, 1989-1992*, translated by David Fernbach (Polity)

Bourdieu, Pierre (2023) *Politics and Sociology, General Sociology, Volume 5: Lectures at the Collège de France, 1985-1986*, translated by Peter Collier (Polity)

Bourdieu Pierre and Jean-Claude Passeron (1990) *Reproduction in Education, Society and Culture*, 2nd ed, translated by Richard Nice (Sage)

Bourdieu, Pierre and Löic Wacquant (1999) 'On the Cunning of Imperial Reason' *Theory, Culture & Society* 16: 41–58

Bourdieu, Pierre, Franz Schultheis, and Andreas Pfeuffer (2011) 'With Weber Against Weber: In Conversation with Pierre Bourdieu' in Simon Susen and Bryan S. Turner (eds) *The Legacy of Pierre Bourdieu: Critical Essays* (Anthem Press) 111–21

Braoudakis, Nikos, Rosanne Craveia, and Clémentine Baldon (2024) 'Neutralising the ECT Sunset Clause Inter Se' *ICSID Review - Foreign Investment Law Journal* 39: 347–70

Breiner, Peter (1996) *Max Weber and Democratic Politics* (Cornell UP)

Breiner, Peter (2023) 'Weber's Concept of Traditional *Herrschaft* Reexamined' in Alan Sica (ed) *The Routledge International Handbook on Max Weber* (Routledge) 382–94

Brekoulakis, Stavros and Anna Howard (2024) 'Impartiality and the Construction of Trust in Investor-State Dispute Settlement' *ICSID Review* 38: 644–69

Breuer, Stefan (2019) 'The Relevance of Weber's Conception and Typology of *Herrschaft*' in Edith Hanke, Lawrence A. Scaff, and Sam Whimster (eds) *The Oxford Handbook of Max Weber* (Oxford UP) 237–57

Broches, Aron (1972) 'The Convention on the Settlement of Investment Disputes Between States and Nationals of Other States' *Recueil des Cours* II: 331–410

Brower, II, Charles H. (2003) 'Structure, Legitimacy, and NAFTA's Investment Chapter' *Vanderbilt Journal of Transnational Law* 36: 37–94

Brower, Charles N. (1976) 'The Charter of Economic Rights and Duties of States and the American Constitutional Tradition: A Bicentennial Perspective on the New International Economic Order' *Int'l Lawyer* 10: 701–709

Brower, Charles N. (2023) *Judging Iran: A Memoir of the Hague, the White House, and Life on the Front Line of International Justice* (Disruption Books)

Brower, Charles N. (2024) 'Foreword to the Second Edition' in Nikos Lavranos and Stefano Castagna (eds) *International Arbitration and EU Law*, 2nd ed. (Edward Elgar Publishing) xxiv–xxv

Brower, Charles N. and Sadie Blanchard (2014) 'What's in a Meme? The Truth About Investor-State Arbitration: Why It Need Not, and Must Not, be Repossessed by States' *Columbia Journal of Transnational Law* 52: 689–777

Brower, Charles N. and Sarah Melikian (2015) '"We Have Met the Enemy and He is US!" Is the Industrialized North "Going South" on Investor-State Arbitration?' *Arbitration International* 31: 19–26

Brower, Charles N. and Lee A. Steven (2001) 'Who Then Should Judge? Developing the International Rule of Law under NAFTA Chapter 11' *Chicago Journal of International Law* 2: 193–202

Brower, Charles N. and John B. Tepe, Jr. (1975) 'The Charter of Economic Rights and Duties of States: A Reflection or Rejection of International Law?' *International Lawyer* 9: 295–318

Brown, Wendy (2023) *Nihilistic Times: Thinking with Max Weber* (Belknap Press)

Brownlie, Ian (1979) *Principles of Public International Law*, 3rd ed. (Oxford UP)

Brubaker, Rogers (1984) *The Limits of Rationality: An Essay on the Social and Moral Thought of Max Weber* (Routledge)

Bruun, Hans Henrik (2007) *Science, Values and Politics in Max Weber's Methodology*, New Expanded Edition (Ashgate)

Bruun, Hans Henrik and Sam Whimster (eds) (2012) *Max Weber: Complete Methodological Writings*, translated by Hans Henrik Bruun (Routledge)

Bücheler, Gebhard (2015) *Proportionality in Investor-State Arbitration* (Oxford UP)

Bungenberg, Marc (2023) 'Democracy and International Investment Law' in Stefan Kröll, Andrea K. Bjorklund, and Franco Ferrari (eds) *Cambridge Compendium of International and Commercial Arbitration*, Volume 1 (Cambridge UP) 186–210

Bungenberg, Marc and August Reinisch (2020) 'From Arbitral Tribunals to a Multilateral Investment Court: The European Union Approach' Julian Chaisse, Leïla Choukroune, and Sufian Jusoh (eds) *Handbook of International Investment Law and Policy* (Springer) 2285–2319

Burke-White, William W. (2008) 'The Argentine Financial Crisis: State Liability Under BITs and the Legitimacy of the ICSID System' *Asian Journal of WTO & International Health Law and Policy* 3: 199–234

Butler, Judith and Cornel West (2011) 'Dialogue' in Judith Butler, Jürgen Habermas, Charles Taylor, and Cornel West (eds) *The Power of Religion in the Public Sphere* (Columbia UP) 101–08

Butterfield, Herbert (1965) *The Whig Interpretation of History* (W. W. Norton and Company)

Butterfield, Herbert (1981) *The Origins of History*, edited by Adam Wilson (Eyre Methuen)

Cahill-O'Calaghan, Rachel, Anna Howard, and Stavros Brekoulakis (2023) 'Influence in Investor-Dispute Settlement: A Dynamic Concept' *Journal of International Dispute Settlement* 14:1–23

Calamita, N. Jansen (2015) 'The Principle of Proportionality and the Problem of Indeterminacy in International Investment Treaties' *Yearbook on International Investment Law & Policy 2014*: 157–200

Calamita, N. Jansen and Ayelet Berman (eds) (2022) *Investment Treaties and the Rule of Law Promise: The Internalisation of International Commitments in Asia* (Cambridge UP)

Cao, Lan (1997) 'Law and Economic Development: A New Beginning' *Texas International Law Journal* 32: 545–59

Carim, Xavier (2016) 'International Investment Agreements and Africa's Structural Transformation: A Perspective from South Africa' in Kavalit Singh and Burghard Ilge (eds) *Rethinking Bilateral Investment Treaties: Critical Issues and Policy Choices* (BothEnds/ Madhyam/Somo) 51–67

Caserta, Salvatore and Mikael Rask Madsen (2022) 'The Situated and Bounded Rationality of International Courts: A Structuralist Approach to International Adjudicative Practices' *Leiden Journal of International Law* 35: 931–43

Cavalli, Luciano (2006) 'Charisma and Twentieth Century Politics' in Scott Lash and Sam Whimster (eds) *Max Weber, Rationality and Modernity* (Routledge) 317–33

Censat Agua Viva (2023a) 'Does Cerrejón Always Win? Between Corporate Impunity for Human Rights Violations and the Quest for Comprehensive Reparation in Times of Transition' at https://www.cinep.org.co/publi-files/PDFS/20231114_Glencore_Report_EN.pdf? (last accessed 1 April 2025)

Censat Agua Viva (2023b) 'Glencore Persists in its Behaviour of Denial and Evasion of Accountability: Response to the Company's Letter dated 2 October 2023' at https://www.fairfinanceinternational.org/media/4teh43se/respuesta-carta-glencore_colombia-rebuttal-letter_en.pdf (last accessed 1 April 2025)

Chang, Ha-Joon (2002) *Kicking Away the Ladder: Development Strategy in Historical Perspective* (Anthem Press)

Chalcraft, David J. (2008) 'Introduction: Interweaving Past and Present' in David Chalcraft, Fanon Howell, Marisol Lopez Menendez, and Hector Vera (eds) *Max Weber Matters: Interweaving Past and Present* (Routledge) 1–14

Charlotin, Damien (2022) 'Swedish Supreme Court Sets Aside PL Holdings v. Poland Intra-EU Award, Relying on the CJEU's Assessment of the Case to Ground a Breach of Public Policy' *Investment Aribtration Reporter* (14 December)

Cheng, Bin (1953) *General Principles of Law as Applied by International Courts and Tribunals* (Steven and Sons Limited)

Chilton, Adam S. (2016) 'The Political Motivations of the United States' Bilateral Investment Treaty Program' *Review of International Political Economy* 23: 614–42

Choudhry, Sujit (2006) 'What is the Real Legacy of *Oakes*? Two Decades of Proportionality Analysis Under the Canadian *Charter*'s Section 1' *Supreme Court Law Review* (2d) 34: 501–35

Coates, Benjamin Allen (2016) *Legalist Empire: International Law and American Foreign Relations in the Early Twentieth Century* (Oxford UP)

Cohen, Ira J. (1985) 'The Underemphasis on Democracy in Marx and Weber' in Robert J. Antonio and Ronald M. Glassman (eds) *A Weber-Marx Dialogue* (U Press of Kansas) 274–99

Cohen, Jean (1972) 'Max Weber and the Dynamics of Rationalized Domination' in Peter Hamilton (ed) *Max Weber: Critical Assessments 2, Volume 1* (Routledge) 84–105

Cohen, Jean L. and Andrew Arato (1992) *Civil Society and Political Theory*. (The MIT Press)

Cohen-Eliya, Moshe and Iddo Porat (2004) 'Proportionality and Justification' *University of Toronto Law Journal* 64: 458–77

Cohen-Eliya, Moshe and Iddo Porat (2010) 'American Balancing and German Proportionality: The Historical Origins' *International Journal of Constitutional Law* 8: 263–86

Cole, Tony, Pietro Ortolani, and Dean Wright (2020) 'Arbitration in its Psychological Context: A Contextual Behavioural Account of Arbitral Decision-Making' in Thomas Schultz and Federico Ortino (eds) *The Oxford Handbook of International Arbitration* (Oxford UP) 910–49

Colen, Lisbeth and Andrea Guariso (2013) 'What Type of Foreign Direct Investment is Attracted by Bilateral Investment Treaties?' in Olivier de Schutter, Johan Swinnen, and Jan Wouters (eds)

Foreign Direct Investment and Human Development: The Law and Economics of International Investment Agreements (Brill) 138–55

Collins, Randall (1980) 'Weber's Last Theory of Capitalism: A Systemization' *American Sociological Review* 45: 925–42

Colliot-Thélène, Catherine (1992) *Le Désenchatement de L'État: De Hegel à Max Weber* (Les Éditions de Minuit)

Colliot-Thélène, Catherine (2008) 'The Disenchantment of Law? Formal and Substantive Rationality in Weber's Work' in Frank Adloff and Manuel Borutta (eds) *Max Weber in the 21st Century: Transdisciplinarity within the Social Sciences* (EUI Working Paper MWP No. 2008/35) 81–89 at https://hdl.handle.net/1814/9110 (last accessed 23 April 2025)

Condorcet, Marquis de (1793) 'On the Principles of the Constitutional Plan Presented to the National Convention' in *Condorcet: Selected Writings*, edited by Keith Michael Baker (Bobbs-Merrill, 1976) 143–82

Connolly, William E. (1993) *The Augustinian Imperative: A Reflection on the Politics of Morality* (Sage Publications)

Cotterrell, Roger (1983) 'Legality and Political Legitimacy in the Sociology of Max Weber' in David Sugarman (ed) *Legality, Ideology and the State* (Academic Press) 61–94

Cottier, Thomas (2017) 'The Role of Lawyers, Courts and Legal Education' in Thomas Cottier and Krista Nadakavukaren Shafer (eds) *Elgar Encyclopedia of International Economic Law* (Edward Elgar) 578–81

Cottier, Thomas, Roberto Echandi, Rachel Liechti-McKee, Tetyana Payosova, and Charlotte Sieber (2017) 'The Principle of Proportionality in International Law: Foundations and Variations' *Journal of World Trade* 18: 628–72

Cottier, Thomas, Katja Gehne, and Maria Schultheiss (2012) 'The Protection of Property in International Law: The Missing Pieces' in Holger Hestermeyer and Rüdiger Wolfrum (eds) *Coexistence, Cooperation and Solidarity: liber amicorum Rüdiger Wolfrum* (Brill/Nijhoff) 367–96

Coutu, Michel (2009) 'Max Weber and the Labour Contract: Between Realism and Formal Legal Thought' *Journal of Law and Society* 36: 558–78

Coutu, Michel (2013) 'Weber Reading Stammler: What Horizons for the Sociology of Law?' *Journal of Law and Society* 40: 356–74

Coutu, Michel (2018) *Max Weber's Interpretive Sociology of Law* (Abingdon: Routledge)

Coutu, Michel (2024) 'Max Weber and the Labour Constitution' *Max Weber Studies* 24: 129–53

Craiutu, Aurelian (2003) *Liberalism Under Siege: The Political Thought of The French Doctrinaires* (Rowman & Littlefield)

Craiutu, Aurelian (2008) 'Guizot's Elitist Theory of Representative Government' *Critical Review* 15: 261–84

Crawford, James (2017) 'The Ideal Arbitrator: Does One Size Fit All' *American University International Law Review* 32: 1003–22

Cruz Trabanino, Patricia (2022) 'State Counterclaims and the "Legitimacy Crisis" in Investment Treaty Arbitration' *European Yearbook of International Economic Law 2021* 12: 203–27

Dafe, Florence and Zoe Williams (2021) 'Banking on Courts: Financialization and the Rise of Third-Party Funding in Investment Arbitration' *Review of International Political Economy* 28: 1362–84

Dale, Gareth (2010) *Karl Polanyi: The Limits of the Market* (Polity)

Dam, Kenneth W. (2006) *The Law-Growth Nexus: The Rule of Law and Economic Development* (Brookings Institution Press)

Dann, Philipp (2023) 'The Law of International Development' in Ruth Buchanan, Luis Eslava, and Sundhya Pahuja (eds) *The Oxford Handbook of International Law and Development* (Oxford UP) 35–60

Danzman, Sarah Bauerle (2019) 'The Political Economy of Bilateral Investment Treaties' in Markus Krajewski and Rhea Tamara Hoffman (eds) *Research Handbook on Foreign Direct Investment* (Edward Elgar) 11–38

Dardot, Pierre and Christian Laval (2019) *Never-Ending Nightmare: The Neoliberal Assault on Democracy*, translated by Gregory Elliott (Verso)

Daseking, Christina, Atish R. Ghosh, Timothy D. Lane, and Alun H. Thomas (2004) 'Lessons from the Crisis in Argentina' IMF Occasional Paper No. 236 (10 February), at https://www.imf.org/external/pubs/NFT/Op/236/op236.pdf (last accessed 7 June 2023)

d'Aspremont, Jean (2020) 'The Control Over Knowledge by International Courts and Arbitral Tribunals' in Thomas Schultz and Federico Ortino (eds) *The Oxford Handbook of International Arbitration* (Oxford UP) 328–45

Dautaj, Ylli (2021) 'Between Backlash and the Re-Emerging "Calvo Doctrine": Investor State Dispute Settlement in an Era of Socialism, Protectionism, and Nationalism' *Northwestern Journal of International Law & Business* 41: 273–323

Davies, William (2017) *The Limits of Neoliberalism: Authority, Sovereignty, and the Logic of Competition*, Rev'd Ed. (Sage)

Davis, Kevin E. and Michael J. Trebilcock (2008) 'The Relationship between Law and Development: Optimists versus Skeptics' *The American Journal of Comparative Law* 56: 895–946

Davitti, Daria (2021) 'Proportionality and Human Rights Protection in International Investment Arbitration' in Ulf Linderfalk and Eduardo Gill-Pedro (eds) *Revisiting Proportionality in International and European Law* (Brill) 70–90

Davitti, Daria and Paolo Vargiu (2023) 'Litigation Finance and the Assetization of International Investment Arbitration' *Journal of World Investment & Trade* 24: 487–500

d'Avray, D. L. (2010) *Rationalities in History: A Weberian Essay in Comparison* (Cambridge: Cambridge University Press)

d'Avray, David (2023) 'Rationalities and Rationalization' in Alan Sica (ed) *The Routledge International Handbook on Max Weber* (Routledge) 63–75

De Brabandere, Eric and Paula Baldini Miranda da Cruz (2020) 'The Role of Proportionality in International Investment Law and Arbitration: A System-Specific Perspective' *Nordic Journal of International Law* 89: 471–91

Defensoría del Pueblo de Colombia, La (DPC) (2025) 'Defensoría del Pueblo verifica derechos fundamentales en la Alta Guajira' (4 March) at https://www.defensoria.gov.co/en/-/defensoria-del-pueblo-verifica-derechos-fundamentales-en-la-alta-guajira (last accessed 31 May 2025)

d'Entrèves, Passerin A. (1970) *Natural Law: An Introduction to Legal Philosophy*, 2nd ed. (Hutchinson)

Derman, Joshua (2025) 'Max Weber, Imperialism, and the Fate of Globalization' in Joshua Derman and Peter E. Gordon (eds) *Max Weber at 100* (Oxford UP) 170–95

Desai, Deval (2023) *Expert Ignorance: The Law and Politics of Rule of Law Reform* (Cambridge UP)

De Vriese, Herbert and Guido Vanheeswijck (2024) 'Do We Need an Alternative to the Disenchantment Narrative? Assessing Joas' Criticism of Weber Against the Enduring Merit of the Concept and Theory of Disenchantment' *Max Weber Studies* 24: 86–113

Dewey, John (1927) *The Public and its Problems* (Henry Holt)

Dezalay, Sara and Yves Dezalay (2017) 'Professionals of International Justice: From the Shadow of State Diplomacy to the Pull of the Market for Commercial Arbitration' in Jean D'Aspremont, Tarcisio Gazzini, André Nollkaemper, and Wouter Werner (eds) *International Law as a Profession* (Cambridge UP) 311–37

Dezalay, Yves and Bryant G. Garth (1996) *Dealing in Virtue: International Commercial Arbitration and the Construction of a Transnational Legal Order* (U Chicago Press)

Dezalay, Yves and Bryant G. Garth (2008) 'Law, Lawyers, and Empire' in Michael Grossberg and Christopher Tomlins (eds) *The Cambridge History of Law in America, Volume III: The Twentieth Century and After (1920-)* (Cambridge UP) 718–57

Dezalay, Yves and Bryant G. Garth (2012) 'Corporate Law Firms, NGOs, and Issues of Legitimacy for a Global Legal Order' *Fordham Law Review* 80: 2309–45

Dicey, A. V. (1908) *Introduction to the Study of the Law of the Constitution*, 7th ed. (Macmillan and Co., Limited)

Dingle, Lesley and Daniel Bates (2009) 'A Conversation with Judge Stephen M. Schwebel' Squire Law Library Eminent Scholars Archive (13 May) at https://www.squire.law.cam.ac.uk/sites/

www.law.cam.ac.uk/files/images/www.squire.law.cam.ac.uk/legacy/Media/Eminent%20Scholars%20Archive%20Transcripts/schwebel_transcript_may_2009.pdf (last accessed 17 February 2024)

Dobner, Petra (2010) 'More Law, Less Democracy? Democracy and Transnational Constitutionalism' in Petra Dobner and Martin Loughlin (eds) *The Twilight of Constitutionalism?* (Oxford UP) 141–61

Dolzer, Rudolf and Christoph Schreuer (2008) *Principles of International Investment Law* (Oxford UP)

Dolzer, Rudolf, Ursula Kriebaum, and Christoph Schreuer (2022) *Principles of International Investment Law*, 3rd ed. (Oxford UP)

Douglas, Zachary (2006) 'Nothing if Not Critical for Investment Treaty Arbitration: Occidental, Eureko and Methanex' *Arbitration International* 22: 27–52

Douglas, Zachary (2009) *The International Law of Investment Claims* (Cambridge UP)

Douglass, R. Bruce (2018) *The Iron Cage Revisited: Max Weber in the Neoliberal Era* (Routledge)

Dyzenhaus, David (1997) *Legality and Legitimacy: Carl Schmitt, Hans Kelsen and Hermann Heller in Weimar* (Oxford UP)

Eberhardt, Pia and Cecilia Olivet (2012) *Profiting from Injustice: How Law Firms, Arbitrators And Financiers Are Fuelling An Investment Arbitration Boom* (Corporate Europe Observatory and Transnational Institute) at https://www.tni.org/files/download/profitingfrominjustice.pdf (last accessed 11 February 2026)

Echandi, Roberto (2011) 'What Do Developing Countries Expect from the International Invetsment Regime?' in José E. Alvarez and Karl P. Sauvant (eds) *The Evolving International Investment Regime: Expectations, Realities, Options* (Oxford UP) 3–21

Ehrlich, Eugen (1936) *Fundamental Principles of the Sociology of Law*, translated by Walter L. Moll (Harvard UP)

Eisenstadt, S.N. (1959) 'Bureaucracy and Bureaucratization' *Current Sociology* 7: 99–124

Eisenstadt, S. N. (1959) 'Bureaucracy, Bureaucratization and Debureaucratization' *Administrative Science Quarterly* 4: 302–20

Eliaeson, Sven (1998) 'Max Weber and Plebiscitary Democracy' in Ralph Schroeder (ed) *Max Weber, Democracy and Modernization* (Macmillan) 47–60

Eliaeson, Sven (2000) 'Constitutional Caesarism: Weber's Politics in their German Context' in Stephen Turner (ed) *The Cambridge Companion to Weber* (Cambridge UP) 131–48

Eliaeson, Sven (2002) *Max Weber's Methodologies: Interpretation and Critique* (Polity)

Elkins, Zachary, Andrew T. Guzman, and Beth A. Simmons (2006) 'Competing for Capital: The Diffusion of Bilateral Investment Treaties, 1960–2000' *International Organization* 60: 811–46

Escobar, Arturo (1995) *Encountering Development: The Making and Unmaking of the Third World* (Princeton UP)

Esty, Daniel (2006) 'Good Governance as the Supranational Scale: Globalizing Administrative Law' *Yale Law Journal* 115: 1490–1562

European Commission (2023) 'Non-paper from the European Commission: Next Steps as Regards the EU, Euratom and Member States' *Membership in the Energy Charter Treaty* (n.d.) at https://www.euractiv.com/wp-content/uploads/sites/2/2023/02/Non-paper_ECT_nextsteps.pdf (last accessed 25 February 2023)

European Federation of Investment Law and Arbitration (EFILA) (2014) 'EFILA final response to the EU Commission's consultation on investment protection and investor-to-state dispute settlement (ISDS) in the Transatlantic Trade and Investment Partnership Agreement (TTIP)' (12 July) online at http://efila.org/wp-content/uploads/2014/07/EFILA_TTIP_final_submission.pdf (last accessed 25 May 2025)

Ewing, Sally (1987) 'Formal Justice and the Spirit of Capitalism: Max Weber's Sociology of Law' *Law & Society Review* 21: 487-

Fauchauld, Ole Kristian (2021) 'International Investment Law in Support of the Right to Development?' *Leiden Journal of International Law* 34:181–201

Favro, Alberto (2022) 'New ICSID Arbitration Rules: A Further Step in The Regulation of Third-Party Funding' *Kluwer Arbitration Blog* (3 June) at https://arbitrationblog.kluwerarbitrat

ion.com/2022/06/03/new-icsid-arbitration-rules-a-further-step-in-the-regulation-of-third-party-funding/ (last accessed 20 May 2024)
Feigenbaum, Harvey, Jeffrey Henig, and Chris Hamnet (1999) *Shrinking the State: The Political Underpinnings of Privatization* (Cambridge UP)
Finger, Matthias and Bérangère Ruchat (2000) 'The Transformation of International Public Organizations: The Case of UNCTAD' Working Paper de l'IDHEAP No. 14/2000 (November) at https://api.unil.ch/iris/server/api/core/bitstreams/92bd086b-7ab6-4483-ba5e-4ff133134 4a8/content (last accessed 4 March 2026)
Finnis, John (1980) *Natural Law and Natural Rights* (Clarendon Press)
Fiss, Owen M. (1983) 'The Bureaucratization of the Judiciary' *The Yale Law Journal* 92: 1442–68
Ford, Laura R. (2019) 'Law and the Development of Capitalism' in Edith Hanke, Lawrence Scaff, and Sam Whimster (eds) *The Oxford Handbook of Max Weber* (Oxford UP) 88–109
Ford, Laura R. (2020) 'Law and Development of Capitalism' in Edith Hanke, Lawrence Scaff, and Sam Whimster (eds) *The Oxford Handbook of Max Weber* (Oxford UP) 89–103
Ford, Laura R. (2025) 'Review Essay: Was Max Weber a Legal Positivist?' *Max Weber Studies* 25: 90–120
Forst, Rainer (2017) *Normativity and Power: Analyzing Social Orders of Justification* (Oxford UP)
Franck, Susan D. (2004–05) 'The Legitimacy Crisis in Investment Treaty Arbitration: Privatizing Public International Law through Inconsistent Decisions' *Fordham Law Review* 73: 1521–1625
Franck, Susan D. (2009) 'Development and Outcomes of Investment Treaty Arbitration' *Harvard Journal of International Law* 50: 435–89
Franck, Susan D. (2019) *Arbitration Costs: Myths and Realities in Investment Treaty Arbitration* (Oxford UP)
Fraser, Nancy (2007) 'Transnationalizing the Public Sphere: On the Legitimacy and Efficacy of Public Opinion in a Post-Westphalian World' *Theory, Culture & Society* 24: 7–30
Friedmann, Wolfgang (1957) *Legal Theory*, 3rd ed. (Stevens & Sons Limited)
Friedrich, Carl Joachim (1961) 'Political Leadership and the Problem of Charismatic Power' *Journal of Politics* 23: 3–24
Friedrich, Carl Joachim (1963) *The Philosophy of Law in Historical Perspective*, 2nd ed. (U Chicago Press)
Friedrich, Carl Joachim (ed) (1967) Nomos V: *The Public Interest* (Atherton Press)
Freund, Julien (1968) *The Sociology of Max Weber*, translated by Mary Ilford (Random House)
Frug, Gerald E. (1984) 'The Ideology of Bureaucracy in American Law' *Harvard Law Review* 97: 1276–1388
Fuller, Lon L. (1936) 'American Legal Realism' *Proceedings of the American Philosophical Society* 76: 191–235
Fuller, Lon L. (1940) *The Law in Quest of Itself* (Foundation Press)
Fuller, Lon L. (1941) 'Consideration and Form' *Columbia Law Review* 41: 799–824
Fuller, Lon L. (1949) *The Problems of Jurisprudence*, Temporary Ed. (The Foundation Press)
Fuller, Lon L. (1954a) 'American Legal Philosophy at Mid-Century' *Journal of Legal Education* 6: 457–85
Fuller, Lon L. (1954b) 'Some Reflections on Legal and Economic Freedoms – A Review of Robert L. Hale's "Freedom Through Law"' *Columbia Law Review* 54: 70–82
Fuller, Lon L. (1955) 'Freedom – A Suggested Analysis' Harvard Law Review 68: 1305–25
Fuller, Lon L. (1956) 'Human Purpose and Natural Law' *Journal of Philosophy* 53: 697–705
Fuller, Lon L. (1956–57) 'Means and Ends' in Lon L. Fuller, *The Principles of Social Order: Selected Essays of Lon L. Fuller* (Duke UP, 1981) 47–64
Fuller, Lon L. (1958a) 'Positivism and Fidelity to Law – A Reply to Professor Hart' *Harvard Law Review* 71: 630–72
Fuller, Lon L. (1958b) 'A Rejoinder to Professor Nagel' *Natural Law Forum* 3: 83–104
Fuller, Lon L. (1968) *Anatomy of the Law* (Frederick A. Praeger)
Fuller, Lon L. (1969a) *The Morality of Law*, revised ed. (Yale UP)
Fuller, Lon L. (1969b) 'Human Interaction and the Law' in Lon L. Fuller, *The Principles of Social Order: Selected Essays of Lon L. Fuller* (Duke UP, 2001) 211–46

Fuller, Lon L. and Melvin Aaron Eisenberg (1972) *Basic Contract Law*, 3rd ed. (West Publishing Co.)
Fyock, Claiton (2025) 'Getting "Real" About ISDS Reform: A Critical Realist View of International Investment Law's Status Quo' *Journal of International Dispute Settlement* 16: 1–22
Gaillard, Emmanuel (2015) 'Sociology of International Arbitration' in David D. Caron, Stephan W. Schill, Abby Cohen Smutny, and Epaminontas E. Trianafilou (eds) *Practising Virtue: Inside International Arbitration* (Oxford UP) 187–203
Garden, Robert (2023) '*Eco Oro v Colombia*: The Brave New World of Environmental Exceptions' *ICSID Review* 38: 17–24
Gardner, John (2012) *Law as a Leap of Faith: Essays on Law in General* (Oxford UP)
Garth, Bryant G. (2018) 'Book Review Essay: One Window into the State of Insiders' Arbitration Scholarship' *Journal of World Trade & Investment* 19: 155–64
Gauchet, Marcel (1994) 'Primitive Religion and the Origins of the State' in Mark Lilla (ed) *New French Thought: Political Philosophy* (Princeton UP) 116–22
Gauchet, Marcel (1997) *The Disenchantment of the World: A Political History of Religion*, translated by Oscar Burge (Princeton UP)
Gava, John (2001) 'The Rise of the Hero Judge' *The University of New South Wales Law Journal* 24: 747–59
Gaviria Díaz, Carlos (2015) 'Carlos Gaviria renuncia a Comisión de Auditoría de tratados de inversión de Ecuador por suscripción de acuerdo comercial con Unión Europea' at https://www.polodemocratico.net/carlos-gaviria-renuncia-a-comision-de-auditoria-de-tratados-de-inversion-de-ecuador-por-suscripcion-de-acuerdo-comercial-con-union-europea/ (last accessed 12 May 2024)
Geertz, Clifford (1983) *Local Knowledge: Further Essays in Interpretive Anthropology* (Basic Books)
Gephart, Werner (2015) *Law, Culture, and Society: Max Weber's Comparative Cultural Sociology of Law*, translated by Johannes Nanz (Vittorio Klostermann)
Gerstle, Gary (2022) *The Rise and Fall of the Neoliberal Order: America and the World in the Free Market Era* (Oxford UP)
Gerth, H. H. and C. Wright Mills (1946) 'Introduction: The Man and His Work' in H. H. Gerth and C. Wright Mills (eds) *From Max Weber: Essays in Sociology* (Oxford UP) 3–74
Gertz, Geoffrey, Srividya Jandhyala, and Lauge N. Skovgaard Poulsen (2018) 'Legalization, Diplomacy, and Development: Do Investment Treaties De-politicize Investment Disputes?' *World Development* 107: 239–52
Ghosh, Peter (2005) 'Max Weber on "The Rural Community": A Critical Edition of the English Text' *History of European Ideas* 31: 327–66
Ghosh, Peter (2006) 'Max Weber and William James: "Pragmatism," Psychology, Religion' *Max Weber Studies* 5: 243–80
Ghosh, Peter (2014) *Max Weber and The Protestant Ethic: Twin Histories* (Oxford UP)
Ghosh, Peter (2019) 'Max Weber's Ethics for the Modern World' in Edith Hanke, Lawrence A. Scaff, Sam Whimster (eds) *The Oxford Handbook of Max Weber* (Oxford UP) 313–34
Giddens, Anthony (1971) *Capitalism and Modern Social Theory: An Analysis of the Writings of Marx, Durkheim and Weber* (Cambridge UP)
Gillman, Howard (1993) *The Constitution Beseiged: The Rise and Decline of Lochner Era Police Powers Jurisprudence* (Duke UP)
Goethe, Johann Wolfgang (1960 [1809]) *Kindred by Choice*, translated by H. M. Waidson (John Calder)
Golub, Stephen (2006) 'A House Without a Foundation' in Thomas Carothers (ed) *Promoting the Rule of Law Abroad: In Search of Knowledge* (Carnegie Endowment for International Peace) 105–136
Graf, Friedrich Wilhelm (1987) 'Friendship Between Experts: Notes on Weber and Troeltsch' in Wolfgang J. Mommsen and Jürgen Osterhammel (eds) *Max Weber and His Contemporaries* (Unwin Hyman) 214–33

Grimm, Dieter (2007) 'Proportionality in the Canadian and German Constitutional Case Law' *University of Toronto Law Journal* 57: 383–98
Guizot, François (1850) *The History of Civilization in Europe*, translated by William Hazlitt (Penguin Books, 1997)
Guizot, François (1861) *History of The Origin of Representative Government in Europe*, translated by Andrew M. Scobie (Liberty Fund, 2002)
Guntrip, Edward, Joshua Paine, and Catharine Titi (2025) 'The Intersection of Substance and Procedure in the Work of UNCITRAL Working Group III: The Questions of Damages, the Right to Regulate and Counterclaims' (20 March) Academic Forum on ISDS Concept Paper 2025/2 available at https://papers.ssrn.com/sol3/papers.cfm?abstract_id=5191001 (last accessed 20 April 2025)
Habermas, Jürgen (1971a) 'Discussion on Value-Freedom and Objectivity' in Otto Stammer (ed) *Max Weber and Sociology Today*, translated by Kathleen Morris (Harper & Row) 59–66
Habermas, Jürgen (1971b) 'Technology and Science as "Ideology"' in Jürgen Habermas, *Toward a Rational Society*, translated by Jeremy J. Shapiro (Heinemann)
Habermas, Jürgen (1974) 'Legitimation Problems in the Modern State' in Jürgen Habermas, *Communication and the Evolution of Society*, translated by Thomas McCarthy (Beacon Press) 178–205
Habermas, Jürgen (1984) *Theory of Communicative Action, Volume One: Reason and The Rationalization of Society* (Beacon)
Habermas, Jürgen (1989) *The Structural Transformation of the Public Sphere: An Inquiry into a Category of Bourgeois Society*, translated by Thomas Burger (The MIT Press)
Habermas, Jürgen (2001) 'The Postnational Constellation and the Future of Democracy' in Jürgen Habermas, *The Postnational Constellation: Political Essays*, translated by Max Pensky (The MIT Press)
Habermas, Jürgen (2002) 'The European Nation State and the Pressures of Globalization' in Pablo De Grieff and Ciaran Cronin (eds) *Global Justice and Transnational Politics* (The MIT Press 2004) 217–34
Habermas, Jürgen (2015) 'The Lure of Technocracy: A Plea for European Solidarity' in Jürgen Habermas, *The Lure of Technocracy*, translated by Ciarin Cronin (Polity)
Halberstam, David (1983) *The Best and the Brightest* (Penguin Books)
Hale, Robert L. (1923) 'Coercion and Distribution in a Supposedly Non-Coercive State' *Political Science Quarterly* 38: 470–94
Hamilton, Alexander, John Jay, and James Madison (1961) *The Federalist Papers*, edited by Clinton Rossiter (New American Library)
Hammill, Graham (2012) *The Mosaic Constitution: Political Theology and Imagination from Machiavelli to Milton* (U Chicago Press)
Hanke, Edith (2001) 'Max Weber's "Herrschaftssoziologie"' in Edith Hanke and Wolfgang Mommsen (eds) *Max Webers Herrschaftssoziologie* (Mohr Siebeck) 19–46
Hanke, Edith (2009) '"Max Weber's Desk is Now My Altar": Marianne Weber and the Intellectual Heritage of Her Husband' *History of European Ideas* 35: 349–59
Hanke, Edith (2025) 'What About Democracy? Approaches to Max Weber's Political Sociology' in Joshua Derman and Peter E. Gordon (eds) *Max Weber at 100* (Oxford UP) 241–74
Hanke, Edith and Wolfgang J. Mommsen (eds) (2001) *Max Webers Herrschaftssoziologie* (Mohr Siebeck)
Hanke, Edith, Lawrence Scaff, and Sam Whimster (2019) 'Introduction: Max Weber Past, Present and Future' in Edith Hanke, Lawrence Scaff, and Sam Whimster (eds) *The Oxford Handbook of Max Weber* (Oxford UP) 2–17
Hart, H. L. A. (1958) 'Positivism and the Separation of Law and Morals' in H. L. A. Hart, *Essays in Jurisprudence and Philosophy* (Clarendon Press, 1983) 49–87
Hart, H. L. A. (1961) *The Concept of Law* (Oxford UP)
Hart, H. L. A. (1965) 'Lon L. Fuller: *The Morality of Law*' in H. L. A. Hart, *Essays in Jurisprudence and Philosophy* (Clarendon Press, 1983) 343–64

Hart, Michael and William Dymond (2002) 'NAFTA Chapter 11: Precedents, Principles, and Prospects' in Laura Ritchie Dawson (ed) *Whose Rights? The NAFTA Chapter 11 Debate* (Centre for Trade Policy and Law) 128–70

Haskins, George Lee (1960) *Law and Authority in Early Massachusetts: A Study in Tradition and Design* (Macmillan)

Hayek, F. A. (1944) *The Road to Serfdom* (U Chicago Press)

Hayek, F. A. (1960) *The Constitution of Liberty* (Routledge)

Hayek, F. A. (1973) 'Liberalism' in F. A. Hayek, *New Studies in Philosophy, Politics, Economics and the History of Ideas* (Routledge & Kegan Paul) 119–51

Hayek, F. A. (1982) *Law, Legislation and Liberty, Volume 2: The Mirage of Social Justice* (Routledge & Kegan Paul)

Hegel, G. W. F. (1820) *Elements of the Philosophy of Right*, edited by Allen W. Wood (Cambridge UP, 1991)

Heller, Hermann (1928) 'Political Democracy and Social Homogeneity' in Arthur Jacobson and Bernhard Schlink (eds) *Weimar: A Jurisprudence of Crisis* (U California Press, 2000) 256–65

Heller, Hermann (1996) 'The Nature and Structure of the State' *Cardozo Law Review* 18: 1139–1213

Henckels, Caroline (2015) *Proportionality and Deference in Investor-State Arbitration: Balancing Investor Protection and Regulatory Autonomy* (Cambrideg UP)

Hendrianto, Stefanus (2018) *Law and Politics of Constitutional Courts: Indonesia and the Search for Judicial Heroes* (Routledge)

Hennis, Wilhelm (1976) 'Legitimacy. On a Category of Civil Society' in Wilhelm Hennis, *Politics as Practical Science*, translated by Keith Tribe (Palgrave Macmillan, 2009) 77–120

Hennis, Wilhelm (1986) 'Voluntarism and Judgement: Max Weber's Political Views in the Context of His Work' in Wilhelm Hennis, *Max Weber: Essays in Reconstruction*, translated by Keith Tribe (Allen & Unwin, 1988) 166–97

Hennis, Wilhelm (1987) 'Personality and Life Orders: Max Weber's Theme' in Scott Lash and Sam Whimster (eds) *Max Weber, Rationality and Modernity* (Allen & Unwin) 52–74

Hennis, Wilhelm (1998) 'The Spiritualist Foundation of Max Weber's "Interpretive Sociology": Ernst Troeltsch, Max Weber and William James' Varieties of Religious Experience' *History of the Human Sciences* 11: 83–106

Hippolyte, Antonius R. (2019) 'Foreign Investment Law and Developing Countries' in Markus Krajewski and Rhea Tamara Hoffman (eds) *Research Handbook on Foreign Direct Investment* (Edward Elgar) 72–125

Hirsch, Moshe (2015) *Invitation to the Sociology of International Law* (OUP)

Hirsch, Moshe (2020) 'The Sociological Dimension of International Arbitration: The Investment Arbitration Culture' in Thomas Schultz and Federico Ortino (eds) *The Oxford Handbook of International Arbitration* (Oxford UP) 717–39

Hobe, Stephan (2015) 'Evolution of the Principle on Permanent Sovereignty Over Natural Resources' in Marc Bungenberg and Stephan Hobe (eds) *Permanent Sovereignty over Natural Resources* (Springer) 1–13

Hobér, Kaj (2014) 'Arbitration Involving States' in Lawrence W. Newman and Richard D. Hill (eds) *The Leading Arbitrators' Guide to International Arbitration*, 3rd ed. (Juris) 927–83

Hodgson, Matthew, Yarik Kryvoi, and Daniel Hrcka (2021) '2021 Empirical Study: Costs, Damages and Duration in Investor-State Arbitration' British Institute of International and Comparative Law (June) at https://www.biicl.org/documents/136_isds-costs-damages-duration_june_2021.pdf (last accessed 18 April 2025)

Hogg, Peter W. (2019) *Constitutional Law of Canada* (5th ed. Supp.) (Thomson Reuters)

Honigsheim, Paul (1961) 'Max Weber' in Paul Honigsheim, *On Max Weber* (The Free Press, 1968) 113–124

Horwitz, Morton (1992) *The Transformation of American Law, 1870-1960: The Crisis of Legal Orthodoxy* (Harvard UP)

Howe, Richard Herbert (1978) 'Max Weber's Elective Affinities: Sociology within the Bounds of Pure Reason' *American Journal of Sociology* 84: 366–85

Hübinger, Gangolf (2009) 'Max Weber's "Sociology of the State" and the Science of Politics in Germany' *Max Weber Studies* 9: 17–32
Hull, Cordell (1938) 'Mexico-United States: Expropriations by Mexico of Agrarian Properties Owned by American Citizens' *American Journal of International Law*, Supp. 32(4): 181–207
Hyde, Alan (1983) 'The Concept of Legitimation in the Sociology of Law' *Wisconsin Law Review* 1983: 379–426
Independent Commission on International Development Issues (1980) *North-South: A Programme for Survival* (Willy Brandt, Chairman) (Pan Books Ltd.)
International Centre for the Settlement of Investment Disputes [ICSID] (1968) *Convention on the Settlement of Investment Disputes Between States and Nationals of Other States, Documents Concerning the Origin and Formulation of the Convention*, Vol. II, Part I (ICSID)
International Centre for the Settlement of Investment Disputes [ICSID] (2023) *Annual Report 2023* (ICSID)
Ihering, Rudolf Von (1877) *Law as a Means to an End*, translated by Isaac Husik (The Boston Book Company, 1913)
Innes, Stephen (1995) *Creating the Commonwealth: The Economic Culture of Puritan New England* (W.W. Norton)
Jackman, Henry (2008) 'William James' in Cheryl Misak (ed) *The Oxford Handbook of American Philosophy* (Oxford UP) 60–86
Jackson, John H. (1997) *The World Trading System: Law and Policy of International Economic Relations*, 2nd ed. (The MIT Press)
Jackson, Trevor (2023) 'The Price of Crypto' *The New York Review of Books* (8 June) LXX (10): 6–10
Jameson, Frederic (1973) 'The Vanishing Mediator: Narrative Structure in Max Weber' *New German Critique* 1: 52–89
Jaspers, Karl (1989) *On Max Weber*, translated by Robert J. Whelan (Paragon House)
Jellinek, Georg (1901) *The Declaration of the Rights of Man and of Citizens: A Contribution to Modern Constitutional History*, translated by Max Farrand (Henry Holt and Company)
Jenks, Chris (1993) *Culture* (Routledge)
Jennings, Ivor Sir (1961) *Cabinet Government*, 3rd ed. (Cambridge UP)
Jensen, Merrill (ed) (1969) *English Historical Documents: American Colonial Documents to 1776* (Eyre & Spottiswoode)
Jessop, Bob (2016) *The State: Past, Present, Future* (Polity)
Jhering, Rudolf von (1907) *Geist des römischen Rechts auf den verschiedenen Stufen seiner Entwicklung*, Vol. 1, 6th ed. (Breitkopf und Härtel)
Johnson, Lise and Oleksander Volkov (2013) 'Investor-State Contracts, Host-State "Commitments" and the Myth of Stability in International Law' *The American Review of International Arbitration* 24: 361–415
Jones, Cree and Weijia Rao (2022) '(Un)stable BITs' *Yale Journal of International Law* 47: 247–307
Josephson-Storm, Jason Ā. (2017) *The Myth of Disenchantment: Magic, Modernity, and the Birth of the Human Sciences* (University of Chicago Press)
Josephson-Storm, Jason Ā. (2021) 'Max Weber and the Rationalization of Magic' in Robert Yelle and Lorenz Trein (eds) *Narratives of Disenchantment and Secularization* (Brill) 31–49
Kahale, III, George (2018) 'The Inaugural Brooklyn Lecture on International Business Law: ISDS: The Wild, Wild West of International Practice' *Brooklyn Journal of International Law* 44: 1–10
Kahn, Paul (1997) *The Reign of Law: Marbury v. Madison and the Construction of America* (Yale UP)
Kalberg, Stephen (1980) 'Max Weber's Types of Rationality: Cornerstones for the Analysis of Rationalization Processes in History' *The American Journal of Sociology* 85: 1149–75
Kalberg, Stephen (1990) 'The Rationalization of Social Action in Max Weber's Sociology of Religion' *Sociological Theory* 8: 58–84
Kalberg, Stephen (2008) 'The Perpetual and Tight Interweaving of Past and Present in Max Weber's Sociology' in David Chalcraft, Fanon Howell, Marisol Lopez Menendez, and Hector Vera (eds) *Max Weber Matters: Interweaving Past and Present* (Routledge) 273–88

Kalberg, Stephen (2009) 'Introduction to *The Protestant Ethic*' in Max Weber, *The Protestant Ethic and the Spirit of Capitalism with Other Writings on the Rise of the West*, 4th ed., translated by Stephen Kalberg (Oxford UP) 7–58

Kalberg, Stephen (2017) *The Social Thought of Max Weber* (Sage)

Kapstein, Ethan B. (2020) 'Private Enterprise, International Development, and the Cold War' *Journal of Cold War Studies* 22: 113–45

Käsler, Dirk (1988) *Max Weber: An Introduction to his Life and Work*, translated by Philippa Hurd (Cambridge: Polity Press)

Kellner, Douglas (1985) 'Critical Theory, Max Weber, and the Dialectics of Domination' in Robert J. Antonio and Ronald M. Glassman (eds) *A Weber-Marx Dialogue* (U Press of Kansas) 89–116

Kelly, Robert F. (1979) 'Historical and Political Interpretations of Jurisprudence and the Social Action Perspective in Psychology' *Journal of the History of the Behavioral Sciences* 15: 47–62

Kemple, Thomas M. and Cornelia Meyer-Stoll (2003) 'The Last Hand: On the Craft of Editing Weber's "Börsenschriften"' *Max Weber Studies* 3: 169–98

Kennedy, David (2004) *The Dark Sides of Virtue: Reassessing International Humanitarianism* (Princeton UP)

Kennedy, David (2006) 'Lon L. Fuller' in David Kennedy and William W. Fisher III (eds) *The Canon of American Legal Thought* (Princeton UP) 209–17

Kennedy, David (2013) 'Law and International Political Economy of the World' *Leiden Journal of International Law* 26: 7–48

Kennedy, David (2016) *A World of Struggle: How Power, Law, and Expertise Shape Global Political Economy* (Princeton UP)

Kennedy, Duncan (1976) 'Form and Substance in Private Law Adjudication' *Harvard Law Review* 89: 1685–1778

Kennedy, Duncan (1997) *A Critique of Adjudication: {fin de siècle}* (Harvard UP)

Kennedy, Duncan (2000) From the Will Theory to the Principle of Private Autonomy: Lon Fuller's "Consideration and Form"' *Columbia Law Review* 100: 94–175.

Kennedy, Duncan (2004) 'The Disenchantment of Logically Formal Legal Rationality or Max Weber's Sociology in the Genealogy of the Contemporary Mode of Western Legal Thought' *Hastings Law Journal* 55: 1031–76

Kennedy, Duncan (2011) 'A Transnational Genealogy of Proportionality in Private Law' in Roger Brownswood, Hans W. Micklitz, Leone Nigla, and Stephen Weatherhill (eds) *The Foundations of European Private Law* (Hart) 185–220

Kennedy, Duncan (2012) 'Political Ideology and Comparative Law' in Mauro Bussani and Ugo Mattei (eds) *The Cambridge Companion to Comparative Law* (Cambridge UP) 35–56

Kennedy, Duncan (2014) 'The Hermeneutic of Suspicion in Contemporary American Legal Thought' *Law & Critique* 25: 91–139

Kennedy, Duncan (2020) 'A Political Economy of Contemporary Legality' in Poul F. Kjaer (ed) *The Law of Political Economy: Transformations in the Function of Law* (Cambridge UP) 89–124

Kennedy, Ellen (2004) *Constitutional Failure: Carl Schmitt in Weimar* (Duke UP)

Ketchen, James C. (2003) 'Revisiting Fuller's Critique of Hart – Managerial Control and the Pathology of Legal Systems: The Hart-Weber Nexus' *University of Toronto Law Journal* 53: 1–35

Kim, Sung Ho (2002) 'Max Weber's Liberal Nationalism' *History of Political Thought* 23: 432–57

Kingsbury, Benedict and Stephan W. Schill (2010) 'Public Law Concepts to Balance Investors' Rights with State Regulatory Actions in the Public Interest—The Concept of Proportionality' in Stephan W. Schill (ed.) *International Investment Law and Comparative Public Law* (Oxford UP) 76–104

Kinsella, W. P. (1980) *Shoeless Joe Jackson Comes to Iowa* (Oberon Press)

Kippenberg, Hans G. (2021) 'Dialectics of Disenchantment: The Devaluation of the Objective World and the Revaluation of Subjective Religiosity' in Robert Yelle and Lorenz Trein (eds) *Narratives of Disenchantment and Secularization* (Brill) 9–30

Kirchheimer, Otto (1933) 'Remarks on Carl Schmitt's *Legality and Legitimacy*,' translated by Anke Grosskopf and William E. Scheuerman in William E. Scheuerman (ed) *The Rule of Law*

Under Siege: Selected Essays of Franz L. Neumann and Otto Kirchheimer (U California Press, 1996) 64–98

Klatt, Matthias and Moritz Meister (2012) 'Proportionality – A Benefit to Human Rights? Remarks on the ICON Controversy' *International Journal of Constitutional Law* 10: 687–708

Kleinfeld, Rachel (2006) 'Competing Definitions of the Rule of Law' in Carothers (ed) *Promoting the Rule of Law Abroad: In Search of Knowledge* (Carnegie Endowment for International Peace) 31–74

Knörich, Jan and Axel Berger (2014) 'Friends or Foes? Interactions between Indonesia's International Investment Agreements and National Investment Law' Deutsches Institut für Entwicklungspolitik (DIE)/German Development Institute (Bonn) at https://www.idos-research.de/en/studies/article/friends-or-foes-interactions-between-indonesias-international-investment-agreements-and-national-investment-law/ (last accessed 12 May 2023)

Kocka, Jürgen (1981) 'Capitalism and Bureaucracy in German Industrialization Before 1914' *Economic History Review* 34: 453–68

Kocka, Jürgen (1987) 'Otto Hintze and Max Weber: Attempts at Comparison' in Wolfgang J. Mommsen and Jürgen Osterhammel (eds) *Max Weber and His Contemporaries* (Unwin Hyman) 284–95

Koselleck, Reinhart (1988) *Critique and Crisis: Enlightenment and the Pathogenesis of Modern Society* (Berg)

Koskenniemi, Martti (1989) 'The Politics of International Law – Twenty Years Later' in Martti Koskenniemi, The Politics of International Law (Hart, 2011) 63–75

Koskenniemi, Martti (2005) *From Apology to Utopia: The Structure of International Legal Argument, Reissue with a New Epilogue* (Cambridge UP)

Koskenniemi, Martti (2006) 'Constitutionalism as Mindset: Reflections on Kantian Themes About International Law and Globalization' *Theoretical Inquiries in Law* 8: 9–36

Koskenniemi, Martti (2017a) 'Between Commitment and Cynicism: Outline for a Theory of International Law as Practice' in Jean d'Aspremont, Tarcisio Gazzini, André Nollkaemper, and Wouter G. Werner (eds) *International Law as a Profession* (Cambridge UP) 38–66

Koskenniemi, Martti (2017b) 'Foreword' in Anthea Roberts, *Is International Law International?* (OUP) xiii–xvi

Kriebaum, Ursula (2018) 'Evaluating Social Benefits and Costs of Investment Treaties: Depoliticization of Investment Disputes' *ICSID Review* 33: 14–28

Krishan, Devashish (2011) 'Thinking About BITs and BIT Arbitration: The Legitimacy Crisis That Never Was' in Todd Weiler and Freya Baetens (eds) *New Directions in International Economic Law: In Memoriam Thomas Wälde* (Martinus Nijhoff Publishers) 107–50

Kröll, Stefan, Andrea Bjorklund, and Franco Ferrari (eds) (2023) *Cambridge Compendium of International Commercial and Investment Arbitration* (Cambridge UP)

Krommendijk, Jasper and John Morijn (2009) 'Proportional by What Measure(s)? Balancing Investor Interests and Human Rights by Way of Applying the Proportionality Principle in Investor-State Arbitration' in Pierre-Marie Dupuy, Ernst-Ulrich Petersmann, and Francesco Francioni (eds) *Human Rights in International Investment Law and Arbitration* (Oxford UP) 421–45

Kronman, Anthony T. (1983) *Max Weber* (Edward Arnold)

Kronman, Anthony T. (1993) *The Lost Lawyer: Failing Ideals of the Legal Profession* (Belknap Press of Harvard University Press)

Kulick, Andreas (2012) *Global Public Interest in International Investment Law* (Cambridge UP)

Kulick, Andreas (2017) 'Reassertion of Control: An Introduction' in Andreas Kulick, *Reassertion of Control Over the Investment Treaty Regime* (Cambridge UP) 3–29

Kumm, Mattias (2004) 'The Legitimacy of International Law: A Constitutionalist Framework of Analysis' *The European Journal of International Law* 15: 907–31

Kumm, Mattias (2007) 'Political Liberalism and the Structure of Rights: On the Place and Limits of the Proportionality Requirement' in George Pavlakos (ed) *Law, Rights and Discourse: The Legal Philosophy of Robert Alexy* (Hart) 131–66

Kumm, Mattias (2010) 'The Idea of Socratic Contestation and the Right to Justification: The Point of Rights-Based Proportionality Review' *Law & Ethics of Human Rights* 4: 142–75

Kurtz Jürgen (2010) 'Adjudging the Exceptional at International Investment Law: Security, Public Order and Financial Crisis' *International and Comparative Law Quarterly* 59: 325–71

Kurtz Jürgen (2014) 'Building Legitimacy Through Interpretation in Investor-State Arbitration: On Consistency, Coherence and the Identification of Applicable Law' in Zachary Douglas, Joost Pauwelyn, and Jorge E. Viñuales (eds) *The Foundations of International Investment Law: Bringing Theory into Practice* (Oxford UP) 257–96

Lacey, Nicola (2010) 'Out of the Witches' Cauldron? Reinterpreting the Context and Reassessing the Significance of the Hart-Fuller Debate' in Peter Cane (ed) *The Hart-Fuller Debate in the Twenty-First Century* (Hart Publishing) 1–42

Lalonde, Marc (2016) 'The New Investment Tribunal under Chapter 8 of CETA' CIGI Investor-State Arbitration Commentary Series No. 2 (6 May) online at https://www.cigionline.org/publications/new-investment-tribunal-under-chapter-8-ceta (last visited 14 July 2024)

Langford, Malcolm, and Daniel Behn (2018) 'Managing Backlash: The Evolving Investment Treaty Arbitrator?' *European Journal of International Law* 29: 551–80

Langford, Malcolm, Daniel Behn, and Ole Kristian Fauchald (2018) 'Backlash and State Strategies in International Investment Law' in Tanja E. Aalberts and Thomas Gammeltoft-Hansen (eds) *The Changing Practices of International Law* (Cambridge UP) 70–102

Langford, Malcolm, Daniel Behn, and Runar Hilleren Lie (2017) 'The Revolving Door in International Investment Arbitration' *Journal of International Economic Law* 20: 301–31

Larrain, Jorge (1979) *The Concept of Ideology* (Hutchinson)

Laski, Harold J. (1927) *Communism* (Thornton Butterworth)

Lassman, Peter (2000) 'The Rule of Man Over Man: Politics, Power and Legitimation' in Stephen Turner (ed) *The Cambridge Companion to Weber* (Cambridge UP) 83–98

Lassman, Peter (2023) 'The Fate of Politics: The Vocation of the Political Educator' in Alan Sica (ed) *The Routledge International Handbook on Max Weber* (Routledge) 371–81

Latour, Bruno (2010) *The Making of Law: An Ethnography of the Conseil d'État*, translated by Marina Brilman and Aalin Pottage (Polity)

Lauterpacht, Elihu (1997) 'International Law and Private Foreign Investment' *Indiana Journal of Global Legal Studies* 4: 259–76

Lawrence, Mark Atwood (2021) *The End of Ambition: The United States and the Third World in the Vietnam Era* (Princeton UP)

Lechner, Frank J. (2023) 'Sociology of Law, Then and Now' in Alan Sica (ed) *The Routledge International Handbook on Max Weber* (Routledge) 327–38

Ledford, Kenneth F. (2004) 'Formalizing the Rule of Law in Prussia: The Supreme Administrative Law Court (1876-1914)' *Central European History* 37: 203–24

Lehmann, Hartmut (2008) 'Max Weber and the Dialectics of Disenchantment and Re-enchantment in Modern History' in Frank Adloff and Manuel Borutta (eds) *Max Weber in the 21st Century: Transdisciplinarity within the Social Sciences* (EUI Working Paper MWP No. 2008/35) 73–80 at https://hdl.handle.net/1814/9110 (last accessed 23 April 2025)

Lejour, Arjan and Maria Salfi (2015) 'The Regional Impact of Bilateral Investment Treaties on Foreign Direct Investment' CPB Discussion Paper No. 298, CPB Netherlands Bureau for Economic Policy Analysis (January)

Leonhardsen, Erlend M. (2012) 'Looking for Legitimacy: Exploring Proportionality Analysis in Investment Treaty Arbitration' *Journal of International Dispute Settlement* 3: 95–136

Leonhardsen, Erlend M. (2021) 'Designing Deference: Towards a Thin Margin of Appreciation Doctrine in International Investment Law?' *European Yearbook of International Economic Law* 151–81

Lestition, Steven (2000) 'Historical preface to Max Weber, "Stock and Commodity Exchanges"' *Theory and Society* 29: 289–304

Létourneau-Tremblay, Laura and Daniel F. Behn (2016) 'Judging the Misapplication of a State's Own Environmental Regulations' *The Journal of World Investment & Trade* 17: 823–32

Levinson, Sanford (1988) *Constitutional Faith* (Princeton UP)

Lieblich, Eliav and Eyal Benvenisti (2022) *Occupation in International Law* (Oxford UP)

Lim, C. L., Jean Ho, and Martins Paparinskis (2021) *International Investment Law and Arbitration: Commentary, Awards and other Materials*, 2nd ed. (Cambridge UP)

Lin, Wei-Chung (2017) 'Safeguarding the Environment? The Effectiveness of Amicus Curiae Submissions in Investor-State Arbitration' *International Community Law Review* 19: 270–301

Lindseth, Peter L. (2020) 'Theorizing Backlash: Supranational Governance and International Investment Law and Arbitration in Comparative Perspective' *The Journal of World Investment & Trade* 21: 34–70

Little, David (1969) *Religion, Order, and Law: A Study of Pre-Revolutionary England* (Harper & Row)

Llewellyn, Karl N. (1930) 'A Realistic Jurisprudence – The Next Step' *Columbia Law Review* 30: 155–89

Llewellyn, Karl N. (1960) *The Common Law Tradition: Deciding Appeals* (Little, Brown)

Llewellyn, Karl N. (1989) *The Case Law System in America*, translated by Michael Ansaldi (The University of Chicago Press)

Loewenstein, Karl (1966) *Max Weber's Political Ideas in the Perspective of Our Time*, translated by Richard and Clara Winston (University of Massachusetts Press)

Löwith, Karl (1982) *Max Weber and Karl Marx*, translated by Hans Fantel (George Allen & Unwin)

Löwy, Michael (1992) *Redemption and Utopia: Jewish Libertarian Thought in Central Europe – A Study in Elective Affinity*, translated by Hope Heaney (The Athlone Press)

Löwy, Michael (2004) 'Le Concept d'affinité élective chez Max Weber' *Archives de sciences sociales des religions* 127: 93–104

Löwy, Michael and Eleni Varikas (2021) 'Max Weber and Anthropology' *Max Weber Studies* 21: 67–83

Luhmann, Niklas (2004) *Law as a Social System*, translated by Klaus Ziegert (Oxford UP)

Lüthy, Herbert (1970) *From Calvin to Rousseau: Tradition and Modernity in Socio-Political Thought from the Reformation to the French Revolution*, translated by Salvator Attanasio (Basic Books)

Maitland, F. W. (1913) *Equity, Also the Forms of Action at Common Law: Two Courses of Lectures* (Cambridge UP)

Malczewski, Eric (2019) 'The Weberian Presuppositional Analytic' *Sociological Theory* 37: 363–80

Maley, Terry (2011) *Democracy and the Political in Max Weber's Thought* (U of Toronto Press)

Manasse, Moritz (1947) 'Max Weber on Race' *Social Research* 14: 191–221

Mann, F. A. (1981) 'British Treaties for the Promotion and Protection of Investments' *British Yearbook of International Law* 52: 241–54

Mannheim, Karl (1927) 'Conservative Thought' in Kurt Wolff (ed) *From Karl Mannheim* (Oxford UP) 132–222

Mannheim, Karl (1959) *Ideology and Utopia: An Introduction to the Sociology of Knowledge*, translated by Louis Wirth and Edward Shils (Harvest Books)

Mannheim, Karl and WAC Stewart (1962) *An Introduction to the Sociology of Education* (Routledge & Kegan Paul)

Marceddu, Maria Laura and Pietro Ortolani (2020) 'What Is Wrong with Investment Arbitration? Evidence from a Set of Behavioural Experiments' *European Journal of International Law* 31: 405–28

Marchand, Suzanne L. (2009) *German Orientalism in the Age of Empire: Religion, Race, and Scholarship* (Cambridge UP)

Marcuse, Herbert (1941) 'Some Social Implications of Modern Technology' in Herbert Marcuse, *Technology, War and Fascism: Collected Papers of Herbert Marcuse, Volume One*, edited by Douglas Kellner (Routledge, 1998) 39–65

Marcuse, Herbert (1968) 'Industrialization and Capitalism in the Work of Max Weber' in Herbert Marcuse, *Negations: Essays in Critical Theory* (Beacon) 201–26

Marcuse, Herbert (1971) 'Industrialization and Capitalism' in Otto Stammer (ed) *Max Weber and Sociology Today* (Harper & Row) 133–51

Maritain, Jacques (1944) 'Human Equality' in *The Social and Political Philosophy of Jacques Maritain: Selected Readings*, edited by Joseph W. Evans and Leo R. Ward (Charles Scribner's and Sons, 1955) 69–77

Marx, Karl (1883) '"Notes" on Adolph Wagner' in Karl Marx, *Later Political Writings*, edited by Terrell Carver (Cambridge UP)

Mayer, J. P. (1955) *Max Weber and German Politics*, 2nd ed. (Routledge, 1998)

McCormick, John P. (1997) *Carl Schmitt's Critique of Liberalism: Against Politics as Technology* (Cambridge UP)

McCormick, John P. (2007) *Weber, Habermas, and the Transformations of the European State: Constitutional, Social, and Supranational Democracy* (Cambridge: Cambridge University Press)

McKinnon, Andrew M. (2010) 'Elective Affinities of the Protestant Ethic: Weber and the Chemistry of Capitalism' *Sociological Theory* 28: 108–26

McLachlan, Campbell (2014) *Foreign Relations Law* (Cambridge UP)

McRae, Donald (2014) 'International Economic Law and Public International Law: The Past and the Future' *Journal of International Economic Law* 17: 627–38

Mehranvar, Ladan and Lisa Sachs (2023) 'The Role and Relevance of Investment Treaties in Promoting Renewable Energy Investments' [unpublished]

Mehranvar, Ladan and Sunayana Sasmal (2022) 'The Role of Investment Treaties and Investor-State Settlement in Renewable Energy Investments' (Colombia Center on Sustainable Investment) (December) at https://scholarship.law.columbia.edu/sustainable_investment/5/ (last accessed 12 June 2023)

Merrill, Thomas W. (2022) *The Chevron Doctrine: Its Rise and Fall, and the Future of the Administrative State* (Harvard UP)

Merryman, John Henry (1985) *The Civil Law Tradition: An Introduction to the Legal Systems of Western Europe and Latin America*, 2nd ed. (Stanford UP)

Michelman, Frank (1967) 'Property, Utility, and Fairness: Comments on the Ethical Foundations of "Just Compensation" Law' Harvard Law Review 80: 1165–1258

Miliband, Ralph (1977) *Marxism and Politics* (Oxford UP)

Mill, John Stuart (1861) 'Considerations on Representative Government' in John Stuart Mill, *Utilitarianism, Liberty, Representative Government* (J. M. Dent & Sons, 1910)

Miller, Perry (1935) 'The Marrow of Puritan Divinity' in Perry Miller, *Errand into the Wilderness* (Harvard UP, 1956) 48–98

Miller, Perry (1938) 'The Puritan State and Puritan Society' in Perry Miller, *Errand into the Wilderness* (Harvard UP, 1956) 141–52

Miller, Perry (1939) *The New England Mind: The Seventeenth Century* (Harvard UP)

Miller, Perry (1953) *The New England Mind: From Colony to Province* (Harvard UP)

Miller, Perry and Thomas H. Johnson (1938) *The Puritans* (American Book Company)

Mistelis, Loukas (2020) 'Efficiency – What Else? Efficiency as the Emerging Defining Value of International Arbitration: Between Systems Theories and Party Autonomy' in Thomas Schultz and Federico Ortino (eds) *The Oxford Handbook of International Arbitration* (Oxford UP) 349–76

Mitzman, Arthur (1969) *The Iron Cage: An Historical Interpretation of Max Weber* (Alfred A. Knopf)

Möller, Kai (2012) The Global Model of Constitutional Rights (Oxford UP)

Mommsen, Wolfgang J. (1977) 'Max Weber as Critic of Marxism' *Canadian Journal of Sociology* 2: 373–98

Mommsen, Wolfgang J. (1981) 'The Causes and Objectives of German Imperialism Before 1914' in Wolfgang J. Mommsen, *Imperial Germany 1867-1918: Politics, Culture, and Society in an Authoritarian State*, translated by Richard Deveson (Arnold 1995) 75–100

Mommsen, Wolfgang J. (1984) *Max Weber and German Politics, 1890-1920*, translated by Michael S. Steinberg (Chicago UP)

Mommsen, Wolfgang J. (1985) 'Capitalism and Socialism: Weber's Dialogue with Marx' in Robert J. Antonio and Ronald M. Glassman (eds) *A Weber-Marx Dialogue* (UP Kansas) 234–61

Mommsen, Wolfgang J. (1989) 'Max Weber on Bureaucracy and Bureaucratization: Threat to Liberty and Instrument of Creative Action' in Wolfgang J. Mommsen, *The Political and Social Theory of Max Weber: Collected Essays* (Polity Press) 109–20

Mommsen, Wolfgang J. (2005) 'Max Weber's "Grand Sociology": The Origins and Composition of Wirtschaft und Gesellschaft. Soziologie' in Charles Camic, Philip S. Gorski, and David M. Trubek (eds) *Max Weber's Economy and Society: A Critical Companion* (Stanford UP)

Mommsen, Wolfgang J. (2021) *The Age of Capitalism and Bureaucracy: Perspectives on the Political Sociology of Max Weber*, 2nd ed. (Berghahn)

Moore, Jonathan D. (2007) *English Hypothetical Universalism: John Preston and the Softening of Reformed Theology* (William B. Eerdmans)

Morcillo Laiz, Álvaro and Klaus Schlichte (2016) 'Rationality and International Domination: Revisiting Max Weber' *International Political Sociology* 10: 168–84

Moyn, Samuel (2023) *Liberalism Against Itself: Cold War Intellectuals and the Making of Our Times* (Yale UP)

Müller, Jan-Werner. 2011. *Contesting Democracy: Political Ideas in Twentieth- Century Europe* (New Haven: Yale University Press)

Myrdal, Gunnar (1956) *An International Economy: Problems and Prospects* (Harper & Bros.)

Nagel, Ernest (1958) 'On the Fusion of Fact and Value: A Reply to Professor Fuller' *Natural Law Forum* 3: 77–82

National Conservatism (2022) 'National Conservatism: A Statement of Principles' (15 June) at https://nationalconservatism.org/national-conservatism-a-statement-of-principles/ (last accessed 25 May 2025)

Nelson, Benjamin N. (1969) The Idea of Usury: From Tribal Brotherhood to Universal Otherhood, 2nd ed. (U Chicago Press)

Nelson, Benjamin N. (1971) 'Discussion on Industrialization and Capitalism' in Otto Stammer (ed) *Max Weber and Sociology Today*, translated by Kathleen Morris (Harper & Row) 161–71

Nelson, William E. (2008) *The Common Law in Colonial America, Volume 1: The Chesapeake and New England, 1607-1660* (Oxford UP)

Netelenbos, Benno (2016) *Political Legitimacy Beyond Weber* (Palgrave Macmillan)

Netelenbos, Benno (2023) 'The Problem of Legal-Rational Domination' in Alan Sica (ed) *The Routledge International Handbook on Max Weber* (Routledge) 395–407

Neumann, Franz (1936) *The Rule of Law: Political Theory and the Legal System in Modern Society* (Berg Publishers Ltd., 1986)

Neumann, Franz (1937) 'The Change in the Function of Law' in William E. Scheuerman (ed) *The Rule of Law Under Siege: Selected Essays of Franz L. Neumann and Otto Kircheimer* (U California Press, 1996) 101–41

Neumann, Franz (1942) *Behemoth: The Structure and Practice of National Socialism 1933-1933* (Harper & Row, 1963)

Neumann, Franz (1953) 'The Concept of Political Freedom' in William E. Scheuerman (ed) *The Rule of Law Under Siege: Selected Essays of Franz L. Neumann and Otto Kircheimer* (U California Press, 1996) 195–230

Newcombe, Andrew and Lluís Paradell (2009) *Law and Practice of Investment Treaties* (Wolters Kluwer)

North, Douglass C. (1990) *Institutions, Institutional Change and Economic Performance* (Cambridge UP)

Nottage, Luke (2023) 'International Arbitration and Society at Large' in Stefan Kröll, Andrea Bjorklund, and Franco Ferrari (eds) *Cambridge Compendium of International Commercial and Investment Arbitration* (Cambridge UP) 389–423

Nowrot, Karsten and Emily Sipiorski (2021) 'Towards a Republicanisation of International Investment Law? Conceptualising the Legitimatory Value of Public Participation in the Negotiation and Enforcement of International Investment Agreements' in Katia Fach Gómez (ed) *Private Actors in International Investment Law* (Springer) 157–73

Oakes, Guy (1975) 'Introductory Essay' in Max Weber, *Roscher and Knies: The Logical Problem of Historical Economics*, translated by Guy Oakes (The Free Press)

Oakes, Guy (1977) 'The Verstehen Thesis and the Foundations of Max Weber's Methodology' *History and Theory* 16: 11–29

Oakes, Guy and Arthur J. Vidich (1999) *Collaboration, Reputation, and Ethics in American Academic Life: Hans H. Gerth and C. Wright Mills* (University of Illinois Press)

Omni Bridgeway (2024) 'About Us' and 'Litigation Finance' https://omnibridgeway.com/about/overview (last accessed 20 May 2024)

Onwuamaegbu, Uche (2017) 'Ad Hoc Investment Arbitration' in Thomas Cottier and Krista Nadakavukaren Shafer (eds) *Elgar Encyclopedia of International Economic Law* (Edward Elgar) 312–14

Orford, Anne (2021) *International Law and the Politics of History* (Cambridge UP)

Organization for Economic Co-Operation and Development [OECD] (2017) 'Inequality: A Hidden Cost of Market Power – Working Paper by the Secretariat' (16 February) available at https://one.oecd.org/document/DAF/COMP(2015)10/en/pdf (last accessed 19 May 2023)

Ortino, Frederico (2012) 'Legal Reasoning of International Investment Tribunals: A Typology of Egregious Failures' *Journal of International Dispute Settlement* 3: 31–52

Ortino, Frederico (2013) 'Refining the Content and Role of Investment "Rules" and "Standards": A New Approach to International Investment Treaty Making' *ICSID Review – Foreign Investment Law Journal* 28: 152–68

Ortino, Frederico (2017) 'Investment Treaties, Sustainable Development and Reasonableness Review: A Case Against Strict Proportionality Balancing' *Leiden Journal of International Law* 30: 71–91

Ortino, Frederico (2019) *The Origin and Evolution of Investment Treaty Standards* (Oxford UP)

Ortino, Frederico (2023) 'The Public Interest as Part of Legitimate Expectations in Investment Arbitration: Missing in Action?' in Charles Brower, Joan E. Donoghue, Cian C. Murphy, Cymie R. Payne, and Esmé R. Shirlow (eds) *By Peaceful Means: International Adjudication and Arbitration Essays in Honour of David D. Caron* (Oxford UP) 399–418

Ostřanský, Josef (2023) 'Fair and Equitable Treatment' in David Schneiderman and Gus Van Harten (eds) *Rethinking Investment Law* (Oxford UP) 126–52

Ostřanský, Josef and Facundo Pérez Aznar (2021) 'Investment Treaties and National Governance in India: Rearrangements, Empowerment, and Discipline' *Leiden Journal of International Law* 34: 373–96

Page, Edward C. (2024) *Weber's Scorecard: State Development, Bureaucracy, and Officialdom in Europe Since Charlemagne* (Oxford UP)

Pahuja, Sundhya (2011) *Decolonising International Law: Development, Economic Growth and the Politics of Universality* (Cambridge UP)

Paine, Joshua (2021) 'Autonomy to Set the Level of Regulatory Protection in International Investment Law' *International and Comparative Law Quarterly* 70: 697–736

Palonen, Kari (2004) 'Max Weber, Parliamentarism and the Rhetorical Culture of Politics' *Max Weber Studies* 4: 273–92

Palonen, Kari (2008) 'The Past, Present and Future of Democratization' in Kari Palonen, Tuija Pulkkinen, and José María Rosales (eds) *The Ashgate Research Companion to the Politics of Democratization I Europe: Concepts and Histories* (Routledge) 405–11

Palonen, Kari (2010) 'Max Weber's Rhetoric of "Objectivity": The Parliament as Paradigm for Scholarly Disputes' *Max Weber Studies* 10: 71–93

Palonen, Kari (2014) 'Was Max Weber Wrong About Westminster?' *History of Political Thought* 35: 519–27

Palonen, Kari (2017) A Political Style of Thinking: Essays on Max Weber (ECPR Press)

Palonen, Kari (2019) *Parliamentary Thinking: Procedure, Rhetoric and Time* (Palgrave Macmillan)

Paparinskis, Martins (2020) 'A Case Against Crippling Compensation in International Law of State Responsibility' *The Modern Law Review* 83: 1246–86

Parkin, Frank (1979) *Marxism and Class Theory: A Bourgeois Critique* (Tavistock)

Parra, Antonio R. (2017) The *History of ICSID*, 2nd ed. (Oxford UP)

Parsons, Talcott (1963) 'Introduction' in Max Weber, *The Sociology of Religion*, translated by Ephraim Fischoff (Beacon Press) xix–lxvii

Parsons, Talcott (1964) 'Introduction' in Max Weber, *The Theory of Social and Economic Organization*, translated by A. M. Henderson and Talcott Parsons (The Free Press) 3–86
Parsons, Talcott (1968) *The Structure of Social Action: A Study in Social Theory with Special Reference to a Group of Recent European Writers, Vol. II: Weber* (The Free Press)
Parsons, Talcott (1977) 'Law as an Intellectual Stepchild' *Sociological Inquiry* 47: 11–58
Paulsson, Jan (2005) *Denial of Justice in International Law* (Cambridge UP)
Paulsson, Jan (2010) 'The Power of States to Make Meaningful Promises to Foreigners' *Journal of International Dispute Settlement* 1: 341–52
Paulsson, Jan (2013) *The Idea of Arbitration* (Oxford UP)
Pauwelyn, Joost (2014) 'At the Edge of Chaos? Foreign Investment Law as a Complex Adaptive System, How it Emerged and How it Can Be Reformed' *ICSID Review* 1–47
Pauwelyn, Joost (2015) 'Rule of Law Without the Rule of Lawyers? Why Investment Arbitrators are From Mars and Trade Adjudicators from Venus' *The American Journal of International Law* 109: 761–805
Pavel, Carmen E. (2015) *Divided Sovereignty: International Institutions and the Limits of State Authority* (Oxford UP)
Peck, Jamie (2010) *Constructions of Neoliberal Reason* (Oxford UP)
Perrone, Nicolás M. (2017) 'The Emerging Global Right to Investment: Understanding the Reasoning behind Foreign Investor Rights' *Journal of International Dispute Settlement* 8: 673–94
Perrone, Nicolás M. (2018) 'UNCTAD's World Investment Reports 1991–2015: 25 Years of Narratives Justifying and Balancing Foreign Investor Rights' *The Journal of World Investment & Trade* 19: 7–40
Perrone, Nicolás M. (2021) *Investment Treaties and the Legal Imagination: How Foreign Investors Play by their Own Rules* (Oxford UP)
Perrone, Nicolás M. (2022) 'Local Communities, Extractivism and International Investment Law: The Case of Five Colombian Communities' *Globalizations* 19: 837–53
Perrone, Nicolás M. (2023) 'Expropriation' in David Schneiderman and Gus Van Harten (eds) *Rethinking Investment Law* (Oxford UP) 64–88
Perrone, Nicolas Marcelo and David Schneiderman (n.d.) 'Lost to History? Latin America and the Charter of Economic Rights and Duties of States' in Liliana Obregón Tarazona, Laura Betancur-Restrepo, Juan Manuel Amaya Castro, and Daniel Ricardo Quiroga-Villamarín (eds) *Oxford Handbook on International Law and the Americas* (forthcoming Oxford UP)
Poggi, Gianfranco (1978) *The Development of the Modern State: A Sociological Introduction* (Stanford UP)
Poguntke, Thomas and Paul Webb (eds) (2005) *The Presidentialization of Politics: A Comparative Study of Modern Democracies* (Oxford UP)
Pohl, Joachim (2018) 'Societal Benefits and Costs of International Investment Agreements: A Critical Review of Aspects and Available Empirical Evidence', *OECD Working Papers on International Investment*, 2018/1 (OECD Publishing)
Polanyi, Karl (1944) *The Great Transformation: The Political and Economic Origins of Our Time* (Beacon Press)
Polanyi, Karl (2001) *The Great Transformation: The Political and Economic Origins of Our Time* (Beacon Press)
Pollack, Mark A. (2014) 'Political Science and International Adjudication' in Cesare P. R. Romano, Karen J. Alter, and Yuval Shany, *The Oxford Handbook of International Adjudication* (Oxford UP) 357–87
Polodemocratico (2013) 'Presidente Correa designa a Carlos Gaviria en comisión de expertos para auditar tratados de inversiones suscritos por Ecuador' at https://www.polodemocratico.net/presidente-correa-designa-a-carlos-gaviria-en-comision-de-expertos-para-auditar-tratados-de-inversiones-suscritos-por-ecuador/ (last accessed 12 May 2024)
Polonskaya, Ksenia (2020) 'Metanarrative as a Trap: Critique of Investor-State Arbitration' *Journal of International Economic Law* 23: 1–23
Posner, Richard (2008) *How Judges Think* (Harvard UP)

Postema, Gerald J. (2010) 'Positivism and the Separation of Realists from their Skepticism' in Peter Cane (ed) *The Hart-Fuller Debate in the Twenty-First Century* (Hart Publishing) 259–79

Potestà, Michele (2013) 'Legitimate Expectations in Investment Treaty Law: Understanding the Roots and the Limits of a Controversial Concept' *ICSID Review* 28: 88–122

Poulsen, Lauge N. Skovegaard (2015) *Bounded Rationality and Economic Diplomacy: The Politics of Investment Treaties in Developing Countries* (Cambridge UP)

Prebisch, Raúl (1986 [1949]) 'El desarrollo económico de la América Latina y algunos de sus principales problemas' *Desarrollo Económico* 26(103): 479–502

Puig, Sergio (2013) 'Emergence & Dynamism in International Organizations: ICSID, Investor-State Arbitration & International Investment Law' *Georgetown Journal of International Law* 44: 531–608

Puig, Sergio (2014) 'Social Capital in the Arbitration Market' *European Journal of International Law* 25: 387–424

Puig, Sergio and Gregory Shaffer (2018) 'Imperfect Alternatives: Institutional Choice and the Reform of Investment Law' *The American Journal of International Law* 112: 361–409

Radbruch, Gustav (1932) 'Legal Philosophy' in Edwin W. Patterson (ed) *The Legal Philosophies of Lask, Radbruch, and Dabin*, translated by Kurt Wilk (Harvard UP) 43–226

Radkau, Joachim (2011) *Max Weber: A Biography*, translated by Patrick Camiller (Polity Press)

Ranjan, Prabash (2014) 'Using the Public Law Concept of Proportionality to Balance Investment Protection with Regulation in International Investment Law: A Critical Appraisal' *Cambridge Journal of International and Comparative Law* 3: 853–83

Rasmussen, Terje (2023) *Political Legitimacy: Realism in Political Theory and Sociology* (Routledge)

Ratner, Steven R. (2015) *The Thin Justice of International Law* (Oxford UP)

Ratner, Steven R. (2017) 'International Investment Law through the Lens of Global Justice' *Journal of International Economic Law* 20: 747–75

Ratner, Steven R. (2018) 'Survey Article: Global Investment Rules as a Site for Moral Inquiry' *The Journal of Political Philosophy* 27: 107–35

Ratner, Steven R. (2022) 'Fair and Equitable Treatment and Human Rights: A Moral and Legal Reconciliation' *Journal of International Economic Law* 25: 568–91

Raz, Joseph (1979) 'The Rule of Law and Its Virtue' in Joseph Raz, *The Authority of Law: Essays on Law and Morality* (Oxford) 210–29

Raz, Joseph (1994) 'The Politics of the Rule of Law' in Joseph Raz, *Ethics in the Public Domain: Essays in the Morality of Law and Politics*, Revised Ed. (Clarendon Press) 370–78

Reed, Lucy, Jan Paulsson, and Nigel Blackaby (2004) *Guide to ICSID Arbitration* (Kluwer Law International)

Reinisch, August (2017) 'The European Union and Investor-State Dispute Settlement: From Investor-State Arbitration to a Permanent Investment Court' in Armand de Mestral (ed) *Second Thoughts: Investor-State Arbitration Between Developed Democracies* (Centre for International Governance and Innovation) 333–76

Reinisch, August (2020) *Advanced Introduction to International Investment Law* (Edward Elgar)

Reinisch, August (2023) 'Investment Arbitration and the Rule of Law' in Stefan Kröll, Andrea K. Bjorklund, and Franco Ferrari (eds) *Cambridge Compendium of International and Commercial Arbitration*, Volume 1 (Cambridge UP) 211–43

Reinisch, August (2024) 'The Rule of Law in International Investment Law and Arbitration as Reflected in the Work of the ILA' *Zeitschrift für europarechtliche Studien – ZEuS* 4: 463–85

Reinisch, August and Stephan W. Schill (2023) 'Introduction' in August Reinisch and Stephan W. Schill (eds) *Investment Protection Standards and the Rule of Law* (Oxford UP) 1–19

Reisebrodt, Martin (1989) 'From Patriarchalism to Capitalism: The Theoretical Context of Max Weber's Agrarian Studies' in Keith Tribe (ed) *Reading Weber* (Routledge) 131–57

Rheinstein Max (1954) 'Introduction' in Max Rheinstein (ed) *Max Weber on Law in Economy and Society* (Harvard UP) xvii–lxiv

Ridi, Niccolò and Thomas Schultz (2021) 'Empirically Mapping Investment Arbitration Scholarship: Networks, Authorities, and the Research Front' in K. Fach Gómez (ed) Private

Actors in International Investment Law (2021) *European Yearbook in International Economic Law* 209–241
Rittich, Kerry (2002) *Recharacterizing Restructuring: Law, Distribution and Gender in Market Reform* (Kluwer Law International)
Roberts, Anthea (2010) 'Power and Persuasion in Investment Treaty Interpretation: The Dual Role of States' *American Journal of International Law* 104: 179–225
Roberts, Anthea (2017) *Is International Law International?* (Oxford UP)
Roberts, Anthea and Taylor St. John (2023) 'The Originality of Outsiders: Innovation in the Investment Treaty System' *The European Journal of International Law* 33: 1153–81
Rodríguez, César (2001) 'The Return of Law and Development' *Beyond Law* 23: 13–42
Rodríguez, José Antonio Moreno (2023) 'Private (and Public) International Law in Investment Arbitration' *Recueil des Cours* 429: 9–702
Rosanvallon, Pierre (2000) *La démocratie inachevée: histoire de la souveraineté du peuple en France* (Gallimard)
Rosanvallon, Pierre (2011) *Democratic Legitimacy: Impartiality, Reflexivity, Prosperity*, translated by Arthur Goldhammer (Princeton UP)
Rostow, W. W. (1960) *The Stages of Economic Growth: A Non-Communist Manifesto* (Cambridge UP)
Roth, Guenther (1968) 'Political Critiques' in Reinhard Bendix and Guenther Roth, *Scholarship and Partisanship: Essays on Max Weber* (U California Press, 1971) 55–68
Roth, Guenther (1993) 'Reviews: Between Cosmopolitanism and Ethnocentrism: Max Weber in the Nineties' *Telos* 96: 148–62
Roth, Guenther (2002) 'Max Weber: Family History, Economic Policy, Exchange Reform' *International Journal of Politics, Culture and Society* 15: 509–20
Ruggie, John Gerald (1998) *Constructing the World Polity: Essays on International Institutionalization* (Routledge)
Runciman, W. G. (1972) *A Critique of Max Weber's Philosophy of Social Science* (Cambridge UP)
Rundle, Kristen (2012) *Forms Liberate: Reclaiming the Jurisprudence of Lon L Fuller* (Hart)
Rundle, Kristen (2017) 'Opening the Doors of Inquiry: Lon Fuller and the Natural Law Tradition' in George Duke and Robert P. George (eds) *The Cambridge Companion to Natural Law Jurisprudence* (Cambridge UP) 428–56
Rundle, Kristen (2021) 'The Morality of the Rule of Law: Lon L. Fuller' in Jens Meierhenrich and Martin Loughlin (eds) *The Cambridge Companion to the Rule of Law* (Cambridge UP) 186–201
Sacerdoti, Giorgio (2013) 'BIT Protections and Economic Crises: Limits to Their Coverage, the Impact of Multilateral Financial Regulation and the Defence of Necessity' *ICSID Review* 28: 1–13
Sahni, Isher-Paul (2006) 'Vanished Mediators: On the Residual Status of Judges in Max Weber's "Sociology of Law"' *Journal of Classical Sociology* 6: 177–94
Sahni, Isher-Paul (2009) 'Max Weber's Sociology of Law' *Journal of Classical Sociology* 9: 209–33
Salacuse, Jeswald W. (2000) 'Direct Foreign Investment and the Law in Developing Countries' *ICSID Review—Foreign Investment Law Journal* 15: 382–400
Salacuse, Jeswald W. (2010) 'The Emerging Global Regime for Investment' *Harvard International Law Journal* 51: 427–74
Salomon, Albert (1934) 'Max Weber's Methodology' *Social Research* 1: 147–68
Sandomierski, David (2020) *Aspiration and Reality in Legal Education* (U Toronto Press)
Santos, Alvaro (2006) 'The World Bank's Use of the "Rule of Law" Promise in Economic Development' in David M. Trubek and Alvaro Santos (eds) *The New Law and Economic Development: A Critical Appraisal* (Cambridge UP) 253–300
Santos, Boaventura de Sousa (2018) *The End of the Cognitive Empire: The Coming of Age of Epistemologies of the South* (Duke UP)
Santos, Boaventura de Sousa (2023) *Law and the Epistemologies of the South* (Cambridge UP)
Sarfaty, Galit (2012) *Values in Translation: Human Rights and the Culture of the World Bank* (Stanford UP)

Sattorova, Mavluda (2018) *The Impact of Investment Treaty Law on Host States: Enabling Good Governance?* (Hart)

Sattorova, Mavluda (2023) 'The Impact of Investment Protection Standards on the Rule of Law: Strengthening or Weakening the Domestic Rule of Law?' in August Reinisch and Stephan W. Schill (eds) *Investment Protection Standards and the Rule of Law* (Oxford UP) 353–70

Sattorova, Mavluda, and Oleksandra Vytiaganets (2022) 'Learning from Investment Treaty Law and Arbitration: Developing States and Power Inequalities' in Daniel Behn, Ole Kristian Fauchald, and Malcolm Langford (eds) *The Legitimacy of Investment Arbitration: Empirical Perspectives* (Cambridge UP) 501–30

Sayer, Derek (1991) *Capitalism and Modernity: An Excursus on Marx and Weber* (Routledge)

Scaff, Lawrence A. (1973) 'Max Weber's Politics and Political Education' *The American Political Science Review* 67: 128–41

Scaff, Lawrence A. (1984a) 'Weber Before Weberian Sociology' in Keith Tribe (ed) *Reading Weber* (Routledge, 1989) 15–41

Scaff, Lawrence A. (1984b) 'From Political Economy to Political Sociology: Max Weber's Early Writings' in Ronald A. Glassman and Vatro Murvar (eds) *Max Weber's Political Sociology: A Pessimistic View of a Rationalized World* (Greenwood Press) 83–107

Scaff, Lawrence A. (1989) *Fleeing the Iron Cage: Culture, Politics, and Modernity on the Thought of Max Weber* (Berkeley: University of California Press)

Scaff, Lawrence A. (2011) *Max Weber in America* (Princeton UP)

Schadendorf, Sarah (2009) 'Investor-State Arbitrations and the Human Rights of the Host State's Population: An Empirical Approach to the Impact of *Amicus Curiae* Submissions' in Norman Weiß and Jean-Marc Thouvenin (eds) *The Influence of Human Rights on International Law* (Springer) 167–81

Scharpf, Fritz W. (1999) *Governing in Europe: Effective and Democratic?* (Oxford UP)

Schauer, Frederick (2003) *Profiles, Probabilities, and Stereotypes* (Harvard UP)

Schauer, Frederick (2024) 'Lon Fuller and the Rule of Law' in Michael Sevel (ed) *Routledge Handbook of the Rule of Law* (Routledge) 112–22

Scheuerman, William E. (1995) 'Is Parliamentarism in Crisis? A Response to Carl Schmitt' *Theory and Society* 24: 135–58

Scheuerman, William E. (2000) 'Social Democracy and the Rule of Law: The Legacy of Ernst Fraenkel' in Peter C. Caldwell and William E. Scheuerman (eds) *From Liberal Democracy to Fascism* (Humanities Press, Inc.) 74–105

Schill, Stephan W. (2007) '"Fair and Equitable Treatment" as an Embodiment of the Rule of Law' in Rainer Hofmann and Christian Tams (eds) *The International Convention on the Settlement of Investment Disputes (ICSID): Taking Stock after 40 Years* (Nomos) 31–72

Schill, Stephan W. (2010) 'Fair and Equitable Treatment, The Rule of Law, And Comparative Public Law' in Stephan W. Schill (ed) *International Investment Law and Comparative Public Law* (Oxford UP)

Schill, Stephan W. (2016) 'In Defense of International Investment Law' in *European Yearbook of International Economic Law* 7: 309–41

Schill, Stephan W. (2023) 'Legitimacy of Investment Arbitration' in Stefan Kröll, Andrea K. Bjorklund, and Franco Ferrari (eds) *Cambridge Compendium of International and Commercial Arbitration*, Volume 3 (Cambridge UP) 1825–52

Schlegel, John Henry (2008) 'Law and Economic Change During the Short Twentieth Century' in Michael Grossberg and Christopher Tomlins (eds) *The Cambridge History of Law in America, Volume III: The Twentieth Century and After (1920-)* (Cambridge UP) 563–612

Schlink, Bernhard (2012) 'Proportionality in Constitutional Law: Why Everywhere But Here?' *Duke Journal of Comparative & International Law* 22: 291–302

Schluchter, Wolfgang (1979) 'Value-Neutrality and the Ethic of Responsibility' in Gunther Roth and Wolfgang Schluchter, *Max Weber's Vision of History: Ethics and Methods* (U California Press) 65–116

Schluchter, Wolfgang (1981) *The Rise of Western Rationalism: Max Weber's Developmental History*, translated by Guenther Roth (U California Press)

Schluchter, Wolfgang (1989) *Rationalism, Religion, and Domination*, translated by Neil Solomon (U California Press)
Schluchter, Wolfgang (2002) 'The Sociology of Law as an Empirical Theory of Validity' *Journal of Classical Sociology* 2: 257–80
Schluchter, Wolfgang (2017) 'Dialectics of Disenchantment: A Weberian Look at Western Modernity' *Max Weber Studies* 17: 24–47
Schmidl, Maximilian (2021) 'The Renewable Energy Saga from Charanne v. Spain to The PV Investors v. Spain: Trying to See the Wood for the Trees' *Kluwer Arbitration Blog* (1 February) at https://arbitrationblog.kluwerarbitration.com/2021/02/01/the-renewable-energy-saga-from-charanne-v-spain-to-the-pv-investors-v-spain-trying-to-see-the-wood-for-the-trees/ (last accessed 15 June 2023)
Schmitt, Carl (1922) *Political Theology: Four Chapters on the Concept of Sovereignty*, translated by George Schwab (The MIT Press, 1985)
Schmitt, Carl (1923) *The Crisis of Parliamentary Democracy*, translated by Ellen Kennedy (The MIT Press, 1985)
Schmitt, Carl (1928) *Constitutional Theory*, translated by Jeffrey Seitzer. (Duke UP, 2008)
Schmitt, Carl (1932) *Legality and Legitimacy*, translated by Jeffrey Seitzer (Duke UP, 1996)
Schmitt, Carl (1970) *Political Theology II: The Myth of the Closure of Any Political Theology*, translated by Michael Hoelzl and Graham Ward (Polity Press)
Schnapper, Dominique (2010) *Une Sociologue au Conseil constitutionnel* (Gallimard)
Schneiderman, David (2008) *Constitutionalizing Economic Globalization: Investment Rules and Democracy's Promise* (Cambridge UP)
Schneiderman, David (2010a) 'A New Global Constitutional Order?' in Rosalind Dixon and Tom Ginsburg (eds) *Research Handbook on Comparative Constitutional Law* (Edward Elgar) 189–207
Schneiderman, David (2010b) 'Investing in Democracy? Political Process Review and International Investment Law' *University of Toronto Law Journal* 60: 909–40
Schneiderman, David (2010c) 'Judicial Politics and International Investment Arbitration: Seeking an Explanation for Conflicting Outcomes' *Northwestern Journal of International Law and Business* 30: 383–416
Schneiderman, David (2011) 'Legitimacy and Reflexivity in International Investment Arbitration: A New Self-Restraint? *International Journal of Dispute Management* 2: 471–95
Schneiderman, David (2012) 'Revisiting the Depoliticization of Investment Disputes' *Yearbook on International Investment Law and Policy, 2010-11*: 693–714
Schneiderman, David (2013a) *Resisting Economic Globalization: Critical Theory and International Investment Law* (Basingstoke: Palgrave Macmillan)
Schneiderman, David (2013b). 'Judging in Secular Times: Max Weber and the Rise of Proportionality' *Supreme Court Law Review* (2d) 63: 557–77
Schneiderman, David (2016) 'The Paranoid Style of Investment Lawyers and Arbitrators: Investment Law Norm Entrepreneurs and their Critics' in Chin Leng Lim (ed) *Alternative Visions of International on Foreign Investment: Essays in Honour of Muthucumaraswamy Sornarajah* (Cambridge UP) 131–55
Schneiderman, David (2017a) 'Investment Law's Unending Legitimacy Project' *Loyola University of Chicago Law Journal* 49: 229–69
Schneiderman, David (2017b) 'Listening to Investors (and Others): Audi Alteram Partem and the Future of International Investment Law' in Armand de Mestral (ed) *Second Thoughts: Investor-State Arbitration Between Developed Countries* (McGill-Queen's University Press) 131–54
Schneiderman, David (2018a) 'The Impossibility of International Investment Law as Formally Rational Law: A Weberian Analysis' in Moshe Hirsch and Andrew Lang (eds) *Research Handbook on the Sociology of International Law* (Edward Elgar) 232–51
Schneiderman, David (2018b) 'Against Constitutional Excess: Tocquevillian Reflections on International Investment Law' *The University of Chicago Law Review* 58: 585–608
Schneiderman, David (2018c) 'North America Investment Law and Policy: 2017' in *Yearbook of International Investment Law and Policy* (Oxford UP) 289–304

Schneiderman, David (2020) 'Investment Arbitration as Constitutional Law: Constitutional Analogies, Linkages, and Absences' in Thomas Schultz and Federico Ortino (eds) *The Oxford Handbook of International Arbitration* (Oxford UP)

Schneiderman, David (2022a) *Investment Law's Alibis: Arguments from Colonialism, Imperialism, Development, and Debt* (Cambridge UP)

Schneiderman, David (2022b) 'International Investment Law and Discipline for the Indebted' *European Journal of International Law* 33: 65–96

Schneiderman, David (2022c) 'Investment Law and its Others' *Temple International & Comparative Law Journal* 36: 77–93

Schneiderman, David (2022d) 'Hayek's Dream: International Investment Law and the Denigration of Politics' *Leiden International Law Journal* 35: 743–59

Schneiderman, David (2022e) 'Local Resistance: At the Margins of Investment Law' *Globalizations* 19: 897–910

Schneiderman, David (2024a) *Constitutional Review and International Investment Law: Deference or Defiance?* (Oxford UP)

Schneiderman, David (2024b) 'National Treatment' in David Schneiderman and Gus Van Harten (eds) *Rethinking International Investment Law* (Oxford UP) 7–37

Schneiderman, David (2024c) 'Weber, Fuller, and Belief in the Legitimacy of Law' *Max Weber Studies* 24: 183–216

Schneiderman, David and Gus Van Harten (eds) (2024) *Rethinking International Investment Law* (Oxford UP)

Schön, Manfred (1987) 'Gustav Schmoller and Max Weber' in Wolfgang J. Mommsen and Jürgen Osterhammel (eds) *Max Weber and His Contemporaries* (Unwin Hyman) 59–70

Schreuer, Christoph H. (2009) with Loretta Malitoppi, August Reinisch, and Anthony Sinclair, *The ICSID Convention: A Commentary*, 2nd ed. (Cambridge UP)

Schreuer, Christoph (2011) 'The Future of Investment Arbitration' in Mahnoush H. Arsanjani, Jacob Cogan, Robert Sloane, and Siegfried Wiessner (eds) *Looking to the Future: Essays on International Law in Honor of W. Michael Reisman* (Brill Nijhoff) 787–803

Schroeter, Gerd (1985) 'Dialogue, Debate, or Dissent? The Difficulties of Assessing Max Weber's Relation to Marx' in Robert J. Antonio and Ronald M. Glassman (eds) *A Weber-Marx Dialogue* (UP Kansas) 2–19

Schultz, Thomas (2014a) *Transnational Legality: Stateless Law and International Arbitration* (Oxford UP)

Schultz, Thomas (2014b) 'Against Consistency in Investment Arbitration' in Zachary Douglas, Joost Pauwelyn, and Jorge E. Viñuales (eds) *The Foundations of International Investment Law: Bringing Theory into Practice* (Oxford UP) 297–316

Schultz, Thomas (2020) 'The Ethos of Arbitration' in Thomas Schultz and Frederico Ortino (eds) *The Oxford Handbook of International Arbitration* (Oxford UP) 235–59

Schultz, Thomas and Robert Kovacs (2012) 'The Rise of a Third Generation of Arbitrators? Fifteen Years After Dezalay and Garth' *Arbitration International* 28: 161–71

Schultz, Thomas and Niccolò Ridi (2020) 'Arbitration Literature' in Thomas Schultz and Frederico Ortino (eds) *Oxford Handbook of International Arbitration* (Oxford UP) 1–32

Schumpeter, Joseph A. (1994) *History of Economic Analysis*, edited by Elizabeth Boody Schumpeter (Oxford UP)

Schwebel, Stephen M. (2015) 'Keynote Address: In Defence of Bilateral Investment Treaties' in Albert J. van den Berg (ed) *Legitimacy: Myths, Realities, Challenges* (Kluwer Law) 1–11

Sciulli, David (1992) *Theory of Societal Constitutionalism: Foundations of a Non-Marxist Critical Theory* (Cambridge UP)

Sebok, Anthony J. (2010) 'Comment on "Law as a Means"' in Peter Cane (ed) *The Hart-Fuller Debate in the Twenty First Century* (Hart) 189–95

Selznick, Philip (1965) 'Review of the *Morality of Law* by Lon L. Fuller' *American Sociological Review* 30: 947–48

Selznick, Philip (1992) *The Moral Commonwealth: Social Theory and the Promise of Community* (U of California Press)

Shaw, Gary J. and Lorena Guzmán-Díaz (2020) 'Looking in on Transparency: A 2020 Review of States' Reactions to the UNCITRAL Rules on Transparency and the Mauritius Convention' *Yearbook on International Investment Law & Practice* 2020: 349–83

Shihata, Ibrahim F. (1986) 'Toward Greater Depoliticization of Investment Disputes: The Roles of ICSID and MIGA' *ICSID Review* 1: 1–12

Shihata, Ibrahim F. (1991) 'The World Bank and "Governance" Issues in Its Borrowing Members' in *World Bank in a Changing World: Selected Essays*, Vol. 1 (Dordrecht: Martinus Nijhoff Publishers) 53–96

Shils, Edward (1981) *Tradition* (U Chicago Press)

Shklar, Judith (1964) *After Utopia: The Decline of Political Faith* (Princeton UP)

Shklar, Judith (1986) *Legalism: Law, Morals, and Political Trials* (Harvard UP)

Sica, Alan (ed) (2023) *The Routledge International Handbook on Max Weber* (Routledge)

Simmel, Georg (1950) 'Superordination and Subordination' in Kurt H. Wolff (ed) *The Sociology of Georg Simmel* (The Free Press) 101–223

Simmons, A. John (1999) 'Justification and Legitimacy' in A. John Simmons, *Justification and Legitimacy: Essays on Rights and Obligations* (Cambridge UP, 2001) 122–56

Simpson, Gerry (2004) *Great Powers and Outlaw States: Unequal Sovereigns in the International Legal Order* (Cambridge UP)

Sipiorski, Emily (2019) *Good Faith in International Investment Arbitration* (Oxford UP)

Smith, David Norman (2013) 'Charisma Disenchanted: Max Weber and His Critics' *Current Perspectives in Social Theory* 31: 3–74

Smith, David Norman (2016) 'Charisma and the Spirit of Capitalism' in Alan Sica, *The Anthem Companion to Max Weber* (Anthem Press) 67–116

Smith, David Norman (2023) 'Capital and the Thrill of Domination' in Alan Sica (ed) *The Routledge International Handbook on Max Weber* (Routledge) 195–207

Soave, Tommaso (2022) *The Everyday Makers of International Law: From Great Halls to Back Rooms* (Cambridge UP)

Sornarajah, M. (2008) 'A Coming Crisis: Expansionary Trends in Investment Treaty Arbitration' in Karl P Sauvant and Michael Cheswick-Patterson (eds) *Appeals Mechanism in International Investment Disputes* (Oxford UP) 39–79

Sornarajah, M. (2013) 'The Case Against a Regime on International Investment Law' in Leon E. Trakman and Nicolai W. Ranieri (eds) *Regionalism in International Investment Law* (Oxford UP) 475–98

Sornarajah, M. (2015) *Resistance and Change in The International Law on Foreign Investment* (Cambridge UP)

Sornarajah, M. (2019) 'The Battle Continues: Rebuilding Empire Through State Contracts' in Jochen von Bernstorff and Philipp Dann (eds) *The Battle for International Law: South-North Perspectives on the Decolonization Era* (Oxford UP) 175–97

South Commission, *Challenge to the South: Report of the South Commission* (1990) (Julius K. Nyerere, Chairman) (Oxford UP)

St. John, Taylor (2018) *The Rise of Investor-State Arbitration: Politics, Law, and Unintended Consequences* (Oxford UP)

Stacey, Richard (2019) 'The Magnetism of Moral Reasoning and the Principle of Proportionality in Comparative Constitutional Adjudication' *The American Journal of Comparative Law* 67: 435–75

Steffek, Jens (2017) 'International Organizations and Bureaucratic Modernity' in Richard Ned Lebow (ed) *Max Weber and International Relations* (ArCambridge UP) 119–42

Stern, Brigitte (2011) 'The Future of International Investment Law: A Balance Between the Protection of Investors and the States' Capacity to Regulate' in José E. Alvarez and Karl Sauvant (eds) *The Evolving International Investment Regime: Expectations, Realities, Options* (Oxford UP) 174–92

Stiglitz, Joseph E. (1996) 'Some Lessons from the East Asian Miracle' *The World Bank Research Observer* 11: 151–77

Stinchcombe, Arthur L. (2001) *When Formality Works: Authority and Abstraction in Law and Organizations* (U of Chicago Press)

Stone Sweet, Alec (2000) *Governing with Judges: Constitutional Politics in Europe* (Oxford UP)

Stone Sweet, Alec (2010) 'Investor-State Arbitration: Proportionality's New Frontier' *Law & Ethics of Human Rights* 4: 47–76

Stone Sweet, Alec (2011) 'Arbitration and Judicialization' *Onati Socio-Legal Series* 1: 7–23

Stone Sweet, Alec and Thomas L. Brunell (2013) 'Trustee Courts and the Judicialization of International Regimes: The Politics of Majoritarian Activism in the European Convention of Human Rights, the European Union, and the World Trade Organization' *Journal of Law and Courts* 1: 61–88

Stone Sweet, Alec and Giacinto Della Cananea (2014) 'Proportionality, General Principles of Law, and Investor-State Arbitration: A Response to José Alvarez' *New York University Journal of International Law and Politics* 46: 911–64

Stone Sweet, Alec and Florian Grisel (2017) *The Evolution of International Arbitration: Judicialization, Governance, Legitimacy* (Oxford UP)

Stone Sweet, Alec and Jud Mathews (2009) 'Proportionality Balancing and Global Constitutionalism' *Columbia Journal of Transnational Law* 47: 72–164

Stone Sweet, Alec and Jud Mathews (2019) *Proportionality Balancing and Constitutional Governance: A Comparative and Global Approach* (Oxford UP)

Stothard, Paul (2023) 'Third-Party Funding for Energy Disputes' *Norton Rose Fulbright International Arbitration Report* 20: 29–30 (May) at https://www.nortonrosefulbright.com/en/knowledge/publications/bc180571/third-party-funding-for-energy-disputes (last accessed 20 May 2024)

Strand, Michael and Omar Lizardo (2022) 'Chance, Orientation, and Interpretation: Max Weber's Neglected Probabilism and the Future of Social Theory' *Sociological Theory* 40: 124–50

Strauss, Leo (1950) *Natural Right and History* (U Chicago Press)

Strazzeri, Victor (2022) *The Young Max Weber and German Social Democracy: The 'Labour Question' and the Genesis of Social Theory in Imperial Germany (1884-1899)* (Brill)

Streeck, Wolfgang (2014) *Buying Time: The Delayed Crisis of Democratic Capitalism* (Verso)

Streeck, Wolfgang (2024) *Taking Back Control: States and State Systems After Globalism* (Verso)

Strong, Tracy B. (1994) 'Max Weber and the Bourgeoisie' in Terry Maley and Asher Horowitz (eds) *The Barbarism of Reason: Max Weber and the Twilight of the Enlightenment* (U Toronto Press) 113–38

Strong, Tracy B. (2002) 'Love, Passion, and Maturity: Nietzsche and Weber on Science, Morality, and Politics' in John P. McCormick (ed) Confronting Mass Democracy and Industrial Technology: Political and Social Theory from Nietzsche to Habermas (Duke UP) 15–41

Suárez Ricaurte, Federico (2015) '"Actuando bajo la ética de la convicción" Carlos Gaviria Díaz en CAITISA, Ecuador' *Instituto de Estudios Constitucionales Carlos Restrepo Piedrahita, Universidad Externado de Columbia* (18 April) at https://icrp.uexternado.edu.co/actuando-bajo-la-etica-de-la-conviccion-carlos-gaviria-diaz-en-caitisa-ecuador/ (last accessed 12 May 2024)

Suárez Ricaurte, Federico (2022) 'Two Tiers and Double Standards: Foreign Investors and the Local Community of La Guajira, Colombia' *Globalizations* 19: 854–64

Suesse, Marvin (2023) *The Nationalist Dilemma: A Global History of Economic Nationalism, 1776–Present* (Cambridge UP)

Summers, Robert S. (1983) 'Lon L. Fuller's Jurisprudence and the Possibility It was Much Influenced by G.W.F. Hegel' *Cornell Law Forum* 10(1): 9–13

Summers, Robert S. (1984) *Lon L. Fuller* (Stanford UP)

Sunstein, Cass (1993) The Partial Constitution (Harvard UP)

Sunstein, Cass R. (2014) 'Constitutional Personae' *The Supreme Court Review*: 433–460

Swedberg, Richard (1998) *Max Weber and the Idea of Economic Sociology* (Princeton UP)

Swedberg, Richard (2018) 'How to Use Max Weber's Ideal Type in Sociological Analysis' *Journal of Classical Sociology* 18: 181–96

Swedberg, Richard and Ola Agevall (eds) (2016) *The Max Weber Dictionary: Keywords and Central Concepts*, 2nd ed. (Stanford UP)

Swigart, Leigh and Daniel Terris (2014) 'Who are International Judges?' in Cesare P. R. Romano, Karen J. Alter, and Yuval Shany, *The Oxford Handbook of International Adjudication* (Oxford UP) 619–38

Symonds, Michael (2023) 'Weber's Theory of Meaning, Modernity and the Value Spheres' in Alan Sica (ed) *The Routledge International Handbook on Max Weber* (Routledge) 49–62

Tamanaha, Brian Z. (2001) *A General Jurisprudence of Law and Society* (Oxford UP)

Tamanaha, Brian Z. (2004) *On the Rule of Law: History, Politics, Theory* (Cambridge UP)

Taylor, Charles (1985a) 'Legitimation Crisis?' in Charles Taylor, *Philosophy and the Human Sciences: Philosophical Papers 2* (Cambridge UP) 248–88

Taylor, Charles (1985b) 'Alternative Futures: Legitimacy, Identity, and Alienation in Late-Twentieth Century Canada' in Charles Taylor, *Reconciling the Solitudes: Essays on Canadian Federalism and Nationalism* (McGill-Queen's UP, 1993) 59–119

Taylor, Charles (1989) *Sources of the Self: The Making of Modern Identity* (Harvard UP)

Taylor, Charles (2007) *A Secular Age* (Harvard UP)

Taylor, Charles (2024) *Cosmic Connections: Poetry in the Age of Disenchantment* (Harvard UP)

Tenbruck, Friedrich H. (1980) 'The Problem of Thematic Unity in the Works of Max Weber' *British Journal of Sociology* 31: 316–51

Tenbruck, Friedrich H. (1987) 'Max Weber and Eduard Meyer' in Wolfgang J. Mommsen and Jürgen Osterhammel (eds) *Max Weber and His Contemporaries* (Unwin Hyman) 234–67

Thomas, Chantal (2006) 'Max Weber, Talcott Parsons and the Sociology of Legal Reform: A Reassessment with Implications for Law and Development' *Minnesota Journal of International Law* 15: 383–424

Thomas, Chantal (2008) 'Re-Reading Weber in Law and Development: A Critical Intellectual History of "Good Governance" Reform' Cornell Legal Studies Research Paper No. 08-034 (9 December) at https://papers.ssrn.com/sol3/papers.cfm?abstract_id=1313718 (last accessed 9 October 2023)

Thompson, E. P. (1975) *Whigs and Hunters: The Origins of the Black Act* (New York: Pantheon Books)

Titi, Catharine (2018) 'Refining the Expropriation Clause: What Role for Proportionality?' in Julian Chaisse (ed) *China-European Union Investment Relationships* (Edward Elgar) 111–30

Titi, Catharine (2020) 'Refining the Expropriation Clause: What Role for Proportionality?' in Julien Chaisse (ed) *China-European Union Investment Relationships: Towards a New Leadership in Global Investment Governance?* (Edward Elgar) 111–30

Titunik, Regina F. (2005) 'Democracy, Domination, and Legitimacy in Max Weber's Political Thought' in Charles Camic, Philip S. Gorski and David M. Trubek (eds) *Max Weber's Economy and Society: A Critical Companion* (Stanford UP) 143–63

Torres Lasso, Juan Diego (2025) 'Corte Constitucional hace seguimiento al cumplimiento de la sentencia sobre protección a indígenas Wayuu' *El Tiempo* (21 March) at https://www.eltiempo.com/justicia/cortes/corte-constitucional-hace-seguimiento-a-la-sentencia-3437520 (last accessed 12 May 2025)

Tortola, Pier Domenico (2020) 'Technocracy and Depoliticization' in Eri Bertsou and Daniele Caramani (eds) *The Technocratic Challenge to Democracy* (Routledge) 61–74

Trebilcock, Michael (2016) 'Between Universalism and Relativism: Reflections on the Evolution of Law and Development Studies' *The University of Toronto Law Journal* 66: 330–52

Trebilcock, Michael J. and Mariana Mota Prado (2011) *What Makes Poor Countries Poor? Institutional Determinants of Development* (Edward Elgar)

Treiber, Hubert (1985) '"Elective Affinities" Between Weber's Sociology of Religion and Sociology of Law' *Theory and Society* 14: 809–61

Treiber, Hubert (2005) 'Max Weber's "Sociology of Domination" in the Light of Recent Publications' *Max Weber Studies* 5: 139–49

Treiber, Hubert (2008) 'Max Weber and Eugene Ehrlich: On the Janus-Headed Construction of Weber's Ideal Type in the Sociology of Law' *Max Weber Studies* 8 (2): 225–46

Treiber, Hubert (2011) 'Insights into Weber's Sociology of Law' in Knut Papendorf, Stefan Machura, Kristian Andenaes (eds) *Understanding Law in Society: Developments in Socio-legal Studies* (LIT Verlag, 2011) 21–79

Treiber, Hubert (2019) 'On Weber's Partiality to "Logic"' *Max Weber Studies* 19: 196–224

Treiber, Hubert (2020) *Reading Max Weber's Sociology of Law*, translated by Matthew Philpotts (Oxford UP)

Treiber, Hubert (2023) 'Critical Reflections on Pollitt and Bouckaert's Construct of the Neo-Weberian State (NWS) in their Standard Work on Public Management Reform' *Theory and Society* 52: 179–212

Tribe, Keith (1983) Prussian Agriculture - German Politics: Max Weber 1892-7' in Keith Tribe (ed) *Reading Weber* (Routledge, 1989) 85–130

Tribe, Keith (2002) 'Review: Börsenwesen: Schriften Und Reden 1893–1898 (WG I/5), Part 1, Part 2' *Max Weber Studies* 2: 242–46

Tribe, Keith (2005) 'Études wébériennes: Rationalités, histoires, droits by Catherine Colliot-Thélène' *Max Weber Studies* 5: 150–55

Tribe, Keith (2010) 'Max Weber and the New Economics' in Yukihiro Ikeda, Tamotsu Nishizawa, and Harald Hagemann (eds) *Austrian Economics in Transition: From Carl Menger to Friedrich Hayek* (Palgrave Macmillan) 62–88

Tribe, Keith (2019) 'Introduction to Max Weber's Economy and Society' in Max Weber (2019) 1–73

Tribe, Keith (2023) 'Capitalism, Contingency and Economic Development' in Alan Sica (ed) *The Routledge International Handbook on Max Weber* (Routledge) 300–12

Troeltsch, Ernst (1922) 'The Ideas of Natural Law and Humanity in World Politics' in Otto Gierke, *Natural Law and the Theory of Society, 1500 to 1800*, Vol. 1, translation by Ernest Barker (Cambridge University Press) 201–22

Troeltsch, Ernst (1931) *The Social Teaching of the Christian Churches*, translated by Olive Wyon (Macmillan)

Trubek, David M. (1972a) 'Max Weber and the Rise of Capitalism' *Wisconsin Law Review* 1972: 720–53

Trubek, David M. (1972b) 'Toward a Social Theory of Law: An Essay on the Study of Law and Development' Yale Law Journal 82: 1–50

Trubek, David M. (1985) 'Reconstructing Max Weber's Sociology of Law' *Stanford Law Review* 37: 919–36

Trubek, David M. (2006) 'The "Rule of Law" in Development Assistance: Past, Present, and Future' in David M. Trubek and Alvaro Santos (eds) *The New Law and Economic Development: A Critical Appraisal* (Cambridge UP) 74–94

Trubek, David M. (2016) 'Law and Development: Forty Years after "Scholars in Self-Estrangement"' *University of Toronto Law Journal* 66: 301–329

Trubek, David M. and Marc Galanter (1974) 'Scholars in Self-Estrangement: Some Reflections on the Crisis in Law and Development Studies in the United States' *Wisconsin Law Review* 4: 1062–1102

Tsakyrakis, Stavros (2009) 'Proportionality: An Assault on Human Rights?' *International Journal of Constitutional Law* 7: 468–93

Tsebelis, George (2002) *Veto Players: How Political Institutions Work* (Princeton UP)

Tucker, Todd (2018) *Judge Knot: How the Crusade for Investor Rights Tangles Our Democracies and Economies* (Anthem Press)

Tully, James (1995) *Strange Multiplicity: Constitutionalism in an Age of Diversity* (Cambridge UP)

Turner, Bryan S. (1981) *For Weber: Essays on the Sociology of Fate* (Routledge & Kegan Paul)

Turner, Stephen (2019) 'Causation, Value Judgments, *Verstehen*' in Edith Hanke, Lawrence A. Scaff, and Sam Whimster (eds) *The Oxford Handbook of Max Weber* (Oxford UP) 575–96

Turner, Stephen (2023) 'The Rule of Law Deflated: Weber and Kelsen' in Stephen Turner and George Mazur, *Making Democratic Theory Democratic: Democracy, Law, and Administration after Weber and Kelsen* (Routledge) 162–76

Turner, Stephen (2025) 'Weber's Countergenealogy of Democracy' in Joshua Derman and Peter E. Gordon (eds) *Max Weber at 100* (Oxford UP) 275–97

Turner, Stephen P. and Regis A. Factor (1984) *Max Weber and the Dispute Over Reason and Value: A Study in Philosophy, Ethics and Politics* (Routledge & Kegan Paul)

Turner, Stephen P. and Regis A. Factor (1994) *Max Weber: The Lawyer as Social Thinker* (Routledge)

Ubilava, Ana (2020) 'Amicable Settlements in Investor-Disputes: Empirical Analysis of Patterns and Perceived Problems' *Journal of World Investment & Trade* 21: 528–57
Unger, Roberto (1976) *Law in Modern Society: Toward a Criticism of Social Theory* (New York: the Free Press)
United Nations Commission on International Trade Law [UNCITRAL], Working Group III (2018) Note by the Secretariat, 'Possible reform of Investor-State Dispute Settlement (ISDS): Consistency and Related Matters' (28 August) A/CN.9/WG.III/WP.150 at https://docs.un.org/en/A/CN.9/WG.III/WP.150 (last accessed 27 May 2025)
United Nations Commission on International Trade Law [UNCITRAL], Working Group III (2019) Note by the Secretariat, 'Possible Reform of Investor-State Dispute Settlement (ISDS): Third-Party Funding – Possible Solutions' Note by the Secretariat (2 August) A/CN.9/WG.III/WP.172 at https://documents.un.org/doc/undoc/ltd/v19/083/90/pdf/v1908390.pdf?token=9A0kQq3X5EiryvMabm&fe=true (last accessed 20 May 2024)
United Nations Commission on International Trade Law [UNCITRAL], Working Group III (2023a) Note by the Secretariat, 'Possible Reform of Investor-State Dispute Settlement (ISDS): Draft Provisions on Procedural and Cross-Cutting Issues,' 46th Session (26 July) A/CN.9/WG.III/WP.231 at https://documents.un.org/doc/undoc/ltd/v23/059/71/pdf/v2305971.pdf?token=Np9q5R7j5fjWuTURfC&fe=true (last accessed 20 May 2024)
United Nations Commission on International Trade Law [UNCITRAL], Working Group III (2023b) 'Singapore's Written Commons on Draft Provisions Contained in A/CN.9/WG.III/WP.231' at https://uncitral.un.org/sites/uncitral.un.org/files/media-documents/uncitral/en/comments_from_singapore.pdf (last accessed 20 May 2024)
United Nations Conference on Trade and Development [UNCTAD] (2015a) *World Investment Report 2015: Reforming International Investment Governance* (United Nations)
United Nations Conference on Trade and Development [UNCTAD] (2015b) *Investment Policy Framework for Sustainable Development* (United Nations) UNCTAD/DIAE/PCB/2015/5
United Nations Conference on Trade and Development [UNCTAD] (2018) *World Investment Report 2018: Investment and New Industrial Policies* (United Nations)
United Nations Conference on Trade and Development [UNCTAD] (2020) *International Investment Agreements Reform Accelerator* (United Nations) UNCTAD/DIAE/PCB/INF/2020/8
United Nations Conference on Trade and Development [UNCTAD] (2023a) *Trade and Development Report Update: Global Trends and Prospects* (April) (United Nations) UNCTAD/GDS/INF/2023/1
United Nations Conference on Trade and Development [UNCTAD] (2023b) *World Investment Report 2023: Investing in Sustainable Energy for All* (United Nations)
United Nations Conference on Trade and Development [UNCTAD] (2023c) *SDG Investment Trends Monitor* Issue 4 (September) UNCTAD/DIAE/MISD/2023/6
United Nations, Human Rights Council, 'Report of the Special Rapporteur on the Rights of Indigenous Peoples' A/HRC/33/42 (11 August 2016) at https://docs.un.org/en/A/HRC/33/42 (last accessed 29 March 2025)
United States National Security Council, (1950) 'NS 68: United States Objectives and Programs for National Security (April 14, 1950)' in Ernest R. May (ed) *American Cold War Strategy: Interpreting NSC 68* (Bedford: St. Martin's, 1993) 21–82
United States Trade Representative (2014) 'The Facts on Investor-State Dispute Settlement' *Tradewinds: The Official Blog of the United States Trade Representative* (March)
Urbina, Francisco J. (2012) 'A Critique of Proportionality' *American Journal of Jurisprudence* 57: 49–80
Vadi, Valentina (2018) *Proportionality, Reasonableness and Standards of Review in International Investment Law and Arbitration* (Edward Elgar)
Valeri, Mark (2010) *Heavenly Merchandize: How Religions Shaped Commerce in Puritan America* (Princeton UP)

Van Aaken, Anne (2014) 'Control Mechanisms in International Investment Law' in Zachary Douglas, Joost Pauwelyn, and Jorge E. Viñuales (eds) *The Foundations of International Investment Law* (Oxford UP) 409–35

Van Den Berg, Albert Jan (2010) 'Dissenting Opinions by Party-Appointed Arbitrators in Investment Arbitration' in Mahnoush H. Arsanjani, Jacob Cogan, Robert Sloane, and Siegfried Wiessner (eds) *Looking to the Future: Essays on International Law in Honor of W. Michael Reisman* (Brill Nijhoff) 821–43

Van Den Berg, Albert Jan (2014) 'Organizing an International Arbitration: Practice Pointers' in Lawrence W. Newman and Richard D. Hill (eds) *The Leading Arbitrators' Guide to International Arbitration*, 3rd ed. (Juris) 415–36

Van Harten, Gus (2010a) 'Investment Treaty Arbitration, Procedural Fairness, and the Rule of Law' in Stephan W. Schill (ed) *International Investment Law and Comparative Public Law* (Oxford UP) 627–57

Van Harten, Gus (2010b) 'Five Justifications for Investment Treaties: A Critical Discussion' *Trade, Law and Development* 2: 19–58

Van Harten, Gus (2012) 'The Use of Quantitative Methods to Examine Possible Bias in Investment Arbitration' *Yearbook on International Investment Law & Policy 2010-2011*: 859–81

Van Harten, Gus (2013) *Sovereign Choices and Sovereign Restraints: Judicial Restraint in Investment Treaty Arbitration* (Oxford UP)

Van Harten, Gus and Pavel Malysheuski (2022) 'Who Has Benefited Financially from Investment Treaty Arbitration? An Evaluation of the Size and Wealth of Claimants' in Daniel Behn, Ole Kristian Fauchald, and Malcolm Langford (eds) *The Legitimacy of Investment Arbitration: Empirical Perspectives* (Cambridge UP) 394–423

Van Harten, Gus and Dayna Nadine Scott (2016) 'Investment Treaties and the Internal Vetting of Regulatory Proposals: A Case Study from Canada' *Journal of International Dispute Settlement* 7: 92–116

Vandevelde, Kenneth J. (1992) 'The BIT Program: A Fifteen-Year Appraisal' *ASIL Proceedings* 86: 532–40

Vandevelde, Kenneth J. (1998a) 'Investment Liberalization and Economic Development: The Role of Bilateral Investment Treaties' *Columbia Journal of Transnational Law* 36: 501–27

Vandevelde, Kenneth J. (1998b) 'The Political Economy of a Bilateral Investment Treaty' *American Journal of International Law* 92: 621–41

Vandevelde, Kenneth J. (2010) *Bilateral Investment Treaties: History, Policy, and Interpretation* (Oxford UP)

Vandevelde, Kenneth J. (2017) *The First Bilateral Investment Treaties: U.S. Postwar Friendship, Commerce, and Navigation Treaties* (Oxford UP)

van Aaken, Anne and Jürgen Kurtz (2009) 'Prudence or Discrimination? Emergency Measures, the Global Financial Crisis and International Economic Law' *Journal of International Economic Law* 12: 859–94

Vauchez, Antoine (2014) 'Communities of International Litigators' in Cesare P. R. Romano, Karen J. Alter, and Yuval Shany, *The Oxford Handbook of International Adjudication* (Oxford UP) 655–68

Veeder, V. V. (2014) 'Whose Arbitration is it Anyway – The Parties' or the Arbitration Tribunal's?' in Lawrence W. Newman and Richard D. Hill (eds) *The Leading Arbitrators' Guide to International Arbitration*, 3rd ed. (Juris) 87–107

Venzke, Ingo (2008) 'International Bureaucracies from a Political Science Perspective – Agency, Authority and International Institutional Law' *German Law Journal* 9: 1401–28

Venzke, Ingo and Philipp Günther (2022) 'International Investment Protection Made in Germany? On the Domestic and Foreign Policy Dynamics behind the First BITs' *European Journal of International Law* 33: 1183–1207

Villa, Dana (2001) *Socratic Citizenship* (Princeton UP)

Villa, Dana (2018) 'Weber and the Frankfurt School' in Peter E. Gordon, Espen Hammer, and Axel Honneth (eds) *The Routledge Companion to the Frankfurt School* (Routledge) 266–81

Von Mises, Ludwig (1944) *Bureaucracy* (Yale UP)

Waddams, Stephen (2011) *Principle and Policy in Contract Law: Competing or Complementary Concepts?* (Cambridge UP)
Waelde, Thomas W. (1998) 'A Requiem for the "New International Economic Order": The Rise and Fall of Paradigms in International Economic Law and a Post-Mortem with Timeless Significance' in Gerald Hafner et al. (eds) *Liber Amicorum: Professor Ignaz Seidl-Hohenveldern* (Kluwer Law International) 771–803
Waibel, Michael (2015) 'Interpretive Communities in International Law' in Andrea Bianchi, Daniel Peat, and Matthew Windsor (eds) *Interpretation in International Law* (Oxford UP) 147–65
Wälde, Thomas (1999) 'Non-Conventional Views on "Effectiveness": The Holy Grail of Modern International Lawyers: The New Paradigm? A Chimera? Or a Brave New World in the Global Economy?' *Austrian Review of International & European Law* 4: 164–203
Wälde, Thomas W. (2000) 'Non-Conventional Views on "Effectiveness": The Holy Grail of Modern International Lawyers: The New Paradigm? A Chimera? Or A Brave New World in the Global Economy?' *Austrian Review of International and European Law Online* 4: 164–203
Wälde, Thomas (2005) 'The Umbrella Clause in Investment Arbitration' *Journal of World Investment & Trade* 6: 183–236
Wälde, Thomas (2006) 'Denial of Justice: A Review Comment on Jan Paulsson, *Denial of Justice in International Law*' *ICSID Review—Foreign Investment Law Journal* 21:449–85
Wälde, Thomas (2007) 'The Specific Nature of Arbitration' in Paul Kahn and Thomas W. Wälde (eds) *New Aspects of International Investment Law* (Martinus Nijhoff Publishers) 43–120
Wälde, Thomas (2008) 'Renegotiating Acquired Rights in the Oil and Gas Industries: Industry and Political Cycles Meet the Rule of Law' *Journal of World Energy Law & Business* 1: 55–97
Wälde, Thomas and Stephen Dow (2000) 'Treaties and Regulatory Risk in Infrastructure Investment' *Journal of World Trade* 34: 1–61
Wälde, Thomas and Abba Kolo (2001) 'Environmental Regulation, Investment Protection and "Regulatory Taking" in International Law' *International and Comparative Law Quarterly* 50: 811–48
Wälde, Thomas and Todd Weiler (2002) 'Investment Arbitration Under the Energy Charter Treaty in Light of New NAFTA Precedents: Towards a Global Code of Conduct for Economic Regulation' in G Ann-Kohler (ed) *Investment Treaties and Arbitration* (Swiss Arbitration Association)
Waldron, Jeremy (2010) 'Legal Pluralism and the Contrast Between Hart's Jurisprudence and Fuller's' in Peter Cane (ed) *The Hart-Fuller Debate in the Twenty-First Century* (Hart Publishing) 135–55
Waldron, Jeremy (2012) *The Rule of Law and the Measure of Property* (Cambridge UP)
Walker, Neil (2003) 'Postnational Constitutionalism and the Problems of Translation' in J. H. H. Weiler and Marlene Wind (eds) *European Constitutionalism Beyond the State* (Cambridge UP) 27–54
Walzer, Michael (1965) *The Revolution of the Saints: A Study in the Origins of Radical Politics* (Harvard UP)
Webb, Beatrice (1948) *Our Partnership* (Longman's, Green and Co.)
Webb, Paul and Thomas Poguntke (2013) 'The Presidentialization of Politics Thesis Defended' *Parliamentary Affairs* 66: 646–54
Webb, Sidney and Beatrice Webb (1935) *Soviet Communism: A New Civilisation?* (Longmans, Green and Co., Ltd.)
Webber, Grégoire C. N. (2009) *The Negotiable Constitution: On the Limitation of Rights* (Cambridge UP)
Weber, Marianne (1975) *Max Weber: A Biography*, translated by Harry Zohn (John Wiley & Sons)
Weber, Max (1894a) 'Developmental Tendencies in the Situation of East Elbian Rural Labourers' in Keith Tribe (ed) *Reading Weber* (Routledge, 1989) 158–87
Weber, Max (1894b) 'Stock and Commodity Exchanges [*Die Börse* (1894)]' *Theory and Society* 29: 305–38

Weber, Max (1895a) 'The Nation State and Economic Policy' in Weber (1994) 1–28
Weber, Max (1895b) '"Roman" and "Germanic" Law' *International Journal of the Sociology of Law* (1985) 13: 237–46
Weber, Max (1896a) 'The Social Causes of the Decay of Ancient Civilization' *The Journal of General Education* (1950) 5: 75–88
Weber, Max (1896b) 'Commerce on the Stock and Commodity Exchanges [*Die Börsenverkehr*]' *Theory and Society* 29: 339–71
Weber, Max (1897) 'Germany as an Industrial State' in Keith Tribe (ed) *Reading Weber* (Routledge, 1989) 210–20
Weber, Max (1902) 'Le Contrat de Travail de Philipp Lotmar, Note Critique (1902)' *Canadian Journal of Law and Society* 24: 147–158 [translation of Max Weber (1902) 'Rezension von: Philipp Lotmar, Der Arbeitsvertrag' *Archiv fur soziale Gesetzgebung und Statistik* 17: 723–734
Weber, Max (1904a) 'The "Objectivity" of Knowledge in Social Science and Social Policy' in Bruun and Whimster (2012) 100–38
Weber, Max (1904b) 'The "Threatening" of the Reich Constitution' *Journal of Classical Sociology* (2023) 23: 95–96
Weber, Max (1904c) 'Roscher and Knies and the Logical Problems of Historical Economics' in Bruun and Whimster (2012) 3–99
Weber, Max (1906a) 'Critical Studies in the Logic of the Cultural Sciences' in Bruun and Whimster (2012) 139–84
Weber, Max (1906b) 'On the Situation of Constitutional Democracy in Russia' in Weber (1994) 29–74
Weber, Max (1906c) '"Churches" and "Sects" in North America: An Ecclesiastical Sociopolitical Sketch' *Sociological Theory* 3: 7–13
Weber, Max (1906d) 'II Knies and the Problem of Irrationality' in Bruun and Whimster (2012) 28–94
Weber, Max (1907) 'Stammler and the Materialist Conception of History' in Bruun and Whimster (2012) 185–226
Weber, Max (1908) 'Weber's Second Reply to Karl Fischer, 1908' in David J. Chalcraft and Austin Harrington (eds) *The Protestant Ethic Debate: Max Weber's Replies to His Critics, 1907-10*, translated by Austin Harrington and May Shields (Liverpool UP) 43–51
Weber, Max (1909a) '"Energetical" Theories of Culture' in Bruun and Whimster (2012) 252–68
Weber, Max (1909b) 'Intervention in Discussion on "The Productivity of the National Economy"' Association for Social Policy, Vienna in Bruun and Whimster (2012) 358–61
Weber, Max (1910a) 'Intervention in the Debate on H. Kantorowicz's Paper on "Legal Science and Sociology"' in Bruun and Whimster (2012) 365–69
Weber, Max (1910b) 'A Final Rebuttal of Rachfahl's Critique of the "Spirit of Capitalism" (1910)' in *The Protestant Ethic and the "Spirit" of Capitalism and Other Writings*, translated by Peter Baehr and Gordon C. Wells (Penguin Books) 282–339
Weber, Max (1910c) 'Max Weber on Race and Society' *Social Research* (1978) 38: 30–41
Weber, Max (1910d) 'Max Weber, Dr. Alfred Ploetz, and W.E.B. Dubois ('Max Weber on Race and Society II)' *Sociological Analysis* (1973) 34: 308–12
Weber, Max (1913a) 'The Meaning of "Value Freedom" in the Sociological and Economic Sciences' in Bruun and Whimster (2012) 304–34
Weber, Max (1913b) 'On Some Categories of Interpretive Sociology' in Bruun and Whimster (2012) 273–301
Weber, Max (1913c) 'Letter to Robert Wilbrandt (2 April 1913)' in Bruun and Whimster (2012) 406
Weber, Max (1915a) 'Introduction to the Economic Ethics of the World Religions' in *The Essential Weber: A Reader*, edited by Sam Whimster (Routledge, 2004) 55–80
Weber, Max (1915b) 'Intermediate Reflections on the Economic Ethics of the World Religions' in *The Essential Weber: A Reader*, edited by Sam Whimster (Routledge, 2004) 215–44
Weber, Max (1915c) 'The Social Psychology of World Religions' in H. H. Gerth and C. Wright Mills (eds) *From Max Weber: Essays in Sociology* (New York: Oxford University Press) 267–301

Weber, Max (1916) 'Between Two Laws' in Weber (1994) 75–79
Weber, Max (1917) 'Suffrage and Democracy in Germany' in Weber (1994) 80–129
Weber, Max (1918a) 'Socialism' in Weber (1994) 272–303
Weber, Max (1918b) 'Parliament and Government in Germany' in Weber (1994) 130–271
Weber, Max (1918c) 'Germany's Future Form of State' *Max Weber Studies* (2021) 21: 23–65
Weber, Max (1919a) 'The Profession and Vocation of Politics' in Weber (1994) 309–69
Weber, Max (1919b) 'Science as a Profession and Vocation' in Bruun and Whimster (2012) 335–53
Weber, Max (1919c) 'The President of the Reich' in Weber (1994) 304–08
Weber, Max (1920a) 'Prefatory Remarks to Collected Essays in the Sociology of Religion' in Max Weber, *The Protestant Ethic and the Spirit of Capitalism with Other Writings on the Rise of the West*, 4th ed. Trans. Stephen Kalberg (Oxford UP, 2009) 205–20
Weber, Max (1920b) *General Economic History*, translated by Frank H. Knight (Dover, 2003)
Weber, Max (1920c) 'The Protestant Ethic and the Spirit of Capitalism' in Max Weber, *The Protestant Ethic and the Spirit of Capitalism with Other Writings on the Rise of the West*, 4th ed., translated by Stephen Kalberg (Oxford UP, 2009) 61–159
Weber, Max (1921) *The Rational and Social Foundations of Music*, translated by Don Martindale, Johannes Riedel, and Gertrude Neuwirth (Southern Illinois University Press, 1958)
Weber, Max (1922a) 'The Protestant Sects and the Spirit of Capitalism' in H. H. Gerth and C. Wright Mills (eds) *From Max Weber: Essays in Sociology* (New York: Oxford University Press) 302–22
Weber, Max (1922b) 'Three Pure Types of Legitimate Rule' in *The Essential Weber: A Reader*, edited by Sam Whimster (Routledge, 2004) 133–45
Weber, Max (1946b) 'Politics as Vocation' in H. H. Gerth and C. Wright Mills (eds) *From Max Weber: Essays in Sociology* (New York: Oxford University Press) 77–128
Weber, Max (1946b) 'Science as a Vocation' in H. H. Gerth and C. Wright Mills (eds) *From Max Weber: Essays in Sociology* (New York: Oxford University Press) 129–56
Weber, Max (1956) *Wirtschaft und Gesellschaft: Grundriss der Verstehenden Soziologie*, 2 Volumes, edited by Johannes Winckelmann (JCB Mohr [Paul Siebeck])
Weber, Max (1958) *The Protestant Ethic and the Spirit of Capitalism*, translated by Talcott Parsons (Charles Scribner's Sons)
Weber, Max (1963) *The Sociology of Religion*, translated by Ephraim Fischoff (Beacon Press)
Weber, Max (1964) *The Theory of Social and Economic Organization*, translated by A. M. Henderson and Talcott Parsons (The Free Press)
Weber, Max (1978) *Economy and Society: An Outline of Interpretive Sociology*. Ed. by Gunther Roth and Claus Wittich (Berkeley: University of California Press), 2 volumes
Weber, Max (1994) *Political Writings*. Edited by Peter Lassman and Ronal Speirs (Cambridge: Cambridge University Press)
Weber, Max (2004) *The Essential Weber: A Reader*, edited by Sam Whimster (Routledge)
Weber, Max (2009) *Allgemeine Staatslehre und Politik (Staatssoziologie)* (Mohr Siebeck)
Weber, Max (2014) *Wirtschaft und Gesellschaft, Recht, Max Weber-Gesamtausgabe: Band I/22-3*, edited by Werner Gephart and Siegfried Hermes (Tübingen: J. C. B. Mohr [Paul Siebeck])
Weber, Max (2019) *Economy and Society: A New Translation*, translated by Keith Tribe (Harvard UP)
Wehler, Hans-Ulrich (1985) *The German Empire, 1871-1918*, translated by Kin Traynor (Berg)
Weiacker, Franz (1995) *A History of Private Law in Europe with Particular Reference to Germany*, translated by Tony Weir (OUP)
Weiler, J. H. H. (2004) 'The Geology of International Law – Governance, Democracy and Legitimacy' ZaöRV 64: 547–62
Weiss, Johann (1987) 'On the Irreversibility of Western Rationalization and Max Weber's Alleged Fatalism' in Scott Lash and Sam Whimster (eds) *Max Weber, Rationality and Modernity* (Allen & Unwin) 154–63
Westad, Odd Arne (2005) *The Global Cold War* (Cambridge UP)
Westerman, Pauline (1999) 'Means and Ends' in Willem J. Wiitteven and Wibren van der Burg (eds) *Rediscovering Fuller: Essays on Implicit Law and Institutional Design* (Amsterdam UP) 145–68

Whimster, Sam (2007) *Understanding Weber* (Routledge)

Whimster, Sam (2017) 'Max Weber's Roman Agrarian History: Jurisprudence, Property, Civilization' in Werner Gephart and Daniel Witte (eds) *Recht als Kultur? Bieträge ze Max Webers Soziologie des Rechts* (Vittorio Klostermann, Frankfurt am Main) 229–77

Whimster, Sam (2019a) 'Max Weber and Federal Democracy' *Journal of Classical Sociology* 19: 346–60

Whimster, Sam (2019b) 'Economics and Society and the Fate of Liberal Capitalism' in Edith Hanke, Lawrence A. Scaff, and Sam Whimster (eds) *The Oxford Handbook of Max Weber* (Oxford UP) 21–46

Whimster, Sam (2021) 'Introduction to "Germany's Future Form of State"' *Max Weber Studies* 21: 11–22

Whimster, Sam (2023) 'Legitimizing Bureaucracy and the Challenge of Caesarism' *Max Weber Studies* 23: 82–108

Whimster, Sam (2025) 'Caesarism and Democratic Agency in Max Weber' in Joshua Derman and Peter E. Gordon (eds) *Max Weber at 100* (Oxford UP) 215–40

White & Case (2021) '2021 International Arbitration Survey: Adapting Arbitration to a Changing World' at https://www.whitecase.com/sites/default/files/2023-05/qmul-international-arbitration-survey-2021-web-single-final-v3.pdf (last accessed 19 September 2023)

Whyte, Jessica (2019) *The Morals of the Market: Human Rights and the Rise of Neoliberalism* (Verso)

Williams, Randall (2009) 'Nothing Sacred: Developing Countries and the Future of International Investment Treaties' IISD The Third Annual Forum of Developing Country Investment Negotiators (November) at https://www.iisd.org/system/files/meterial/developing_countries_and_the_future_of_IIAs.pdf (last accessed 6 October 2023)

Winston, Kenneth I. (1981) 'Introduction' in Lon L. Fuller, *The Principles of Social Order: Selected Essays of Lon L. Fuller* (Duke UP) 11–44

Winston, Kenneth I. (1988) 'Is/Ought Redux: The Pragmatist Context of Lon Fuller's Conception of Law' *Oxford Journal of Legal Studies* 8: 329–49

Winston, Kenneth I. (1994) 'Legislators and Liberty' *Law and Philosophy* 13: 389–418

Winston, Kenneth I. (1999) 'Three Models for the Study of Law' in Willem J. Wiitteven and Wibren van der Burg (eds) *Rediscovering Fuller: Essays on Implicit Law and Institutional Design* (Amsterdam UP) 51–77

Winston, Kenneth I. (2021) 'Good Order and Workable Arrangements: Lon Fuller's Critique of Legal Positivism' in Torben Spaak and Patricia Mindus (eds) *The Cambridge Companion to Legal Positivism* (Cambridge UP) 651–74

Wolin, Sheldon S. (1991) 'Max Weber: Legitimation, Method, and the Politics of Theory' in Sheldon S. Wolin, *Fugitive Democracy and Other Essays*, edited by Nicholas Xenos (Princeton UP, 2016) 195–213

Wolin, Sheldon S. (2004) *Politics and Vision* (expanded edition) (Princeton UP)

World Bank (1969) *Partners in Development: Report of the Commission on International Development* (Lester B. Pearson, Chairman) (Praeger)

World Bank (1993) *The East Asian Miracle: Economic Growth and Public Policy* (Oxford UP)

World Bank (1997) *The State in a Changing World: World Development Report 1997* (Oxford UP)

Wrong, Dennis (1970) 'Introduction: Max Weber' in Dennis Wrong (ed) *Max Weber* (Prentice-Hall, Inc.) 1–76

Yackee, Jason Webb (2011) 'Do Bilateral Investment Treaties Promote Foreign Direct Investment - Some Hints from Alternative Evidence' *Virginia Journal of International Law* 51: 397–442

Yackee, Jason Webb (2012) 'Controlling the International Investment Law Agency' *Harvard Journal of International Law* 53: 391–448

Yilmaz Vastardis, Anil (2020) 'Investment Treaty Arbitration: A Justice Bubble for the Privileged' in Thomas Schultz and Frederico Ortino (eds) *Oxford Handbook of International Arbitration* (Oxford UP) 617–40

Yu, Chen (2022) 'Advancing Predictability via a Judicialized Investment Court? A Fresh Look Through the Lens of Constructivism' *Journal of International Dispute Settlement* 13: 370–92

Zarbiyev, Fuad (2023) '"These are My Principles. If You Don't Like Them I Have Others": On Justifications of Foreign Investment Protection under International Law' *Journal of International Economic Law* 26: 525–41
Zaret, David (1985) *The Heavenly Contract: Ideology and Organization in Pre-Revolutionary Puritanism* (U Chicago Press)
Živković, Velmir (2022) 'ISDS and Nazis or History Without Context: A Reply to Gary Born' *Journal of International Arbitration* 39: 575–92
Živković, Velmir (2023) *Fair and Equitable Treatment and the Rule of Law* (Edward Elgar)
Zimmerman, Andrew (2006) 'Decolonizing Weber' *Postcolonial Studies* 9: 53–79
Zürn, Michael, Martin Binder, and Matthias Ecker-Ehrardt (2012) 'International Authority and Its Politicization' *International Theory* 4: 69–106

Cases/Awards

Alberta v. Hutterian Brethren of Wilson Colony [2009] SCR 567
Antaris GmbH and Göde v. Czech Republic (2018), Award, PCA Case No 2014-01, IIC 1413 (2 May)
Clayton v. Canada (2015), Award on Jurisdiction and Liability, Permanent Court of Arbitration (PCA) Case No. 2009-04 (17 March)
Eco Oro Minerals Corp. v. Republic of Colombia (2021), Decision on Jurisdiction, Liability and Directions on Quantum, ICSID Case No. ARB/16/41 (9 September)
Eiser Infrastructure Limited v. Spain (2017), Award, ICSID Case No. ARB/13/36 (4 May)
Electrabel v. Hungary (2015), Award, ICSID Case No. Arb/07/19 (25 November)
Mathis Kruck v. Spain (2022), ICSID Case No. ARB/15/23 (13 September), Partial Dissenting Opinion of Prof. Zachary Douglas KC
Metalclad Corp v. Mexico (2000), Award, Ad hoc—ICSID Additional Facility Rules, ICSID Case No ARB(AF)/97/1 (25 August)
Mohamed Abdel Raouf Bahgat v. Egypt (2019), Final Award, PCA Case No. 2012-07 (23 December)
Montauk Metals v. Colombia (2024), Award, ICSID Case No. ARB/18/13 (7 June)
Pantechniki SA Contractors and Engineers v. Albania (2009), Award, ICSID Case No ARB/07/21 (30 July)
Philip Morris Brands Sàrl, Philip Morris Products S.A. and Abal Hermanos S.A. v. Oriental Republic of Uruguay (2003), Award, ICSID Case No. ARB/10/7 (8 July)
PV Investors v. Spain (2020), Final Award, PCA Case No. 2012-14 (UNCITRAL) (28 February)
RWE Innogy v. Spain (2019), Decision on Jurisdiction, Liability and Certain Issues of Quantum, ICSID Case No. ARB/14/34 (30 December)
Sevilla Beheer SV v. Spain (2022), Decision on Jurisdiction, Liability and the Principles of Quantum, ICSID Case No. ARB/16/27 (11 February)
Suez v. Argentina (2010), Decision on Liability, ICSID Case No. ARB/03/19 (30 July)
Técnicas Medioambientales Tecmed SA v. Mexico [Tecmed] (2003), Award, ICSID ARB(AF)/00/2 (29 May)

Index

For the benefit of digital users, indexed terms that span two pages (e.g., 52–53) may, on occasion, appear on only one of those pages.